DON'T LET THE BASTARDS GRIND
YOU DOWN

DON'T LET THE BASTARDS GRIND YOU DOWN

How one generation of British actors changed the world

ROBERT SELLERS

preface
publishing

Published by Preface Publishing 2011

10 9 8 7 6 5 4 3 2 1

Copyright © Robert Sellers 2011

Robert Sellers has asserted his right to be identified as the author of this work under the Copyright, Designs and Patents Act 1988

First published in Great Britain in 2011 by Preface Publishing
20 Vauxhall Bridge Road
London SW1V 2SA

An imprint of The Random House Group Limited

www.rbooks.co.uk
www.prefacepublishing.co.uk

Addresses for companies within The Random House Group Limited
can be found at www.randomhouse.co.uk

The Random House Group Limited Reg. No. 954009

A CIP catalogue record for this book is available from the British Library

Hardback ISBN 978 1 84809 297 6
Trade paperback ISBN 978 1 84809 298 3

The Random House Group Limited supports The Forest Stewardship
Council (FSC), the leading international forest certification organisation. All our
titles that are printed on Greenpeace approved FSC certified paper carry the FSC logo. Our paper
procurement policy can be found at www.rbooks.co.uk/environment

Mixed Sources
Product group from well-managed
forests and other controlled sources
www.fsc.org Cert no. TT-COC-2139
© 1996 Forest Stewardship Council

Typeset in Dante MT by Palimpsest Book Production Limited,
Falkirk, Stirlingshire
Printed and bound in Great Britain by Clays Ltd, St Ives PLC

To Mum and Dad for their love and continued support.

Contents

Contents

Acknowledgements

I'd like to thank the following, who agreed to be interviewed for this book:

Sheila Allen
Paul Almond
Michael Anderson
David Andrews
John Arden
Jane Asher
George Baker
Trevor Bannister
Keith Baxter
Ann Beach
Lord Birkett
Tony Britton
Michael Cacoyannis
John Cairney
Peter Cellier
Margaretta D'Arcy
Glynn Edwards
Anthony Field
Derek Fowlds
Cyril Frankel
Sonia Fraser
Sidney J. Furie
Colin George

Richard Goodwin
Denys Graham
Philip Grout
Guy Hamilton
Edward Hardwicke
Robert Hardy
Elizabeth Harris
Pamela Howard
Barbara Jefford
Gemma Jones
Walter Lassally
Phyllida Law
Dyson Lovell
Millicent Martin
David McCallum
Brian Murphy
Monty Norman
Conrad Phillips
Alvin Rakoff
Gary Raymond
William Russell
Philip Saville
Michael Seymour

Acknowledgements

Sara Shane

Victor Spinetti

David Storey

Virginia Stride

Rita Tushingham

Paul Williamson

Susannah York

Special thanks must go to Trevor Dolby, my editor at Preface, and a salute to my agent Tim Bates.

'I thought people from my background didn't become actors. I thought actors were bred in special places – a stud farm in Mayfair.'

Albert Finney

'My memory of that whole, wonderful time is that everything was possible and no holds were barred. Looking back with joy, I see that we were all free to do our thing, whatever it was, and to the maximum extreme. Kitchen-sink drama didn't only release language on the stage, it liberated the actors. And not only from their performing conventions and style, but from the image, particularly of the West End actor, of being Public School and Best BBC, who dressed immaculately, even for an audition, attended the best clubs and would never be seen in the Public Bar. That all changed from 1956 and we were given our new uniform: jeans, T-shirts and Hush Puppies. Thus attired, we went into battle to lift the hitherto underprivileged and denied, to a place in the sun they deserved. The rest is history.'

John Cairney

Introduction

'For the first time in British history the young working class stood up for themselves and said, "We are here, this is our society and we are not going away."' So said Michael Caine; loud and proud.

The late 1950s and early 1960s saw the most exhilarating burst of creativity in the history of British popular culture. Plays such as John Osborne's *Look Back in Anger* and films of the calibre of *Saturday Night and Sunday Morning* blew away the middle-class monopoly that was strangling the life out of the arts in Britain and gave a voice to a working class that for the first time was gaining some economic power.

It all started at the Royal Court, a theatre that dared to stick two fingers up at the elitist West End, dared to be different and unleashed the rallying cry upon the nation in 1956 with *Look Back in Anger*. The reaction was shock. Audiences had never seen anything like it; it was so savage. Repulsive to the establishment, it spoke clearly to a disaffected youth whose unquestioning obeisance to authority could no longer be taken for granted. This was a time of political unrest, of protests against British military intervention in Suez and anti-nuclear marches. From out of that melting pot poured revolution. And at its forefront was a group of remarkable young actors who brought a dynamism and gritty edge to their performances that was startlingly fresh and unparalleled: Alan Bates, Michael Caine, Sean Connery, Tom Courtenay, Albert Finney, Richard Harris, Peter O'Toole, Robert Shaw and Terence Stamp were all rightly hailed as a new kind of star. 'All those guys had one thing in common,' says actor/producer Dyson Lovell. 'A savage truth, they were real. It was gutsy, but it wasn't the kind of American method acting that people like Marlon Brando were doing, it was a different kind of reality; it wasn't even a method, I don't think. It came from the gut. Their performances were so truthful and natural.'

Each of them was different, unique; all had their own strong and individual personalities, and they were islands unto themselves. David McCallum was their contemporary, worked with them, drank with them. 'Nowadays, like the group of actors that I work with on American television, we work as an ensemble company, there is no question of egos. Whereas in those days the egos seemed to be the most important thing. They were tremendously powerful actors, all doing terrific work, but with tremendous egos.'

The country was certainly ready for change. For years there had been a period of cultural stagnation during which nothing much very interesting was going on in either theatre or film. Then – bang! 'I think there was a kind of zeitgeist,' says *This Sporting Life* author David Storey. 'An emergence of almost proletarian energy, which was probably the result of the Second World War and the lower classes being engaged in it. And there was the 1944 Education Act which quite changed the notion of educating the lower orders, as it were, and out of that mix came this sudden assertion from the lower part of society; they came along with a great deal of energy and animation which drew away from the until then rather middle-class conception of stage work and film-making. It was a class that hadn't articulated itself in any significant way until then.'

This was a revolution not solely concerned about class, though. 'We were moving towards classlessness in the fifties,' says Elizabeth Harris. 'Our mindsets were not on class.' What really made those actors so good was their anti-establishment stance; they had an attitude bolstered by a real sense of grievance and a natural anger. 'It was a revolt against the establishment that was pre-1960s, which is when everybody got involved,' says producer Richard Goodwin. 'But these guys got everybody thinking in the right direction.'

More than class divisions it was about breaking down barriers, opening up opportunities for those who had been denied it for so long purely because of how they spoke and where they came from. Terence Stamp stated that he didn't believe there had been any genuine working-class actors before, 'just caricatures of the working class'. At the Royal Court Lindsay Anderson would audition young actors and actresses and then have to ask them where they came from, and then to repeat their audition pieces, 'not in the "acceptable" accents into which they had been drilled at drama school but in the natural accents of their youth. The results were almost always revelatory.'

Everyone had been brought up not only to attend auditions and interviews in their best suits, or with a collar and tie, but to speak in, for want of a better expression, BBC drama standard English. That all changed. 'And with that came an image,' says Trevor Bannister. 'We didn't wear suits any more to interviews. And to maintain that image some actors were going around talking with voices that were totally alien to them. Instead of greeting you with "Hello, my dear, how are you?" it was "'Allo, luv, 'ow yer doin'?"'

It was now no longer a hindrance for an actor to hail from the provinces, indeed it had become something of an advantage and reached the point where nicely spoken drama students were trying to acquire regional, working-class accents in order to get work. Derek Fowlds recalls this odd phenomenon well. 'Everyone who was speaking posh couldn't get a job whereas before if you had a regional accent you couldn't get a job, so the roles were reversed completely.'

Although a lot of the plays and movies from this era have dated, understandably so, the bulk of them have lasted the test of time because there is something universal and eternal about the anti-establishment stance of, say, *The Loneliness of the Long Distance Runner*. To enjoy a movie you have to care about the characters. We go to the cinema and identify with the people we see on screen, it's a huge part of moviegoing. 'That's why everybody goes to see Harrison Ford movies, because you just like him,' says David McCallum. 'Back then you were going to see Albert Finney or Alan Bates, all these people that audiences identified with, and they'd go to see those movies because what was happening to Albert Finney was happening to them.'

By 1963 over a third of British film output dealt with contemporary life in Britain. Then the success of James Bond and, ironically enough,

Tom Jones, which hailed from the creative talents behind the Royal Court (John Osborne and director Tony Richardson), opened the floodgates for Hollywood dosh to flood the British film industry, and the new wave with its accent on gritty realism and regional nuances, was an early casualty.

Still, its echoes resonated throughout the sixties and beyond, influencing later films like *My Beautiful Laundrette* and *The Full Monty*. 'Looking back on that time,' says Rita Tushingham, 'the fifties was to me like a pale black and white, then you get to the sixties and suddenly there's colour added. And I think it was added by the energy of young people suddenly given the opportunity to express themselves.'

That was the key: energy; an energy that hadn't been seen before, that had been suppressed. 'I think all the people I was mixing with realised this was an explosion of energy,' says Elizabeth Harris. 'It was very exciting. It was a very liberating time; nobody felt bound by constrictions of what you could and couldn't do. You didn't think long term, either; you didn't think what am I going to be doing when I'm thirty. Thirty seemed so old! We never planned ahead because then you are being cautious, you're not gambling with life, you're thinking, Do I need a pension? That never entered one's head. And that's the sort of liberation we had that the poor kids today don't have.'

This, then, is the story of that remarkable group of actors, who in just a few short years, from 1956 to 1964, changed the cultural landscape of Britain, took the fight to the establishment, ripped apart the staid British film and theatre industries and paved the way for the Swinging Sixties, at the same time becoming some of the most bankable and successful film stars Britain ever produced.

1
RADA Fledglings

Peter O'Toole arrived in London at the age of twenty in the back of an open-top lorry, keeping several empty beer barrels company. He hadn't drained them dry, they were empty already. After jumping out at Euston station he made his way to a men's hostel in Tottenham Court Road, cutting through Gower Street. Halfway down he stopped in his tracks; there in front of him was the most famous and accomplished drama school in the world, the Royal Academy of Dramatic Art. The nondescript stone entrance wasn't nearly as imposing as he'd thought it might be for such an august institution, so he decided there and then to case the joint, as it were. This in spite of the fact that the previous evening had been spent under the stars in a haystack in Stratford-upon-Avon and the windswept journey down had done little to erode the odour of fertiliser that still clung to him like a too-tight demob suit.

Trudging round the entrance hall, O'Toole's eyes fell immediately upon a bronze bust of George Bernard Shaw, an idol of his and as it happened an avid patron of the academy. While he was admiring it a scholarly looking gentleman, ancient in years and bearing, came up from behind to enquire whether he was a RADA student. 'Indeed not,' said O'Toole. 'But I fully intend to become one.'

Indeed, that was the very reason he was in London that autumn of 1953, having cadged lifts all the way from Leeds in the industrial north. En route he had stopped at Stratford-upon-Avon, his own personal Mecca, where he had bedded down in the bus station before walking to the Shakespeare Memorial Theatre next morning and spending a good portion of what little money he had left on a ticket to see Michael Redgrave play *King Lear*. The rest of the day was spent doing the whole touristy bit, visiting Shakespeare's house and Anne Hathaway's cottage; those memories would stay with him for the rest of his life. Killing the hour before curtain-up, O'Toole took a stroll along the river that snakes past that grand old theatre, watched as people fed the swans and occasionally glanced up at the shifting figures in the windows of the dressing rooms, hoping that one day he might be one of them.

Once in the auditorium O'Toole was, like the rest of the audience, swept along by Redgrave's mesmerising performance. After several pints had been downed in the predictable trip to the pub, there followed a rather rapid local survey for a convenient resting place for the night. O'Toole found one in a bale of hay in a farmer's field, only to discover as he nestled himself in for the night that the straw was merely a soft covering for a very large chunk of manure. 'Did you ever find yourself in the dark up to your shoulders in hot shit?' O'Toole was able to say years later with some authority.

After cleaning up as best he could in the biting cold river next morning O'Toole took breakfast at a roadside café, making a bolt for it without paying when the waitress wasn't looking. A few years hence and the toast of Stratford, O'Toole made a point of revisiting that very café, this time leaving a generous tip.

In the RADA entrance hall, with the trials of the last few days still fresh in his mind, O'Toole rallied enough to offer a few choice Shaw anecdotes that made a dent in his elderly interlocutor's mouth that just about qualified as a smile. The man introduced himself as Sir Kenneth Barnes, principal of the academy. A crashing snob who came to work almost every day dressed in a frock coat and cravat looking like something out of *Tom Brown's Schooldays*, Sir Kenneth had run the academy since 1909, an incredible forty-four years.

With impeccable timing on O'Toole's part it turned out that auditions were being held that very week for the new term; alas, the candidates for these highly sought-after places had already been carefully selected from previous interviews. O'Toole agreed that such rules were important, but hoped in his case they might be bent ever so slightly, perhaps, just this once. Barnes looked at his watch. It was 2 p.m. 'Be at my office at four forty-five this afternoon.'

A broad grin spread over O'Toole's face. 'Thank, you, sir,' he said and raced out into the street.

At the Tottenham Court Road hostel O'Toole took a bath, shaved, borrowed a suit and arrived on the dot at RADA. Barnes welcomed the eager youngster into his office and explained that he'd be required to perform two speeches before a panel of judges. 'Choose something from that,' he said, passing over a sheet of typed paper. 'The other speech you can select yourself. The audition is set for two days' time.' O'Toole's nerves ran riot: forty-eight hours wasn't a very long time to decide one's future. As he scanned the list he was elated to see a favourite speech of his by Professor Higgins from Shaw's *Pygmalion* that he already knew by heart. Things suddenly didn't look so bad. For his other piece O'Toole had decided to go with 'O, what a rogue and peasant slave am I' from *Hamlet*. Now a bit of sartorial elegance was called for: a brand-new tie and a red rose for his lapel bought from Covent Garden. O'Toole was ready.

When destiny called he was shown into a large room to face his inquisitors and gave it everything he'd got. As he was turning to leave a voice struck out: 'How tall are you?' And then another: 'Do you have any professional experience?' O'Toole spun back to face them. 'Six foot two, and no, no professional experience.' 'Take a seat downstairs,' they said. Desperate for a smoke, O'Toole considerately stepped outside onto the pavement and lit up. He'd barely stubbed the thing out when he was requested back inside and told a place at the academy was his. He felt pure joy.

O'Toole always said that he got his love of the arts from his genteel and well-read mother Constance and his sense of style and showmanship from his racecourse-bookie dad Patrick, a dashing gentleman who nearly always drank too much and ended up fighting with the police. One day Patrick sat his son up on the mantelpiece: 'Jump, boy. I'll catch you. Trust me.' When O'Toole jumped his father withdrew his arms, leaving his son painfully spreadeagled on the hard stone floor. The lesson, said his father, was 'never trust any bastard'.

On the north-west coast of Ireland, in County Galway, is the picturesque Connemara, birthplace of Peter O'Toole. He arrived on

2 August 1932. Being Irish has been the most definitive aspect of O'Toole's life, accounting for his passion, his unruly behaviour, his disregard for authority and, of course, his love of the hard stuff. Perhaps O'Toole's attachment to Ireland is so strong because he was forced to leave it at an early age. When his father couldn't find suitable work he moved the whole family to a working-class area of Leeds. O'Toole was a year old. The area was well known for its large population of Irish expatriates. 'A Mick community,' O'Toole described the place, with its narrow back-to-back properties, outside privies, cold-water-only taps and alleyways smelly and filthy black from the waste spewed out by factories. The people were as hard as the conditions; three of his playmates grew up to be hanged for murder: one strangled a girl in a lover's quarrel, one killed a man during a robbery, another dispatched a warden in South Africa with a pair of shears. 'It was a heavy bunch,' he remembered.

Hitler did his best to provide the area with a bit of urban redevelopment. After the first air raid O'Toole stood by a bomb crater and looked around him at the shattered, burned-out buildings. Another night he and his dad opened the front door to watch the spectacle of searchlights in the sky and tracer bullets whirring about, to hear the roar. Suddenly a white flash and an immense blast of heat threw them backwards and halfway up the stairs. They were alive, if slightly singed.

O'Toole attended a Catholic boys' school where the teachers used to rap his knuckles brutally every time he attempted to write with his left hand. He detested the place and left at the earliest opportunity, having sat not a single exam. With the help of a local priest O'Toole managed to land a job on his local paper, the *Yorkshire Evening News*, steadily moving his way up from tea boy to junior reporter. 'But I soon found out that, rather than chronicling events, I wanted to be the event.'

Already O'Toole sensed that his life was not going to follow the more conventional path of his contemporaries. As a teenager he scribbled an oath in his notebook: 'I will not be a common man because it is my right to be an uncommon man. I will stir the smooth sands of monotony.'

While still a reporter O'Toole attended a local arts theatre. He'd a vague notion of perhaps a career working backstage or as a poet or a playwright, but when he appeared briefly in the Christmas pantomime

4

he was singled out and asked to play the lead in their next amateur production. A regular cinema- and theatre-goer, the thought of acting had played across his mind but he'd never given it an ounce of credence. Now here he was, learning lines, attending rehearsals and shaping a proper performance for the first time. When the whole thing became a success he took to writing to drama schools, reading books on drama and taking private lessons from dowager former actresses. But always on the horizon was London and RADA.

So off he went with the good wishes of his parents, a fair wad of cash in his pocket, a hundred Gold Flake cigarettes and a rather natty dressing gown. 'For a few months I swanked around my various London digs, peacocking about in it,' O'Toole recalled. Alas, on his return from a brief holiday he found his flat turned over and most of his possessions stolen, the natty dressing gown amongst them.

O'Toole's life changed from the first morning he attended RADA – 'I thought I'd died and gone to heaven' – not least because of two other striking talents that he found himself in company with: Albert Finney and Alan Bates. 'That was the most remarkable class the academy ever had,' said O'Toole. 'Though we weren't reckoned for much at the time. We were all considered dotty.'

One brilliant afternoon the head boy burst into class asking if young Finney could be excused; the headmaster, Mr Simms, wanted to see him in his office. 'What the hell have I done now?' was the obvious question floating around the Finney cranium as he waited outside the door. Finney was summoned inside and asked to sit down by Mr Simms, who unexpectedly enquired whether he'd ever considered studying drama at RADA. 'What's that?' Finney asked, thinking it might be a school for backward kids. 'It's in London, and you'd be there two years and you'd train to be an actor.' Mr Simms handed over a letter he'd written for Finney's parents which explained the whole thing. He'd also arranged for RADA to send a prospectus and the forms for an audition.

Finney looked at the letter and scratched his head but was in no doubt that he was at a crossroads in his life. Acting had never been a burning ambition; he was fifteen before he even saw his first play in a proper theatre, and that was a school trip he'd gone on only because it got him out of work for the day. Sure it was fun and he enjoyed it, encouraged in the activity by Simms's belief that acting might prove an outlet for his bottled-up energy; he'd even shown some genuine talent for it. So why not give it a bash?

Finney couldn't wait to tell his mum about the headmaster's plans for him but she was less than convinced, having read a newspaper article describing how the great majority of actors were usually out of work. 'It doesn't seem like a very secure job, does it?' Albert's dad, a bookie by trade, always the gambler, looked on the positive side: 'Let him go, if he doesn't like it he can always come back into the family business and I'll make him honest Albert the bookie.' Mother shuddered; the last thing she wanted was her little Albie becoming a bookie.

Before off-course betting became legit bookies like Finney Sr plied an illegal trade from their backyards. They were, in the main, tolerated by the authorities: every now and then the police might pay a friendly visit to arrange a mutually convenient time for a raid. Little Albert often went to race meetings with his father. Over the breakfast table he'd often be asked, 'What lessons have you got today, son?' If the answer was along the lines of, 'Sports, art, a free period, not much, really,' a smile would beam across his face. 'May as well come to Haydock Park, then.' And there he'd be, little Albert mingling with the toffs and toughs of the racing world.

Albert Finney was born on 9 May 1936 in Salford, Greater Manchester, and raised in a two-up, two-down terraced house with a pair of older sisters. He was five years old when a Nazi bomber mistook the local racecourse for the docks and dropped its payload just a few streets away. The family was unhurt, but their home was declared unsafe and the Finneys were moved a mile and a half away to a slightly more upmarket neighbourhood. In the seventies Finney made a pilgrimage to that part of Salford in a bid to relive his childhood memories, because that's all that was left by then: the terraced houses in the streets he grew up in had all been pulled down, the residents moved to live in the sky in characterless tower blocks twenty storeys high. It had been a close-knit community, women chatting on doorsteps, kids playing in the street; the tower blocks took all that away.

There was one constant: school and its difficulties, as if the sole purpose of the place was to test and rile him. He was a bright lad, though, no question – passed the eleven-plus to get into Salford grammar, arriving in the top stream – 'but I regarded the homework rather as an imposition'. When the subject of homework was first broached his immediate thought was: 'What, work at home?' The idea was scarcely believable. So unbelievable, in fact, that he plain didn't do any. He once ran away from home because he was terrified of facing his teacher the next morning having not done his maths homework. The young Finney got as far as the railway station, with Rhyl as his intended destination; yes, he'd live up in the mountains as they'd done on holiday once. To his great disappointment no trains were leaving for Rhyl that day so he sloped off home again, climbing back in through the toilet window.

His lack of application had the inevitable effect, and by the following term he'd slid to the bottom class. Some respite came from acting in school plays, not that young Finney saw himself as a thespian: his primary motive was that during performance week the cast were excused homework.

'Finney!' roared his language master one afternoon as he scanned through the class's returned assignments and saw that one was missing. 'Finney! You haven't done your French. You're here to learn, boy. Why haven't you done your homework?'

'I'm excused from homework, sir,' Finney replied. 'We're doing the play.'

'Oh, I beg your pardon, please forgive me.' The teacher hoped his sarcasm was sufficiently clear. 'I wouldn't dare suggest that learning could interfere with your life as a schoolboy actor.'

It was fun, of course, to pull that kind of stunt in class, and he genuinely loved the attention acting brought him, but not for one second did it enter his head that there was a career in it. Finney had no understanding or love for legitimate theatre; his heroes were all from the cinema, a result of afternoons spent watching the murderous exploits of Cagney and Bogart. That said, there is evidence to suggest that he was capable of taking his acting responsibilities seriously, such as when the school put on the Eugene O'Neill play *The Emperor Jones*, about an

African-American who escapes from prison and lands on a Caribbean island where he sets himself up as ruler. Finney was given the lead (his make-up was boot polish) and went down to the local docks to spend hours studying how the West Indian labourers talked and behaved; he was sixteen at the time. Perhaps it was this attention to detail that caught the eye of Mr Simms.

Somewhat belatedly, he'd also decided to knuckle down academically in his final year. Finney took particular care when it came to geography spending hours drawing maps, shading the edges round coastlines, until one day a teacher saw what he was doing and said, 'That's unnecessary.' Bugger that then, thought Finney, and went back to his old ways. Finney sat his exams and failed the lot, except geography. (For years afterwards he'd find the relatively simple act of writing difficult due to its associations with punishing exams. 'I can always hear the school clock clicking away.') Career-wise, acting was the only option left.

Since Finney was just seventeen it was decided that Mother would accompany him to London for the week of the RADA auditions. 'Be a bit of a change for her,' was the thinking. His sister Marie had written off to several hotels but everywhere was packed out. Father took charge and, flicking through a London guide book, stopped at one page, 'The Dorchester looks all right. Try there.' Marie did, and Finney and his mum surprised the cabbie outside the railway station by asking to be taken to the Dorchester. It certainly beat anything back home in Salford; they were even shown to their room by a man in a tailcoat. As they looked around at the ornate furnishings severe doubts began to emerge; this was posh, maybe too posh. 'Albie,' said Mum, 'be a love and go down and ask how much the room is.' Off he went to reception. 'Excuse me, how much is the room?'

The receptionist looked up, 'Three pounds fifteen shillings a night, young man.' A bloody fortune, then.

'Does that include breakfast?' asked Finney.

The receptionist returned a blank stare.

Finney's dad, who, as a bookie, always dealt in cash, had given his wife a large roll of notes and a big bag of sixpences. She emptied the whole lot onto a coffee table and began to count. They'd just enough, but would have to be frugal, which meant egg and chips every night at the Lyons Corner House near Marble Arch, after which they returned to the Dorchester for their evening entertainment, watching the other guests, dressed in their finery, going into the grand ballroom. 'Isn't it nice sat here watching the elite going to dance?' said Mrs Finney, sipping her nightly gin as Albert enjoyed his glass of cider.

Once back home, news soon drifted up that a place at RADA had been awarded and a scholarship to boot. Finney left home with a full suitcase and a warning from his dad ringing in his ears: 'If anyone stops you on the street, say no.' Most northerners were still mistrustful of London, which was too cosmopolitan by far. So back down he went on the train, alone this time, arriving into a new and wonderful world. 'A fiver a week in my pocket, aged seventeen, in London! My God, what delights!'

Stage-struck from an early age, Alan Bates was just fifteen when he first sat down and wrote to RADA asking how to apply for a place. 'I was attracted to the glamour and the famous people.' In this he was strongly encouraged by a well-known local figure in the area of Derby he'd grown up in: actor and budding director John Dexter. Dexter, the working-class son of a coal miner, saw nearly every play put on in Derby and always seemed to be either going to London to see the latest West End opening or just returning from Stratford. He must have appeared a dazzling figure to the adolescent Bates. He was also ten years his senior and openly homosexual. Their friendship was regarded by Bates's father with about as much equanimity as a herd of rhinos charging through the outside lavatory would generate. Words were had, reassurances requested, but the friendship continued.

'From the age of eleven I knew I had to be an actor,' Bates once revealed. 'What made me so certain? Well, when everyone else said what a ridiculous idea it was then I became certain out of sheer bloody mind-edness.'

The oldest of three brothers, Alan Bates was born in Allestree, Derbyshire, on 17 February 1934. It was his mother Florence Mary, an accomplished pianist, who instilled in Alan a love of theatre and music.

At eight he was enrolled in an academy school that specialised in drama, and because Florence had always insisted her son speak with good diction and grammar, the teachers often singled him out to read poems at morning assemblies and inveigled him into school plays. It was something he resisted at first – 'I would panic and withdraw from it' – but slowly the quiet and reserved little boy, cosseted too much by a smothering mother, opened up like a flower before the sun. In time he became instinctively attracted to acting and was nurtured by an astute teacher who recognised his talent.

He'd an ongoing love affair with the cinema, too, his taste ever evolving, from the moronic laughs of George Formby and the thrills of Tarzan to more sophisticated fare like Olivier's film of *Hamlet*, which he saw no fewer than three times. And there was the theatre. Bates went whenever he could and one evening returning home with his mother suddenly blurted out, 'I can do what we've seen on that stage tonight!' That was it, his career path settled, and in the autumn of 1948 set in concrete when he joined a group of students on a trip to Stratford where he watched a young Paul Scofield triumph.

Both parents received the news with a sort of battlefield weariness, hoping this obsession was a childhood fancy that might disappear in the hormonal vapour of pubescence. Bates's father Harold had attended London's Royal College of Music and was a gifted cellist but never quite adapted to the hurly-burly life of a touring orchestra, and with a young family to support settled into the life of an insurance salesman which offered more stable income.

He hoped his son might also come to his senses and opt for a proper job, but Alan was perceptive enough to see that his father's short temper and sudden bursts of bitter anger were perhaps the result of thwarted ambition and he was determined not to repeat the mistake. Besides, academia had been a distinct disappointment; study bored him and he'd barely scrapped together an adequate portfolio of grades. Acting was something he did well and something where this still rather private boy could show off.

His parents, now sympathetic to their son's artistic ambition, got him a place in the Derby Shakespeare Society where he quickly gained his first speaking role in a production of *King John*, playing Prince Arthur, whose most impassioned speech is his plea for mercy at the hands of an assassin. 'I was smashing,' Bates would later vouch. 'Even though I forgot to take off my wristwatch while I was playing a thirteenth-century prince.' Impressed, the heads of the society had no hesitation in casting Bates in their next production.

Perhaps it was time to make a second approach to RADA, his first having been rejected because he wasn't old enough, but his parents and teachers expressed concern that he was still perhaps too young at seventeen and really ought to stay one more year at school. But Bates was intensely bored with his life in Derby and desperate to get out. He found the atmosphere of suburbia stifling and inhibiting. He felt frustrated. Finally, his parents caved in and when Bates heard he'd been accepted by the academy his joy was tempered only by the reality of how his career was going to be financed. The fees were far beyond his father's means. Generously, Bates's teachers petitioned Derby County Council with an endorsement of his talents and a handsome grant was eventually forthcoming.

Arriving in London full of trepidation, Bates discovered that John Dexter was living in a flat in Hampstead. He moved in, ignoring the inevitable rumours their sharing would generate. The rowdy antics of the theatricals who were also frequent guests wasn't his scene at all, though, and Bates soon moved out.

RADA students tended to change digs as the rest of us change underwear. Peter O'Toole lived in a succession of dingy bedsits; even for a time on a barge that sank one night during a party after too many revellers came aboard. 'We all took turns at the pumps,' recalled classmate Frank Finlay. The barge was but one of what O'Toole estimated to be twenty-five different places he rested his noggin during his tenure as a student. This kind of haphazard existence led to regular greetings of, 'Hello, Peter, which hedge did you sleep under last night?' as he bounded through the academy's door. One night after seeing the musical *Guys and Dolls* in the West End and endeavouring to walk home with a bottle of whisky for company he spent the night under the stars on the old bandstand in Green Park.

Albert Finney took small lodgings in Finchley Central in north London; after paying the rent, there was just enough out of his allowance for tube fare, five fags a day and then either two cups of coffee or a pint of beer. He'd bypass lunch altogether. When Kenneth Barnes got to hear of this from the canteen staff he called Finney to his study, telling him of his concern that he might become undernourished. 'That shows how they kept an eye on you,' said Finney. To save money he used to send his laundry home, as many students did, as laundromats were expensive and very few and far between.

In comparison with O'Toole and Finney, Bates, having taken voice lessons and played Shakespeare, was reasonably prepared for RADA; although lacking confidence, he believed this helped him at least to understand what the teachers were talking about. For the young Finney RADA was a complete culture shock, he felt inadequate amongst his fellow drama students, who numbered almost seventy, blaming his poor education. Dubbing himself 'a bit uncouth', this lack of sophistication battered any self-confidence he might have brought with him, his knowledge of literature and theatre was practically nil and here he was rubbing shoulders with some folk who had degrees dropping out of their pockets.

And then there was his Salford accent, which made him feel more out of place than anything else. 'I was surrounded by the accents of a world I didn't know about. I was conscious of what I was and where I came from for the first time.'

As for the female students, they were untouchable goddesses. O'Toole's very first day had him standing in the hall listening not at all to instructions about where to hang his donkey jacket and the like, instead ogling the constant parade of women going up and down the staircase, a beautiful Indian girl in a sari, a blonde bombshell in tight slacks and an even tighter sweater; his eyes were on stalks. Finney felt unattractive and awkward around them: 'I was a bit porky in those days and I'd had a crew cut which must have looked terrible.'

Besides O'Toole, Finney and Bates the roster of RADA students around at that time was remarkable, add the names of Peter Bowles, Roy Kinnear, Ronald Fraser, John Stride, Julian Glover, Richard Briers and Frank Finlay, capable actors every one who enjoyed substantial careers. Inevitably there was fierce rivalry, excellent training for the harsh realities of the theatrical profession. 'It was because we all knew we had potential,' said Peter Bowles. 'Finney, O'Toole and Bates were all swaggering around. They threw down the gauntlet. They said, "There, that's my Macbeth – beat that!"' Being competitive in that environment became almost an automatic reflex. A student would see a performance given by a colleague and think, God, I'll have to find something quick if I'm going to keep up.

Easily likeable and with a friendly disposition, Bates had quickly established himself as one of the most popular pupils, certainly one to watch. When he was cast in the lead in a production of *She Stoops to Conquer* classmates recalled how on the very first day of rehearsal Bates was already word perfect. He'd also begun to elicit some very persistent female attention, but those smitten found it difficult to stir within him anything other than a basic friendship. The gossip of the time centred on his closeness to certain male colleagues. It was all very secretive, not so much because of society's taboo surrounding homosexuality, but the personal horror Bates had of any such notion reaching his mother's ears.

Finney, though, was still finding his feet and for the first two terms was deeply unhappy. The problem was simple. Acting had been fun and uninhibited in school plays; now it became rather more like work, something he'd not particularly cared for through his adolescence. The craft behind acting worried him, too; teachers would say how many steps to take in a scene, how to control one's breathing and use the pitch in one's voice. It was all too rigid an approach, too stifling, lacking emotion, feeling and freedom. The whole place felt like just another school, as student Virginia Stride recalls: 'In the reception area there was the sergeant, he was quite strict, he took a dim view of us all rushing up and down the stairs, it was that kind of thing, you felt an eagle eye on you all the time. Some of the staff were rather like school teachers.'

RADA was also stolidly traditional in its approach to drama tuition, concerned almost entirely with technique. 'Some of them good and some of them not so good,' said Bates. 'How to speak, how to move, how to dance – never how to think.' It was a policy imposed from on high, from Sir Kenneth Barnes, and therein lay the problem. 'Sir Kenneth's attitude was entrenched in a kind of theatre that had already disappeared,' says Keith Baxter, a fellow RADA student. The sort of theatre typified by grandstanding actor-manager types like Sir Herbert Beerbohm Tree who dominated the London stage at the end of the nineteenth century. 'That was the sort of theatre Kenneth Barnes represented and believed in,' says Baxter. 'But even we knew that that had gone. And we also knew that what we were being schooled in was not right.'

Barnes had populated RADA with a staff drawn largely from a sort of cobweb-strewn twilight world, theatrical equivalents of Miss Haversham. There was Ernest Milton, a Shakespearean actor very definitely of the old school. Finney recalled seeing Milton once huffing and puffing after a departing train, yelling at the top of his voice, 'Stop! Stop! You're killing a genius!' And there was Nell Carter, whose claim to fame was that she had been Narissa to Dame Irene Vanbrugh's Portia before the First World War. Dame Irene was the older sister of Kenneth Barnes; it was all very much like that. And it was this sort of elitism that coloured Barnes's thinking when it came to RADA, although to be fair to him more than one ex-student admitted that the principal had a gift for spotting talent. He did, however, believe that West End theatre was the reserve of middle-class actors whose mothers took tea in Tunbridge Wells. Keith Baxter knows that only too well. After a year at RADA he was asked to play Claudio in *Much Ado About Nothing*. 'After the performance we all had to have a critique individually by Sir Kenneth and I couldn't work out what he was getting at, except that he was advising me that he didn't think I would have a life in the theatre. Later on I realised that what he was saying was that I was too common. I came from Wales.' That suddenly so many students were turning up from the Midlands and the north and further afield was mystifying to the old guard. 'It was a fact that Sir Kenneth couldn't cope with at all,' says another RADA alumnus of that time, Shirley Dixon.

Hardly a surprise, then, that film technique or how to act on television was completely ignored, all part of the inherent snobbishness that existed in every brass handle and marble slab of the place. One was taught how to perform for the Stratford stage, not BBC Lime Grove. Finney never forgot one teacher belittling cinema, saying it was OK for making a quick buck but the theatre was an actor's true calling. 'Even at seventeen I knew the man was a fool.'

Finney held his tongue for the most part, leaving the rebel rousing to O'Toole, who could display sheer contempt for the tutors, sometimes screeching during rehearsals, 'My God, what the hell does he know? If he were any good he wouldn't be teaching here, would he?' There was a wildness in him, inherent, God-given, that simply would not be subsumed. 'He'd never take direction,' remembered Roy Kinnear. 'That's the confidence of youth. Peter would tell the director how he was going to do a scene and then do it.'

Students were required to attend voice production lessons with a prepared speech which they'd perform and then submit to a critique. O'Toole arrived one day with nothing prepared. 'That's all right,' said the teacher, handing him a book. 'Read something out of that.' O'Toole started. 'No, no,' said the teacher. 'Do it again.' O'Toole sighed audibly before beginning once more. Just a few lines in, the tutor interrupted again, 'No, no, no!' O'Toole threw the book at him and stormed out, not returning to the class for a week. He later apologised.

Finney and O'Toole shared many a lesson and got along heartily; even ballet classes saw the two of them contorting their bodies into shapes no earthly being would ever require of them again. Both men were near-cripples after their first lesson. 'Pain grinds through every inch of me,' O'Toole testified to the torture. 'And I have grave worries concerning the whereabouts of my testicles.' The sheer gusto and exuberance of O'Toole must have filtered through into Finney for by his fourth term he'd gained a belief and a confidence in his abilities that he was never to lose. Instead of going into lessons thinking the rest of the class were laughing at him he thought, no, they're going to learn from me. It was a positivity that allowed him to surge forward. Much of it also came about after playing Toby Belch in *Twelfth Night*, a role he could really get stuck into. Blocking his moves at the first rehearsal, Finney asked where he should enter from. 'Come in from where you like,' said the teacher. A breath of fresh air: not having a way of acting imposed on him was liberating to Finney. 'Now, with training, I did feel that I had a bit of a knack for the old acting.'

By this time Finney was sharing a flat with Peter Bowles. The two became very close and shared many a domestic mishap. He was now doing his own laundry, and wash day could be a trial. To dry their damp clothes when the weather was poor they'd resort to hanging them all over the kitchenette and turning the gas rings up full blast. The landlady was apoplectic when she saw her gas bill. Bowles fondly recalled an evening of discussion about how one day they'd both like to play Macbeth. Bowles went first, declaring an honest intent to research thoroughly the historical period depicted by Shakespeare, perhaps a foray into the proper make of kilt to wear, an appreciation of the legends of the Highlands and the clans. 'How would you approach it, Albie?' Finney looked across almost scornfully. 'I'd learn the fucking lines and walk on,' he said. Bearing in mind his earlier conscientious research for *The Emperor Jones*, however, this dismissive response perhaps owed as much to bravado as arrogance.

Attending as many theatre performances as possible was definitely encouraged, which for the poorer students meant queuing for hours for cheap seats to become available. In the autumn of 1953 Richard Burton reigned supreme at the Old Vic. Back from his first foray into Hollywood for the lumpen biblical epic *The Robe*, tickets were like gold dust with the twenty-eight-year-old hailed as the new Olivier. A group of RADA students, O'Toole amongst their number, decided to see *King John*, with Burton playing Philip the Bastard. After queuing in shifts they got their tickets and sat up in the gods, crackling with anticipation. They were not to be disappointed, Burton's sheer presence and charisma were awesome, and few eyes dared drift away to the other performers.

Robert Hardy was in that production and recalls an incident that amply demonstrates the sheer power of Burton's personality at the time. 'There must have been twenty people on the stage, all looking out front, and Richard came on as the Bastard and behaved so wickedly and subtly with us all that the entire cast had to turn upstage with our backs to the audience; we'd absolutely collapsed. That was presence.'

The curtain that evening fell to applause like thunder and O'Toole stepped outside into a cold, windy Waterloo Road almost traumatised by what he'd seen. One of the girls insisted on going round to the stage door, hoping to catch a glimpse of her idol. Everyone followed.

Conveniently located nearby was a pub and O'Toole made haste inside, sure from what he'd read about Burton that he'd most likely be in at some point. O'Toole sat down, lit up and put the bitter to his lips while he tried to make sense of the evening.

Sure enough the cast arrived, headed by Burton who was soon calling for a pint. O'Toole watched him like a hawk, impressed now as much by the man's drinking as by his acting; 'Burton lifted his pint with an ease and sure-handedness that told of diligent practice.' Another thought played around in his mind. Here he was sitting in the same pub as the actors who hitherto had entertained him so grandly; there was laughter, good humour. It delighted him, yes, 'but though I can see and hear all this, I cannot yet touch it'. They were professionals while O'Toole was still very much the apprentice.

Eventually the rest of his group joined him, only for Burton to suddenly look over and catch the hero-worshipping gaze of the giggling girls. No doubt he could tell that they were all most likely drama students. A brief pause, then Burton looked straight into O'Toole's face. 'A grin as big as it was friendly,' O'Toole recalled. 'He raised his glass to me, to my friends, we raised our glasses to him, and then with the grin still on him he ambled away' to join his fellow players at the far end of the bar.

2

When Connery Met Caine

Of course, the prospect of attending RADA or any of the other London drama schools was enhanced for these working-class provincial lads by the allure of the capital itself: the promise of opportunity amidst the gaudy neon lights of Piccadilly and Soho. The first time Sean Connery ever left Scotland was to come down to London with some pals in 1951 for the Festival of Britain, an experience that left a lasting impression on him, especially in those austere post-war years; 'We were caught up in its sense of optimism that a new era was beginning.'

It didn't seem like it when he returned to the drab stone edifices of Fountainbridge. The streets Connery grew up in were a far cry from the tourist image of Edinburgh; you'd be hard pressed to find a post-card with Fountainbridge's wretched, depressing face on it. Never was 'Auld Reekie' more apt, for all day the local brewery and manufacturing plants spewed out stench into the air. But in spite of the poverty, or maybe even because of it, there was a sense of community, people could keep their doors unlocked safe in the knowledge no urchin would dare thieve from them, probably because there wasn't anything worth nicking inside.

Connery's father Joe worked at the local rubber mill. He was a simple, hard-working man, unashamedly old fashioned in his attitude and bearing. Back in those days it just wasn't done for the father to be present at the birth of his children, which suited Joe fine as he celebrated the news of his firstborn down the local pub on 25 August 1930.

The young Connery, who was christened Thomas, grew up in a rented flat consisting of just two rooms: a large kitchen-cum-living room and a bedroom. Legend has it that Connery's first cot was the bottom drawer of a wardrobe at the foot of his parents' bed. When he got too big for that he was transferred to the other room to sleep on a bed-settee. Twelve other families shared the tenement block. There was no hot water and no bathroom and the communal toilet was outside. For a bath, Joe doused the child, when he was still small enough to fit, under the cold water tap in the sink. He later graduated to a tin tub in front of the fire.

His mother Effie (short for Euphemia) worked as an office cleaner and was, according to her son, the 'engine' of the family. She was thrifty and needed to be, never frittering away her pennies on luxuries, so even when money was tight the family didn't go hungry. Victor Spinetti, who later befriended Connery, recalls meeting Effie during a visit to Fountainbridge. 'I remember going up the steps to this flat and hanging outside their front door was this mirror, an oval mirror, and I thought, isn't that marvellous having a mirror on the outside; it was the bottom of the tin bath. Mrs Connery was such a marvellous lady she cleaned this bath till it sparkled. And the flat was so tidy and clean; it was so spotless you could eat off the floor. She was an amazing lady, Effie.'

Like most kids in the area Connery grew up fast. He had little choice; life's training ground was the streets. With no parks nearby to roam the kids played football in the road, goalposts chalked on the walls, or fished using jam jars in the Union Canal; carefree pleasures amidst the grinding poverty, although they were largely oblivious to their under-privileged background. 'Looking back, I think it's fair to say that we were disadvantaged,' recalled Craigie Veitch, an old school chum. 'We grew up in an area of social deprivation. But in those days, of course, we didn't have social workers to tell us that. Consequently we were as happy as pigs in shit.'

There was the odd glimpse of how the other half lived. During the war Fountainbridge's children were taught in the houses of the middle class, for fear bombs might fall on school buildings. Connery remembers being made to feel distinctly unwelcome. 'A lot of people didn't want certain kids in their houses, and I was one of them.' For maybe the first time in his life Connery understood what privilege meant, and it stank of injustice.

At school Connery was hardly an enthusiastic pupil. Darroch Secondary School specialised in technical subjects such as metalwork and carpentry, preparation for a life of manual labour, like their fathers before them. Discipline was harsh; one teacher used his large Chambers dictionary to wallop errant pupils. And football ruled the sporting field; the rugby playing swots over at the nearby grammar school were viewed with disdain. Academia simply passed Connery by, and he didn't care a jot. At fourteen he'd had enough and left school without a single qualification. 'I never remembered anybody making school sufficiently stimulating or interesting to make me want to stay. I couldn't wait to go to work.'

Since the age of nine Connery had been employed as a milk-delivery boy, getting up at five in the morning and helping on the horse-drawn wagons before going off to school. Now he was offered a full-time post at the dairy at a little over two pounds a week, all of which he gave to Effie to help with the housekeeping. To earn spending money he took an evening job delivering newspapers, covering two miles of Edinburgh's busy streets on foot.

Out on his milk round one day the horse's harness broke and Connery, by now riding solo, panicked, leaving the animal and his cargo in the middle of a busy thoroughfare while he ran back to the stables for help. 'It's as well he made it as an actor,' observed his boss years later, 'because he'd no' have made it as a milkman.'

By the age of fourteen Connery already cut an imposing figure, becoming almost too big for the flat; he turned the glass doorknob to his parents' bedroom on one occasion and crushed it in his hand. Regular visits to a boxing gym meant he could certainly handle himself. One night at a dance hall he was menaced by a gang of local thugs who cornered him on the balcony, drawing him closer to the edge and the fifteen-foot drop to the main dance floor below. It was then that Connery made his move, grabbing one by the neck and hurling him to the ground while decking two of the others. They left him alone after that.

Bored with the grinding routine of life, the seventeen-year-old Connery saw the navy as a way out and signed on for seven years. He had visions of sailing to exotic ports, but in the end never got further than Portsmouth. When not scrubbing decks he was fighting for the ship's boxing team, usually against men twice his age. 'It wasn't exactly a bundle of laughs. When you box in the services, all they want is blood; it was usually my blood they got.' He was given a medical discharge at the age of nineteen thanks to a duodenal ulcer.

Probably just as well, for life in the navy obviously wasn't suitable for a rugged individualist who found it hard to conform to the service's rules and rigid structure. It wasn't the discipline, hell he'd been slogging his guts out since the age of nine, it was the class-riddled pecking order and his reluctance to take orders from chinless wonders who'd become officers purely through privilege. His only souvenirs of his time at sea were a pair of tattoos on his right forearm, as synonymous with naval life as vomiting over the stern in a gale: 'Scotland forever' and 'Mum and Dad'.

Connery returned home a little humbled; his first attempt to better himself and break free had failed. During the next few years he took a succession of dead-end jobs: delivering coal, bricklaying, cement mixing, lifeguard, digging ditches and dance-hall bouncer. For a while he worked as a coffin polisher on the other side of the city and to save bus fare would sometimes stay overnight, sleeping in one of the coffins. Connery had inherited his father's work ethic and was never afraid of hard graft, but at the same time he had no grasp of what he wanted to achieve, no sense of the future or clear ambition beyond getting his pay packet at the end of the week.

His real passion was bodybuilding and he'd joined a weightlifting club that met several times a week in an old air-raid shelter that stank of liniment and body odour. 'It was not so much to be fitter but to look good for girls.' Connery's well-toned body was soon in demand as an artist's model, posing semi-nude for students at the Edinburgh School of Art, though he found it sometimes embarrassing that girls in the class always wanted to sketch him up close and very personal. Then in the autumn of 1952 he answered an ad in the local paper for male extras to play guardsmen in a touring production of *Sixty Glorious Years* starring Anna Neagle, a glamorous British film star of the thirties and forties. For a kid raised on football, comics and Saturday-morning flicks the cultured atmosphere of Edinburgh's Empire Theatre held a curious fascination. He stood about in crowd scenes dressed in a fancy uniform doing nothing of any import, but it was certainly less back-breaking than digging ditches.

Early in 1953, working in the noisy printing room of the *Edinburgh Evening News*, Connery was persuaded to try his luck at the Mr Universe contest, which that year was being held in London. The contest ultimately proved a disappointment. The American competitors were hulking behemoths; beside the winner Connery looked like a seven-stone weakling who was liable to get sand kicked in his face. But the trip wasn't to be an entirely wasted venture. Hearing from a colleague that chorus parts were available in the musical *South Pacific*, then closing a successful West End run in preparation for a national tour, Connery remembered how much he'd enjoyed his previous time as an extra and decided to have a crack, undaunted by his complete lack of experience. 'I knew there and then I didn't want to go back to my job in Edinburgh.'

The auditions were held at the Theatre Royal in Drury Lane, where *South Pacific* had been packing them in for three years. His first reading was a disaster. After just a few seconds on stage he succumbed to nerves and dropped his script, the pages fluttering to the floor. 'Hurry up,' said a voice from the darkened stalls as Connery began picking them up. 'We haven't got all day.'

'Neither have I,' Connery replied and stormed off.

'Hey, bring that guy back here.'

Connery returned. Lying that he could sing like Crosby and dance like Astaire, Connery launched into a sailor's shanty, dredged up a few nifty moves from his dance-hall days and read the dialogue in as near an American accent as he could muster. To his utter astonishment he was hired, though physique as much as ability probably won him the job. Director Joshua Logan had been on the lookout for hefty lads to sing, 'There is Nothing like a Dame' with a degree more conviction than the average limp-wristed West End male chorus line.

'What's the wage?' Connery asked, bold as brass.

'That doesn't concern me,' Logan snapped.

'Well, it concerns me.' From the get-go Connery was taking no nonsense.

A deal for twelve pounds a week was reached, twice as much as Connery had ever earned in his life, and all he had to do was work nights, the days were pretty much free – it was money for jam. Back in Fountainbridge, friends received the news with mild surprise: Tommy going into show business, fancy that. Work colleagues were a little more sceptical, believing he'd return soon enough asking for his old job back. But Connery made an impact straight away, particularly on the female members of the company. And there's a witness to this. Millicent Martin was then understudy to *South Pacific*'s American star Mary Martin and had been with the show for two years. The memories of the young and inexperienced Connery showing up for rehearsals are still vivid in Millicent's mind and bring a tingle of sweet nostalgia to her cheery voice. 'He came in and he was just lovely, all the girls fell in love with him. He stood out. He didn't have a word to say in the show, but he looked so stunning, we all thought he would make it because he was so gorgeous to look at.'

For three days, though, no one would talk to him; it wasn't that he was physically intimidating, it was his accent, heavy and tar-thick. Millicent decided to take matters into her own hands. 'Drury Lane has this very big lobby and after rehearsals everybody was streaming out, so I grabbed Sean and took him over into a corner and said, "Maybe you're wondering why we haven't spoken to you, it's because we can't understand you." And he said, "What the +*~#?*" I said, "If you could speak a little slower, just for a few days." He said, "Will . . . this . . . be . . . all . . . right?" I said, "That's perfect. If you can hold it down to that then we'll all be able to talk to you." And, bless his heart, he did.'

Sometime in the 1990s, having not seen Connery for twenty years, Millicent was at a party at the house of Julie Andrews and Blake Edwards in Malibu when Sean turned up as the surprise guest. 'And over dinner he brought up this story. "Do you know," he said. "Millie was the only one who had the guts to come over and tell me how heavy my Scots accent was? She didn't know how I was going to react to that, it was so sweet of her, and I'll always remember that." I was absolutely dumbstruck that he'd remembered.'

During those final few shows in London Millicent's apartment was broken into and several personal items taken. She came in very shaken and upset the next day but like a trouper did that evening's perform-ance. As she was preparing to leave there was a knock on her dressing-room door. It was Connery, offering to take her home. 'So he drove me back, and when we arrived he looked all round the apartment to make sure everything was OK and then said, "Look would you like me to sleep in one of the other bedrooms and stay if you're nervous?" I said I'd be fine, and so he had a quick cup of tea and then went. Very, very sweet.'

When the curtain finally fell on *South Pacific* in London Millicent didn't go on the provincial tour, having been offered another musical. Of course she kept tabs on Connery's career, thrilled by his eventual success: 'We were all very proud of him because as far as we were concerned, all the people in *South Pacific*, he was ours.'

One Saturday night after the show Connery attended a house party. It was clearly an actors' party because most of the guests looked half famished, being either out of work or appearing in rep on lousy wages. When Connery walked in, looking like Charles Atlas, all muscles and brimming with health, every eye fell on him: Who the hell is that? It can't be an actor; he doesn't look like he's been starving all week.

One of the youngest amongst the crowd grew curious and walked over to introduce himself as Michael Scott. There seemed to be an immediate rapport between the two men and they promised to keep in touch, but wouldn't in fact meet up again for another few years when they forged what would become a long and famous friendship. Michael Scott had just changed his name from Maurice Micklewhite. The following year he changed it again, to Michael Caine.

A good deal of the glue that has kept these two men bonded over some sixty years is the stark similarity of their childhoods. Caine's father was a porter at London's Billingsgate fish market, up at four in the morning and carrying crates of fish packed in ice for eight hours solid. His Mother Ellen worked as a charlady and was your typical working-class mum, devoted to her family and as tough as nails. Money was scarce and much of her husband's wages ended up in the local bookies or sometimes the pub, but Caine never went hungry as a kid or felt bereft of comfort and love.

Michael Caine was born on 14 March 1933 and named after his father. The Micklewhites lived in a two-room flat in Camberwell, a pretty shabby part of a pretty shabby south London suburb, at the top of a tall Victorian terraced house, five flights away from the outside toilet that was shared by four other families. That was especially tough for little Maurice, who wore special shoes because his bones had been weakened by rickets. Mum and Dad lived in one room and their son occupied the other, which, like the Connerys', was a combined kitchen and dining room. The Micklewhites had a tin tub, too, which was also used for the laundry. Cramped became positively overcrowded when a second child, Stanley, arrived. Famously proud of his working-class roots, Caine felt less nostalgic about his birthplace itself and shed no tears when the area was redeveloped in the sixties and whole swathes of his past fell to the bulldozer.

The war arrived when Caine was six and upended his life utterly. He and Stanley were given a gas mask each at school one day and then told to wave goodbye to their sobbing mother before walking two miles to Waterloo station and a train that would evacuate them to leafy Berkshire, far from Hitler's bombs. Separated from his brother, he was entrusted to what seemed like a smiling and charitable couple who proved to be psychos of the highest order when they locked him in a cupboard for twenty-four hours. Ellen arrived in true cavalry style to cart her boys back home to London, thinking the Luftwaffe was more friendly.

Bombs had begun to drop unnervingly close to the Micklewhite homestead and Maurice Sr dug a shelter in the garden. After he was called up to serve in the Royal Artillery, Ellen took her boys to live on a farm in Norfolk that was inhabited by several other London evacuees. Caine loved his time there – the animals, the freedom, the fresh air; such a change from the Smoke. But for the parents in surrounding villages this invasion seemed only a little less disagreeable than a Nazi one and they kept their own children at arm's distance, fearful they'd catch lice, 'or worse, our cockney accents', said Caine.

For a time Ellen landed a job as a cook in a nearby manor house and for the first time in his life Caine saw for himself how the other half lived; things that were luxuries to him, like hot running water and electric lights, were commonplace here. And fridges – what a marvel! Back home the milk bottles were kept in a bucket of cold water outside in the summer. And there were the dinner parties, with caviar, pheasant, port and brandy, cigars, the works. 'I'm going to live exactly like this,' he decided there and then.

Often the family trudged back to London, mainly to see if their house was still standing, and experienced some of the worst nights of the Blitz. Caine was never to forget the sheer terror instilled in people by the V-1 rocket or 'doodlebug', a pilotless flying bomb that landed indiscriminately. If you heard its engine cut out you knew it was time to duck. These were slingshots, however, compared to the V-2 which arrived in 1944. Caine survived one attack that occurred without warning, just a sudden blinding flash and the street next to the Micklewhites and everyone in it were gone.

After the war the euphoria of victory quickly subsided as rationing continued to blight the lives of the populace, while London seemed like one large bomb site. The only bright spots for Caine were his regular trips to the cinema, an escape route for a couple of hours from the sheer bloody drabness of it all. He noticed something strange, though: British movies always seemed populated by frightfully posh people with strangulated vowels, while Hollywood movies embraced the ordinary man, and heroes that people like Caine could identify with.

With their house unfit to live in owing to bomb damage, the Micklewhites were moved into prefabricated accommodation. The prefab was small, but had all the mod cons, including an inside toilet – what luxury! Their new address was the Elephant and Castle, a rough area full of gangs and spivs who carried razor blades and weren't afraid to use them. 'The streets were as dangerous as it was possible to get without anybody actually declaring war,' Caine recalled.

After passing his eleven-plus Caine went to the local grammar school but grew rebellious and restless, often deliberately antagonising teachers and fellow pupils, a self-styled loner with a 'stay away' attitude. Such behaviour combined with a penchant for truancy meant that both his work and his backside suffered. Escape arrived once again in the form of the cinema, only now Caine knew that's what he wanted to do with his life, become an actor. Unfortunately he had not the slightest idea how someone from his situation went about it. He decided that a good start would be to join a local drama club, where he loved the thrill of putting on a show. It was the greatest sense of achievement he'd ever felt, even though his father viewed his son's acting ambitions with scarcely concealed suspicion, asking on more than one occasion, 'Are you a nancy boy?'

At sixteen Caine left school, a development that delighted him. 'The feeling, I was assured on my last day by the headmaster, was mutual.' After a few dead-end jobs National Service beckoned and Caine spent the next two years in Germany, exhibiting much the same level of commitment as his fellow sufferers: 'Survive and get out.' The survival aspect seemed less certain when he went off to fight in the Korean War with the Royal Fusiliers. Much time was spent in dirty trenches, where rats wandered over his sleeping body, near several thousand warring Chinese who occasionally attacked only to be mown down by machine-gun fire. Suicide squads were sometimes dispatched by the enemy to blow themselves up in the minefields or hurl their disposable bodies across the barbed wire, leaving the path free for the crack troops. When he saw the bodies that they picked off the wire Caine wondered about the merits of communism. The suicide squads were all old men and boys, some as young as twelve.

After all that the Elephant and Castle must have seemed like paradise when Caine returned in 1952, but he moped about the house, wondering how to get started as an actor. 'Why don't you get up off your arse and go and get a job?' his father helpfully suggested. He was glumly employed in a factory when a work colleague who knew of Caine's theatrical ambitions explained that his daughter was a singer and there was a newspaper she found useful called the *Stage* which carried advertisements for the entertainment profession. He bought a copy and sat on a bench in Leicester Square to leaf through it. The only suitable vacancy was a job as assistant stage manager and bit-part player at a small repertory theatre in Horsham, Sussex. Determined to do things properly, he had his photograph professionally taken and, having recently come to the conclusion that Maurice Micklewhite just wouldn't do at all, changed his name to Michael Scott – quite dashing, he thought. Off went the photograph and application and not long afterwards came a request to see the company's proprietor, a chap by the name of Alwyn Fox, who turned out to be very 'theatrical' indeed. 'Well, I suppose you'll be all right for those small butch parts like policemen that *we* have so much difficulty with.' Caine was hired. And quids in, too, certainly with the ladies in the company since most of the male actors were very much batting on Mr Fox's team.

It's interesting to note here that Caine, just like Connery, had set about becoming an actor literally from the bottom up. There was never any thought of going to a drama school like RADA, which both men equated with the class system, churning out acting clones with plums in their throats. Even then Caine's ambition was to portray real people accurately on stage and film, the sort of people he grew up and lived amongst, the class who were either ignored or not properly represented in British films.

Caine's professional debut was a disaster. Coming on as a policeman at the end of a thriller to arrest the villain he forgot to do up his flies, got a huge laugh from the audience and consequently forgot his line. A helpful actor whispered it and Caine shouted back, 'What?' Other disasters followed, like the time he wore a top hat too big for the flimsy set and as he entered it took the top of the doorway off. But as the months went by his roles grew in stature and he gained valuable experience. Then one night during a performance of *Wuthering Heights* Caine suddenly collapsed on stage and was rushed to hospital. Coming round, through blurry vision he saw a nurse and, sensing the mist of unconsciousness descending once again, quickly blurted out, 'I've got malaria.' The nurse looked quizzically at him. 'You can't catch malaria in Sussex.' It was his Korean misadventure coming back to haunt him. It turned out to be a rare virulent strain, and quite incurable; in twenty years Caine could be dead. It was Fox who raised his spirits from the floor, telling him that as soon as he was ready and able the whole company wanted him back. And there was renewed hope from the doctors too; they were looking for volunteers to test a new drug for this very type of malaria. Still in the experimental stage, it was risky, possibly fatal, but what was the alternative? A life with a death sentence attached to it. Caine signed on.

The gamble paid off; the treatment was an unqualified success and after a few weeks of recuperation Caine packed his suitcase and caught a train back to Horsham. When he arrived at the theatre everything looked decidedly quiet. Of Mr Fox and the others there was no sign. The company had gone bust. He never saw any of them again. Flash forward to the 1970s, Caine is a major star living in Beverly Hills. His agent tells of a letter he's received from social services in Hammersmith about an utterly destitute and dying man in one of their hospitals who has been telling everyone that he used to be a theatre producer and that Michael Caine was his discovery. No one believed him, of course, but the authorities were writing just in case there was any truth in his tale and if Mr Caine might send some money so the poor man's last few weeks might pass in relative comfort.

Caine was astounded and wrote back saying it was all true and enclosing a handsome cheque. Two weeks later the cheque arrived back uncashed, with a note. It said the dying man had been thrilled beyond words to receive his letter and proudly showed it round the hospital. That night Mr Alwyn Fox went to bed the happiest he'd been for years, and passed away.

3

On the Road

For most of 1954 Connery criss-crossed the country with *South Pacific*, playing to packed houses every night as it became one of the most successful touring productions ever staged in Britain. At first it was an adventure, nothing more. 'It all seemed like a giggle.' Certainly Connery never considered himself a budding actor, but the adrenalin rush of being on stage, the applause and the attention soon became addictive. The crowds of women who flocked to the show, not so much for the famous tunes but to ogle the bicep-bulging chorus line, helped too.

More importantly, acting offered him a direction and a purpose; like the navy, it was an escape route from a bleak existence back home. The only thing that irritated him was having to share a dressing room with a frightfully old thespian type who preened himself in front of the mirror for hours on end. When he finally left, Connery breathed a huge sigh of relief but feared the worst when his replacement arrived wearing a fur coat and clutching a teddy bear. It was Victor Spinetti, who may have felt the same trepidation about Connery, who was completely starkers and pissing in the sink when he walked into the dressing room. It's a memory he's never forgotten. 'Sean turned round and put his hand over his bollocks and said, "Hello, a pigeon sitting on two eggs," and I said, "That's not a pigeon, darling, that's a crow."'

Spinetti had been brought in to understudy one of the leads and had been with the show for only two weeks when the actor in question tripped and smashed his kneecap on one of the large stage microphones. 'He was carried off and I was in the wings and got a shove from Sean who said, "You're on." I managed to get through the best I could, everyone was supportive, and that night in the digs – Sean and I shared digs – he said, "Right, you got through it on nerve, but now you've got to give a performance." So we sat up all night and he went through the lines with me. He was fabulous. And we were so naive, there were no drugs or anything, it was black coffee that kept us awake.' The following night Spinetti excelled and was asked to take over the role permanently. After that Connery and Spinetti often shared digs. 'In Dublin we even shared a bed! Because it was cheaper, nothing else. And Sean used to fall out of bed laughing onto the floor. He had a tremendous sense of humour. He was full of fun.'

It was this kind of genuineness mixed with a beguiling charm that made Connery many friends in the company, including Robert Henderson, an American actor/director twenty-five years his senior. Often they chatted for hours about acting and drama, and during one of these conversations the name Ibsen was mentioned; Connery shook his head, he'd never heard of him. 'Then you should acquaint yourself with this great dramatist,' advised Henderson. 'Read *Hedda Gabler* and *The Wild Duck*.' Expecting to hear no more about it – 'Most young men are keen to be stars but they're also dead lazy' – Henderson was surprised when Connery returned for more. So he drew up a list of ten import-ant works of which any would-be actor ought to have at least a working knowledge, including Tolstoy's *War and Peace*, Proust's *Remembrance of Things Past*, James Joyce's *Ulysses*, Stanislavsky's *An Actor Prepares*, plus the obligatory Shakespeare, Shaw and Wilde.

It was a hell of a list, especially for someone who'd left school with no qualifications, but Connery diligently worked his way through it, then read further: Hemingway, Thomas Wolfe, Dickens. Travelling around on a motorbike, Connery always joined the local library in what-ever town or city *South Pacific* hitched up in and caught as many theatrical matinees as his budget allowed. He also frequented courtrooms to observe human behaviour. It was a programme of self-education that made up for the one society had failed to give him. 'He was the most dedicated man I had ever met,' recalls Spinetti. 'We were all from the provinces and most of us were in our first jobs, but Sean was deter-mined to pull himself up by the bootstraps and become something.'

Henderson saw in Connery the potential for an interesting acting personality, someone who looked like a truck driver but could converse on Dostoevsky; 'Speak one thing, look another.' But from the start he identified Connery's gruff accent as a major handicap and told him to work on his diction. Connery invested in a tape recorder and spent hours practising speeches from Ibsen and Shaw, while at the same time always careful not to lose the Celtic burr in his voice, for that was who he was, where he'd come from. Connery was to spend not even an afternoon in a drama school. He was dismissive of the 'poetry voice' and standard house style adopted by drama pupils, believing the emotion inherent in the language should be allowed to speak for itself.

Midway through the tour, as it landed for a long run in Manchester, Connery's newfound interest in acting was to be sorely tested. He'd been playing on the *South Pacific* football team, tackling local provincial teams, and quickly proved to be the star player, having in his youth appeared as a semi-pro. At a game against a Manchester United junior side a certain Matt Busby sat watching in the stands, later turning up at the theatre to see the show and present the whole cast with football strips. Out of the blue a few days later Connery was offered a trial at Old Trafford, with the possibility of joining the Busby Babes, the group of young players on their way to becoming the most exciting team in the English league. It had always been a dream of his to play professional football, and now Connery faced the toughest choice of his young life.

It was to Henderson that he turned for guidance. 'Look,' he told him. 'With hard graft and the regulation good luck I'm convinced you can make it as an actor. Besides, what can football guarantee you? Maybe eight years at the top, if you're lucky.' It was solid advice but still Connery sweated over the dilemma. In the end he made his choice and turned Busby's offer down, a decision that may well have saved his life. Who knows if Connery would have made it into the squad that fell victim to the Munich air crash of 1958?

When *South Pacific*'s producer Jerome White heard what Henderson had done he exploded with rage and confronted him after an evening performance. 'Are you fucking mad? You've built up this kid's hopes with baloney. United was offering him a career chance. In this business

he'll probably sink like a stone. This boy will never make it as an actor.'
A cloud of doubt did indeed hang about Connery for weeks afterwards;
often he'd sidle over to Spinetti asking, 'Vic, have I just made a huge
mistake?'

Mistake or not, the decision was made. Connery knuckled down to
work and began to win more responsibilities, understudying two roles
until finally his diligence was rewarded when he took over the part of
Lieutenant Buzz Adams, originally played in London by future *Dallas*
star Larry Hagman. When asked if he was nervous about speaking for
the first time on stage Connery replied, 'Oh no, what for?' He'd reached
another milestone, too, dumping the name Thomas in favour of Sean.
Spinetti watched Connery grow in the many months they were together
in the show and gain in confidence but on stage he was a natural; there
was something there that no drama school could teach: charisma, presence. 'Yes he was raw but the point is when Sean was on stage you
didn't look anywhere else. When I was going out to do my bits I used
to say to him, "Don't stand too near me, you bastard!" Otherwise the
audience wouldn't notice me at all.'

Spinetti was also a friend and a rock to cling to when Connery's life
fell apart. He was dating a girl in the company, an actress called Carol
Sopel. 'He was madly in love with her,' says Spinetti. 'But she turned
him down. And I remember walking through Dublin with him, it was
snowing, oh God, he was in a terrible state, and we walked and we
talked, sat up all night. And then one day it was over, that's it, it was
put behind him and he moved on, and that's very Sean. But he was very
upset over it, in fact his mother was convinced that this was the girl he
was going to marry.'

When *South Pacific* arrived in Edinburgh Connery's parents occupied
the best seats in the house, bursting with pride at seeing their son on stage.
Afterwards he brought some of the cast back to Fountainbridge for supper.
'Shows he's not ashamed of his home, doesn't it?' said Effie. It wasn't the
house but the welcome that mattered, Connery told his mum.

While Connery was horsing it round the country with *South Pacific*,
Caine found work with another repertory company, this one on the

Suffolk coast at Lowestoft. Back then all rep theatre was very much alike, certainly in the kind of plays they put on, mostly whodunnits set in manor houses, creaking melodramas and drawing-room comedies with twits coming in through the French windows. In other words they catered mostly for a middle-class audience. And there's no better example of this than the kind of costumes that many actors were contractually obliged to supply at their own expense once hired: a smart suit and blazer, plus the inevitable dinner jacket for the gents; a cocktail dress and tennis outfit for the ladies.

Despite their unambitious repertoires, the companies were run by dedicated people and over at Lowestoft Caine found another great old pro from whom he was to learn an awful lot. Take the time during one rehearsal when, after Caine had said his line, the air was dented by a loud yell, not dissimilar to a Zulu war cry. 'You, Michael, what the hell are you doing?' Nothing, said Caine; he'd no lines for a while, so there was nothing he had to do. 'Of course you have, Michael! You are listening to everything that is being said and you are thinking of wonderful lines to say and then deciding not to say them.' In other words, always listen. 'That's half of acting, Michael.' It was a lesson he learned well; just watch Caine's movies and you'll see.

Repertory theatre was the quintessential training ground for any actor, a place to learn the trade and how, quite literally, to avoid bumping into the furniture. 'The marvellous thing about rep is that it taught you how to think on your feet,' recalls Trevor Bannister, who did years of it up and down the country before coming into the West End in the early sixties. 'It also taught us to be resourceful and to be a quick study. And it taught you to work as a team, to not be selfish and to be generous to your fellow actors because you relied on each other. Inevitably we all used to get into terrible mucks sometimes and you relied on your fellow actors to get you out of it and you'd do the same for them, so it was a very good training ground and I feel very sorry for the young actors today that don't have it because the rep system as it was back then just doesn't exist any more.'

It was no picnic, though; doing weekly rep meant performing a brand-new play every seven days, which was quite an undertaking. The evenings were spent performing and the days were spent learning the lines for next week's production. The turnaround was frantic; even fortnightly rep wasn't a great deal easier. But what grounding for actors these places provided. 'Once you got into the swing of it then it was all right,' says Philip Grout, another rep veteran. 'You got by on the camaraderie, and luck. A lot of people dismissed rep as a treadmill, it was more living dangerously – and surviving. If we hadn't done that extraordinary training, that sort of hanging-on-by-your-teeth training, we couldn't have survived working later on for people like Joan Littlewood.'

In the hierarchy of repertory theatre the leading players of the company rarely got involved with the lower plebs who played juveniles and sundry nondescript parts. Plebs like Michael Caine. But for quite some time the young actor had felt strong stirrings for the leading lady, Patricia Haines, who hailed from Sheffield and wasn't long out of RADA. At a party he plucked up enough courage to finally string a sentence together in her presence, only to discover she shared similar emotions. It was a fast affair and their marriage took place in April 1954. At the reception Caine got hammered on barley wine with his father-in-law and spent much of the festivities under the table with him. It was a bad start to what turned out to be a brief marriage.

4

The Irish Invader

Caine and his new wife left Lowestoft rep to try their luck in London at much the same time as a young, slightly lanky Irishman was making his way to the capital, a chap by the name of Richard Harris. Keen to become an actor but unsure how to go about it, Harris heard that the famous actor/manager Anew McMaster was arriving in his home town of Limerick. For decades McMaster toured Ireland bringing Shakespeare and the classics to towns and villages, trawling the local amateur groups for bit-part players. Harris auditioned and was accepted, but required to do little more than stand around in a few scenes, but nevertheless it marked his professional stage debut. More importantly, he questioned McMaster about his desire to act. The veteran's advice was simple: 'If you want to be an actor, my boy, you must go to London.'

When the news broke, Harris's mother wailed her objection, begging him to reconsider. His father's only comment was, 'For God's sake, let him go.' Harris had been a bloody handful since his birth on 1 October 1930. His father, Ivan, was the owner of a local mill and bakery and his house was a large affair with maids and gardeners and big cars in the drive. Then suddenly, almost overnight, it was all gone when the bakery closed down. 'One day was luxury, the next morning my mother was on her knees scrubbing floors,' Harris recalled.

The Harris brood was a large one, as families were back then, and the young Harris was all but lost amidst the scrum of seven brothers and sisters. 'What's his name again?' Ivan frequently asked over the top of his newspaper. 'Dick,' said mother. 'Oh yeah, Dick, I remember.' Harris learned early on to be a rabble-rouser, an attention seeker; it was the only way he could make his presence felt. School and Harris didn't mix either. 'Wild and uncontrollable' in his own words, Harris set fire to the toilets and on another occasion infamously attacked a nun. She took exception to his manic behaviour and thwacked him with a ruler, as nuns in Irish schools tended to do. Harris wrestled the ruler back from her and hit out violently. He went to Crescent College, under the educational instruction of Jesuits, and was placed in a class of fellow dunces and troublemakers, a class academically excluded from the rest of the school, like the mad brother locked in the attic in gothic Victorian fiction. It was the class the school did its best never to mention.

In the classroom Harris tended to doze off or fart to get attention, the lesson going completely over his head. The teachers simply gave up on him. Even caning didn't work. When a reporter arrived in Limerick to research a story on the now-famous Harris he visited Crescent College and was informed by the headmaster, 'I would prefer it if you did not mention him in connection with this school.'

Academically a dead loss, rugby was seen as an escape route and he became obsessed with the sport, dreaming of one day playing for his country. Aged thirteen, Harris was already a big bugger and a real bruiser on the pitch, able to dish out punishment as well as take it. During the lead-up to a crucial match against a rival school Harris had his eyes on the opposite team's danger player and practised numerous ways of nobbling him. During practice their coach Father Guinane called Harris over. 'I'm utterly appalled,' he said, a fag dangling from his mouth like an extra from *Father Ted*. 'We'll win this match by fair means or not at all.' Come match day the danger player was doing his stuff. 'Harris, a quiet word,' it was Father Guinane again, ciggie in place. 'You may continue with your plan.'

After leaving school Harris played for a local semi-pro side that went on to win the Munster Senior Cup. For a lot of fans he was the star player and wore his various injuries as a swordsman would his duelling scars. However, he met his match one afternoon on the field. 'If the stand was full of surgeons they couldn't have done anything for my nose, I got such a wallop.' Carried off, his face smeared in blood, Harris sportingly returned heavily bandaged to be greeted with shouts of, ''Tis the return of the Phantom!' 'No 'tis the Mummy!' He'd end up breaking his nose a further eight times in subsequent collisions with various walls, doors and fists, even ploughing head-first through the windscreen of a car. It was reconstructed using bone from his hip as there was so little left up his nostrils.

Besides rugby another obsession had taken over Harris: the cinema. As a kid he'd go to Saturday-morning pictures and ape the heroes he saw on the screen, once memorably flinging himself down the cinema's great staircase emulating a cowboy taking a bullet. Now in his late teenage years he exhibited a keen eye for the art of the film-maker, staying to watch the matinee and the evening show, studying the actors' performances. His absolute hero was Marlon Brando, who'd just exploded as a star, responding to this new way of acting that was 'raw and provocative, with the smell of real life'.

It was always hoped that Harris would go into the family business. The bakery had gone but the flour mill was still in operation, if struggling. He coped with the job for a while, but his heart just wasn't in it. His idea of fun was brawling on the rugby pitch and going off to the pub to get royally hammered. 'I was pissed from the day I was out of short trousers,' he told his friend Ronald Fraser. One of Harris's favourite teenage tales involved driving a massive haulage truck to Dublin aged seventeen, on an errand for his dad. Ordered to be back home promptly by 7.30 that evening he headed for the nearest pub after making the delivery. 'Fuck it,' he said. 'I'll make it on the back roads in no time.' A pissed Harris set off and soon up ahead was a bridge warning: 'Clearance 12 feet.' Thinking he could just manage it, Harris sped on but hit the thing, lifting it off its pillars. An unimpressed copper flagged him down. Harris opened his window and said, 'Sorry, officer. You see, I'm just delivering this bridge to Limerick.'

Perhaps this kind of wild exploit was indicative of a restless nature, and as he toyed with thoughts of emigrating to Canada, away from the religious bigotry and hypocrisy of rural Ireland, Harris's whole world fell apart when he was diagnosed with TB. Canada was out, as were any hopes he may have fostered about a rugby career. He never did play again. His widow, Elizabeth Harris, was convinced that had it not been for the TB Harris would have assuredly pursued a professional rugby career. 'And I've no doubt he would have played for Ireland. Rugby was his first love and it remained a passion all his life.'

Instead Harris was confined to bed for countless months, 'playing a staring game with the damp Irish walls that caused my TB in the first place'. Those months, endless months of solitude and soul-searching, was where his love of literature began, says Elizabeth. 'Gradually people dropped off coming to see him and so he spent more and more time on his own and he began to read and write poetry. I remember him saying to me, "I've got to make it as an actor and then people will read my poetry, they won't read it before then." And he was passionate about Dylan Thomas.'

After finally beating the disease, Harris promised himself never to be shackled and imprisoned again, and set out to pursue a life of sensory overload, willingly embracing his demons. 'I had a terrible desire to let nothing pass me by.' Acting was the perfect outlet for such strong emotions and he joined a local amateur drama group. Those at the club remember his arrival, this shy young man in his early twenties whose inhibitions vanished entirely when he acted and the natural born showman within sprang out. They also remember his bullish unwilling-ness to learn, mainly because he thought he knew it all already. Planning to head for Dublin in the hope of joining the prestigious Abbey Theatre, McMaster's words that he should study in London prompted a drastic rethink.

The friends and family who waved him off at the station couldn't help thinking he'd be back in Limerick soon, tail between his legs. Harris was determined to prove them wrong. In London he headed for Earls Court Road, then a popular area with the Irish, and took the cheapest lodgings he could find. He'd already written in advance to the Central School of Speech and Drama and on his second day in the capital turned up for his audition full of naive expectation that was shot down swifter than a partridge over Balmoral. There he was, aged twenty-four, sitting amongst other applicants barely out of their teens. He felt immediately out of place, isolated, and this was before he'd even opened his mouth.

If Harris felt awkward amongst his fellow wannabe drama students then the auditioning panel, made up of 'aristocratic-looking ladies and gentlemen', in his words, must have seemed like something out of an Edwardian nightmare.

'What are you going to do for us, young man?' one of them asked.

'Something from Shakespeare,' said Harris. He took a deep breath and began.

When he'd finished, the panel looked at one another and there was an unnerving period of silence which eventually was shattered rather than broken. 'What right do you think you have to enter our profession?' Harris wasn't going to take that one on the chin. 'The same right you have to judge me.' He was shown the door. Was it plain snobbery that didn't get him into Central or, as Harris confessed later, was it just that he hadn't been very good?

Where next? Someone mentioned the London Academy of Music and Dramatic Art. LAMDA wasn't up there with RADA or Central, granted, but it was conveniently located in Earls Court, just a few minutes from his tatty bedsit. On the day of his audition, set for 4 p.m., Harris went for a long walk to compose himself, ending up in Hyde Park, going through his speech and unnerving enough walkers to warrant a police investigation. 'You all right, lad?' asked a passing bobby.

Harris looked up. 'I'm rehearsing. I'm an actor.'

The policeman laughed. 'That explains it. One of those.'

Suddenly Harris realised the time and raced over to LAMDA, arriving an hour late. A gentleman was locking up. 'Quick, quick,' shouted Harris, almost out of breath. 'Take me to the principal, Michael Macowen.'

The man turned round to face this bedraggled creature. 'I am Michael Macowen.'

'Good,' said Harris, not missing a beat. 'You've discovered me.'

Unfortunately not, as Macowen explained that the LAMDA course was now full. 'But you must take me,' cried Harris. 'I've checked out the record of your academy and you haven't had one success. Not one. Now I am going to be your first success.'

Macowen had to hand it to the cheeky bugger, and so unlocked the door, showing him into a small theatre. Alas, Harris's doorstep performance was a whole lot better than he was able to muster on stage. Macowen's heart sank a little at the lack of talent on display, but there was no doubt this Irish rogue had charm to spare; certainly he'd got balls. 'I'm going to take a chance on you,' he said. 'You're in.'

Twenty years later the two men met again quite by chance and Harris asked for an honest appraisal of that audition. 'You want the truth,' said Macowen, before taking a deep breath. 'It was the worst audition I have ever sat through. It was truly awful.'

It didn't take Harris very long to fall in love with London, the neon-lit nightlife of Soho, the smells and new experiences, those first few months were a kind of 'wide-eyed hysteria'. And then there were the women, the kind of fascinating women he could only have dreamed of meeting along Limerick High Street. Inevitably Harris turned almost overnight into a gung-ho womaniser, often moving from flat to flat as love affairs dictated.

Money was his only problem and when funds were at an all-time low he slept for a while on the counter of a bar in a pub owned by a mate, then under piles of coats on the Embankment. When it rained he scraped enough cash for a bed in a local doss house, sure to sleep with his hands wrapped round the suitcase that held all his belongings. 'If you removed as much as a dirty handkerchief from your pocket somebody would steal it by the morning.' When one day he collapsed from hunger during class a fellow student took pity and offered him accommodation at his small flat.

At LAMDA, besides being slightly older than everyone else, Harris looked physically out of place too. Though his accent was moderately decipherable his native brashness and swagger, combined with a natur-ally loud personality, grated with some people. Frank Windsor recalled that Harris was not your average greenhorn drama student. 'He gave off an aura of command, like Look at Me! I have arrived!' And budding actor James Booth, a drinking companion, said Harris's self-confidence bordered on 'offensive arrogance'.

He had a problem with the teachers too; old fogeys in grey suits telling him to treat Shakespeare with reverence and pronounce his verbs like Olivier. Fuck off, thought Harris, he wasn't going to say it the correct way, he was going to say it the way he felt. 'I was an outsider in my own family and at LAMDA,' he said. 'It was like, oh Jesus, here he is again. He doesn't conform. He doesn't do what we tell him.' That would be the story of his life.

5

Received Pronunciation

On his first day at RADA O'Toole had reconnoitred the old place, gone up on the roof, where many a student went to roll their own cigarettes and have a puff, walked into rehearsal rooms and prop stores. At one point he came across a mêlée of workmen, humping cement around, sawing and hammering, making a right clatter. They were constructing RADA's new theatre, to be christened the Vanbrugh, on the site of the old stage that had been destroyed in 1941 at the height of the Blitz. For years that area had lain waste. David McCallum, a student at RADA in 1949, still vividly remembers it. 'RADA was essentially two buildings, one on Gower Street and one at the back in Malet Street, and right in the very middle there had at one time been a theatre and it was hit by a German bomb, so it was completely derelict and as students you went from one side of RADA to the other to get to your next class across this bomb site.'

Leaving the workers to their labours, little did O'Toole realise that several months later he would be appearing in the inaugural production at the Vanbrugh, in front of Queen Elizabeth the Queen Mother. It would be an illuminating performance, and one that Keith Baxter has still not forgotten. The opening night was reserved for dignitaries and few, if any, students got in, attending instead a special performance put on just for them. The play was George Bernard Shaw's *Great Catherine* and O'Toole had been cleverly cast as Catherine's brother Prince Potemkin. 'It was a real knockabout part,' says Baxter. 'And Peter was falling over, doing pratfalls, the whole works.' Baxter had gone with Roy Kinnear and afterwards they joined a bunch of other students at a nearby café. 'And they were doing what actors all do, pulling the production apart and saying how awful it was, but Roy and I weren't talking very much and then we decided to go home, and so we walked from Gower Street back to Battersea where we lived.' A distance of some miles, but in those days because the tubes stopped early and there were no late-night buses, and with taxis a financial no-no, there was no other option. 'It wasn't unusual as a student to walk everywhere in those days,' says Baxter. 'Roy had a girlfriend at that time in Hampstead and sometimes he would walk from a party in Hampstead all the way back to Battersea, and that's a very long walk.'

On this particular night Baxter and Kinnear had been pounding the pavement hard for two hours almost in complete silence. 'And then we crossed Battersea Bridge and there was a roadside café for late-night lorry drivers and so we sat and had a cup of tea, we really hadn't talked much, then Roy looked at me and said, "He's fucking incredible, isn't he?" And I said, "Yes." There was something about Peter that was absolutely irresistible, overwhelming. As an actor he was just something beyond any of us, any of us.'

O'Toole's performance that night was perhaps a culmination of all he'd learned so far at RADA. One of the very few directors he'd any time for there was Hugh Miller, who was hot on stagecraft, those little bits of business despised by a lot of actors; you pick up your fork on this line, you put it down on that line, but a valuable asset all the same, says Baxter: 'Peter was an instinctive actor, but in this play he was doing head falls, he was jumping about, he was doing all the Hugh Miller shtick you might call it, but it was underpinned by his own genius.' Whatever else RADA bestowed upon the likes of O'Toole, Finney and Bates it was perhaps this bedrock of stagecraft that empowered them the most. 'The technique I learned at RADA is my lifeline,' Bates admitted years later. 'It prevents my being undermined by insecurities or directors who play the power game.'

Baxter hadn't been back long from National Service when he witnessed that O'Toole performance. In those days conscription into the armed forces was still compulsory and RADA's male students could choose to do a year at drama school and then go off and do their bit for Queen and Country and return again for their final year, which is what most of them did. Alan Bates had to suffer in silence at an RAF base in Syerston; a period of utter drudgery and a complete waste of time. To prevent himself going completely round the bend he joined a local amateur dramatics group in nearby Nottingham run by a gentleman called Conrad Monk, who couldn't help but sense there was something different about this new recruit, whose easy-going charm and dark looks made everyone naturally gravitate towards him.

Finney also had to leave RADA halfway through his studies to do his National Service but returned some weeks later, to the general mystification of his colleagues. 'Albert managed to get out of it,' recalls Baxter, 'and we never quite understood why because he gave various stories as to how he'd done it, some said he had a nervous breakdown in the interview.'

Years later Finney was chatting with Tom Courtenay and the subject came up. 'Is it true that you got out of the army by sitting on top of your locker?' asked Courtenay. 'That's how rumour had it.'

Finney shook his head. 'I sat on one of the rafters in our Nissen hut. I didn't eat anything and from time to time I fainted.'

'You fell off the rafter?'

'I didn't faint while I was on the rafter, silly bugger. I waited till I was on the ground.'

'How soon before they let you out?'

'Eight weeks. They would have let me out sooner, but they knew I was a drama student and the officers wanted me to direct their Christmas show.'

Other students, like O'Toole, had already done their National Service prior to drama school and therefore were a very different commodity, as Elizabeth Harris, then a RADA student, describes. 'You found that the men were much more worldly wise, if wise is the right word, certainly more worldly than the girls. The girls would go straight from school to RADA. And in the classes the girls were used to being at a school where you didn't argue with the teacher, you accepted what they said. RADA at that time was still very much in the mode of a sort of finishing school for young ladies. Of course a lot of the guys had been in the forces and they didn't let the teachers get away with anything, they were much more challenging and much more dominant.'

O'Toole's stint had been in the navy and it didn't take him long to realise it had all been a ghastly mistake. 'What was I doing marching to the left and marching to the right? What was I doing darning socks? It was a bloody nightmare.' Several times he did a Finney, trying to con his way out. One attempt consisted of drinking eighteen bottles of wine, taking a lot of aspirins and a drug that was supposed to turn one's features a deathly grey, but it didn't work. Insubordination followed. He was once arrested for taking extra rations of rum: 'Because it was a cold day.' It did look as if the navy and O'Toole made an ill-matched pair. 'I would stand alone on deck at night talking to seagulls for hours.'

When his ship visited Copenhagen, besides patronising the local hostelries, O'Toole did at least manage to find an unorthodox cure for a stammer and lisp that had plagued him since childhood. Playing in a naval rugby team against a bunch of thugs from the Swedish police force, O'Toole fell on the ball only for a hulking great Swede to kick him full on the chin, slicing his tongue in half. He was rushed to hospital, where the tongue was stitched back together, resulting in his speech impediment disappearing completely. The doctors discharged him before his ship was due to sail and O'Toole caught a train back to the dock, discovering half an hour later that it was going the wrong way. He eventually reached the harbour just in time to see the fleet sailing off into the distance. O'Toole swore he hired a funfair boat and paddled out until it came alongside the supply ship and they threw a rope ladder down to him.

After eighteen months O'Toole was discharged as temperamentally unsuitable. He'd later describe his time with the navy as 'A total waste for everybody, particularly His Majesty.'

When Bates was officially discharged from the RAF late in 1954 he returned to finish his studies at RADA at about the same time as Baxter, who, like Michael Caine, had been in Korea. 'When I came back I had nowhere really to stay and Alan came up to me in the canteen and said, "Listen, you can come and live in The Mansions, there's a bed there." And that was an extraordinary place; it was dubbed the best knocking shop east of Suez.'

The Mansions was a large flat in Battersea owned by RADA student Ian White, whose parents had bought him the lease. The rent was something like a pound a week; Bates lived there, as did others from RADA including Brian Bedford, Roy Kinnear and sometimes Finney. 'What a crew!' Bates later recalled. 'Did we have fun!' The place became a bohemian hostelry for just about any drama student or acquaintance who wanted a place to stay for the night, or sometimes longer. 'Some were straight, some were gay,' recalls Baxter. 'And some didn't know quite what they were. It was a sort of crash pad. People would sleep on the floor. If you had nowhere else to go you ended up at The Mansions.'

Baxter remembers one particular evening when he and Bates had gone out and returned to The Mansions to find a party in full swing. 'Alan and I went up the stairs and ahead of us was a Canadian actor deep in conversation with a young Sean Connery, who had done nothing yet with his life, and I remember Alan taking one long look at Sean and saying, "I don't think that's gonna go anywhere."'

It hadn't taken people like Bates or Baxter long to realise that in their absence things had changed at RADA. 'The atmosphere was different,' says Baxter. The main change was that Sir Kenneth Barnes had been pensioned off in 1955; not before time, most would say. More than one student would recall the old boy falling asleep during his own lecture. Even back in 1949 David McCallum recognised that their aged leader was past it. 'Sir Kenneth would watch our productions and then the next day all the cast would assemble in his room for a critique. But very often he would critique one class with the plays that another class performed because he was getting somewhat senile.'

Barnes's successor was John Fernald, who'd had a long career in the theatre as a director, and it was he who was largely the instigator of a little more modern thinking at RADA. He was a much more down-to-earth type and fervently against the notion that RADA was a snobby place. But some of the old habits refused to be killed off, notably voice production. 'The Queen's English was taught at RADA,' explains television and theatre director Philip Saville. 'I remember when I was there all these guys and gals came down from the Midlands and the north and they all had their voices ironed out.' Finney was having none of that. 'I simply refused to let RADA wipe my personality clean.'

Back then drama schools, epitomised by RADA, felt required to teach any working-class scruff who passed through their door how to speak 'standard' English, aka received pronunciation, so once let loose upon the big bad world they could be serviceably employed playing the kind of roles that dominated English theatre, namely middle-class characters or toffs. 'But the thing that was wrong with RADA is that it taught you to come out like sausages, all speaking the same way,' says Elizabeth Harris. 'Some of the teachers would be quite scathing if somebody had a regional accent. All that was blown away by the guys.'

Some like Finney did indeed rebel, others like Bates were more philosophical about the need to eradicate the regional tone in his voice. 'It's nice to be able to use it when necessary,' he'd say later. 'But not to be forever saddled with it.' Looking back now, Baxter also sees the value of those diction classes. 'I remember Finney had a very strong Salford accent, while I was from Wales. One of my teachers told me that I sounded as though my mother dug for coal with her fingernails. It wasn't that we wanted to talk posh, that's not it, we didn't want to talk like the royal family, we just wanted when we got into the theatre to talk like Olivier, or Ralph Richardson or Gielgud, actors who spoke beautifully, we all wanted to do that. But the important thing is none of us lost our regional accents. Even now Albert uses it some-times, when he played Winston Churchill a little bit of Salford sneaked in every now and then, you can't lose everything.'

In 1957 Lindsay Anderson warned: 'A young actor with a regional or Cockney accent had better lose it quick. For where are his chances of stardom?' When Sheila Allen left RADA in 1952 she immediately faced prejudice, thanks to a Hereford accent that remained despite the best efforts of her teachers to get rid of it. 'I didn't know I'd got an accent, it didn't occur to me I'd got an accent. And I was refused a job after I graduated. I went for an interview at one of the big seaside weekly reps, very famous, Worthing. I met up with the gentleman and at the end of the interview he said, "Well, Sheila Allen, I can't possibly employ you, you've got a dark R and a dark L, we can't have that at the Worthing theatre company."'

Millicent Martin had been born in Romford and studied at the Italia Conti School with Anthony Newley, whose broad London accent was equally indecipherable to the teachers. 'They weren't sure about us because we had cockney accents; they didn't know whether we would get anywhere in the business. A lot of people couldn't understand cockney, so we had to soften it. But I remember Tony Newley and myself making a stance at the school; OK, they think we're not going to make it because of our accents, we're going to prove them wrong; we'll make our accents popular.'

And that really was the secret, this was the first generation of actors to keep their authentic voice, but their speech was underpinned by vocal techniques learned at drama school. So when Finney played Arthur Seaton in *Saturday Night and Sunday Morning*, audiences recognised the regional accent, but also heard and understood every word spoken. 'There was also a lot of emphasis on how to project your voice,' says McCallum. 'I played in *Julius Caesar* in Central Park in 2000 and that's a huge venue, maybe fifteen hundred seats or more. And my mike went out one night and I did the whole of the first act without a microphone and there were people in the audience who afterwards said it was wonderful to hear a voice for the first time that wasn't amplified, and I said, well it was wonderful to be able to do it because that's what we were taught at RADA, to project. But I wouldn't want to do something like that more than once.'

After his stunning performance in *Great Catherine* O'Toole had continued to make his mark at RADA. Few who attended classes with him ever forgot the wild man from Ireland, the born eccentric. A former student recalled that O'Toole once took an ironing board into Gower Street right outside the academy building and did his shirts. 'You couldn't be at RADA and not have memories of O'Toole,' says Elizabeth Harris. 'He had enormous charisma, even then. He was larger than life. There was so much excitement when he was around, anything could happen and you never knew if it was going to be good or bad or whatever. Also I very rarely saw O'Toole without a plaster or a bandage somewhere about him. He'd always been in some scrape or other.'

This may have had something to do with the fact that O'Toole was doing stunt work in minor films and on television, regularly falling off horses or hurling himself through windows. He enjoyed it, in spite of the bruises and scars, and would perform under various pseudonyms such as Walter Plings, Charlie Staircase and Arnold Hearthrug. Certainly odd things seemed to happen to O'Toole and O'Toole alone. On his way to a RADA production he was a passenger in a car that hit a ten-ton lorry on the A1. Following hospital X-rays, his leg bursting with pain, O'Toole limped off after waiting in vain for hours for the results, took a train back to London and found a sympathetic doctor to bind up his injured leg and pump him full of painkillers so that he could perform. He returned to hospital the next day and was told that the X-ray had showed a broken leg.

Over the next few years cars and O'Toole were never truly the best of friends. He once fell asleep while driving on the M1 and woke up to find himself careering down the grass of the central reservation. 'There was nothing for it but to put my feet up on the dashboard and wait for the crash.' One woman who accepted a lift from O'Toole swore afterwards that she would never do so again. During the journey he ignored a keep-left sign on the grounds that it was 'silly' and narrowly avoided driving down a flight of steps.

There was also the odd skirmish with the law during his RADA days, usually following over-indulgence in a pub. O'Toole didn't run with any particular crowd at drama school, though he'd a nose for finding where the best parties were and the pubs that sold the cheapest beer. Sometimes his drunken antics landed him in court, where he'd turn up in a typically dishevelled state, and on one occasion not wearing socks.

'Don't you have any?' asked a policeman.

'Of course, I have,' replied O'Toole, aghast at the absurdity of the question.

'Well, where are they?'

'They're here,' and O'Toole produced a mangy green pair from his pocket.

6

'We Don't Want Any of That!'

Michael Caine's first marital home was a small two-room flat in Brixton. It was agreed that Patricia, by far the more established and experienced partner, would continue with her acting career while Caine supplemented her income by taking any dreary dead-end job going: laundryman, plumber's mate, dishwasher. 'I was merely keeping alive while waiting for my next chance at acting.'

Far from giving up hope, Caine had decided to become a fully paid-up member of the actor's union Equity, but the discovery of a Michael Scott already on their books meant an alternative name was required. Resurrecting Micklewhite was out for a start. One evening he was in Leicester Square, looking at the glittering cinema marquees and trying to come up with a name that would look suitably epic and grand up there, when he noticed that one of the theatres was showing Humphrey Bogart's latest, *The Caine Mutiny*. One imagines a little bell going off in his head. And so Scott was jettisoned to be replaced by Caine. Michael Caine, it had a nice ring to it.

On the actor's grapevine Caine heard there was a job going with maverick director Joan Littlewood that winter of 1954, an adaptation of Dickens's short story 'The Chimes'. He auditioned successfully, but Caine didn't fit in with what he later described as not so much a theatre company, rather 'a communist organisation'. The wages were certainly working class, two pounds ten shillings a week; at least each cast member was given free vitamins daily.

Littlewood, the illegitimate daughter of a cockney maid, had dreamed of becoming an actress and attended RADA, quitting after just a few months the place she condemned as little more than a finishing school for debs. Fuelled by her socialist principles her ambition was for a theatre that served the community, a people's theatre. She opened her Theatre Workshop in a near-derelict Victorian playhouse in a rundown area of the East End in 1953, shunning everything she associated with the commercial West End she despised: elaborate sets, footlights, stage make-up and mannered acting.

Caine and she were an accident waiting to happen. At the first day's rehearsal Caine walked on stage and had barely begun acting when he heard a yell from the stalls. 'We don't want any of that! Come on again.' Caine duly came on again, unsure quite what was required of him. There was another yell from Joan. 'This is a group theatre; we don't want any of that.' Third time lucky, Caine must have thought. 'I'm not having it,' Joan said. 'Not having what?' asked Caine innocently. 'Any of this star nonsense. You bury your individuality in the character for the good of the group and the play as a whole.'

As the production moved forward Caine did his best to try and get a handle on Joan's way of working but was never accepted by her. 'Best thing you can do is fuck off to Hollywood and be a star,' she admonished before firing him. 'You don't need to know anything about acting there.' A 'star' was a dirty word to Joan. Her company was a collection of actors, with no individual taking the limelight.

Caine's treatment at the hands of Joan Littlewood is strange, since you would have thought a lad from the Elephant and Castle would be right up her street. But even back then Caine had little patience with trendy lefties. His time there, however, was not wasted, learning one important lesson that would serve him well in movies. Joan taught Stanislavsky, the first time Caine had been exposed to the method-acting technique, and one of her mantras was: 'Rehearsal is the work, performance is the relaxation.' Caine never forgot that.

Joan Littlewood was very much part of what was a new kind of theatre just beginning to happen in Britain. She was one of the pathfinders, both in her methods and in her outlook, theatre for the masses and a two-finger salute to the middle-class West End. 'Joan had an extraordinarily unique way of working,' recalls Ann Beach, who was part of Joan's company for many years. 'Mainly using improvisation, which back then was quite new, then everybody started doing it. Sometimes it was aggravating, and sometimes marvellous and magical and very often tremendous fun. She was a school in herself, quite honestly. She was so clever, she just knew so much about theatre. Not all actors could work with her. But she would draw everything out of you that you had to offer.'

Still at LAMDA, Harris caught a sniff of this burgeoning theatrical revolution. There was quite definitely an underground buzz happening, 'The buzz that would spark Osborne and Pinter – but it was a slow fuse.' Harris recognised it and wanted to be a part of it. Frustrated after months of non-progress at drama school, he came up with the hare-brained scheme of producing and directing his own play, a reworking of *The Country Girl* by Clifford Odets. Auditions were held in a basement room at the Troubadour, a coffee bar in Earls Court and a popular haunt for actors back then.

Elizabeth Harris had just been unceremoniously chucked out of RADA, and was feeling very sorry for herself as she walked back in the snow to her parents' flat. 'Just then an actor called Peter Prowse stopped his car next to me and said, "You look cold, do you want a lift?" And remembering everything my mother said about never accepting lifts from strangers, I was in such a bolshie mood I immediately got in.' Prowse could see that Elizabeth was feeling miserable and when he heard why explained that he was an actor and that he was on his way to an audition. 'He said, "Why don't you come along, there might be a part for you?"' So off they went together to the Troubadour. 'And that's the first time I met Richard.'

Elizabeth had grown up in a rarefied environment. Her father was David Rees-Williams, the 1st Baron Ogmore, who sat in the House of Lords, and her education had ended at a finishing school in Switzerland. But despite the trappings of privilege she was a rebellious spirit and intrigued to meet this new director that Prowse was giving the big sell.

When they arrived at the Troubadour it was quiet; Harris was sitting in almost complete darkness at a table in the corner reading a book. 'He had this massive red hair and wasn't wearing any shoes,' Elizabeth recollects. 'When Peter came in and introduced me Richard looked up and said, "All right, come down," and he took us to the basement and flung books at us to read from. I have to say, he was very scary, his shirt was all out, in those days it wasn't fashionable to have your shirt out, it wasn't fashionable to have torn jeans, he had torn jeans. He was well ahead of his time, not because he was planning it, but because that's how he was. He was quite crazy, actually.'

Elizabeth read only to be waved away almost instantly. She began her ascent of the stairs unaware that Harris had already decided to cast her. The play itself was put on in January 1955 at the intimate (read 'small') Irving Theatre just off Leicester Square, a venue so grubby it later found better use as a strip joint. Rehearsals were tough, egos flooded the place and it was not uncommon for furniture to be thrown around to make a point. Harris had also learned of Elizabeth's high-born origins and was livid, blasting one day: 'The first time she's late for rehearsals she's out on her social arse.' This was no act of bravado, as Elizabeth was to find out; Harris made an Olympic sport out of railing against the establishment. 'He always used to bash against the House of Lords because of my father; he bashed against the establishment, to the very end.'

The play was not a success, hardly helped by the directorial antics of Harris, who constantly ran up and down the aisles during performances letting out roars of disapproval whenever one of the actors did something he didn't like. 'By the end the audience was paying more attention to him than what was happening on the stage,' says Elizabeth. 'It was crazy.'

The day after the play's final performance Elizabeth returned to the venue to collect some belongings. Harris was there. With the pressure off he seemed to Elizabeth gentler, less a fierce tornado. They got talking and Harris wondered if she'd have dinner with him. He chose a rather flash restaurant where the menu was in French. He couldn't decipher a word, agreeing instead to what Elizabeth suggested; the date set him back the equivalent of two weeks' rent. It was the beginning of a relationship that Elizabeth particularly felt serious about at an early stage. 'He certainly wasn't somebody who was run of the mill.' Still a deb at the time, the sort of men Elizabeth was meeting at high-society balls didn't compare to Harris; they were, to use her word, 'shadows'. They were incredibly strait-laced for a start, while the Harris crowd was wonderful and exciting to be around. She also saw a more vulnerable side to his nature. 'And that was part of his charm. He was actually quite a softie, which he tried hard to hide.'

7

The Cuckoos Leave the Nest

RADA students were sometimes required to put on a grand end-of-term production. In those days it was quite an event: theatre managers, agents, PR people would attend; it was a terrific shop window, a chance to be noticed, maybe even get a job or a contract. It was one of the reasons the place was so popular. Bates never forgot one particular show. He'd chosen to do a scene from *Richard II*, 'and I absolutely blew it. Everyone else did well except me. I felt terrible that night. I was so shattered that I just walked around London for hours saying to myself, this will never happen to me again.' It was the young Bates's first experience of abject failure, 'a feeling of having thrown everything away'. He thinks it probably gave him the determination to go on and succeed. Bates knuckled down for the short remaining time he had left, and his final report was positive: 'He has real talent,' it summarised. 'We look forward with interest to his future on the stage.'

As he usually did, Frank Dunlop, the artistic director of the Midland Repertory Company, arrived at RADA looking for new talent and was struck by the young Bates playing Romeo in his last production at the academy. 'I was bloody marvellous,' said the actor modestly. Dunlop invited Bates to join his theatre, which was based in Coventry but also toured extensively. It wasn't a big salary but it was his first professional opportunity and Bates grabbed it.

Like Dunlop, Nat Brenner was another regular attendee of the end-of-term RADA showcase. Brenner was one of the men behind the enormous recent success of the Bristol Old Vic, his staging of radical and important plays turning it into perhaps the most important theatre outside London, with the exception of Stratford. One young actor in the company was Glasgow-born John Cairney. 'It was a proud thing to belong to the Old Vic at Bristol,' he says, 'because it managed to combine the best of the old, yet contain all the surging talent of the new.' In 1954, for instance, the first production outside of America of Arthur Miller's *The Crucible*, which dramatised the infamous Salem witch trials of the 1690s, the playwright's metaphor for the McCarthy witch hunts that gripped America in the early fifties, went to Bristol rather than London, mainly because no producer in the West End would mount it.

As Brenner watched O'Toole he immediately sensed something special – 'He was absolutely riveting. I was smitten' – and hurriedly made arrangements for him to join the company. Already established for a year at Bristol was Edward Hardwicke: 'Nat approached me one morning and said, "Listen, we've got this young actor coming soon; would you mind if he shares your dressing room?" And I said fine and I clearly remember Peter arriving and we instantly hit it off.'

It was traditional for any newcomer to have a couple of lines in the local paper announcing his arrival. Hardwicke has good reason to remember O'Toole's particular entry. 'It said that he was related to a Victorian actor called J. L. Toole who played the fool to Henry Irving's King Lear, and I was terribly impressed by this. Then years later we were chatting and I'd recently been to the Garrick Club and in the lobby somewhere was a bust of J. L. Toole and I asked Peter, "Did you ever follow up your connection with J. L. Toole?" and he said, "It was bollocks, dear boy, pure bollocks." So the whole thing was an utter invention.'

Why had he done it? O'Toole offered Hardwicke this revealing explanation: 'Peter said that when he first auditioned at RADA he was standing in the foyer and there used to be a sergeant who looked after the front door and there were students coming down the stairs and the sergeant said to Peter, "You see that guy there, his father is an actor, Cedric Hardwicke." And it was me! And Peter told me, "I remember looking at you, Edward, and you had a bow tie on and suede boots, you looked frightfully confident, so the next day I went to look to see if I could find an O'Toole in the acting profession. There wasn't one but there was a J. L. Toole." So he turned himself into a relation.' Even then, O'Toole was devising ways to make an impression.

The generation of O'Toole and Bates and Finney was lucky to leave drama school when they did. Most towns had a repertory theatre, thus making it relatively easy for actors to find work, especially those leaving such an august institution as RADA, and certainly a lot easier than it is today. 'Take the year I left drama school,' says Hardwicke, 'which was only a couple of years before Peter. Of the ninety students who graduated only two didn't immediately find work, that's because one was ill and the other one just gave up. That's an enormous number of actors immediately being employed from drama school.'

The Bristol Old Vic was an extraordinary theatre, one of the oldest in Britain, retaining much of its original Georgian splendour; it had, for example, a proper thunderer above the auditorium down which cannon balls were rolled to create sound effects. Bristol also had the luxury of putting on a play every three weeks, as opposed to the one- or two-week turnaround of other reps, so the actors could spend more time exploring and improving what they were doing instead of running round like headless chickens.

At first O'Toole was engaged in small roles, one production at a time, 'because they were always worried that he wasn't going to turn up', reveals Hardwicke. 'I can remember being in the dressing room at one point and he hadn't showed yet and the taxi was sent up to his digs and he was still fast asleep with a smashed alarm clock lying about the floor. So Peter was a bit of an enfant terrible but did become enormously successful at Bristol.'

Although O'Toole, even at this early stage was, in Hardwicke's estimation, 'an extraordinary personality', he had a long way to go yet. 'This may sound odd, but in those early days at Bristol Peter was just another actor. It's only when you look back and you think, I suppose the seeds of what he turned into were there, you don't necessarily at the time recognise any of that, he's just another mate in a company of actors.'

One early stage performance required O'Toole to ramble on stage as a Georgian peasant to speak one line in Chekhov's Uncle Vanya – 'Dr Astrov, the horses have arrived' – and then amble off again. Trying to make the most of this meagre role, O'Toole decided that his character was really the young Stalin. After working on his make-up for hours using early photographs of the dictator, O'Toole entered the stage smouldering with resentment for the aristocracy, and could feel an electric spark of anticipation from the audience. He glared at Dr Astrov, paused, and snarled quietly. 'Dr Horsey, the Astrovs have arrived.'

The audience fell about laughing. O'Toole's mortification remained written all over his face for days. Phyllida Law was a young actress at Bristol and remembers being quite taken by the actor's public show of remorse. 'He was rather charming because he was so depressed, saying how awfully bad he'd been. Very cast down he was by it all, which I thought was enchanting.'

The actress playing the lead was less forgiving, recalls Hardwicke. 'She invited Peter and me out to lunch, which was quite a thrill, and Peter went off to the loo and she leaned over to ask me, "Is he a good friend?" I said, "Yes, we get on very well." She said, "Well do try and persuade him to give it up."'

John Cairney remembers O'Toole as 'a whirling windmill of passion and enthusiasm. I can still see Peter and me wrestling on the Green Room floor of the Theatre Royal, Bristol during some kind of young-blood quarrel – why, I cannot remember. We worked together in *The Matchmaker*, where I was one of the juvenile leads and he was a character juvenile, playing a carriage driver. He carried a big whip, which I'm glad to say he never used on me.'

By far Cairney's most memorable stage performance at Bristol was one Christmas during the annual panto, playing Marmaduke in *Dick Whittington*. 'And Peter was being Peter in whatever he was playing. I do remember trying to cope with those long gangling legs and arms and wild eyes. At one stage, he and I corpsed ourselves to such effect that neither of us could remember the next line and we couldn't hear what the prompter was calling out because of the laughter from the audience. So we both marched into the prompt corner and lifted the girl out on the high stool and put her centre stage and made her point to the place in the script. Then, to further laughter, we carried her off again and resumed the action. As a result of this, we were both on the carpet before John Moody, the director of the company, and threatened with instant dismissal. But fortunately for theatre, especially in Mr O'Toole's case, he changed his mind the next day. The incident was all part of our mutual excess.'

Even then the O'Toole style was much in evidence, the highly theatrical performances which for some observers were perhaps too BIG. 'I think a lot of really extraordinary actors, people with big personalities, can sometimes in a very small part in a play completely distort that play,' says Hardwicke. 'But if things are done with sufficient confidence they'll convince.' O'Toole, to some extent, was a throwback to actors like Edmund Kean.

Having had no formal education to speak of, RADA, and now the Bristol Old Vic, constituted O'Toole's only real schooling, and he revelled in it, not least the social activities, which meant largely going to the pub. And when he wasn't at the pub O'Toole was busy producing his own whisky. 'We made gallons of it. We had a distillery. The only trouble was we couldn't find anything to store it in. So we got some of those big carboys they keep acid in and filled them with the stuff. Judging by the taste of the whisky, we left some of the acid in.'

O'Toole had a tendency to drink in some real sawdust-and-spit dives; he liked the tinge of anarchy and pent-up violence that might erupt at any moment. He also made friends with those types on the fringes of society, drunks and miscreants. As Nat Brenner observed, 'He cultivated the friendship of people who were plainly psychopathic.' One afternoon O'Toole turned up at the Old Vic's stage door with cuts and bruises; obviously he'd been in a scrap. 'Why do you court this kind of trouble?' reprimanded Brenner. O'Toole's reply was chilling. 'I need it. I need to feed on it in order to inform myself about these people.' More than once Brenner would get calls from the local hospital reporting that a Mr O'Toole was there, not feeling terribly well.

Sheila Allen had also just joined the company and very swiftly got caught up in the weird universe of O'Toole and the shady company he kept. 'He had a rather strange friend who was nothing to do with the theatre community; he was very odd, bordering on dangerous. And they got into some kind of argument, two or three a.m. down some part of Bristol, and Peter ran to us and stayed on our sofa for a bit; it wasn't a very big sofa and he had very long legs. Peter was adorable, but impossible.'

Without fail, it seemed, most of the cast headed to the pub after the curtain fell. 'Often you'd follow O'Toole,' says Sheila, 'because we knew that's where the action would be. And there was this young man, very nice, very quiet, with him one night. "This is my friend Tom; he writes for one of the Bristol rags." He was a young journalist. And he had in the top pocket of his jacket a red exercise book folded in half and every now and then he'd bring it out and jot things in it. "What are you doing?" we asked. "Oh, I just write things down that I like," he replied. "This going in the newspaper?" we queried. "Oh no, this is for me." And that was Tom Stoppard.'

O'Toole continued to appear in minor roles, even in another of the company's pantomimes playing Mrs Ali Baba in *Aladdin*. 'What was good about Peter was that he didn't sneer at playing in a pantomime,' says Phyllida Law. 'He hadn't got any big starry pretensions.' O'Toole didn't even mind having to sell ice creams in the interval. One evening, still dressed as Mrs Ali Baba, he sold an ice cream to Cary Grant. 'He was constantly going round and round, seemingly unsure of which way the wind was blowing,' recalls Cairney. 'But there was no denying the innate power that was there, though it had yet to be applied fully to the talent. But, he was all go – and he went.'

With Bates and O'Toole having moved on and found coveted positions, all eyes now fixed on Finney, the last big gun left at RADA. In fact, he'd been one to watch for quite some time now. Fellow student Gillian Martell was reminded of James Dean in the way he'd wander round with his head down, all mean and moody-looking. She plucked up the courage to ask him one day why he did this. 'I go downstage with my head down, then I look up and give the audience *my eyes!*'

One afternoon the teachers informed the students that some television producers were arriving the following day to cast a TV play, so they'd better turn up in their best clothes. Finney still shared a flat with Peter Bowles, who was ecstatic about the chance and busy dressing into his finery. 'Fuck 'em,' was Albie's attitude, putting on a jumper with more holes in it than the Maginot Line. He'd barely any dialogue anyway in the play being performed and when told to sit with everyone else at the feet of the producers he refused to budge, staying in the far corner of the rehearsal room. When asked who they wanted, the producers pointed straightaway at Finney. 'We want that boy, for a start.'

Standing out more and more, Finney made perhaps his greatest impact in a modern-dress production of *Troilus and Cressida* in January 1956, playing the lead. Kenneth Tynan, amongst the leading drama critics of the day, singled him out as having 'a smouldering talent' that would 'soon disturb the dreams of Burton and Scofield'. Such was his promise that one newspaper, the *News Chronicle*, ran a competition for its readers to select a new name for this brilliant young actor, since Albert Finney was obviously too plebeian to be acceptable in West End lights.

While all this was going on Binkie Beaumont, the top theatrical impresario of the day, invited Finney to his private office at the Globe Theatre and more or less dangled a year's contract in front of his face. It was rejected. Next to try and snare Finney was Rank. Mary Duff, who coached at RADA, also happened to be a talent scout for the film company, always on the lookout for new faces to put into their infamous charm school or to develop as interesting new screen personalities. On her recommendation Finney was asked to go to Rank's head office in London. There on the table was a seven-year contract that started at £1,500 and would eventually rise to £10,000 a year.

Either a bit of shrapnel from the bomb that had landed near his house was still lodged in his brain or the young Finney had balls of steel, for Rank was also summarily dispatched into the long grass. A long-term contract meant commitment, and Finney didn't want to know what he was going to be up to next week, let alone in seven years' time. Where was the excitement in that! So after spurning the chance of West End fame and cinema idolisation, what did Finney choose? Why, Birmingham rep at ten pounds a week, of course.

Actually it was a smart move, a place to learn his craft away from the spotlight. And Birmingham rep wasn't any old suburban theatre, but one of the country's most respected: Olivier, Richardson and Scofield had all been members of its august company. According to theatre critic

Michael Billington, who as a young man regularly attended it, Birmingham was 'the Oxford or Cambridge of repertory theatre, so any young actor who wanted to earn his spurs usually went to Birmingham'. Not for nothing did the likes of Kenneth Tynan regularly travel up to see their productions.

Birmingham also had the distinct advantage over many other theatres of being a monthly rep. 'So you had plenty of time to rehearse properly,' says Paul Williamson, who was there at the same time as Finney. 'To take a play apart and put it back together. Whereas with weekly rep you just got the bloody thing on, fortnightly rep sometimes you fell between the two stools because you just had time to start to take the play apart but not time to put it together again. Monthly rep was a luxury.'

Finney had been recommended to them by RADA's John Fernald and auditioned before the theatre's director Douglas Seale and actor Bernard Hepton, his second in command, who thought the young actor had 'something special. Though we didn't know quite what.' Even so, Finney went straight into a production of *Julius Caesar*. 'We were all saying amongst ourselves that he'd better prove himself, this upstart,' recalled Geoffrey Bayldon. But arriving late for rehearsals on his first morning, looking cold and dishevelled and not a little nervous, didn't do much to endear Finney to the company. When everyone broke for lunch and went to the local pub, Finney stayed behind to sort a few things out. Over drinks the actors all looked at each other and it was understood: the guy was a star, something blazed out of him. 'I think we did know he was fairly special,' says Paul Williamson. 'And that he was supposed to be the white hope of the English theatre. And I do remember being out front sometimes watching rehearsals and the thoughts just came pinging out of his eyes, which is the mark of really great acting. He seemed to be able to convey his thoughts right across an audience. I would contrast that with myself when the director said to me, "What about trying so-and-so, Paul, in that scene?" and I'd say, "I was doing it," and he said, "Well, I didn't notice." Whereas Albie could just convey thoughts with great efficacy.'

While Finney had started with a bang at Birmingham, over in Coventry

Bates was having to make do with minor roles and work as an assistant stage manager. Colin George was there at the time and appeared with Bates in *The Comedy of Errors*, in which they played identical twins. 'Then I did another play with them that Alan wasn't in, he was just doing props, and in one scene I had to come on stage carrying a suitcase. Anyway, on the last matinee tricks were played and I went to pick up my bag and Alan had filled it with stage weights, I could hardly get it off the floor. And when I looked into the wings he was killing himself with laughter.'

Phyllida Law had lots of friends over at the Midland Repertory Company and the name Alan Bates often cropped up during cosy chats. 'They used to call him Daisy Bates and worry about him because he was so nice. They adored him but didn't believe he was any use at all as an actor. I think because he wasn't strong or tough enough to push himself forward. They said, what are we going to do about Daisy? We've got to get him a job. He'll never get a job by himself. They were all very felicitous about Daisy Bates.'

One of the actresses decided to take matters into her own hands. Hearing about a new company being formed in London, she urged Bates to go and audition for them. It was something based at the Royal Court Theatre with an aim to promote new and challenging British playwrights. Bates thought it all sounded interesting. 'I didn't really know what I was getting into. I went in quite innocently.' Little did Bates realise that he was about to become part of theatre history.

8

Osborne's Little Bastard

England in the 1950s was a rather grey place. There was rationing, high unemployment and poverty, homosexuality was illegal – it really was a whole different world. When John Gielgud was arrested for cottaging in a public lavatory in 1953, the following evening police stood guard all down the side of the stalls and the circle in case there was a demonstration against him when he appeared on stage. (Instead, the audience gave him a standing ovation.) Abortion was also illegal and the country remained polarised by the class system; Prime Minister Anthony Eden was an old Etonian with a cabinet full of fellow Etonians and Oxford men. The licensing laws were also both primitive and punitive. So, not a very Merrie England. Did the West End theatre indicate that rebellion against any of this was in the offing? Of course not. As Kenneth Tynan summed it up: 'The bare fact is that apart from revivals and imports there is nothing in the London theatre that one dares discuss with an intelligent man for more than five minutes.'

Compare this with Broadway, where there existed a theatre culture bursting with energy and passion and where the likes of Tennessee Williams and Arthur Miller were producing radical plays that dealt with real social issues and were populated with characters the average Joe off the street could relate to. The West End was stiflingly highbrow in comparison, run as it was by an established theatrical mafia reluctant to tamper with the existing state of affairs. And Binkie Beaumont, managing director of H. M. Tennent, was the most influential of the lot. His productions were, admittedly, beautifully mounted star vehicles, an antidote to post-war blues and austerity in England. His playwrights of choice were Noël Coward and Terence Rattigan. But they were designed to please a middle-class audience who still came to the theatre dressed in dinner jackets and cocktail dresses. As for the commoners, the theatre portrayed a different world that they couldn't possibly engage in, represented only by the servant or the policeman who might come in at the odd moment, say a couple of lines and then disappear again. Where was their voice? When would they be heard?

The instrument of change came from a very unlikely source, a man who was every bit as establishment as the clowns in charge, but someone who could see that English drama was suffocating and close to terminal arrest. His name was George Devine. Educated at Oxford, Devine was president of the university's dramatic society, where he'd been friends with fellow student Terence Rattigan. He'd acted with all the distinguished thesps from Olivier to Redgrave in all manner of period classics, ran the Old Vic Theatre School and directed at Sadler's Wells and at Stratford. His knowledge of stagecraft was perhaps unequalled. Yet he'd become bored to death by it all. Drama in the whole of Britain just hadn't evolved; the West End scene in the mid-fifties was a mirror image of twenty years before. 'I have it in my bones that we have got to start on the *young* generation right away.'

Hired to appear in a BBC production of a Chekhov play, Devine's attention was caught by the brilliant energy of its young director. Tony Richardson, the son of a chemist from Shipley in Yorkshire, had also studied at Oxford and with his friend Lindsay Anderson had co-written film essays for the university's highbrow cinema magazine. But he yearned to make movies. Richardson was accepted on a BBC director trainee course and quickly rose through the ranks to become the corporation's 'hot' new talent. In an effort to disguise – indeed, eliminate – his northern accent Richardson had taken speech lessons, with the result that he now had a highly inflected voice.

Devine discovered that Richardson shared his passion about making English theatre more relevant in the life of the nation and together they hatched an audacious plan to create their own theatre company, but things looked bleak when a search for funds drew a blank. At much the same time another group of fairly diverse people had arrived at much the same opinion, while progressing quite a bit further; they were playwright Ronald Duncan, theatre producer and member of the Communist Party Oscar

Lewenstein, no lover of West End middle-class dirge, and Lord Harewood, cousin to the Queen and the royal family's keenest patron of the arts. It was Lewenstein who heard of Devine and Richardson's idea and decided it benefited everyone if both parties merged. Thus was the English Stage Company born, with Devine elected artistic director and Richardson as his associate; Devine saw Richardson as his link with the new generation.

Next came the search for a suitable venue. The Royal Court Theatre stands on the east side of Sloane Square in Chelsea, a convenient distance from the glitz of theatreland. It was as clear a statement the new company could make that they weren't just miles away in metaphorical terms from the West End, but a literal distance, too. Built in 1888 and having suffered bomb damage during the war, the Royal Court was a bit run down to say the least, with rain streaming in through the roof and some rather dodgy equipment; the switchboard was a death trap, touch it and risk getting a 1,000-volt connection! Other than that, the place was perfect.

Devine's mission statement was clear, to seek out fresh and unheralded British writing talent and to mount new plays that other theatres had either rejected or wouldn't dream of putting on, plays that reflected more closely the times they were living in, as opposed to the drawing-room comedies and revivals of the West End. 'As I saw it,' said Bates, 'the Royal Court's function was to bring a new force, new thinking, a new provocation into the theatre.'

And so a beacon of light and hope was sent out from Sloane Square to all those hungry playwrights in bedsit land. It took the form of an advertisement in the *Stage* and within weeks Devine's office was inundated with some 700 submissions. Amongst what was, let's be fair about it, mostly a pile of rubbish, one play stood out, it was called *Look Back in Anger* and was written by twenty-seven-year-old John Osborne.

Osborne was the son of an advertisement copy-writer and a barmaid. When his father died in 1941, the young Osborne used the payout from his life-assurance policy to fund a private education but was kicked out of boarding school for whacking the headmaster, after he himself had been struck for listening to a forbidden radio broadcast by Frank Sinatra.

For years Osborne struggled as an actor in repertory theatres, having eradicated his London accent in order to be accepted into the middle classes. He knew the world of the theatre was riddled with class, play after brain-numbing play set in either a manor house or Lady Whatsit's drawing room; it was like some ghastly waxwork exhibition that Osborne was determined to let loose on with a blow torch.

Dispirited by his lack of progress as an actor, Osborne began to play the arse. While appearing in a melodrama he applied spirit gum to the outer surface of his fake moustache so that after snogging the leading actress she was left looking like Lord Kitchener. He also sprinkled condoms amidst plates of food that were used as props. Unsurprisingly, producers grew less and less fond of employing Osborne so he turned instead to writing. In order to exorcise some of the emotional turmoil following a divorce from his first wife, the actress Pamela Lane, he set to work on a play about an individual trapped in a combative marriage. Osborne was on the dole at the time, and living in the cheapest accommodation he could find: a barge moored on the Thames near Chiswick with a gay actor by the name of Anthony Creighton, who fussed over him like a neurotic mother hen. Close to penury, the odd couple sometimes boiled and ate nettles they found growing on the riverbank.

Osborne finished *Look Back in Anger* in little over a month, putting the final touches to it while sitting on a deckchair at the end of Morecambe pier, where he was appearing in rep. The play's hero was Jimmy Porter, who, while his better-born young wife bends over an ironing board and his friend Cliff sprawls over the Sunday papers, lets loose in machine-gun fashion on everything within range: art, religion, England, but especially his wife and the dreaded mother-in-law. Jimmy Porter was to a large extent the mouthpiece of Osborne, venting anger on behalf of an educated generation that wanted to see some sense of meaning and purpose injected into Englishness now the empire had passed away. Was it any wonder, then, that every West End producer and agent turned the thing down? Even the Bristol Old Vic thought he'd gone too far. Then he saw the English Stage Company's ad in the *Stage* and sent it off to the Royal Court. 'It was just what we were looking for,' Devine later wrote. 'The bomb that would blow a hole in the old theatre and leave a nice-sized gap, too big to be patched up.'

So desperate was Devine to meet the play's creator that instead of sending word for him to come to his office, all business-like, he borrowed a friend's dinghy and furiously paddled the short distance from his riverside home near Hammersmith bridge to Osborne's barge. After scrutinising the author as a scientist would some newly discovered organism under his microscope, trying to ignore the posters of Marlon Brando and other bare-chested beefcake that adorned the scant wall space, Devine offered Osborne twenty-five pounds for a year's option on his play.

Meanwhile a recruitment drive was under way for a supreme ensemble of young actors to make up the English Stage Company's inaugural season; discoveries included Joan Plowright, known to Devine from the Old Vic Theatre School, Keith Michell, Mary Ure, Kenneth Haigh, Nigel Davenport and Robert Stephens, talent-spotted by Devine in a production of *King Lear* at the Library Theatre, Manchester. Richardson also organised a series of auditions and it was to one of these, held in February 1956, that Alan Bates turned up.

Much to his own surprise, Bates was asked to join and was rewarded with a small role in the Court's first production, *The Mulberry Bush* by novelist Angus Wilson, which opened in April under Devine's direction. Alas, the play found little critical favour and played to poor houses. The Royal Court was off to a bit of a stinker. It had been planned to open with a bang with *Look Back in Anger*, but Osborne's play was becoming something of a hot potato. Devine's enthusiasm for it was not matched by a succession of actors approached to star. Some turned it down because it was too radical; others were simply horrified. One 'revered theatre dame', in Osborne's phrase, not only rejected Devine's approach but dismissed the play altogether, saying, 'It should be thrown into the river and washed out to sea so that it may never be seen again.'

The Court's second play was the London debut of Arthur Miller's *The Crucible*, and although it attracted a better critical response the box-office takings were still dismal. Bates must have wondered whether he'd made the right choice in leaving Coventry. Maybe even Devine was thinking he'd made a terrible mistake in coming to the Royal Court. Chelsea was hardly the swinging place in 1956 that it would eventually become; the King's Road was then predominantly the reserve of antique sellers, greengrocers and cake shops.

However, everything would change with the Court's next production, for Devine had decided it was time to unleash Osborne's little bastard.

With Kenneth Haigh cast as Jimmy Porter and Mary Ure as his put-upon wife Alison, Bates decided to go up for the role of Cliff, Porter's friend and the play's most sympathetic character. He faced a number of competitors including John Cairney, whom Devine had spotted over at the Bristol Old Vic. 'George seemed quite happy with my audition,' recalls Cairney, 'and asked me to join him for a beer at the pub next door, during which I managed to talk myself out of the part as he did not regard me as an ideal company man.'

Osborne would later reveal that he helped 'stage manage' Bates's audition, making sure he got the role; 'He was definitely the best choice.' Other reports suggest that Osborne in fact favoured Nigel Davenport and it was Richardson who insisted on Bates. Whatever the case, Bates found himself cast in a production that would change the theatrical landscape for ever: 'Of course none of us realised this at the time, how important the play was going to become.'

Richardson, who'd been installed as director, was a huge fan of *Look Back*, telling Osborne at their first meeting, 'I think it's the best play written since the war,' but rehearsals were anything but enjoyable, instead they were nervy and tense. 'Kenneth was sullen and argumentative,' Osborne recalled. 'Alan was agreeable and bent on pleasing.' Haigh and Richardson were very often at each other's throats; at one point it got so bad that, unable to watch the spectacle any longer, Osborne left the auditorium. Richardson would later label Haigh as 'gifted but self-indulgent whose moods and pouting shed a gloom that I wasn't experienced enough to dispel.'

Bates, still living at The Mansions, asked Keith Baxter for some tips on the Welsh accent required for the role and also invited him along to the dress rehearsal. 'It didn't blow me away, you know,' Baxter says today. 'Although I thought Alan was terribly good. He was perfectly cast as Cliff. I went with Roy Kinnear and then we went back to The Mansions and Alan came along soon after, ran into the living room and asked, "So what do you think of it?" And we said, "Terrific, it's great," as you do, but we didn't feel it was going to become this iconic piece of theatre.'

As opening night loomed Devine's confidence in the play began to slip, not from an artistic standpoint – he still understood its value – but whether it would draw in the crowds and please the critics. Lord Harewood had shown the play to a friend and received this response: 'Well, it's very excitingly written, but you can't put that on in a theatre! People won't stand for being shouted at like that, it's not what they go to the theatre for.' The company's press officer told Osborne to his face that he was appalled by his play and doubted he could interest any journalists in it. Pausing, he then offered this evaluation of the playwright: 'I suppose you're really . . . an angry young man.' It was the first time Osborne recalled that phrase ever being used.

Considering the effect *Look Back in Anger* was to make, the opening night on Tuesday, 8 May 1956 gave little indication of it, although those in attendance came away at the end of the evening fully aware they'd seen something the like of which British theatre had never staged before. Even the set – a drab attic bedsit – was so radically different from the norm that the mere sight of Alison's ironing board on stage is said to have drawn a collective intake of breath from the audience. Once the play started, Osborne, watching anxiously, sensed that much of that first-night crowd felt ill at ease: 'They seemed transfixed by a tone of voice that was quite alien to them.' Some walked out; others were cast adrift 'like Eskimos watching a Restoration comedy'.

One of those who left at the interval, no doubt sporting a face of purple indignation, was Binkie Beaumont. Terence Rattigan was of a mind to follow suit but was persuaded to remain to the end by the theatre critic of the *Financial Times*, T. C. Worsley. Stepping out into the night, Rattigan and Worsley had a stand-up row about what they'd just witnessed; Worsley saw it as a breakthrough, Rattigan couldn't believe that nice decent West End audiences wanted to watch plays about the social outcry of the working class; it just wasn't cricket.

A witness to that historical first night is Anthony Field, then just starting out as a theatre producer and soon to make his own little piece of history. 'It really knocked you for six,' he says of it today. 'It was certainly a new style of theatre, people were suddenly standing on stage and being *you*, and thinking like you and talking like you, and it wasn't like a normal West End play. You suddenly thought, these are real people talking about what is happening *now*. I remember there was enormous applause at the end; people recognised they were seeing something new and different.'

The next morning, nursing a horrendous hangover, Osborne collected the newspapers and scanned the review sections. It was then that his world fell apart. Milton Shulman in the *Evening Standard* called it 'self-pitying snivel'. *The Times* thought the play 'inadequate' and consisting largely of 'angry tirades'. The *Birmingham Post*'s critic thought if more plays like Osborne's were produced at the Royal Court the place was done for. But the *Daily Worker* took the biscuit for the most imaginative critique, suggesting *Look Back* was 'the kind of play Tennessee Williams might have written if he had spent a month of rainy Sundays in Birmingham'.

Later that afternoon Osborne and Richardson sat depressed in a café opposite Sloane Square tube station, convinced the play would barely last a month, if that. Osborne was bemoaning the critics. 'But what on earth did you expect?' responded Richardson. 'You didn't expect them to like it, did you?' As for Devine, he was even more downcast; believing the very future of the Royal Court was now in jeopardy.

With his hopes dashed, Osborne was like a man walking to the scaffold as he trudged to his local newsagent that weekend for the Sunday papers, maybe he could take some solace in those. And there it was, Kenneth Tynan in the *Observer*: 'All the qualities are there, qualities one had despaired of ever seeing on the stage . . . I doubt if I could love anyone who did not wish to see *Look Back in Anger*. It is the best young play of the decade.' It was a godsend and Tynan's rave had an almost immediate effect, turning *Look Back* into *the* play to see, especially amongst actors and others associated with the entertainment business, almost all of whom recognised it as a real breakthrough. 'It was the play that changed everything for the working-class actor in the British theatre,' is how Michael Caine saw it. For him, though, it wasn't so much the vindictive spiel that Porter spouted, but the accent of the actor playing him; Kenneth Haigh hailed from a mining village near Doncaster and sounded like it.

Sonia Fraser saw the play as an actress of just eighteen and has never forgotten the experience. 'It was so exciting to hear, not so much a working-class voice, but an alternative voice. I was so excited, I actually came out of the theatre and I walked the streets of London all night. It was unbelievably exciting and it's terribly difficult to convey now how exciting that particular production was.' For Sonia and many others like her *Look Back* wasn't just momentous because it was going to break the barriers down. 'It was more than that, this was the first time one completely related to something that was happening on stage. You know how sometimes you can read a book and you read something and you think, that's exactly what I've always felt but I've never seen it expressed before. It was an identification. It was that something was happening on stage which wasn't separate from oneself, it completely resonated within oneself.'

So, all the right people were seeing *Look Back*, but not enough to make any meaningful difference to the box office. It got so bad that Devine went to extraordinary lengths to try and save the company from closure, such as getting his wife to pop round to next-door neighbour Anne Piper, a successful novelist, to see if she and perhaps some friends would attend a performance and cause a disturbance that might get reported and make a bit of publicity. 'The idea was that we should go and stand up in the middle of the play and say, "This is rubbish" or "How disgusting!" and walk out really obviously.'

As it was, such play-acting wasn't required, though Anne was rewarded by becoming the first reader for the Royal Court, trawling through some six hundred new scripts that had arrived. Just when it seemed that *Look Back* was doomed it was saved by, of all things, television. The BBC decided to screen a short extract, with an introduction by Lord Harewood. Within days the sale of tickets skyrocketed, bringing with it a totally new kind of audience. 'All these people started arriving,' recalled the Court's stage director Michael Halifax. 'People you never see in theatres. Young people gazing around wondering where to go and what the rules were. A completely new audience: just what we were trying to find.'

That July the playwright Arthur Miller arrived in London, accompanying his new wife Marilyn Monroe who was due to begin filming *The*

Prince and the Showgirl opposite Laurence Olivier. During that first encounter between America's foremost playwright and England's greatest living actor, Olivier asked Miller what plays he wanted to see while in London. Unfamiliar with the current West End scene, Miller chose *Look Back in Anger* simply because he liked the title, not knowing the play from Adam. Olivier was aghast; he'd seen the thing and told Miller to choose something else. 'You don't want to bother with that, it stinks. Besides, it's a travesty on England, a lot of bitter rattling on.' The actor's furore over the play only served to intrigue Miller even further, so it was arranged that both men would see it the following night. As Olivier settled into his seat to steady himself once again for an assault on his beloved country, Miller sat entranced. Not only did he find the play astonishing; much to the bemusement of Olivier, Miller went further, describing West End theatre in general as 'hermetically sealed off from life', naming *Look Back in Anger* the single exception, it was for him the only modern British play. Only in Osborne's play did he feel as though he knew the characters, understood their plight and their fears, and that they shed more light on England than anything else he was to see during his stay.

In a few short weeks the Royal Court had become, in the words of Richardson, 'The theatre of the moment, the place where it was happening, take it or leave it, love it or hate it.' And there were plenty who did hate it, or were certainly wary of its impact. As John Gielgud remarked, 'When I saw *Look Back in Anger* I thought my number was up.' Others felt it didn't really impinge on them; Robert Hardy for one: 'I remember thinking that *Look Back in Anger* was indeed a very angry play but I couldn't see quite why everybody was so cross in it. I didn't see it as a new wave of theatrical expansion, because if you've done a great deal of Shakespeare there really is no need for expansion, it's all there; the whole thing, the kitchen sink is in Shakespeare.'

John Cairney, who'd been up for Cliff, remember, was also rather less blown away by the revolutionary nature of the play. 'Coming from the Citizens Theatre and their naturalistic style, the play was no great surprise. I thought it was a series of almost operatic speeches, which Kenneth Haigh used to great effect. Haigh was a tour de force of the first order. The part was exactly right for his attacking style. But, my particular memory of that production was of the exquisite Mary Ure, who had little to do other than ironing, but did it very smoothly.'

Haigh was indeed the star of the show, but Bates's Cliff was a beautiful study in restraint and touching sensitivity, a welcome counterpoint to Haigh's blistering rants. It was also a huge bolster to his career, so early on, too. 'It was the first time I was seen in a recognised play, and people took notice. It was a real stroke of luck in terms of finding my feet and getting on and being acknowledged.'

Having failed to bag Finney, Rank now homed in on Bates with a similarly lucrative contract but they were given equally short shrift. 'Even though it offered security, I felt it meant being owned by somebody. I didn't want to be somebody else's property and be told what to do.' And Bates had no desire to become anything as bland as a 'star', following a very deliberate calculated course, mapped out for him by a studio. He wanted to make films, to be sure, but wanted with it the freedom to make his own choices. Years later, looking back on that decision, Bates was amazed that his younger self had the nerve to resist, 'but I'm glad I did'.

Kenneth Tynan remarked that *Look Back in Anger* lanced a boil which had been coming to a head for some years. Not least in the mind of John Osborne, increasingly bitter that his generation had no voice. In one letter to a friend he wrote, 'What a deep and bitter division there is in this country. There's no one to take the lead, no one to jolt and inspire the angry ones among us.'

With *Look Back* that post-war generation was finally heard, the vitality of its language, the long pent-up attitudes and its unstoppable grievance. And the anger and class hatred that Osborne unleashed shocked the establishment to its core. 'Osborne felt that middle-class England had to be shaken up,' says Keith Baxter. 'And that the general populace was not being addressed in terms that they would understand.' *Look Back* enabled common life to be seen on the stage. Out went country houses, French windows and anyone for tennis; within just a few months that kind of play looked positively archaic, replaced by a new wave of British playwrights like Harold Pinter, Arnold Wesker and Shelagh Delaney.

Poor old Rattigan and Coward and others like Emlyn Williams and J. B. Priestley were dismissed as fuddy-duddies, their work unjustifiably derided and unperformed in the West End for years. 'I think these writers saw *Look Back in Anger* and its ilk as a threat,' says Anthony Field. 'That they couldn't write that sort of play and they didn't want this to be the theatre of the future. It was all right as long as it was done in a tiny, off-West End theatre, but when it started to come into major theatres they saw it very much as a threat.' The Yorkshire-born Priestley once protested to a group of young Royal Court writers in the early sixties, 'Angry! I'll give you angry. I was angry before you buggers were born!'

Osborne's play also had the good fortune to open around the time of the Suez crisis, which sounded the death-knell of the empire and demolished any pretence that Britain was still a major player on the world stage. This was also the time of the Hungarian revolution and the Campaign for Nuclear Disarmament. The plays and films that followed in the wake of Osborne's offspring were a symbol for rebellion and dissent amongst the creative chattering classes, a weapon to strike against the political and cultural establishment.

The success of *Look Back in Anger*, its revivals and the sale of film rights, essentially kept the English Stage Company afloat. Whenever the Royal Court suffered a duff play, more often than not *Look Back* arrived like the cavalry to take over and get bums on seats again. So much so that one of the businessmen on the theatre's board of directors made the suggestion that there should be a permanent company of actors available to play *Look Back* at a moment's notice.

Perhaps the biggest irony of all is that Osborne's play has dated quite awfully. It looks formulaic now, almost quaint, a museum piece. Sonia Fraser recalls taking her young daughter to see the 1989 London stage revival directed by Judi Dench with Kenneth Branagh as Jimmy Porter and Emma Thompson playing Alison. Having gone on and on about the impact the play wrought on her and her generation, she remembers the evening as being rather depressingly anticlimactic. 'It just didn't stir the blood any more.'

9

The Hurricane After the Storm

Just two and a half weeks after the opening night of *Look Back in Anger* London's theatre scene was rocked by another earth tremor, this time delivered by Joan Littlewood, the self-proclaimed 'vulgar woman of the people', with the aid of two Irishmen, Richard Harris and Brendan Behan.

Still a LAMDA student, Harris was staying in a succession of dirty bedsits, when he could find one that didn't have a 'No Irish' policy. Sometimes Elizabeth, persevering with her career in rep theatre, would come down at weekends and get Harris a new room. 'You always had to pay your first week and your last week in advance, so I'd pay the first week and the last and then that's about as long as he'd last. It wasn't the Irish accent so much; somehow landladies were a red rag to him, and he to them. They represented authority I guess – you've got to do this, you can't do that. "Why?" he'd say.'

Harris was always being thrown into the street, either for being the worst tenant imaginable or for other indiscretions. He was in a pub one evening giving a drunken impersonation of his current harridan of a landlady when the saloon doors opened and the very she-devil herself appeared in the bar. 'And you, Mr Harris,' she shrilled, 'you can piss off out of my house right now and never come back!'

His luck changed another time in a bar when he overheard a couple of theatrical types saying how they hadn't finished casting Joan Littlewood's new production over at Theatre Workshop. 'Jesus Christ,' he yelled, 'I'll have a try for that.' Borrowing fourpence for the phone, Harris called them up. Gerry Raffles, the company's general manager and Joan's right-hand man, answered. 'There's only one part we haven't cast yet, but it's for a fifty-year-old man.'

75

Such a trivial obstacle didn't stop Harris. 'I look fucking fifty,' he bellowed down the line. 'I haven't had a good meal for four months and I haven't slept for days. Just take a look at me!'

There was a pause, then: 'Be here at ten tomorrow morning.'

That necessitated borrowing more money for the tube journey to Stratford East, and then a brisk walk through a bustling market to reach the theatre. Inside he was handed a script. Particularly bad as a cold reader, Harris stumbled. 'Perhaps,' said Raffles, 'if the script is too difficult you would like to try an improvisation.'

Harris knew he'd blown it and went into a rant, a rant that was aimed at his mates later that evening in the pub back in Earls Court. 'That Raffles guy, what a cold insensitive bastard. A man with no imagination, a fellow with no compassion and no understanding. Wouldn't you know such a man would turn me down?'

Harris was just getting started when he was interrupted by a solitary handclap that as it grew louder could be seen to belong to a small, plain-looking woman stepping out of the shadows of the rear stalls. It was Joan Littlewood. 'I think we've found our Mickser,' she said, referring to the character Harris was to play. And it was a name that Joan insisted on calling him from then on. Somehow it suited him.

According to Elizabeth, when the authorities at LAMDA heard that Harris had joined Joan Littlewood they went spare and chucked him out. 'They said, "You can't be working in the theatre if you're a student here," and Richard reasoned it by saying, "I'm coming here to get a job in the theatre so how can you chuck me out?" And he was furious with them; anyway, he went.'

The play in question was *The Quare Fellow* by a then unknown Irish play-wright called Brendan Behan. Based on his own experiences as a Republican prisoner on terrorist charges, it was set in a jail on the night of a hanging and was a powerful plea against capital punishment. Behan sent this, his first play, to Joan, who immediately sensed its passion and potential, despite the beer stains over nearly every page, and invited him to London. Behan wired back saying he hadn't the fare, so Joan sent him money. 'And he drank it,' she'd recall. 'I'm not an alcoholic,' he told her, 'but I'm saving up to be one.' With her next letter Joan enclosed a ticket to London and an AA map.

Behan attended rehearsals, sitting chain smoking and coughing in the stalls, occasionally interrupting the actors saying, 'Did I write that? I'm a fucking genius.' He'd also regale everyone with stories of his life that were later used as improvisations by the cast and incorporated into the show. The play was literally being rewritten and reshaped by Joan as it went along. She also invited ex-prisoners to come and give talks, explaining slopping out and other details of prison life, such as how to pass cigarettes to your mate without the screws catching on.

Most unorthodox of all, Joan took her actors onto the roof of the theatre. She wanted them to get the feel of what it was like to walk around a prison exercise yard, and with the stage space too limited, up onto the roof everyone went. For hours and hours, day upon day, the actors trudged around in circles getting mind-numbingly bored; and that was the point. Whenever anyone spoke or cracked a joke Joan screamed at them, 'Stop it! You wouldn't be allowed to talk, none of you, you've got to do it so secretively that nobody else will see you.' Some of the cast asked Behan how he'd managed and he told them the prisoners spoke out of the corners of their mouth. In the end it was a worthwhile exercise; Joan hoped to instil in her actors not just how to act as though they were in a prison, but how to actually feel it, pushing through the barriers of boredom.

Harris saw all this as a game, but enjoyed the method of it and persevered. According to Elizabeth, Joan took to Harris in a big way. 'She adored Richard and he adored her. They'd have terrific fights and arguments, but he always listened to her and had great respect for her till the very end. He learned more from Joan than he ever did at LAMDA. What he loved was that she wanted improvisation, she wanted new things, she wanted you to challenge and see what you could develop, and LAMDA and RADA, that was not what they were teaching in those days.'

Joan employed rather unusual methods to get her new charges acquainted with her style. Harris found this out when he stood before her on a bare stage. 'Right,' she said. 'Take them all off.' Harris was required to strip. First his shirt, his shoes, then his trousers, until he stood there in just his underpants. 'And your underwear. Get them off.'

'What?' Harris did as he was told, standing there stark naked.

'Now,' said Joan, 'make me believe you are fully dressed. That's what actors do. Until you're prepared to expose yourself and vomit up your secrets on stage you'll never be any good as an actor.'

Harris also fitted in well with the company, befriending in particular Brian Murphy. 'We got on rather well and I liked Richard very much. He was incredibly determined. He said to me that he was going to be a film star and I say to this day, he's the only person that I have worked with who set his sights high on becoming a film star and achieved it in a very short time. He seemed to me to be very calculated.'

Neither has Murphy forgotten the opening night of *The Quare Fellow*. Amongst the audience were East End criminals with their strumpet molls, all earrings and fur coats, and the Kray brothers who turned up in a Rolls-Royce, all rubbing shoulders with IRA members who'd managed to smuggle themselves in, having earlier threatened to blow up the theatre. Noisy Irishmen of all sorts filled the place and when Joan blasted their national anthem from out of the loudspeakers they all stood to attention and the sound of their seats flying back was like a hail of machine gun fire and people ducked in panic.

The atmosphere was electric that night. Not least the play's denouement when the prisoner is hung. The cast were positioned all over the theatre: front of house, backstage, up in the flies, banging on metal pipes the way the inmates did when a man was being topped, it was exhilarating.

One of the performances was attended by producer Anthony Field, who ran the Comedy Theatre, and was determined to bring *The Quare Fellow* into the West End, in spite of Joan's fierce resistance. 'Joan had always said no to transferring her plays,' Field remembers. 'She used to say, we have this atmosphere at the Theatre Workshop, I don't want it moved into a glossy West End theatre. And it was only because Gerry Raffles and I said to her that financially it made sense, that they had no money to put on other shows they wanted to unless they did this West End run, that she was finally persuaded.'

The role of Gerry Raffles in Theatre Workshop has often been overlooked. He wasn't just the company's backbone, he was Joan's life partner, they never married but one sensed they never needed to. He was always around, the mad paddling feet to Joan's creative swan. 'He kept the thing going, really,' says Philip Grout. 'What she would have done without him is obvious – she wouldn't have. It was as simple as that. He was calm, on the whole, genial, and it was quite obvious that he was a rock for her.'

In the West End Behan's influence still loomed large, he'd arrive with a crate of Guinness to talk and share stories with the actors minutes before curtain-up. Anthony Field was forced at one point to lock him in a dressing room because of his drunken state and the chaos he was causing. 'I think the only person who could cope with Brendan was Joan,' he says. 'She had this amazing way of establishing a relationship with people who worked with her. Everyone was very much in awe of Joan, although she was a very down-to-earth, basic person.'

On the eve of the transfer Behan was invited to be interviewed on the BBC by Malcolm Muggeridge. Arriving decently lubricated, Behan continued drinking in the hospitality room, downing two bottles of whisky. When a headmistress of a finishing school and her charges arrived Behan awoke from his drunken slumber with a start. 'I'd like to fuck you,' he growled. 'The lot of you!' The poor females about turned and quickly marched out again.

As Behan grew increasingly lathered the show's producer began to wonder whether all this was a good idea, turning to Muggeridge to advise, 'If he uses the word cunt, don't laugh.' Propped up by Joan, Behan found it difficult to speak, nay to stay conscious. After the transmission both he and Joan were ignominiously expelled from the premises but the next day the driver of every passing lorry or taxi slowed down to shout, 'Oi, Brendan! You was properly pissed on the telly last night. Good on yer!'

The success of *The Quare Fellow* brought Behan international recognition, critics hailed him as another Sean O'Casey. It did much for Joan's theatre, too. Barely subsisting before with no grants or subsidies, the Behan play brought them much-needed box-office revenue as Field had predicted. It also, as Field had hoped, did much to shake up the status quo a bit. 'I don't think we'd ever had such an earthy play in the West End like *The Quare Fellow*. Many of us were trying to establish a new sort of theatre to get away from the plays of Noël Coward and Terence Rattigan and people coming through French windows with a bouquet of flowers. And it's very interesting that now we've got back to thinking of Rattigan and Coward as classic plays, whereas at the time people thought they were rather superficial, glossy West End fare and that these new writers were the way forward and would establish a wider range of plays.'

Two years later Joan put on Behan's *The Hostage*, again a successful West End transfer. Ann Beach was in that production and remembers it vividly. 'Brendan used to watch the show every night. He'd sit in the stalls and he'd start talking to us on the stage during the performance, "That's right, Eileen, you tell her off, yeah you tell her off, that's a good thing," that sort of stuff. We loved it because we'd talk back to him, Joan loved it because we had a banter going, and the audience loved it. He'd also come onto the stage for the curtain call and was there for ages telling his jokes and stories.' The only people who took umbrage were the theatre bosses who barred Behan from attending any more performances. 'So we used to sneak him in through the stage door,' says Ann. 'Just as long as he sat quietly in the prompt corner and didn't interrupt. I'll always remember him sitting on the stool in the corner, poor Brendan, complaining, "I can't get in to see me own fucking play!" Sometimes he'd try and get onto the stage and we'd have to hold him back.'

10

Game of Squash, Anyone?

Besides *Look Back in Anger* and *The Quare Fellow* there was another play at the same time courting controversy, but this one was to quickly slip into obscurity. *Off the Mainland* was about an unnamed Eastern-bloc country that uses an island to interrogate and torture prisoners; curiously prescient thanks to Guantanamo Bay. Like John Osborne, the author was a down-at-luck actor who hoped the play would set him off on a new career as a writer. By sheer gumption he'd managed to get the play produced at the Arts Theatre in London with himself in the lead. Alas he had the misfortune to open in the same week as *Look Back in Anger*. The actor's name was Robert Shaw.

It was lousy timing, although *Off the Mainland* met with much the same public outcry in some quarters as Osborne's play, mainly from women who stood up in the auditorium and shouted, 'Disgrace! I shall write to the management.' Shaw had thought his play marvellous, but friends were brutally honest about its failings; Lindsay Anderson thought it pretty risible, though 'with flashes of good writing'. Playing to dismal houses, the critical notices were even worse, notices that Shaw read and re-read, turning them over in his head; his own private torture.

Robert Shaw was born on 9 August 1927 in rural Westhoughton, Lancashire, the heart of the cotton industry. He was the oldest of five children. Before embarking upon a career as a GP Shaw's father Thomas was a talented rugby player and amateur boxing champion; also decorated in the First World War. But behind the dashing, handsome gent who charmed the socks off the local lasses and was well liked by his patients, there was an inner darkness, an addiction to alcohol that he seemed unable to control. Too young to see the pain behind his father's smiles, it was an idyllic early childhood for Bob Shaw, who loved to entertain the girls on their way home from the mills by dancing with his dad's top hat and cane atop a narrow ledge on the ground-floor bay window of their house, not caring if he fell off. 'I don't know what's to be done with the boy,' a neighbour said to his father one day. 'He's a born actor.'

When he grew old enough to comprehend his father's drink problem, Shaw could see how hard his mother Doreen fought to keep the family together. 'She was a remarkable woman,' he'd say. 'Extraordinarily independent.' He'd remember his father as a 'flamboyant' character, but when drunk, 'he was trouble'. Sometimes Dr Shaw would creep into his son's room after a night on the sauce and cry at his bedside.

Determined to face his demons, Thomas Shaw moved his family to Stromness in the Orkney Islands, hoping for a new start; Bob was just six years old. The local populace lived a tough, simple life and Thomas quickly endeared himself to them, going off by boat in all weathers to visit his patients. But the drinking continued, so too the tearful nocturnal visits to little Robert's room. 'The poor in Scotland like their doctors to take a drink,' Bob Shaw later said. 'They trust doctors who drink.' More disturbing, however, were growing signs of manic depression. It got so bad that Doreen felt she had no option but to take the children away from his disruptive influence and stay with her sister who had a farm in Cornwall.

Bob was ten when his parents reconciled, Thomas once again promising a fresh start if they all joined him at his new practice in Somerset. Doreen relented. What could she do? They were his children, too, and maybe he deserved another chance. Tragically this was thrown away as he became ever more troubled and erratic. He'd drive his children at breakneck speed to the coast, ramming on his brakes just near a cliff edge. 'Shall I drive us over?' he'd say, and then turn to Robert, 'Shall I? End it all, eh?' Such harrowing events, according to Shaw, happened more than once.

'I'm going to kill myself,' Thomas declared to his wife one day. 'Don't do it in front of the children,' was the reply, or so the family story goes. This wasn't the first occasion he'd threatened suicide, but it was the last. A short while later he took poison in his surgery. In the years that followed Shaw's memory of this incident grew ever more blurry and confused; and who could blame him for wanting to try and erase it completely? In some recollections he said he was at school when the headmaster came into class to collect him and impart the shocking news. Other times he'd tell of his father coming into his room saying he was going to do himself in, 'because I can bear the world no longer'.

The death of Shaw's father was a wound, a deep, savage wound that never healed. Even into adulthood Robert Shaw often dreamed of his father and conducted conversations with him about his career and what was happening in his life. Doreen coped by insisting it had been an accidental overdose, not a proper suicide at all, as she battled to bring up the family in a strict but loving manner. Leaving behind Somerset and its painful memories, Doreen had returned to Cornwall, finding work as a part-time nurse. Thanks to a scholarship, Shaw enrolled in boarding school in Truro, excelling in sports and developing the competitive spirit that reached near-lunatic proportions in later life.

In spite of a tendency to be lazy and his moody and introspective nature, with a demeanour that made him unapproachable, Shaw did well in his lessons and also discovered a love of drama. Acting was merely another facet of his competitive instincts, going on stage to prove he was the best actor was very much like running up and down a field to demonstrate he was the best rugby player. At sports, like everything else, he wanted to win, hated losing. To win was all consuming. He saw it as a challenge to choose a new sport or activity and work flat out until he was able to beat everyone else into the ground at it. Little wonder he was made head boy and Shaw loved the responsibility: 'I didn't like school before I was made head boy but the power made it palatable.'

Aged fourteen he won a drama prize and the sound of the applause and approval from his peers had a major effect on him. 'For me, at school, and for a long time after that, acting was a matter of showing off.' And he did so frequently. In one play, in which Shaw's character was required to descend into madness, his performance was so alarming that the audience of schoolboys were positively terrified. Shaw's talent had already come to the attention of one of the masters, Cyril Wilkes, who encouraged him to read the works of classic literature. Wilkes also made a habit of taking a small group of favoured pupils with him to see plays in London. It was on one of these trips, in the autumn of 1944, that Shaw watched his first legitimate stage production, John Gielgud in *Hamlet* at the Haymarket. It made a huge impression on him, so much so that when he returned to his hotel room he picked up a copy of the play and read it from start to finish. It was a spellbinding trip; over the course of a few days the group also caught Margaret Leighton and Ralph Richardson in *Peer Gynt* and Olivier in *Richard III*.

Strangely, when Shaw confided in Wilkes his ambition to be an actor, the teacher strongly advised him not to pursue it, saying he had the wrong temperament, was too rebellious and wanted his own way too much. Shaw recognised the flaws in his character, but his mind was already made up.

Doreen certainly raised no dunces, with one glaring exception all her children went to either Cambridge or Oxford University; that exception was Bob Shaw. His exam results were sufficiently impressive to warrant an offer from Cambridge, but he was obliged to take a Latin exam to qualify and couldn't stomach the thought of cramming for it, especially since he'd already decided on an acting career. The news was met with dismay and surprise in equal measure by his family; Shaw's brother Alec recalls seeing jaws literally dropping open.

He wrote to RADA asking for an audition. When the day came Shaw travelled by train to London with Alec and walked to the doors of the academy, where a great clunking fist barred his brother's entry, 'Where are you going, sonny boy?' Shaw left him on the steps and walked inside, confident in his ability to impress the auditioning panel. Alec kicked his heels in the street for two hours before catching sight of his brother running through the lobby, his face beaming and shouting, 'I'm in!' They caught the train back to Cornwall, Shaw in a state of complete euphoria.

That first year at RADA was a struggle for Shaw, the blame for which he placed squarely on inferior teaching standards, claiming he learned more from the older students. He later described the place as like staying in a concentration camp. His general demeanour didn't help; he was

aggressive and uncooperative, no longer a head boy, the centre of attention, and he kicked out in frustration. Teachers also tried to eradicate
his accent, which had a Cornish lilt to it, he was too energetic and not
graceful enough in his acting delivery: that was frowned upon, too. And
so he was largely ignored, resulting in a poor selection of roles. It didn't
help that he was up against some rather formidable pupils in Laurence
Harvey, John Neville and Edward Woodward.

When his first-term report suggested he consider very seriously
whether to continue trying to be an actor, Shaw ignored it and kept
going: 'In those days, I was completely without nerves.' Fellow student
Peter Barkworth thought Shaw arrogant and boastful, 'He paraded
himself in front of us and swaggered.' Most of Shaw's friends at this
time saw two very different men: the contemplative artist, at his most
content writing poetry or a short story; then the maniac, the man who
had to win at all costs.

One of Shaw's closest friends at RADA, with whom he continued a
relationship for years, was Philip Broadley, who in the sixties swapped
acting for a highly successful TV script-writing career. Their friendship,
however, began on an odd note. Shaw heard that Broadley owned a
table-tennis table, though it was in a dilapidated state, and one evening
arrived unannounced at his door asking for a game. Broadley, an experienced player, beat Shaw hands down. Shaw demanded another game
and was again comprehensively beaten, leaving with his tail between
his legs. The next night Shaw turned up again, only for Broadley to
emerge once more victorious. This went on for several weeks, with
Shaw arriving at all hours ready to play, and with each successive game
edging closer to beating Broadley, until he finally triumphed.

When he graduated from RADA in 1949 Shaw had been supremely
confident of success. 'He is the kind of personality who might become
remarkable in the professional theatre,' said his final report. He just
needed the right break, and began writing to rep companies and scanning the pages of the *Stage*. The most positive response came from the
Memorial Theatre in Stratford, at the time under the directorship of
Anthony Quayle. Shaw auditioned and was given a contract there and
then at six pounds a week. Determined to make his mark, Shaw's vigour

and boundless energy, attacking the text with the brutality of a white hunter hacking through dense jungle, was matched only by his rebellion. 'As a young man I had no charm. I was all aggression. I had no social graces. I insisted on speaking my mind which no one wanted to hear. I was a troublemaker.'

Shaw was determined to prove himself the most talented young actor in a company that included a number of new bucks like Harry Andrews, Nigel Green and Alan Badel. And there was Robert Hardy, making his first proper professional stage appearances after being spotted at the Oxford Playhouse while still a student at the university, where his tutors were C. S. Lewis and J. R. R. Tolkien. Very quickly Shaw made an impression on Hardy. 'Bob was a great character. He was in some ways a rough character and in some ways a very sophisticated, well-informed person. A psychiatrist would put him in the alpha male group; that's what he wanted to be, he couldn't bear losing. He was competitive to an obsessive degree. But we got on very well. And that competitiveness translated to his acting as well. You are as an actor basically what you are as a person. Some actors can escape from what is their basic self into other parts and other people, but Bob wasn't, I don't think, in that category. I think he played most of his parts as Shaw.'

At Stratford Shaw felt educationally superior to most of his fellow actors, conversed as they were only in the world of the arts. 'They seemed to me to be so effete, so physically run down. I was quite intolerant of them.' He grew to despise their ritualistic Shakespeare performances, the assuming of grand postures and put-on dramatic voices, it smacked of dishonesty, retrograde acting that belonged to another age. These actors were assuming personalities rather than grasping the reality of the role.

As the season began Shaw felt marginalised, playing minor roles in the background, scraping against the scenery instead of centre stage where he imagined he belonged. Sometimes he'd come on with a two-line message for the lead actor and carrying a spear. 'Looking back, I am dumbfounded that I didn't chuck the spear straight at them one night.' Worse, Shaw watched helpless as far too many for his liking 'safe' company players strode ahead of him. 'I'm not surprised he got frustrated by his lack of good roles because of this intense competition and ambition he had,' says Hardy. 'He thought he was worth the real big parts, but he wasn't, any more than I was.'

Pissed off and, worse, bored, Shaw started to misbehave and often sat backstage playing chess until it was time to go on. As a gnome in *A Midsummer Night's Dream* Shaw tied the wings of one of his fellow performers to a tree live on stage. Later reprimanded by the embarrassed actor for his unprofessionalism, Shaw was suitably guilt-ridden, but his rebelliousness continued. Playing Jupiter in *Cymbeline* required a covering of gold paint that took several tubs of make-up remover to clean off. Once done he often went straight home, refusing to take part in the curtain call. Three times he was warned that he faced the sack.

These frustrations were born out of the fact that Shaw understood his only real chance of success as an actor was on the stage: he wasn't the Richard Todd or Jack Hawkins type so beloved by British producers at the time, so that ruled out a career in cinema. Unbeknown to him, however, he was getting noticed. Sybil Burton would recall seeing Shaw in a play at Stratford in a lowly part but being nevertheless impressed. 'There was something about his presence that made it impossible for you to take your eyes off him. You could pick him out instantly in a crowd.'

Hired for the next season, Shaw and Robert Hardy decided to rent a cottage together just outside Stratford. Hardy remembers it well: 'I'd been living in this house with the most extraordinary landlady, a one-eyed Irish woman who lived on Guinness. She had her eye shot out by a ricocheting pistol bullet over the gaming tables of Boulogne, and had in her days of youth and beauty been the model for the statue of Britannia which still stands on the pediment of Birmingham town hall. And Bob used to visit, because of the myth of this extraordinary woman, the little house where we lived without electricity, without hot water, without a loo; it was pretty primitive. And eventually he said to me in the theatre one night, "Why don't we get a cottage together? I hate the place I'm in." He was staying in a sort of company house and he found it boring to be with all those other actors all the time. So we rented a cottage and had a wonderful season. His family used to come up from Cornwall and visit, sisters and a brother. They were all very nice people.'

The two men shared the cooking duties, existing on stews and curries, cheap but wholesome. 'We did set fire to the kitchen once, I remember,' says Hardy. 'We had a raw ham that had come from my family and we probably put it on too high a temperature in the oven and when we came back the whole thing was smoking. We flung the oven open and tried to put it out but it spread and we did a lot of damage to the kitchen, all of which my mother had to pay for, because neither of us had a bean.'

Hardy recalls a veritable cavalcade of girls that seemed to swarm around Shaw, and a proclivity to drink too much. But then there was a prominent drinking culture at Stratford; almost everyone went to the pub after a performance. 'It was the rule, practically,' said Shaw. 'We'd all congregate at the Dirty Duck pub.' This wholesale drinking, to some extent, was a hangover from the war years. 'It was in the forces, because of the massive times of hanging around, that we all drank,' says Hardy. 'Some of us killed ourselves and some of us survived very handsomely. I remember coming back from Torquay once with Richard Burton and a group of others having consumed an untold amount of cider. I suddenly got the hit of the drink at the top of this rather steep flight of stairs in our hotel and I tumbled all the way down. And I got such applause at the end that I picked myself up, apparently unhurt, went up and did it again, by popular request. We were all absolutely mad.'

More disturbing than the drink was the occasional foray into depression that Hardy observed in Shaw, usually followed by the dredging up of black memories about his father. 'Some ghastly tragedy like that occurring in your family when you're a youngster has an enormous effect. Maybe it made him more and more determined to exist on his own and to make a great show in the world.'

This moroseness was not helped by a continuing dearth of good roles. 'I hadn't got the gift of charm like Burton,' Shaw later revealed. 'So I felt my individuality was being stifled and I showed my resentment.' Playing a very small role in *King Lear*, Shaw was instructed to stand in the corner during a scene by director John Gielgud. 'I can't possibly give any idea of the majesty of the Duke of Burgundy with my back to the audience!' Shaw responded in front of the whole company. Gielgud recoiled somewhat and later had a quiet word in Shaw's ear. 'I do admire you,' he said, 'and think you've got a lot of ability, and I'd like to help you, but you make me so nervous.'

Finally, Shaw's persistence paid off when Gielgud offered him the role of Conrade in *Much Ado about Nothing*, replacing an actor who'd been fired. It was his biggest role yet. Barbara Jefford was in that production and remembers Shaw as a good Shakespearean actor. 'He was an extrovert, Robert, a wild character. He stood out on stage. He was lively and his intelligence and his spirit were very attractive. He was an extremely intelligent man, but not one of those introverted intelligent people, he was very much an extrovert.'

Barbara didn't see Shaw again until 1963 at Pinewood Studios, when she came in to dub the voice of Italian actress Daniela Bianchi in *From Russia with Love*. 'On the same day I was doing Daniela's voice, Robert and Sean were in the dubbing studio doing the sound for the Orient Express train fight. They were grunting and groaning, just putting in noises for the fight. It was extremely funny to watch them.'

Looking back, Hardy can see that the actor he knew at Stratford wasn't too far removed from the actor that Shaw would eventually become. 'His power was always there. Sometimes it was absolutely obtrusive and he gave much too much power to quite a small and unimportant part. Of course, as time went on he finessed it. His downfall at Stratford was his belligerence, though not with me, which is why we got on so well. But he had an itching shoulder when he met authority. He didn't like being told what to do.'

One night after coming off stage as Conrade, Shaw was relaxing in his dressing room when there was a knock at the door. 'Enter!' Shaw cried, as he was wont to do in suitably dramatic fashion. Shaw immediately recognised the man who came in; it was Alec Guinness. He decided, or maybe it was pure instinct, not to show any deference whatsoever, instead he remained seated, his legs up on the make-up table. Not there merely to congratulate him on his performance, Guinness had called to offer Shaw a role in his forthcoming production of *Hamlet*.

'What part?' enquired Shaw, playing it cool and still not looking up at Guinness's face, instead fixing upon his own gaze in the make-up mirror.

'Er, I thought Rosencrantz,' Guinness answered in a velvety tone.

'How much?' said Shaw.

Guinness, taken aback somewhat by the actor's plain arrogance, but also impressed with the sheer ungrateful balls on display, replied that his producer would sort out his salary and bade him goodnight. When it came time for Shaw to meet the producer he played the scene with a deft poker face. 'What we do is you write what you want to pay and I'll write what I think I'm worth and we'll split the difference.' He got twenty pounds a week, not bad for his West End debut.

Shaw left Stratford at the end of 1950, just missing Richard Burton who arrived for the 1951 season. 'I didn't see Bob for a long time after that,' says Hardy. 'I don't think I really saw him again until we were both in the film *Young Winston*. But I liked Bob very much. He was in many ways admirable.'

Guinness's *Hamlet* opened in May 1951 and Shaw loved working with him, the first 'star' actor he'd ever felt truly at ease with, someone who treated him as an equal. Shaw decided to play Rosencrantz as a dark figure, with a piratical black eyepatch. But there were boos at the end of the first performance, which was marred by various technical hitches, such as the lighting board failing and the whole play having to be performed with the bland overhanging working lights, which hardly made the entrance of the ghost very atmospheric; the production never really recovered. Dismantled by the critics, its disastrous reception has been singled out as a major factor in Guinness turning his back on the classics and Shakespeare to embrace his film career. He shot the classic Ealing comedy *The Lavender Hill Mob* at around the same time and offered Shaw a small uncredited role in it as a police chemist. It really is a blink-and-you'll-miss-it appearance, but nevertheless marked his film debut.

By now Guinness and Shaw had grown close, with the younger actor often visiting the star at his home. For Shaw's twenty-fourth birthday Guinness organised a party at an exclusive London restaurant. With the rumour mill spinning frantically, Guinness invited Shaw to a weekend in Brighton. Shaw must have known of the older man's feelings towards him, but decided to risk the excursion simply because it meant a free holiday away from his miserable bedsit. He'd recall a certain atmosphere when once or twice Guinness would softly touch his hand briefly, and then take it away. There's a story too of Shaw on stage delivering his line as Rosencrantz, 'My Lord, you once did love me,' in a luridly suggestive manner that earned a slap in the face from Guinness.

In October 1951 Shaw joined the Old Vic company at the invitation of the renowned Tyrone Guthrie, who had directed him at Stratford. At last Shaw got the chance to play meatier roles, but his attitude still stank, a kind of surly arrogance worn as vividly as his stage make-up that he wasn't being offered the lead roles his near contemporaries like John Neville and Richard Burton enjoyed. With his rugged looks Shaw was at least receiving plenty of gushing fan mail, but for some time now had eyes only for a young actress in the company by the name of Jennifer Bourke, a white Jamaican, born and raised in Kingston. They'd met during the production of *A Midsummer Night's Dream*, where Jennifer was playing one of Titania's three fairies; the others were essayed by a young Joan Plowright and Jill Balcon, who'd later sire Daniel Day-Lewis. Jennifer was blonde and very beautiful, also very unobtainable, which got Shaw's dander up: it was another thing to master. Problem was, the lust turned to genuine love, love that was reciprocated and they married in the summer of 1952 as they travelled on tour to South Africa.

On their return Shaw found himself out of work – tough, since he was now the sole financial provider, Jennifer seemingly happy to eschew what had been a promising acting career to become a full-time wife and mother. Shaw had wanted children right away. Tyrone Guthrie came to the rescue, offering him a place at Stratford in what would be a vintage season with Peggy Ashcroft and Michael Redgrave headlining, supported by newcomers like Charles Gray and Donald Pleasence. Shaw enjoyed the season; his performance as Gratiano in *The Merchant of Venice* was hailed as 'fiery and determined' by Kenneth Tynan.

The atmosphere at Stratford was still pretty laid-back, as Tony Britton recalls: 'You'd play a scene and then come off stage and go into the green room for a coffee where there was always a table with four or five people playing poker, all in costume and make-up. You maybe had ten or fifteen minutes before you went on stage again so you sat down and joined the poker school. Ten minutes later back onto the stage you'd go, play another scene, come off and play another hand of poker. It was great. And that's how it was. It's all changed today, it's got a little bit more serious. Now people do crosswords instead.'

During the season Britton got to know Shaw well: 'He was a one-off, an extraordinary personality, a great character. He had high intelligence and a great talent. Besides acting he also wrote and painted, would try his hand at everything.' The two men sometimes played golf together at a nearby course, once in near darkness and minutes before they were due on stage. 'But I never won, no way did I win,' laments Britton. 'On the stage he would act beautifully, he would never attempt to steal a scene, but outside of the theatre, like at golf, or playing bridge, he was going to win! And made sure that he did one way or another.'

When the season ended at Stratford Shaw was informed that there was nothing for him in their 1954 season. 'And that amazed me,' says Britton. 'Because he was a bloody marvellous actor and had something that was completely his own and I'm not surprised he enjoyed a highly successful career. But back then, to be honest, one didn't say, this is a chap who's clearly going to make it big.'

With Jennifer pregnant with her second child work was essential, and with no acting offers in sight Shaw suffered the humbling experience of having to borrow money to exist. 'I can remember praying for a job at one point, though I wasn't religious.' Amazingly these desperate straits did not diminish a belief in his acting abilities and he was rewarded when Donald Pleasence introduced him to Richard Hatton, a new agent who was going places fast. Hatton took Shaw on and got to work quickly, helping him land the role of Richard Todd's flight captain in the now-classic war picture *The Dam Busters*, based on the true story of the development of the 'bouncing bomb' and the daring RAF squadron attack on the Ruhr dams in Germany. Although this was Shaw's first speaking role on film, most of his lines were cut out and so he made little impact; which was a shame since the film proved to be Britain's top box-office draw for 1955.

Also in the film was George Baker, and when he was approached to take the lead role in a British war picture entitled *A Hill in Korea* he suggested to the producer Anthony Squire that Shaw would be a very useful member of the cast. Roped in to play a soldier, Shaw used his fee to buy a second-hand car and pay off some of his debts. He then flew out to Portugal for the location shoot and according to Baker pretty quickly got under the skin of everyone. 'Robert was an aggressively macho actor and liked nothing better than having a bet. We all got rather tired of Robert's pushy ways and the camera operator Arthur Ibbotson found a way of silencing him. He told Bob that he'd once been a champion runner and challenged him over a hundred yards across the desert. Arthur was a small round man who could never possibly be a runner so Robert took up the challenge. Arthur's one stipulation was that Robert should drink a glass of water at the start line. The course was marked and Harry Andrews would fire the pistol for the runners to start. The camera crew had been brewing up the kettle and they handed Robert a boiling hot glass of water. Of course Arthur was able to walk quietly down the course singing "Roll out the Barrel". Robert Shaw nearly died of apoplexy but could not get out of the bet and that silenced him for the rest of the film.'

Shaw's misplaced testosterone was forced upon another member of the cast, an actor making his film debut, Michael Caine. Each night the cast and crew ate together in the hotel, plates of not very appetising food, swimming in olive oil and big chunks of garlic. Caine always sent his meal back for the cook to take out all the garlic, a ritual that grated with Shaw until one night he exploded. 'Eat it, you fucking cockney philistine! It's the best food you've ever had in your life, and you're sending it back.'

Caine wasn't standing for that and reached across the table to grab hold of Shaw's shirt collar. 'Who do you think you're fucking talking to?'

'I'll fucking well show you!' hollered Shaw, and the fight was on.

Caine was only there in the first place because of his real-life experiences in the Korean War, helping out in an advisory capacity while also playing a very tiny role. The film was amongst the first to depict that recent campaign and told the story of a small band of British soldiers under attack by a much larger Chinese force.

Prior to landing the job Caine had fallen into a deep depression because of a lack of work and an illness that had struck down his father that turned out to be cancer of the liver. He could do nothing but watch a once proud man literally fade away in front of his eyes. When an ambulance came to take him into hospital Caine knew it was time for him to die. As he lay suffering and in terrible pain, Caine implored a doctor to do something, anything; this wasn't living, nor was it a dignified death. He was told to come back later that night, and there was an almost serene expression on his father's face as he took his hand and held it for the next hour. Outside a clock sounded one in the morning. His father's eyes opened and focused on Caine; then he whispered, 'Good luck, son,' and died. It was the only time Caine remembered his father ever encouraging him. As he was about to leave, a nurse ran after him and thrust some items into his hand. 'This was in your father's pockets.' It was only some loose change, three shillings and eightpence, not much after fifty-six years of hard graft. Caine left that night with a new determination that he would never be poor like that.

How to manage it would be the trick, there was no work around, just a barren landscape of opportunity, even though he'd recently taken on an agent. He was a beguilingly charming Scotsman by the name of Jimmy Fraser, part of an agency called Fraser and Dunlop, with smart offices in Regent Street. They were big-time and Caine was bewildered they'd even considered putting him on their books, but at a meeting Fraser had looked across his desk at the out-of-work actor, pondered and said, 'You've got something, Michael. For the life of me I can't see what it is and therefore I don't know how to sell it, but I'll take you on for a while and see if it becomes a little clearer.'

The *Hill in Korea* offer had come out of the blue via telegram; Caine didn't have a telephone at home. 'I don't believe it!' he said. 'Who'd have me in a film? I haven't even had a speaking part in television yet!' Upon starting work, all the hardships Caine had faced in recent years melted away, despair was replaced for the first time by something new: hope. Here he was hanging out with a bunch of equally thirsty young actors such as Stanley Baker and Stephen Boyd. But the prospect of appearing on film for the first time terrified Caine and when it came time to speak his measly few lines he almost froze, sometimes forgetting them altogether. His role as technical adviser was also pretty much ignored. When he told the director that the actors playing the soldiers out on patrol should spread out wider, the correct military procedure, he was told they didn't have a wide enough camera lens to fit them all in.

During location filming Caine shared a hotel room with fellow Londoner Harry Landis, whose role in the film was vastly more substantial. Often they'd stay up late chatting and Landis recalls one conversation particularly well.

'I'm going to be a star,' Caine said, without much prompting. 'And then I'm going to be a director, a film director.'

'What about the theatre?' asked Landis, already associated with London's Unity Theatre, whose political agenda was even further left-leaning than Joan Littlewood's.

'Oh I can't be bothered with doing the same part every night,' said Caine.

'You won't get anywhere if you don't love the theatre first,' replied Landis, rather pompously as he later admitted. 'That's the roots and all the other media are the branches so I think you've got the wrong idea.'

Maybe he did, for when *A Hill in Korea* came out Jimmy Fraser, who had hitherto thought the actor might have something, suddenly decided that, actually, no he didn't and dropped him. It didn't do much for Shaw, either. They were both back on the acting scrap heap.

11
No Road Back

It was the autumn of 1955 and Connery had been in London for some months, ever since the curtain fell on the tour of *South Pacific*. More determined than ever to forge ahead with an acting career, he'd attended audition after audition, even one for the Old Vic where the theatre's director Michael Benthall personally interviewed him, only to say no: 'You don't fit into the composition here,' he said. 'Take elocution lessons. Study your diction.'

It was Robert Henderson who came to the rescue when he offered Connery the non-speaking role of court usher in his production of *Witness for the Prosecution* at Richmond's Q Theatre. To compensate for his lack of dialogue Connery put to flamboyant use the traditional swirling robes of his office, yet his mannerisms proved so captivating that they diverted the audience's attention from the main action and the costume had to be removed.

At this small rep theatre Connery performed in several other productions, meeting and befriending another young actor, Ian Bannen, who on first encountering Sean thought he looked more like a gangster than an actor. 'He was a towering, huge fellow with hair everywhere, huge eyebrows like a squirrel's tail. He looked formidable. I felt I wouldn't have liked to meet him down some alley.'

Sadly the Q Theatre closed in February 1956 for lack of funds and a valuable breeding ground that churned out actors for the West End was lost for ever, replaced by a faceless office block. The likes of Vivien Leigh, Peggy Ashcroft, Flora Robson and Roger Moore had all trod the boards at Q early in their careers.

To survive the long periods between work Connery took odd jobs and was canny with money. For a time he shared a basement flat just off the King's Road with his old *South Pacific* cohort Victor Spinetti. 'Sean had a pension from the navy and I had a pension from the army and occasionally we'd put our pensions together and buy lots of food and he would make piles of wonderful soups and stews and that's what we survived on.'

The two remained friends for years. In the sixties when Spinetti found fame with Joan Littlewood and the Beatles films he hosted his own talk show on Welsh television and for his final show Connery, then playing James Bond, came down to be his last guest. 'And he sat opposite me and I had on the floor a goodbye speech written out in Welsh, because I didn't speak Welsh, and Sean very quietly as we were talking put his foot on this piece of paper on the floor and pushed it under a chair. Luckily I remembered it. But he was still very playful then, Sean.'

In other digs he bought a second-hand bed at a cheap price, mainly because it had only three legs. No problem, Connery borrowed his land-lord's thirteen volumes of the Collected Works of Stalin to lend literary support. These tough times necessitated him selling his beloved motor-bike and replacing it with a rusty old bicycle, which he raced round London on to save money on bus fares to his various auditions. It was a carefree existence and he had the loving support of a girlfriend, Julie Hamilton, a freelance photographer and step-daughter of future Labour Party leader Michael Foot. They first met in a pub, an encounter Julie walked away from with the belief that Connery was a rather coarse and arrogant man. A month later they met again at the wedding of a mutual friend, Ronnie Fraser. Connery turned up in a kilt and, well, that was it.

Under Julie's instruction Connery began taking elocution lessons to try and refine the hard edges of his accent. But what Connery lacked in training and craft he certainly made up for in sheer presence and enthusiasm, leaving a lasting impression on the Canadian director Alvin Rakoff. Beginning his career at the BBC in 1953, Rakoff was amongst the first Canadian film-makers to come to England. 'And when we arrived we set up a Friday-night poker party. We used to rotate whose house we'd be in and Sean would join in. Actually he was a pretty good poker player; I think he took quite a bit of money off me.'

Rakoff first used Connery as an extra in his TV play *The Condemned* in August 1956. Much of the location shooting took place at Dover Castle and involved an attack by rebel fighters bidding to free their leader. Connery, playing one of the rebels, had no more than a mere walk-on, but approached it with such zeal that Rakoff hired him for other roles. 'In one sequence I had him play both the soldier lobbing a grenade and the poor bandit coming over the castle wall who gets killed. When we edited it together audiences never twigged it was the same actor. And then we got him to do a third role, as an aging prisoner who'd gone off his head after being in prison so long. I just needed a shot of him walking by a cell as an old man covered in white hair with a metal cup tapping the bars.'

As shooting progressed Rakoff got to know Connery a little better, especially during evenings spent in the pub with the rest of the cast, when everyone was in a more relaxed mood. Certainly Rakoff was aware of how raw the guy was, impaired still with a strong accent and bushy unkempt eyebrows, 'but he was a helluva nice guy'. If anything, Rakoff appreciated Connery's complete lack of drama-school artifice. 'He was less pushy, less of the "look at me" or "I'm an artist" attitude. He was actually a very quiet guy.'

It was jobs like this that kept Connery just above the bread line. There was also a small role at the Lyric Theatre, Hammersmith, in *The Good Sailor*, a dramatisation of Herman Melville's novel *Billy Budd*, with Leo McKern and Bernard Bresslaw. But from the outset Connery's ambition was to make it in movies. However, his film debut was hardly auspicious, as is so often the case. *No Road Back* was the kind of quota-quickie crime thriller British studios excelled in during the fifties; rope in some dodgy American has-been (or here in Skip Homeier's case, hardly-ever-was), to sell the film internationally and surround him with chirpy natives. It was a crime drama that managed to make a diamond robbery, murder and romance look about as lively as an episode of *Dixon of Dock Green*.

Connery played Spike, the slow-witted lackey to Alfie Bass's petty crook. Cast because of his brawny physical appearance, Connery dutifully turned up for work at Pinewood Studios that summer of 1956 only to be suckered into a rotten prank perpetrated by Bass and Canadian actor Paul Carpenter, who was playing the chief heavy. As green as spinach on his first film, Connery was persuaded to confront the director Montgomery Tully about some of the feeble dialogue he had to speak and the lame-brained concept of his character stuttering like an idiot all the time. This he did, only to discover Tully suffered from a similar speech impediment, and had co-written the script: 'Who the f-f-fuck do you think you are, L-L-Larry Olivier?'

Things did seem to be going well when Connery was hired for another picture not long after, this one a gritty drama called *Action of the Tiger* about a troubleshooter helping a beautiful woman free her brother from Communist scumbags in Albania, all shot in colourful CinemaScope with locations in Spain. Again Connery was cast largely because of his physique, playing a slovenly sailor whose main scene was an attempted rape of starlet Martine Carol. 'Am I supposed to run away from that?' remarked Martine, eyeing his bulging torso.

Struck by his charisma, the French actress voiced the opinion that Connery should have been playing the lead instead of Hollywood import Van Johnson, who had all the sex appeal of a haddock. 'This man has big star quality,' she told the director, a certain Terence Young. It was a remark that made Young look again at this 'hunk for hire' and over the next few days he observed him at closer quarters. 'He was a rough diamond, no question, but already he had a sort of crude animal force, like a younger Burt Lancaster or Kirk Douglas.'

At the end of shooting Connery approached Young hesitantly, asking, 'Sir, am I going to be a success in this?' Young didn't want to lie to the eager actor of whom he'd grown fond, knowing already he'd botched the film and it had as much chance of being a hit as a Blackpool donkey winning the Grand National. 'No,' said Young. 'But keep on swimming. Just keep at it, Sean, and I'll make it up to you.' Young would indeed keep his promise.

12

The Pirate Shaw

While Shaw licked the wounds of *Off the Mainland*'s failure, in the board-room of the Independent Television Company cigar-chomping TV mogul Lew Grade was wondering how best to exploit the huge success of his *Adventures of Robin Hood* TV series, which had the nation's young-sters running about their gardens in green tights bow-and-arrowing the neighbour's cat. Grade wanted more swash, and certainly a lot of buckle, and a pirate series was the obvious choice, so *The Buccaneers* was conceived, salty tales of derring-do by reformed brigand Dan Tempest, who joins the British colonists in their battles against the Spanish in the Caribbean. Sold to CBS in the States, screen tests were arranged and out of twenty-four actors put through their paces Shaw's rugged physique and manner seemed ideally suited and he was cast. There is one story that Shaw won the role when original choice Alec Clunes was condemned by the Americans as being too British and mild mannered to convince as a scurvy cut-throat. 'Get me the one with balls,' a CBS executive is supposed to have decreed upon seeing Shaw.

At first the action and energetic quality of the Dan Tempest role appealed to Shaw greatly, 'because I am an intensely masculine man and throwing myself around a set, snarling, had its compensations'. He also wanted to use his Cornish accent, still there despite RADA's best efforts to obliterate it. But when he spoke his lines at the first rehearsal the American producer Hannah Weinstein took him to one side and politely explained that not a lot of people in America were going to understand one goddamn word of what he was saying. Shaw concurred and dropped the accent.

While representing a real breakthrough, Shaw's pirate odyssey soon turned sour as the pounding production schedule of thirty-nine episodes over a seven-month period took its toll. Aimed at a youth audience on prime-time Saturday nights, *The Buccaneers* began airing in September 1956 and was deliberately light-hearted and so contained very little for Shaw to actually do, save look heroic. He enjoyed the swashbuckling, of course, a touch of the Errol Flynns, and in the various sword fights looked utterly convincing, the result of taking daily fencing lessons, but from the beginning Shaw had no faith in the scripts, which he labelled 'a joke', and later admitted to rarely committing much of his dialogue to memory. 'I didn't bother to learn more than the first two lines and the last two lines; I paraphrased the rest. That was the only way to keep sane.'

The show was physically draining too, up at four each morning in order to arrive at the studio by six for work that often stretched into the evening, leaving Shaw little time for home life. But the professional rewards were vast. Shaw had never earned more than £1,600 in a single year before, so to be paid £200 an episode was pretty good. He splashed out in style, buying a yellow-and-black 1933 Rolls-Royce and a set of expensive golf clubs.

The Buccaneers took up two stages at Twickenham Studios, where a conveyor belt of guest stars were rolled in; Hammer starlet Hazel Court, Sid James, Paul Eddington, future film director John Schlesinger and a ten-year-old child actress called Jane Asher, who found Shaw a quite intoxicating personality. 'I think I was desperately in love with Robert Shaw, he was just magic. And he was the sort of man who would treat you as an adult, quite flirty and wonderful. You know what those feelings are like when you're a child, they're just desperate, and I can certainly remember being very smitten with Robert Shaw.'

Exterior sea sequences were shot off the coast of Falmouth aboard a schooner that had featured in the film *Moby Dick*. Shaw's competitiveness rose to the surface on location when he bet the cast that he couldn't swim across Falmouth harbour at the ungodly hour of three in the morning. He did it, too, with the actors promising to pick him up afterwards in a boat. 'But while I was swimming in pitch blackness in an ice-cold sea, the whole bunch were warming themselves with swigs of whisky. They never came.'

Shaw's friend and neighbour at the time William Russell, himself bogged down in another TV action series playing Sir Lancelot, identifies this competitive quality as a major facet of Shaw's make-up. 'He'd get easily bored and when we were in the pub would say things like, "I bet a fiver a blonde comes through the door next." He was also very mischievous. There was a sort of naughty-boy quality about him. But a dangerous little boy.'

Although creatively stifling, *The Buccaneers* turned Shaw into something of a star; 'Television makes you a household face, films make you a household name,' he was to say. Also rather disconcertingly, he began to be recognised in public for the first time. During a trip to Battersea funfair he was surprised to be accosted by hundreds of schoolchildren with autograph books. This pattern was repeated Stateside, where CBS sponsored Shaw to come to New York for a promotional trip, his first visit to America. Poor Shaw was obliged to pose with various scantily clad nubile young ladies, all sporting eyepatches and waving wooden cutlasses. He was scheduled to appear in the famous Macy's Thanksgiving Day parade, marching down Broadway dressed as Dan Tempest swashing his buckle at the crowd. On the way there, Shaw found himself sharing a limo with Basil Rathbone and Roy Rogers. While they were stuck in traffic Rogers showed off his prized pair of pistols that had real diamonds in the holsters. Shaw was never to forget this first glimpse of real fame. His own first taste of it would prove fleeting.

13

The View from Here

One night after a performance of *The Quare Fellow* Arthur Miller introduced himself to Harris backstage and asked if he was interested in appearing in a production of his play *A View from the Bridge*, due to be put on at the Comedy Theatre. Any prospect of a job Harris naturally jumped at, but this was different and he couldn't have failed to see the significance of the offer. But how had it happened? *The Quare Fellow* was Harris's first professional engagement, he wasn't long out of drama school, and yet America's foremost modern playwright had personally singled him out.

Over at the Comedy Miller had been tearing his hair out in frustration during auditions. His play was set in a tenement block in Brooklyn's Italian community and its author, having already mouthed off about London's 'middle-class and bloodlessly polite' theatre scene, was sinking lower and lower in his chair, 'listening in some pain as one actor after another who seemed to have arrived fresh from Oxford recited the words of Brooklyn waterfront Italo-Americans'. At one point he turned to director Peter Brook to ask why all the actors had such cut-glass accents; 'Doesn't a grocer's son ever want to become an actor?' In desperation Miller suggested auditioning 'cockney hawkers' off the street.

Instead he'd gone to see *The Quare Fellow*, no doubt because he thought he'd see a more down-to-earth actor there. He was right, and it was Harris that impressed him the most. The role on offer was small, however. He'd not enough experience yet to play any of the stronger supporting roles; they were taken up by Mary Ure, Brian Bedford and Ian Bannen. For the lead role of Eddie, a tough New York docker, Peter Brook cast a Rugby-educated lawyer's son called Anthony Quayle – hardly Marlon Brando, though Quayle did turn in an excellent performance, his first on the London stage after an eight-year break spent directing at Stratford.

Quayle was a strange choice, one imagines a compromise choice. He represented very much the previous generation of actor, 'And he wanted the respect due to him,' says Elizabeth Harris. 'And couldn't understand all these thugs that were coming in, it was that attitude.' An attitude perfectly summed up when Elizabeth bumped into Quayle years later and he confessed he'd actually tried to get Harris fired from the play. 'I used to complain about Richard all the time to Arthur Miller, I used to say, "Why the hell have we got to have him?" And Miller said, "You wait, he's going to be a big star, you just wait and see what's going to happen to him."'

Incredibly, if it hadn't been for a strange quirk of fate *A View from the Bridge* would never have seen daylight. The Lord Chamberlain, the official censor for the theatre, had banned it due to one specific scene involving two male characters kissing, the first homosexual kiss ever on the legitimate stage in Britain. The play had been well received in New York the previous year, so Miller point-blank refused to cut it out. Yet if the play was put on they would face certain prosecution. Stalemate.

Out of the hundreds of plays submitted to Anthony Field over at the Comedy Theatre he'd chosen just three that he wanted to stage, *A View from the Bridge* and two other contentious dramas, Robert Anderson's *Tea and Sympathy* and Tennessee Williams's *Cat on a Hot Tin Roof*, all of which were American and all of which were banned by the Lord Chamberlain's Office from being put on in Britain. 'So I had these plays on the shelf and forgot about them, really,' Field recalls.

Just by chance, Field had lunch one day with Muriel Large, who ran the Watergate Theatre Club, situated under the arches at Charing Cross railway station. She was keen to stage the banned plays herself; as a membership club, the Watergate was beyond the reach of 'that anachronistic bogey, the Lord Chamberlain', as Kenneth Tynan called him. Field thought the idea impractical: the plays had large casts and the royalties were too high. 'Then why don't we move my club into your theatre?' said Muriel. For a moment Field was taken aback. 'Don't be ridiculous, we'll all end up in prison. Added to which, financially you can't run an 850-seat West End theatre as a club, it's never been done before.' But Muriel wasn't taking no for an answer. 'Over the following few weeks she kept pestering me about this, asking me to talk to the lawyers and the accountants to see if something could be done. I thought the whole thing was mad.'

In the end Muriel wore Field down and the Comedy Theatre was essentially turned into a private club so it could open *A View from the Bridge*. The *Picture Post* gleefully reported the foiling of the Lord Chamberlain's 'pious attempt to spare London the shock of this play – a play New Yorkers withstood without pain for some months'. Essentially how it worked was like this: you had to become a member for five shillings, you could then after twenty-four hours book seats for you and three guests. 'And the police were monitoring all this very carefully,' says Field. 'Any transgression, I think they'd have come down on us like a ton of bricks. Two plain-clothes officers popped by twice a week to the box office to see that everybody who bought tickets showed a membership card and could only have three guests. It was pretty ludicrous.' Especially since punters could walk up nearby Windmill Street and ogle naked women on the stage all afternoon and evening. But two men kissing, shock horror!

This strange procedure to see a play certainly attracted news coverage, but the opening night that October turned into a media scrum when Miller attended with his wife Marilyn Monroe. For once Larry Olivier and Vivien Leigh, who were also guests, fed off the scraps. Field recalled that Monroe never once attended rehearsals, though often sat outside the theatre in a car waiting for Miller. 'She was very reticent about taking over the limelight from what she felt was his moment. She admired him enormously, intellectually, and she really wanted to take very much a back seat.'

Opening night was different and the crowds and pressmen flooded Panton Street awaiting her appearance. She didn't disappoint, arriving in a tight, strapless dress that she had to keep pulling up. At the after-show party Field remembers being introduced. 'I'd like to say she was very much as she was on screen but she wasn't really. I think she was a little overawed with the whole English scene, she wasn't quite sure what her place was in all this, and the attention she was getting I think she felt was unjustified.'

Even so, it got the play off to a resounding start and it eventually ran for six months, a success that enabled Field to follow it up with the London stage debut of *Cat on a Hot Tin Roof*. The Lord Chamberlain could do nothing, his powers neutered. And there would be other battles to follow.

14

Restoration Work

Back at the Royal Court, after the hullabaloo of *Look Back in Anger* things had gone off the rails a bit. Two verse plays by Ronald Duncan, one of the instigators of the English Stage Company, were utter disasters and hurriedly taken off. A dramatisation of the satirical novel *Cards of Identity* by Nigel Dennis fared much better and featured a marvellous cast; Bates was reunited with Kenneth Haigh and there was Joan Plowright, Robert Stephens and even John Osborne.

It was not without controversy, however, notably the scene in which George Devine took on the persona of a preacher and delivered a mock sermon: 'I stink, therefore I am,' that sort of thing. Some nights he'd have to battle on through shouts of 'get off' and 'rubbish' and the slamming of seats as people walked out. Bates would later recall that with *Look Back* it had been a case of individual patrons taking offence, with *Cards* it was group protests, who all booed – loudly.

In December the Royal Court's fortunes turned around dramatically when they revived William Wycherley's classic Restoration comedy *The Country Wife* and packed the theatre out night after night. It was put on precisely for that reason, ostensibly as a crowd pleaser, but it was also Devine's intention to launch Joan Plowright as a leading actress with the star part. Sitting in the audience one night was Olivier, a good friend of Devine's. He invited himself backstage afterwards to pay his congratulations to 'the young people'. One who wanted nothing to do with him was Joan Plowright. In her eyes Olivier, Lord Larry, represented everything that was wrong with the kind of theatre she'd joined to smash down, he was titled and like a patronising dinosaur resting on past glories. Curiously that was the night Olivier fell in love with her and from that moment his marriage to Vivien Leigh was dead.

One bit of casting Devine was never happy with was Laurence Harvey. Handsome, certainly, and talented, but he'd pretensions to grandeur that were starkly at odds with the Court's philosophy. For example he had a manservant who went everywhere with him and during rehearsals when Harvey was watching proceedings from the stalls would hover in the aisle, ready to pour him a glass of wine whenever Harvey put out his hand. Some were outraged by the behaviour, others thought it highly amusing.

At the time Harvey was attached to Margaret Leighton. They'd soon marry, an odd couple to be sure and both terrifyingly thin. According to one Royal Court actress the pair ate hardly anything; at restaurants they used to order steak and salad and chew on the meat and spit it out.

With the actors wearing eighteenth-century costumes, long wigs and ridiculous hats, it was a trying production. Even worse were the high-heeled buckled shoes that were crippling to walk in, and each night Bates approached the stage with dread. 'It's the only time I can ever remember having drunk before a first night to get myself on.' Even then he wished he wasn't there. Devine came up to him in the wings one night and said, 'For Christ's sake, boy, enjoy yourself.' But he couldn't, he was in a waking nightmare. 'It was a dreadful part, which I played very, very badly,' he later admitted. 'We were all bad, come to think of it, but I was the worst by far.' Such was its horror that Bates refused to do another classical play for five years.

His worst experience at the Royal Court, then, but all in all Bates thrived in the family atmosphere at Sloane Square. And to many at the Court Devine was the father figure. Once a week he went round the building, dropping into every department to sort out problems. His door was always open. Many remember him in his shirt sleeves smoking a pipe; very down to earth and very hands-on. And every first night there was always a party on the stage afterwards where, according to some of the actors, appallingly cheap red wine was served. But at least Devine made the effort; it was a nice touch. And it wasn't just the actors and other principals who were invited, but everyone associated with the theatre.

For Bates it was exciting to be around terrifically intelligent and artistic people. Although the Royal Court was very much a writer's theatre, with Devine gently nurturing and coaxing them (the actors were just expected to be already equipped with the skills to interpret the author's work), Bates and the rest found the place stimulating largely because of that. Instead of doing the same old Shaw, Shakespeare and other stiffs, they were bringing to life new plays by intoxicating new writers. And often the playwright was on hand during rehearsal or to argue the toss with in the pub afterwards. Incredibly rewarding. And the social life was great, too, lots of parties and a pub just next door. Some of the cast occasionally ventured to a small bistro just behind the theatre run by a rather eccentric woman who only agreed to serve if she took a liking to the person.

One evening Bates was sitting alone in his dressing room when there was a knock at the door. The man who entered had just seen *The Country Wife* and been so impressed by it that he was overwhelmed by a desire to congratulate Bates in particular. His name was Peter Wyngarde. He cut an impressive figure standing in the doorway and was an actor very much on the rise, and very much in the classical mould. 'Peter was incredibly charismatic,' remembers Keith Baxter. 'Both Edith Evans and Peggy Ashcroft adored him.'

Something happened that night; the two men were drawn to each other and within weeks Bates had left The Mansions and they were living together. As a result Bates and Keith Baxter gradually grew apart as their lives and careers took different paths; 'But whenever we did sometimes bump into each other it was exactly like we were back at The Mansions.'

Although only six months older than Bates, Wyngarde was far more experienced and worldly wise and Bates was completely won over, even a little subsumed by Wyngarde's dynamic personality. Unsurprising, since this was his first serious long-term relationship and for the next few years he lived in quiet terror that the true nature of their 'friendship' would be made public, though it was common knowledge within theatrical circles. 'He and Alan were very together,' says Baxter.

This terror was justified. According to Victor Spinetti, gay couples lived in constant fear that not only would their lives be exposed, but they'd run foul of the law; they had no rights whatsoever. 'Maxwell Fyfe, when he was Home Secretary, swore to get rid of this curse on the land, these faggots, these poofs, these gays, and made all these policemen go out and be agents provocateurs. And if you shared a flat with another man, the police could come into that flat without any search warrant and look around in case they found anything to show that you were gay. They could just walk in.'

15
Meet the Parents

Connery was continuing to win work in movies, in unchallenging and minor parts, mainly because of his muscular frame. He was cast as 'second welder' in *Time Lock* precisely because he looked like a labourer; your average thespian clueless as to which end to hold an acetylene torch. 'Sean was a hard worker,' recalled Peter Rogers, the producer of this fairly nail-biting melodrama about a boy trapped in a bank vault, 'although no great talent at the time. But he was ambitious, always watching other actors on the set to see if he could learn anything. Everybody liked him, mostly because he wasn't one of those show-off actors. But he had a quiet assurance about him, like he knew exactly where he was going.'

At the close of the year Connery landed a better role in *Hell Drivers*, a hard-hitting exposé of the cut-and-thrust world of . . . road haulage. Hardly a subject to get the pulse racing, but this is a minor gem thanks to a quite exceptional cast of future famous faces: Stanley Baker, Patrick McGoohan, William Hartnell, Sid James, Herbert Lom, David McCallum and Gordon Jackson.

Connery played one of a motley crew of lorry drivers hauling ballast at breakneck speeds over dangerous roads. He doesn't do very much save look tough and scowl occasionally and in a dance-hall scene show off some nifty footwork with the future Mrs David McCallum and Charles Bronson, Jill Ireland. At the helm was the reliable Cy Endfield, who had to contend with the occasional threat to shooting due to fuel shortages resulting from the ongoing Suez crisis.

When money permitted, Connery returned home to visit and always found it reassuringly unchanged: mother's home cooking, the laundry drying in front of the coal fire in the living room and the gleaming tin bath still hanging on the wall outside. He'd meet up with old friends, go to the pub or bring everyone back to his place with a crate of beer and they'd chat and sing all night. Big Tam was back home and for a while it was just like the old days, though many remained bemused by his decision to carve out an acting career. 'Why go buggering about in the theatre?'

These were sentiments shared by the potential in-laws of Richard Harris; why oh why was their daughter hanging out with an actor, and a pretty bedraggled one at that? Harris had purposefully put off meeting Elizabeth's rather grand and mighty parents for months, but a recent decision made a showdown unavoidable.

Poor old Elizabeth had grown exasperated with the succession of appalling bedsits she kept seeing Harris in.

'This has got to be the bottom of the fucking barrel,' he said when she walked through the door of one particularly disgusting room.

Elizabeth looked around, an expression of rancid disapproval on her face. 'Richard, we can't go on like this.' He knew she was right. 'Perhaps we could stay somewhere together.'

'Get married, you mean? Is that what you're saying?'

It was time to meet the parents. Invited for dinner, Harris had to scrounge a suit off a friend, only to forget to wear socks so spent the whole evening trying desperately to keep his trouser legs tugged down. Worse, when he first arrived the elderly maid mistook him for the cleaner. 'There you are, boy,' she said upon opening the door and throwing a bag of laundry at him. 'And don't forget the starch.'

The dinner was progressing remarkably well until Harris gave the game away, as Elizabeth recalls. 'Richard sat there and went on about this house that his mother would leave him in Limerick, he went on and on about it for ages and my father finally said, "Are you trying to say that you want to marry my daughter?" And Richard said, "Yes." And my mother got up and howled the length of the corridor, and we just all sat and listened to her.'

Lord Ogmore was dubious to say the least about Harris's ability to look after his daughter. 'I'm a thespian!' Harris blasted. 'I can command high fees. I've wonderful contacts, you know, old Ralphie Richardson and Johnny Gielgud and all those splendid theatre queers.' It was glorious bullshit and Lord Ogmore couldn't help but develop a grudging liking for this mad Irishman his headstrong daughter had fallen head over heels for. 'Actually my father was always very fond of Richard, and had no question in his mind about his ability. He said, in life you look to the people coming up, in politics, in anything, and he saw that in Richard.'

In spite of a genuine fondness for each other, both men endured a tempestuous relationship because they were so very different. Elizabeth recalls one memorable occasion when her father visited them at their flat to impart some privileged information he'd managed to uncover about the Harris family heritage. 'He came out with this theory that the Harrises went from Pembrokeshire to Ireland three hundred years ago. He told Richard this, "So you see, you're Welsh originally." Well that was a red rag to a bull and my father was ordered out of the house by Richard. "How dare he think for a second that I'm bloody Welsh!" Poor, poor Father had to leave the house. So there were always these scraps happening and always my father was completely astounded and confused and didn't know what the hell was going on.'

The wedding took place on 7 February 1957. It was a grand affair at the Church of Notre Dame in Leicester Square with a reception at the House of Lords, attended by 300 guests, most of them Lord Ogmore's friends and family. Here was Harris, living at the time in a tiny bedsit and on poor wages, rubbing shoulders with Lord So-and-So and Lady Whatsit. The irony of it all must have brought a huge smile to his face.

There was a smattering of the Harris clan. His father failed to show up but did send twenty-five pounds towards a honeymoon which the couple blew staying at a posh hotel. Harris was still performing in *A View from the Bridge* and everyone in the cast was invited. Happily, they all showed up with the exception of Anthony Quayle, 'who didn't go because he didn't socialise with people in the cast who were not above the title', according to Elizabeth.

A rough and tough new actor marrying a baron's daughter was obviously going to attract press attention and *The Times*, *Daily Telegraph* and

Daily Express covered the wedding. It was Harris's first media exposure. However, one of Elizabeth's society friends saw the union as doomed from the start. 'They were so different it was farcical to imagine how they came to know each other. Here was this elegant young woman, sometimes awkward but always charming, marrying a loud uncouth Irishman who looked so out of place in his morning suit and haircut that you wonder if there was any future in it.'

16
The Pilgrims' Progress

Over at the Bristol Old Vic, with Nat Brenner as his champion, O'Toole had begun steadily to gain more prominent roles. Phyllida Law had watched O'Toole's procession from timid, if a little wild, apprentice to, as she calls it 'hot stuff'; almost untouchable. Her impression of the O'Toole of this period was 'very bad behaviour. He was so badly behaved at Bristol. I used to get very puritan about it and look disapprovingly at him and be fed up because he would alter our rehearsal time because he would have been in London having a lovely time and fib about it majestically; we all knew what he'd been up to. Having said that, on stage he was an incredibly generous performer, he wasn't an idiotic upstager. If he did distract attention it was just pure talent. And he was always very generous in talking to me about the work. And there was I being very disapproving of his behaviour, being late to rehearsal, making us rehearse on Christmas Eve or something ghastly; wicked boy. But secretly I used to lurk in the wings to see some of his performances.'

Warren Jenkins, a guest director at Bristol, was dumbfounded by O'Toole's habit of arriving late or sometimes missing rehearsals altogether and complained to Brenner. 'This man's behaviour is disgraceful. A young actor like he ought to be sacked – or horse whipped.' But nothing was ever done, which didn't surprise Phyllida in the least. 'Peter had a bit of power at Bristol. The authorities were pretty pathetic with him. The director of the theatre John Moody was fairly innocuous and would have known by that time that Peter was important and would have given him free rein. He was gold dust. He was Bristol's star and he was spoiled.'

It wasn't just O'Toole's wildness that got him into trouble; he'd acute insomnia that would plague him for years. It got so bad that Brenner hired someone to get him up in the morning, actually the city's rat catcher who'd arrive at his lodgings, let himself in and then forcibly remove O'Toole from bed. But mostly it was self-inflicted. He could sniff out a party like a veteran bloodhound and was often to be found in the pub. One Bristol student, walking early in the morning to the university, recalled coming across a distraught O'Toole sitting in a doorway looking at a hole in his sock and crying. Had it been a long night or was he studying a part? Maybe even he didn't know.

No clearer example of the esteem in which Bristol held O'Toole was his casting in *the* role of the moment – Jimmy Porter in the Old Vic's production of *Look Back in Anger*. Phyllida Law appeared opposite him. 'Playing Helena, I had to biff him one, didn't I? Had to smack him round the chops and he took it on the chin, so he did.' John Osborne travelled up for a performance and later declared O'Toole the best Porter he ever saw. 'I would think that was the case,' says Phyllida. 'Peter was Jimmy Porter really, in many ways.'

By far Phyllida's fondest memory at Bristol was the occasion of her marriage to Eric Thompson midway through the run of *A Midsummer Night's Dream*. Phyllida was playing Titania and her husband to be was playing Puck. 'And we got married on the morning of the matinee day. Peter came. And he was playing Lysander and in the evening performance he threw rice all over the stage and there were fairies skidding all over the joint.'

As for Finney over at Birmingham, he was enjoying similar success to O'Toole. One of his earliest roles saw him as the orphaned boy in Christopher Fry's *The Lady's not for Burning*, a part that the young Richard Burton played to such dramatic effect in John Gielgud's West End production of 1949. Finney impressed so much that when they came to do *Coriolanus* the producers briefly considered giving him the title role, before realising that his age and inexperience might cause friction within the company and deciding against it.

It wasn't just his acting that dazzled, his personality was radical too.

One witness to the raw and vital Finney of this period is Pamela Howard, just out of Birmingham art school and an apprentice scene painter at Birmingham rep. 'Albert was completely different from anybody else in the company. The first thing was he wore a thing which we'd never seen in Birmingham called jeans, and I'm talking early 1957 here. Well, we'd never seen jeans in Birmingham. And he wore a thing called a T-shirt instead of a proper shirt, which we were completely amazed about. And he had a beret on his head and he said "fuck" and we'd never, absolutely never heard that word in Birmingham, I mean we simply hadn't.'

What's more, Finney was unlike many of the others in that he engaged with everyone working at the theatre, he didn't just hang out with the actor crowd. It was a marked difference from what had gone before for people like Pamela. 'I can only say that to us workers in the dark bowels of the old rep in Station Street, we never imagined an "actor" would actually talk to us. It was still the period where everyone called each other Mr or Miss, and he was the new generation and a breath of fresh air. He got to know us; he was the first actor I think we had ever known.'

Finney also brought vitality to the place, that sense of the revolution that was happening down in London and had yet to fully penetrate north-of-Watford Britain. Pamela still recalls an excitable Finney telling them all about a new theatre being built in nearby Coventry, the first civic theatre built since the war. As part of a large-scale redevelopment of the city, much of which was still scarred by bomb damage, the people of Belgrade had donated money and construction materials to help build what would become known as the Belgrade Theatre. 'I remember Albert telling us they were going to put on plays by John Osborne and Arnold Wesker who were writing plays about people like us, which we simply did not believe. We thought plays were only about other people's lives, rather grand people who had drawing rooms. We certainly didn't think there would be plays about our lives.' Finney kept his promise and would drive Pamela and her friends often to the Belgrade to see this raft of new, challenging drama. 'We saw Wesker's *The Kitchen* and *Chicken Soup with Barley*. Our lives changed at that moment.'

Finney was certainly enjoying his time at Birmingham; he liked the fact that the audience knew him, saw him develop in successive plays and were on his side. When veteran actress Gwen Ffrangcon-Davies arrived for a season, having played the same theatre some twenty-five years previous, she singled out Finney as the one with the brightest future.

Colin George, who'd arrived at Birmingham rep on the very same day as Finney, recalls a man who was certainly at ease with himself and great fun to have around. 'He had an energy and a love of life. I remember at a party he picked up a dustbin and hammered on it and walked around the room. That sounds very childish but in fact it was part of that energy.'

In February Finney played his first lead role in *Henry V*, bringing energy and wry humour to the role, along with the radical idea of not wearing stage make-up, in the belief that this would help emphasise the character's callow youth and insecurity. The production was a huge success, one of the biggest the theatre had known in recent years. As if he needed it, this only served to boost Finney's self-confidence even more, as fellow actor Paul Williamson recalls. 'Without being arrogant, Albert was very confident. I'd already been in the business much longer than he had and yet I found myself being not pushed around so much by him as being almost directed at times.'

17
Requiem

Alvin Rakoff had heard good things from the States about the play *Requiem for a Heavyweight* by Rod Serling, a prolific writer and later creator and host of *The Twilight Zone*. Aired in October 1956 to critical acclaim, and now classed as one of the key plays of 1950s American television drama, it starred movie actor Jack Palance as washed-up boxer Mountain McClintock, one-time contender for world champion now exploited by a seedy manager.

Fed up with the current state of television drama, which tended to be highbrow literary adaptations or filmed stage productions, Rakoff was beginning to be influenced by what was happening over in America. 'I wanted to do plays about reality. I was tired of stories about the middle and upper class. American television were doing plays by people like Paddy Chayefsky and Rod Serling, plays about blue-collar guys, or lower middle class or working class in British terms, but to me they were just good stories about real people, and I said, why aren't we doing those?'

Because *Requiem* went out live Rakoff was unable to see it, so asked Serling to send the script to his London home. Sensing its qualities, Rakoff wasted little time in arranging to produce it for the BBC and in a huge coup persuaded Palance to fly to Britain to reprise his role. 'Then on Friday evening before the Monday rehearsal,' recalls Rakoff, 'and three weeks before we were due to go out live as the Sunday-night play, I got a call from a Hollywood agent saying Mr Palance ain't gonna be there. Panic. It was not an easy part to cast. I said to my production team, "Who can we think of? What about so-and-so?" I ended up phoning all the agents and spent the weekend auditioning until I'd exhausted everybody.'

By Sunday it was getting desperate. All of a sudden Jacqueline Hill, Rakoff's girlfriend and later wife, threw a curve ball that took him completely by surprise. 'I've an idea,' she said. 'Have you thought of Sean?' Rakoff's mind went back to *The Condemned* and the sheer enthusiasm and work ethic Connery brought to his meagre role, but could he sustain a leading performance over ninety minutes – and live, a daunting prospect even for a seasoned pro? Rakoff wasn't convinced. 'Sean? What are you talking about? You can't understand a word he says with that Scots accent of his.' But then Jacqueline, who was playing the female lead, said something that gave the director pause. 'The ladies will like it.'

Rakoff put a hurried call through to Connery's agent and arranged a meeting at his office at the BBC. 'Sean arrived,' recalls Rakoff, 'and I auditioned him in depth, made him read every scene. Finally I narrowed it down to just two actors, Sean and this other guy, who was much shorter and much less likely to be a heavyweight but a much more polished actor and good with the American accent. I called the two of them back later on Sunday and I was convinced this other guy was going to be Mountain McClintock, but Sean had something in the interview, I guess there was a spark of likeableness, vulnerability.' *Requiem* is about a has-been boxer, so the vulnerability was very important; here was a man who was once almost at the top of the pile, that's the poignant thing about it, it's not about a champion, it's about one of life's losers. 'It was the thing of the fifties,' says Rakoff. 'You weren't talking about winners any more, you were talking about the guys who almost became champions; "I could have been a contender."'

Connery's physique had to be taken into account, too, the fact that he looked like he could handle himself in the ring. Rakoff intended the play to open with a pre-filmed boxing match that McClintock loses and the credits roll as he's being led away down a corridor to his dressing room. Finally it was gut instinct that made Rakoff go with Connery. 'I knew I was taking a massive gamble. But he had something. You can try and define what that something is, but he had an inner belief in himself, you could see he was capable, he was saying, give me a chance and I won't let you down.'

Others were less convinced, notably head of BBC drama Michael Barry, who came down to see rehearsals, so concerned was he about Connery's inexperience. That element of doubt was also around on the first day of rehearsals, which took place in a large room in a London working men's club. 'You could be in the midst of some intimate scene and two guys would come in to deliver the beer,' remembers Rakoff. That first morning the cast were all introduced to each other. Eric Pohlmann, who was a big, burly character actor, arrived last and went around saying good morning to everybody. 'And then he saw Sean,' says Rakoff, 'and said, "Hello, what are you doing here?" And Sean said, "I'm playing Mountain McClintock," and Eric just burst out laughing, thought that was the funniest joke ever, and then he suddenly realised, my God, he is.'

Far from being fazed, Connery remained supremely confident that he could pull off this acting feat, such was the confidence and belief he had in his own abilities. 'But then that whole generation of actors had that,' says Rakoff. 'They all thought, what the hell, if Laurence Olivier can do it, I can do it, they all believed that. They were worried about how they were going to get there, and when's it going to happen, but they all believed it.'

Still, Connery did need nurturing and he certainly needed direction. There was a rough quality to his acting and a tendency to stiffen up; Rakoff often impressed on him the need to relax. One can't help feeling, though, that Connery's inexperience lent itself to the character's punch-drunk innocence. 'And the rest of the cast adored him,' remembers Rakoff. 'Warren Mitchell, George Margo, they all got behind him. I knew from the audition that you could put the ideas into Sean's head and let them germinate, and they did. But we rehearsed a lot with Sean to get things right and to soften his accent. A couple of times I did some scenes alone with him. A few of the actors found working with Sean unrewarding in that they felt they weren't getting anything back. Acting is like a tennis match, you rise to the standard of your opponent, so I would then do scenes with Sean to try and get him up a bit.'

Rakoff soon faced another problem. In America the production was shown with commercial breaks between acts, but with no advertising on the BBC there was going to be a problem getting Connery off and into a new costume for one of the scenes. Rakoff contacted Serling for help, and he suggested incorporating an additional scene lasting a couple of minutes that would give Connery time to change. 'Just have two fighters talking about the old days,' said Serling. 'And I hear you're also a writer, Alvin, so you write it.' Rakoff sat down and composed something and then cast a walk-on actor called Reginald Atkinson to play one of the boxers. 'But I couldn't think of who to cast as the second fighter. Again it was Jacqueline who at rehearsals said to me, "Have you noticed that young man over there, there's something about him." This guy was just an extra, so I cast him, and it was Michael Caine.'

In the preceding months things had not been going at all well for Caine. A lack of work meant little money, which led to domestic strife. Often he and Patricia had blazing rows about how they were going to survive on the pittance he was bringing in. A desperate Caine often went to a casting agency on St Martin's Lane near Leicester Square, sitting all day with other hopeful actors praying a studio might need someone to be an extra or even play a small part. Sometimes you'd be cast simply because you fitted the costume. It was soul-destroying stuff.

Then Julian Amyes, who'd directed Caine in *A Hill in Korea*, asked for him to appear in a live TV play he was directing called *The Lark* by Jean Anouilh about the life of Joan of Arc. It was only a minor role, the guard who transports Joan to Paris to meet the Dauphin, but maybe things were starting to happen. He'd a new agent for a start who got him an audition for a part in a movie called *How to Murder a Rich Uncle*. Caine arrived at the production company's Mayfair office and saw that he was up against the bodybuilder guy he'd met a couple of years back at that party – Sean Connery. There was only one role on offer and two candidates. Caine started to sweat. The film's producer walked in and one by one interviewed the actors before finally making his choice – Caine. 'No hard feelings,' he said, shaking Connery's hand. Not at all, it was all part of the game. The name of the producer was Albert R. Broccoli.

It turned out to be a bitter-sweet victory, for most of Caine's scenes ended up cut out of the film. This pretty much summed up his career so far: hope when it came, which was seldom, was usually dashed. Life was pretty much a hand-to-mouth existence, with friends helping out when work was scarce. Now, on *Requiem for a Heavyweight*, here was the bodybuilder guy again, and he had the bloody lead role! Caine just had to grin and bear it.

As the day of the broadcast drew nearer tensions began to rise. The challenges for Connery were substantial: this wasn't just his first ever lead role, but he'd the technical aspects of live television to contend with, such as four cameras following his every move. One time during a technical rehearsal Rakoff called for Connery to get into his position on set and he shouted back, 'I can't move, Alvin. I've got a camera up my arse!'

Then it was the hour of transmission, Sunday evening, 31 March 1957. As Rakoff took his position in the control booth at the BBC's Lime Grove studio he saw Michael Barry arrive. Oh God, he's really worried about Sean playing the lead. 'Michael, what are you doing here?'

Barry tried to look inconspicuous, 'Nothing, nothing.' It wasn't working.

'Come on, what is it?'

'The electricians have threatened to strike,' said Barry. 'They're going to pull the lights out as you go on the air.'

The joy of live television. Also, that's a very effective strike, when you think about it. 'That's a strike and a half,' says Rakoff. 'What had happened was Michael had got various executives in the department to stand by the breakers and if they were pulled Michael and the other suits would push them back up. It never happened, but it didn't help the nerves.'

The transmission went ahead unimpeded and Connery, drawing on his experiences as a boxer in the navy, gave a formidable performance, earning every penny of his measly twenty-five-pound fee. In Edinburgh the Connery clan crouched around a newly purchased television set to watch their boy. Afterwards Effie was overcome by emotion while Joe declared, 'By heavens, that was smashing.' Even Connery's old *South Pacific* mentor Robert Henderson tuned in. 'Sean was sensational. It was a performance that absolutely burst the television camera open. He looked like a prizefighter, and he had this magnetism.'

The Sunday-night play on the BBC was always the drama highlight of the week and grabbed the bulk of the viewing audience. In the papers the next morning much of the critical praise was reserved for Connery, something that didn't surprise Rakoff in the least. 'We both sort of expected it. It was a very showy part and he was good enough in it to get noticed.' *The Times* highlighted Connery's, 'Shambling and inarticulate charm,' while *The Listener*, unmoved by the play itself, thought, 'The dramatist ought to go down on his knees to Sean Connery.' Best of all was the London *Sunday Pictorial*, which picked out Connery for future success, 'Physically he has the strength of a Marlon Brando type.'

Anyone with even half a brain in the business watching Connery that night couldn't have failed to see someone who, yes, may have been a little rough round the edges, but possessed undeniable screen presence. And sure enough Connery's agent Richard Hatton was flooded with enquiries, notably from Rank and also Hollywood in the shape of 20th Century Fox, both with enticing contracts that lesser actors might have killed for. But Connery would not be rushed and went back to Edinburgh to visit family and friends, a relaxing atmosphere in which to mull over a decision that might very well change the course of his life. On returning to London he decided to sign a lucrative seven-year contract with Fox, hoping their considerable clout would turn him into a film star. Ecstatic with the news, Connery called Rakoff at his home to offer thanks for all he'd done for him on *Requiem*.

All this almost didn't happen, according to director Cyril Frankel, who had recently tested Connery for a film. 'And I was so impressed with him that I immediately signed him up. After a few weeks his agent rang and said, "I'm afraid we've had an offer from 20th Century Fox for Sean Connery so would you release him from the contract?" Well I couldn't say no. So I released him.'

18
Entertaining Larry

The night Laurence Olivier saw *Look Back in Anger* for the second time at the behest of Arthur Miller made the actor re-evaluate his opinion of the sea change that was occurring in the British theatre. During the interval he'd asked Miller why he was enjoying it so much, interrogated him almost. Across the bar he spied Devine and went over. 'Is Osborne in tonight?' He wasn't, said Devine. 'Well, get him in by the end of the show,' ordered Olivier. 'Tell him Arthur Miller's here and likes his play.'

Osborne duly made an appearance backstage by the time the curtain dropped; 'A young guy with a shock of uncombed hair,' Miller described, 'and a look on his face of having awakened twenty minutes earlier.' The two chatted, endlessly it seemed to Olivier, who bided his time before seizing his chance during a conversational lull to manoeuvre Osborne to one side. 'Er, you're not writing anything which might have the littlest opportunity for . . . well . . . me, are you?' As it happened, Osborne was – something about a third-rate music-hall comedian called Archie Rice. The play was called *The Entertainer*.

A couple of days later Olivier met with Devine again. 'Do you really think that young Osborne might be serious about a play for me?' If there was any progress in that direction Olivier wanted to be informed straight-away. Devine hurriedly telephoned Osborne and as tactfully as possible enquired how he was getting on with things, then asked, 'Have you got a part in it for Laurence?'

In all innocence Osborne replied, 'Laurence who?'

'Olivier,' said Devine. Osborne, like many theatricals knew Olivier simply as Larry, not Laurence.

When the first act of *The Entertainer* was complete Devine sent it to

Olivier, who read it and phoned Devine immediately to accept the role. 'I could be run over and killed at the beginning of act II for all I cared.'

The more he thought, the more Olivier wanted to get in on the act of this theatrical new wave. Osborne was to call his U-turn a highly intuitive one, not about his play, 'but what was afoot'. Was this merely Olivier sensing where the wind was blowing, desperate to place himself at the heart of this new acting movement, to make himself still relevant, or was it something deeper, more personally profound? Approaching fifty, this was a man desperate for new challenges; his life had become empty thanks to a disintegrating marriage to Vivien Leigh, and his career had grown stale and predictable: 'I really felt that death might be quite exciting compared with the amorphous, purgatorial *nothing* that was my existence. And now, suddenly, this miracle was happening.'

Some of Larry's friends were surprised to find him at the Court, 'in a theatre associated in their minds with kitchen sinks and dustbins', according to Oscar Lewenstein. Hadn't the Court deliberately stuck two fingers up at the theatre establishment to which Olivier belonged? Even during rehearsals of *The Entertainer* colleagues and close friends were telling him he was making a fatal mistake. But his defection, as it might be seen, walking into that bear pit of his own volition, was a major turning point; 'The establishment's first bow to "the angries",' wrote Tynan. 'It meant they had officially arrived.' As the first of the old guard to join the new movement, and in the process creating one of his most famous characterisations, others were to follow Olivier's example: Guinness, Gielgud and Richardson would all perform at the Royal Court over the next few years.

Within ten days of the announcement of Olivier starring in *The Entertainer* every seat at the Royal Court was sold for the four-week run beginning in April, which was to be followed by an even more successful West End transfer. Even without Olivier's name, as a follow-up to Osborne's *Look Back in Anger* few plays have been more eagerly anticipated. And in many ways it's a more admirable work. Archie Rice is one of the great theatrical creations, a faded comic reduced to performing in dried-up seaside resorts to half-empty and half-dead houses. Facing bankruptcy, by the end of the play he's a broken man after learning that his soldier son has been killed at Suez doing his National Service. A clear statement about the decay of

Britain, the crumbling music-hall setting a metaphor for the country's post-colonial decline, *The Entertainer* predictably ran foul of the Lord Chamberlain's Office, whose narrow-minded objections centred on the use of such calamitous words as shagged, poof, rogered, turds and balls.

One interesting witness to the show's power is Michael Seymour, then a postgraduate student at the Royal College of Art, who thanks to a friend landed a part-time job at the Royal Court as a stagehand. He knew absolutely nothing of the play that was about to be put on, nor the significance of the theatre at which he was working. Duly turning up for his first evening, which was a public dress rehearsal for *The Entertainer*, Seymour was sent to work up in the flies, a raised bridge platform about forty feet above the stage from where scenery descended or rose. Not having the best head for heights, Seymour was nervous at first but soon put at ease by his fellow stagehands, Ted and Alfie, salt-of-the-earth cockneys.

When the curtain rose Seymour looked down on the stage and caught a glimpse of an actor he was convinced he'd seen before. 'That looks like Laurence Olivier,' he exclaimed. Ted rolled his eyes contemptuously; 'That's because it is, you silly cunt!'

Seymour conquered his vertigo enough to enjoy watching the play night after night from above, impressed no end by Olivier's performance and professionalism. At one point in the play he had to perform a little song-and-dance routine with a cane. Before every show, without fail, Olivier would appear half an hour before the audience was let in and with the pianist religiously rehearse this same routine over and over.

However, for Seymour there was still one major hurdle to conquer, a bridge that crossed from one side of the stage to the other, just behind the proscenium arch. And for one particular scene it proved very necessary indeed to cross it. 'I think it was the second act,' says Seymour. 'It starts with a tableau of an actress sitting there holding a trident depicting Britannia and naked to the waist. Well, all the stagehands came up from below because they were dying to see this and they would go out in the middle of the bridge and gaze down at those naked breasts. I unfortunately couldn't overcome my fear of heights sufficiently at that time to do this. The part was played by an actress called Vivienne Drummond and her breasts were indeed admirable.'

At the end of the week, on the Saturday after the evening perform-ance, a party took place on the stage with sundry actors, writers and critics. 'As the philosophy of the Royal Court was inclined to be egali-tarian at that time all us stagehands were invited too,' says Seymour. 'And Ted, Alfie and I duly trooped down the stairs from the flies to the metal door that led to the stage.' There was a crowd of people already mingling and no sooner had Seymour pushed open the door and entered than a young female journalist rushed over and heartily shook him by the hand. 'How do you feel now that it is all over?' she enquired breathlessly. Quite taken aback, Seymour didn't know how to respond, saying feebly that he felt a bit 'hot and sweaty'. Almost immediately the interest faded and the woman made a lame excuse and departed. 'It was not until some time later that I realised that I bore a striking resemblance to John Osborne at that time and the poor woman had mistaken me for him. I was often accosted as I walked towards the stage door in the evenings by enthusiastic autograph hunters who plainly did not believe me when I denied that I was him. Later when I told John Osborne that I was constantly being asked for his autograph he just said, "Sell it to them!"'

On another occasion, when Osborne had begun to date Mary Ure, Seymour was sitting with his wife in the pub next door to the theatre when the saloon bar door opened and Mary looked in, spotted Seymour and blew him a big kiss. As she started to walk to their table she suddenly realised that he wasn't Osborne and turned tail and fled. That took some explaining to the wife.

Michael Seymour became a permanent member of the backstage crew at the Royal Court and was involved next with a revival of *Look Back in Anger*, with Bates returning to his role as Cliff. Once again it packed them in, and would do for successive revivals, but more interesting was the atti-tude of those critics who had reviled the play when it first opened, but were applauding its virtues now it was an established success. 'I hadn't seen the original and had little idea of its content,' says Seymour. 'But I soon found it absorbing and wickedly funny. I never tired of watching it. All in all, during the time I worked there I was to see it sixty-four times, a fact that I conveyed to Alan Bates many years later at a party, causing him to go quite pale, assuming that I was some mad obsessive fan.'

19
Harris Heads to Moscow

When Elizabeth turned twenty-one she decided to invest her £150 inheritance in a home for Harris and herself; a five-year lease on a flat opposite Earls Court tube station. They occupied three of the top floors of the building. By the time they'd furnished it there was no money left over for carpets so instead they painted the stairs and the floors. Quickly the place became populated by Harris buddies, sleeping in hallways. In the end Elizabeth decreed that if people were staying over they may as well pay for the privilege and so rented out the two top rooms. With Harris still earning meagre wages with Joan Littlewood, it was a good source of income, but things were still extremely tight. 'I was doing bits and pieces, too,' says Elizabeth. 'I sold ice cream at Olympia for a couple of days and one night the royals came round and in their party was Elizabeth Abel Smith, who was a deb with me and a cousin of the Queen, and there I was dressed in my Lyons Maid outfit holding a tray of ice cream and she saw me and said, "Elizabeth what on earth are you doing!" There I was, captured. But one just carried on. I used to buy a pound of bacon scraps for sixpence and that would last us a couple of days with potatoes, and that's how you lived and one didn't think anything of it. We were all broke, everybody I knew was broke, but nobody felt broke, you just got by. And it never crossed anybody's mind about going on the dole; it just didn't happen. I remember when Richard was a drama student and he wanted to see his parents over Christmas so got a job at King's Cross as a porter, that's what you did.'

There was something romantic and bohemian about it almost. 'On our first wedding anniversary I bought Richard a second-hand book and he bought me a single rose. Actually, I think that's the only time we remembered our wedding anniversary.' Certainly Elizabeth was too proud to call on her family for aid and had completely cut herself off from that whole high-society world when she married Harris. 'I used to think, well the way I'll keep them friends was never to let them meet Richard because he would have been so rude to them, but on the other hand I didn't mix with them any more because our worlds were a million miles apart. There was no crossover at all.'

By the late spring of 1957 *A View from the Bridge* had closed but Harris got another job offer from Joan Littlewood, who was putting on a production of *Macbeth* and for a time had considered him for the title role. 'Richard had fire in his belly, but his speech rhythms were pure Irish. I'd have to stay up all night showing him how to use the iambics.' Instead the role went to Glynn Edwards, after Sean Connery apparently declined Joan's offer. Other cast members included a couple of newcomers to Theatre Workshop: Dudley Sutton ('It was my first job after being booted out of RADA a few months before. I thought, "Fuck 'em"') and Philip Grout, who arrived after a couple of years in rep. His first meeting with Joan was in a tea shop near the theatre. 'I went in and there was this little lady with a Queen Mary-type hat and velvet jacket. "Hello, you're Philip, aren't you." And there was this extraordinary, elegant, delightful, gracious, charming woman. She's not a tiger, I thought, she's sweet. I discovered the tiger a bit later. I was in the dressing room putting on make-up and suddenly the door opened and a tornado came into the room and it was Joan Littlewood. "What are you doing? Are you a transvestite?" I didn't know what a transvestite was, but I certainly wasn't it. When I discovered later I thought, no I don't think so. That was very frightening. And I found it hard to connect the little lady in the tea shop with this tornado. But she didn't like any form of support which didn't come from inside.' Joan was anti most West End gimmicks, fancy scenery, effects, certainly make-up, she didn't want her actors hiding behind masks, she wanted the real person. 'Acting wasn't deception, acting was revelation,' says Grout.

Joan's *Macbeth* was a modern dress production, all First World War tin hats and duffel coats, 'and the script', remembers Grout, 'had all the blank verse shape of it taken right out, it was like an ordinary play script. In other words it was Joan saying, don't you dare be Shakespearean with me.' She also did her usual thing of stripping away the mainstream accoutrements, no Highland mist or the like. She also had an aversion to some of the traditional violent overtures of the story. Watching one scene in rehearsal, where an assassin plunges a dagger into someone's guts, she was appalled. 'I don't like knives at all,' she trumpeted. 'Can you do without?' The actors looked perplexed to say the least and instead came up with an elaborate mime. 'That'll do, that's fine,' said Joan. One night Peter O'Toole came to see the show and went backstage afterwards to congratulate everyone. He was particularly impressed with the assassin death scene. When it was explained to him that the actors hadn't used a prop knife he couldn't believe it. 'But I saw the blade flash.' Goes to show that you can get away with anything if you do it with enough conviction and you've got a good director.

Harris played Ross, a minor character, but was still proud enough to invite his family to attend the first night. As he marched onto the stage, dressed as a soldier brandishing a sword, his mind went blank. As he opened his mouth, hoping the line, any line, would come out, it wasn't his voice that filled the auditorium but his mother's, booming out from the front row. 'That's my son. Isn't he marvellous?' Stranded on the stage, utterly alone and with everyone looking at him, Harris needed to get off fast. Raising the sword high he yelled the first thing that came into his head – 'Grrrr' – before exiting ignominiously stage right. 'As a Shakespeare debut it was a bloody shambles,' said Littlewood. 'But it was bloody marvellous theatre.'

In spite of the fact that the production wasn't well received critically, Harris was happy to be back at Theatre Workshop. 'And he loved doing that production,' says Elizabeth. 'It would be a breath of fresh air even today, that production, but it was like a gale in 1957.' There's one amusing incident Elizabeth recalls, not about Harris, but an actor who'd obviously been in an accident and turned up for the performance with his eye heavily bandaged. Unfortunately he was required to play several background characters in key scenes, he'd be a peasant one minute, a soldier the next, then he'd turn up during the banquet, 'but because of the bandage you couldn't fail to spot this same guy, it was very funny'.

Such was the esteemed light in which Joan was now seen that she was invited to bring her *Macbeth* to Moscow, one of the few English stage companies allowed behind the Iron Curtain. To get there the company travelled by train, stopping en route to perform in Zurich. On the way, Harris managed to get himself stranded. When the train stopped in Lille Harris, Brian Murphy and a couple of others got off to have a bite to eat in the station's café. 'We leisurely strolled back,' recalls Murphy, 'but then we saw that our train was leaving so we ran like hell and got to the end only for this huge guard to push us off back onto the platform. So there we were, alone, and we had nothing on us because our jackets were in the train along with our passports. We tried explaining what happened but our French was minimal, so Richard tried demonstrating: he ran up and down the platform pretending to be the train and the guard pushing us off. Of course the looks on the faces of the station officials, they were totally blank. They must have thought, who the bloody hell have we got here?'

Adding to their woes was the fact that it was Sunday so the nearest British consul was off somewhere playing golf. With hardly any money and nowhere to go, the group ended up sleeping in a field. 'For much of the time Richard was regaling us with stories or impersonations to keep us amused,' says Murphy. 'He was a brilliant mimic and on trips and things would have us all quite helpless with laughter. Then when he ran out of steam his head would drop forward and he'd go to sleep. The next morning we woke up surrounded by cows looking very inquisitive.'

Back at the station, the British consulate informed the lost actors they could take any train bound for Zurich. 'Joan and the company had landed the day before, of course, greeted with a red carpet and a small brass band,' says Murphy. 'Although apparently much of the company was scattered rather like us in distant places.' With half an hour to go before curtain-up, Joan heard a noisy crowd outside and looked to see Harris, Murphy and the others arriving at the theatre escorted by a gang of rowdy students, who turned out to be that evening's audience.

One afternoon in Zurich Grout took a walk with Harris along the famous lakeside, 'and we were both looking out over the water and I heard myself say – how dare I, but nevertheless I did – "Richard, you are going to be a big star." I just said it and it was not me saying it, it came right from inside, you are going to be a big star. "Fuck, don't talk such bloody nonsense," he said. But I do remember saying that and I remember knowing bloody well it was going to happen.'

Back on the train they continued their journey and crossing into Russia everyone was gripped by a sense that something special was happening. Towns had obviously been alerted to their presence and came out in force to welcome them through.

'It was extraordinary,' Grout remembers. 'There were crowds on every bloody platform. And this went on all through the night. It was immensely exciting. By the time we got to Moscow the train's corridor was piled high with flowers, you could hardly get out, there were so many flowers; absolutely astonishing. We were sort of swept into Russia.'

In all the company stayed almost three weeks in Moscow. Audiences received them with enthusiasm and they were given free rein to roam around the city. 'We sort of splashed about in a totally non-political manner and enjoyed ourselves,' says Grout. 'Everyone was on such a buzz being there and everybody one encountered was so full of goodwill that one felt very safe in Moscow. There was absolutely no feeling that we were being watched, although we had an enchanting interpreter, she was absolutely delightful, but of course we all knew she was informing.'

By contrast the return journey was depressing, after being on such a high it was back to Britain, back to normal life, back to the daily grind. It took a long time for some to adjust, for others it was just a feeling of, well, top that!

20

A Show of Confidence

While still at Bristol O'Toole engaged in the odd television play, the parts weren't substantial but the pay more than compensated. There's no better example than when he was asked to be a gang member in a gritty drama about teddy boys. Kenneth Griffith, who'd played supporting roles in numerous British film comedies, a lanky sort of neurotic-actor type, was inexplicably playing the leader. By the third day of rehearsals it was pretty obvious that there were only eight gang members when there should have been nine. 'Where's this other chap, then?' Griffith asked the director.

That morning O'Toole had awoken pissed, with no clue as to where the hell he was, remembering only that he'd written down on a piece of paper that he had to turn up to rehearsals for a TV play. Unable to locate all his clothes, he sort of threw on a bedraggled ensemble from bits lying around, 'and somehow found wherever this bizarre place was where we were rehearsing'.

The cast were reading through the script when these big swing doors opened, 'and there was what appeared to be a tall young tramp', Griffith recalled. O'Toole fixed his eyes on the scene. 'Sorry I'm late, darlings,' he said, then tripped and fell over. Recovering, he focused upon Griffith, thundered across the room, picked him up and kissed the startled actor on the cheek. 'I think you're bloody marvellous.' It was an odd introduction.

Griffith was perturbed, this was a small-part player and there was a certain decorum to be observed, one didn't get out of line. Anyway, they'd only the one scene together and Griffith suggested they run through it now. 'Bang! He gave a performance which was devastating,' Griffith later related. 'I knew immediately that this was the most formidable competition I'd ever come across. I felt as if I had just met the young Edmund Kean. I had no doubt whatsoever.'

Occasionally the Bristol Old Vic brought its shows down to London, those that they were particularly proud of, like the musical *Oh! My Papa*. 'It went down terribly well in Bristol and everyone got wildly excited,' remembers Phyllida Law. 'And then we came into the West End and got hammered, apart from Peter, who got picked out.' On the opening night in July people booed from the stalls of the Garrick Theatre and the show never recovered. Afterwards O'Toole got drunk on home-made mead and was arrested at three in the morning for harassing a building in Holborn. He spent the night in the cells and in the morning told the court, 'I felt like singing and began to woo an insurance building.'

One of the leads was Rachel Roberts, who shared a duet with O'Toole in the show. The daughter of a Baptist minister and RADA graduate, Rachel's earthy manner and acting passion endeared her to the whole cast. 'I loved Rachel,' says Phyllida. 'Very Welsh and generous hearted. When she had a flat in north London, her lodger was a young man, a young actor who she never thought would do anything, terribly nice she thought, very strong Scottish accent, Sean Connery.'

Over at Birmingham, Finney's star continued to ascend. Kenneth Tynan, who'd noticed Finney at RADA, was still keeping tabs on him and wrote in his *Observer* column: 'Birmingham is perhaps the only city on earth that has a population of more than a million and only two legitimate theatres. It may therefore be the right place for a potentially great actor to learn his craft unobserved, and that is what Albert Finney is doing.' That other theatre was the nearby Alexandra, which Finney himself had slammed as 'middle aged, musty and middle class'.

Taking Tynan's lead, other critics began to latch on to Finney. Caryl Brahms in that August's issue of *Plays and Players* wrote: 'He is raw, for this is his first season of professional playing. But he has a fine sense of timing, attack and dramatic urgency.' Another theatre magazine, *Encore*, was probably the first to throw together Finney and O'Toole, placing both of them on their cover. 'What have these young actors in common? Above all, the magic touch of personal magnetism. Love them or loathe them, you can't ignore them. On stage they never relax that special actor's tension which is always in the eyes, in the voice and in the moves. With worlds of technique and experience still before them, they are fortunate to have the quiet apprentice worlds of Bristol and Birmingham in which to learn.'

Sonia Fraser had just been head-hunted from the Bristol Old Vic to appear at Birmingham rep and found herself in several plays with Finney. Having observed O'Toole in the flesh, the young Finney was someone else who stood out in much the same way. 'Like O'Toole he had a charisma, he had an excitement and supreme confidence.' Similarly she didn't detect any rawness round the edges, considering he'd not long left drama school. 'His Henry the Fifth had amazing passion and drive and was an accomplished Shakespearean performance.' Already Finney's use of language was exemplary. 'Albert did have this amazing voice,' says Sonia. 'He was a joy to listen to, he made sense of the language, but he also relished it. It was like listening to someone play music wonderfully.'

Many have since commented on Finney's rich vocal talent. 'He has God's gift of a voice,' says television director Philip Saville. 'The perfect voice roots in the stomach and blossoms in the mouth.' For Sonia, hearing Finney speak was much like listening to Richard Burton doing *Under Milk Wood*; 'It wasn't an accent but the rhythm of the Welshness was in there. With Albert, he didn't have an accent, but he had that kind of energy of the provincial voice.' It seemed as though Finney was the real deal and Sonia was bowled over by him. 'He had a real sense of his own value. He was quite the most magical thing I'd ever met. Lots of girl-friends? Every three minutes I should think; he was devastatingly charming.'

It was that confidence thing again. With Finney it wasn't anything so vulgar as being conceited; no, it was just a genuine and central belief in what he could do within himself. There was an assurance and a faith in what he could achieve. Take a production of *The Alchemist*, a Restoration comedy in which no one in the company placed any trust, either in the play itself or in how it was being handled. Anxiety ruled amongst the actors, was it going to work? Sonia recalls waiting in the wings with Finney on opening night, chatting about everyone's desperate nerves. 'Are you all right, Albert?' Finney looked at her, exhibiting pure calmness, and replied, 'Oh, I've just decided to go on and be terrific.' It was said without a trace of arrogance, that's exactly what he was going to do: go on and make the damn thing work for him.

21
Hard Times

From a distance, Robert Shaw watched the unfurling events at places like the Royal Court with envious eyes. The man who was still appearing on television as pirate Dan Tempest was desperate to gain entry to the intellectual high table of the British theatre. He socialised with many of the big hitters, went drinking with them, probably fell out of cabs with them, but not for one moment did these people ever consider him part of their clique. 'I felt intellectually equal if not superior to John Osborne and I couldn't understand why he was successful instead of me.'

Soon even the gold-plated straitjacket of TV popularity would be denied him. Word came from Hollywood that western shows were the new thing, so with no American backing *The Buccaneers* was cancelled. 'And I'd spent all the money. And there I was unemployed again.' Worse, his artistic credentials had taken a dent within the stuffy theatre community who now looked upon him with disdain for having done commercial television. 'After *The Buccaneers* stage producers no longer considered me a serious actor.' David McCallum confirms that this rather crude snobbery did exist in those days. 'If you worked in television at that time you were considered persona non grata in the theatre, so you just didn't work in theatre.'

Shaw was equally taboo on TV, thanks to his identification in the public's mind as Dan Tempest. As a result Shaw was out of work for a considerable time and faced renewed financial hardship. The Rolls-Royce was the first thing to go. It was a period he'd later describe as 'the lowest point in my life'. But maybe there was another outlet for his frustrated creative urges. Recalling what one London producer had said in the midst of rejecting one of his plays – 'The third act is bad. It's like a novel' – a light bulb flashed inside Shaw's mind. He would write a book. Retreating with his family, that now included three children, to a remote cottage in Suffolk lent to them by a friend, Shaw found it difficult to concentrate with all the stress of his stagnant career and lack of money. He called on his friends again for support, asking Donald Pleasence to lend him £100 just to tide the family over while he pursued this literary endeavour. Pleasence agreed and with that pressure lifted Shaw knuckled down. After thirty pages he knew he could do it, though the finished book wouldn't see daylight for another two years.

As for his friendship with his fellow swashbuckler William Russell, that was maintained for several more years. 'We both had young families and would go down to the seaside for the day and other places,' says Russell. But gradually as time passed and Shaw's career took off Russell began to slowly lose touch, easily done when you're dealing with the kind of fame Shaw eventually had. 'It's always slightly off-putting if you've known someone very well that you ring up and hear, "Mr Shaw's secretary here. Can I get you an appointment?" And I'm thinking, I want to talk to him, I don't want to talk to you, or book an appointment. Those are the things that separate you when people become super-successful.'

Money was a chronically rare commodity in the Caine household, as was work, and his marriage, while not yet on the critical list, was threatening cardiac arrest at any moment. So it wasn't the best time for Patricia to announce that she was pregnant. A daughter was born in August and christened Dominique. If anything, a baby in the house made things worse, certainly from a financial standpoint. It was now that Patricia urged her husband to get a proper job, to dump acting altogether because now more than ever they needed a steady income. But Caine couldn't do it, he knew he'd have hated himself and taken out all his frustrations on his wife and child. Unable to handle the situation, he walked out on his young family, and has blamed no one else but himself for the failure.

At probably his lowest ebb, both personally and professionally, Caine struggled on, barely existing on small roles in television. He did a *Dixon of Dock Green* episode that surprisingly elicited his first bit of fan mail. Even more surprising was that it came from a fellow actor, a distinguished one too, Dennis Price, who'd starred in the Ealing classic *Kind Hearts and Coronets*. 'I always pride myself that I can spot star quality when I see it and you, Mr Caine, have it,' went the letter. 'I know that *Dixon* is not the greatest show but don't give up. You have what it takes. Good luck.' It was a huge boost to Caine's battered confidence, but it didn't pay the bills and he was forced to take a job as a night porter in a small hotel in Victoria. It was a pretty seedy place, more of a knocking shop than a hotel, and when one night he rescued a young prostitute from a savage beating by one of her clients he ended up with a bottle smashed over his head for his troubles. That was it. Caine handed in his notice and was never to work in 'civilian' life again.

More than ever Caine put himself about, knocking on casting directors' doors, turning up for endless auditions. Alvin Rakoff for one was endlessly collared for work. 'Michael was one of those people who kept on ringing. "Is there anything for me?" I'd say, "Michael I'm sorry I've got nothing." He was a pain in the arse. One time he called and I said, as usual, I had nothing at all, then I said, "Wait a minute, Michael, hold on." I'd been sitting in the house all afternoon thinking about the opening credits of this television drama I was directing about communism and repression and I wanted the feet of a guard pounding along castle ramparts as the credits came on. I got back on the phone. "I've just been thinking of something you could do, Michael. I could use your feet." And he agreed. So I used Michael Caine's feet on this production.'

Nothing else better demonstrates just how desperate Caine was for work, and with child maintenance to pay he even once suffered the ignominy of his mother having to dole out the money. 'I remember another time,' says Rakoff. 'I was in an actors' bar off Charing Cross Road and Michael came in and saw me and said, "Hello, Alvin, can I buy you a drink?" I'm sure he felt in his pockets before he made the offer to make sure he had enough money.'

22
The Sex Kitten from Oz

Philip Saville had been running an improvisation class in a warehouse in Soho for a couple of months when news reached him of an extremely statuesque young actor who'd been modelling swimwear at a men's clothes shop in Carnaby Street. Saville invited him to attend one of the classes, but he didn't appear to be in a hurry to come along. 'Anyway, he did turn up on one occasion,' Saville recalls. 'He was tall, dark and very charismatic. He had the kind of physique that was built to climb mountains, together with a natural flair and dominance. He was a born hero figure, in adversity able to come to the rescue of his country, but not yet, then he was a star in the waiting room, that place where so many wannabes falter, but not him. Britain's superstar in the making was perched on a stool sipping a drink in the tea break. I couldn't believe my luck. He was perfect casting for my next production.' The young actor was, of course, Sean Connery.

Saville had been asked to direct a TV adaptation of Eugene O'Neil's Pulitzer Prize-winning play *Anna Christie* for Lew Grade's ATV. It was quite a coup for the young director who only a few years before had been at RADA studying to be an actor. After coming out of National Service Saville had been spotted while on holiday with his parents by an American film producer who put him under contract and packed him off to RADA to learn how to act. 'I didn't do very much there,' Saville confesses, 'except make severe sexual introductions to a number of gorgeous women.'

He had been at the Academy for a little over two months when he was summarily ordered to see Sir Kenneth Barnes in his office. 'And there he stood, literally beside the fireplace with his hands behind his back like a Victorian headmaster and he said, in frightfully pukka English, "You haven't been doing very well. And I'm getting reports from various young ladies that you're obstructing their progress," which is one way of putting it. I said, "I'm very sorry," I was ever so humble. He carried on, "I really think you're wasting your time here. Do you really wish to continue? There are a lot of very young actors who would love to be in your position." I felt really awful.'

Saville left not long after that and following some minor acting jobs in film and television turned to direction. 'But the thing that I remembered about RADA, which has stuck to me all my life, is discipline. If you said you would learn a part by the time of the dress rehearsal, which is fairly standard, you did. But when you're very young and you're burning the candle at both ends, you don't know about those things, so it really taught me what it meant to be disciplined and I'm eternally grateful.'

Anna Christie was Saville's most prestigious directorial assignment yet and he was determined to make it a success. Eugene O'Neill described the play's lead male character Mat Burke as a 'powerful, broad-chested, six footer, handsome, hard, rough, bold with a defiant manner and traditional attitudes about women'. Is it any surprise that when Saville saw Connery step into his improvisation class he had to give him the role? 'Next to John Wayne, here he was.'

Anna Christie tells the story of a man who falls in love with a former prostitute but is unaware of her sordid past. The part of Anna had been played by none other than Greta Garbo in the 1930 film version, so Saville had his work cut out finding a suitably strong actress to take it on. 'There was a young actress making a buzz in theatre and film at that time, a very striking personality from Australia, Diane Cilento. I took the script round to her flat hoping she would accept the role. She was a very no-nonsense lady with a very palpable sex appeal. She agreed to do it.'

Diane Cilento was born in Queensland in 1933 to an Australian knighted for his contribution to tropical medicine and Lady Cilento, an eminent physician. Strikingly independent from an early age, Diane left home at fifteen to study acting in New York and at RADA. Refusing any financial support from her affluent parents, she supported herself by working odd jobs, even for a time in a circus.

Although making her British television debut with *Anna Christie*, Diane was a vastly more experienced performer than Connery. Under contract to Alexander Korda she'd appeared in starring roles in films like *The Admirable Crichton* opposite Kenneth More and acted on Broadway, where she was lauded by the likes of *On the Waterfront* director Elia Kazan. With her distinctive husky Aussie drawl, pouting lips and blonde hair Diane was a screen natural and her 'high-IQ sex kitten' press tag was not misplaced. Still a rebel, and in many ways ahead of her time, she rode a scooter round town and smoked cigars. She was also married to an Italian writer called Andre Volpe, though crucially by the time of *Anna Christie* it was a union on shaky ground.

Diane's fierce independent spirit captivated Connery almost from the word go. On the pretence that, to get the chemistry right between them they should rehearse after hours, Connery invited himself round to Diane's flat. Instead of plonking himself on the nearest chair he stretched out on the carpet as if he owned the place. Was he deliberately trying to antagonise her, to shock her, get her angry? 'At first I thought Sean wore a terrific chip on his shoulder.' Only later did she realise he was merely being himself. Or was it that friends had told him that Diane could be something of a snob and he wanted to prick that balloon of pomposity?

Saville is a witness to the growing affection these two dynamic performers began to feel for each other. 'Each day of rehearsal was extraordinary because I just watched this pair hit it off BIG. They would go off together at the end of the day or at rest periods wander away to kiss in the shadows. I soon realised that any chance for me with Diane was a lost cause.'

This was still early days for Connery and he had to earn his acting stripes next to Diane and the respected Leo McKern, who was also in the cast. 'At that time, although formidable in terms of appearances, you didn't know too much about Sean,' says Saville. 'All you knew was that there was a powerful magnet in the room. Really Sean was like a piece of blotting paper, absorbing everything. And he was quite remark-able as Mat Burke. Indeed, the play was very well received by the press.'

Connery was now living in St John's Wood in a large flat above a garage in a private mews. It was a place in which many women were wined and dined. Although he cared for Diane, he had no intention of settling down; he was having too much fun. 'There's always some girl trying to move in on me,' he said. 'It's getting rid of them that's the problem.'

Comfortably off financially thanks to the Fox contract, Connery was starting to feel less like an actor, more of a commodity. Pretty quickly he'd realised he'd landed himself in a nightmare situation; put up for roles in films he felt utterly unsuited for he'd turn them down, saying, 'I used to live on spaghetti and nothing else for weeks because that's all I could afford. And if necessary I'll go back to that.' Fox, running out of ideas about how to use him, basically gave up and instead got their money back by loaning Connery out to make movies with other companies. One Fox publicist blamed 'that damned accent. Sometimes it seemed tolerable, but when he speeded up, like all Scotsmen, you couldn't interpret the babble.'

Then Lana Turner arrived in London, looking for a young actor to play her lover in a new Paramount weepie called *Another Time, Another Place*. Known as the 'sweater girl', a top pin-up during the Second World War and one of Hollywood's most artfully manufactured glamour queens, by 1957 Lana Turner was in decline somewhat, but still had co-star approval and after trawling through hours of footage featuring a hatful of hopefuls personally selected Connery. Credit must go to Miss Turner here as the first high-profile artist to seize upon Connery's star potential.

Having previously been cast as unshaven heavies, Connery was groomed to match matinee-idol expectations in his role of a married BBC war correspondent during the Blitz who enjoys an illicit affair with Lana's visiting American before being killed off halfway through the film. Despite the melodramatic trappings this was potentially a star-making role for Connery, with the chance of exposure in America; he was even given a special 'and introducing' credit.

Working at Borehamwood Studio that September, Connery and Lana got on well, although he once shocked her by turning up for a date on a battered scooter wearing a T-shirt and jeans, and there she was in formal fur and jewels. 'But she'd hop on anyway,' he said. 'A good sport. I adored her.' There was a definite chemistry between them. Lana's daughter Cheryl, then fourteen, was in London at the time and recalled that her mother and Connery 'had a certain familiar air with each other'.

Amidst growing speculation of romance, Lana's boyfriend Johnny Stompanato arrived in Britain from the States and began making uninvited appearances on the set. Stompanato wasn't a nice fella: a flashy thug who wore little pistols for cufflinks, he'd been a bodyguard for gangster Mickey Cohen and had a temper that went dangerously out of control all too easily. At the rented home in Hampstead the film company paid for Lana to stay in there were blazing rows; the housekeeper once overheard him threaten to break every bone in the star's body. No wonder some nights Lana was too terrified to go back there. Once Scotland Yard officials arrived at the house to see smashed doors literally hanging by their hinges.

Ordered to stay away from the set Stompanato paid no heed, turning up one day armed with a revolver that he pointed straight at Connery, threatening to blow a hole in his head if he didn't keep clear of his girl. This proclamation was met with a stern Scottish fist. Stompanato was politely asked to leave the country by the authorities. But it wouldn't be the last Connery heard of him.

23

An Angry Young Man in New York

David Merrick was a New York theatre producer fast on his way to becoming a legend in his own lifetime, 'the abominable showman', they called him. 'He liked writers in the way that snakes like live rabbits,' John Osborne once said of him. Oscar Lewenstein called Merrick 'a difficult man, tough and mean, who enjoyed his reputation as a hard unscrupulous bastard and in many ways played up to it'. But he was a great promoter and the ideal candidate to bring *Look Back in Anger* to Broadway.

The play was to be staged with its original cast, so rehearsals were swift and easy, as Tony Richardson recalled: 'The atmosphere was slightly like the morning after a party where everyone knew they'd behaved badly the night before and so were now on their most proper behaviour.' It opened in October at the Lyceum Theatre on West 45th Street, a famous old venue but, with a thousand-seat auditorium, far too big and imposing for such an intimate play, a worry that only added to Richardson's fear that Osborne's drama might not hit with American audiences. The likes of Miller and Tennessee Williams had been writing about youthful rebellion for years, so Broadway might find *Look Back*'s angst rather less controversial.

The opening night proved his point, drawing a mute response and only polite applause at the close. No one came backstage afterwards to offer their first-night congratulations, as was traditional; the omens looked bad. Merrick escorted everyone to nearby Sardi's restaurant and handed out drinks to try to calm them all down while they awaited the reviews. Bates recalled that it went unspoken that no one should ask for any food. 'We all felt,' Richardson remembered, 'as though we were carrying some unnameable, unspeakable social disease.'

As the hours crawled along Merrick looked more and more anxious and edgy. The tension was broken at 2 a.m. when early copies of the *New York Times* arrived. It was a rave. 'Menus were produced,' said Richardson. 'We were invited to order. We were a hit.' Mary Ure left to go to the ladies and when she returned to her table the now busy restaurant recognised her as one of the stars of the show and burst into spontaneous applause. On seeing this, Kenneth Haigh surreptitiously walked out and straight back in again, eliciting much the same response as Mary had.

For the first few weeks the play sailed along thanks to favourable critical reaction. But when Richardson and Osborne attended one night they were shocked at Haigh's performance, or lack of one, for he'd got into the habit of cutting some of Osborne's best monologues. Richardson gathered his cast together the next day and laid into Haigh. The actor, his pride dented, pointed at his co-stars Bates and Ure. 'Why do you always pick on me? Why don't you blame them?'

Richardson remained stern faced. 'But they are giving impeccable performances. And why are you cutting speeches?'

'Because I didn't feel those lines deeply enough last night. Do you want me to give the audience lies?'

'Yes,' replied Richardson. 'I want "To be or not to be" whether the Hamlet feels it or not!'

After four months on Broadway, with the box office beginning to slow, the play attracted front-page headlines when a young woman clambered onto the stage during the third act and gave Haigh a wallop round the head. 'He reminded me of all the rotten men I've known,' she told reporters. Of course the whole thing was a publicity stunt: Merrick had hired an actress to feign outrage and the press fell for it. *Look Back* settled into a healthy year-long run. Merrick was nothing if not a wily producer.

More or less celebrities around town, the cast remained on low wages compared to, say, film actors and after tax and his agent's commission there wasn't much left for Bates to find decent accommodation. He resided 'in little more than a red-light apartment block on a sleazy street', according to Osborne. As for the playwright and Richardson, they stayed at the famous Algonquin Hotel, whose management was rather dismayed by this scruffy bunch of Brits in their sneakers and

Portrait of a frustrated actor. Robert Shaw grew bitter and rebellious at his non-progress at Stratford. John Gielgud was terrified of him.

Peter O'Toole was a roaring boy at the Bristol Old Vic, often turning up late for rehearsals or not at all. 'Peter was adorable, but impossible,' says actress Sheila Allen.

Two super spies of the future. Sean Connery plays chess with Patrick McGoohan on the Pinewood set of *Hell Drivers*.

As a struggling actor Michael Caine incessantly phoned round directors and casting agents pleading for work. 'He was a pain in the ass,' recalls director Alvin Rakoff.

A quiet evening in with Mr and Mrs Richard Harris.

Albert Finney as Arthur Seaton in *Saturday Night and Sunday Morning*, perhaps for the first time a working class person was authentically portrayed on film.

The wild man of Stratford. O'Toole broke the Dirty Duck pub's house record by downing a yard of ale (two and a half pints) in forty seconds.

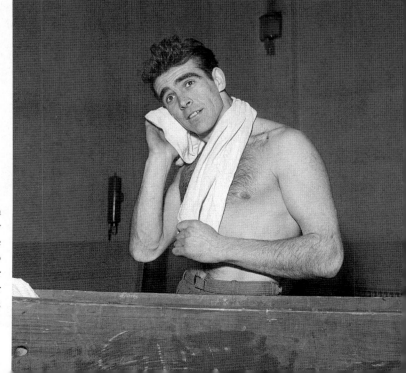

A beef-cake for hire in his early years Connery had, 'the kind of physique that was built to climb mountains, together with a natural flair and dominance,' says director Philip Saville.

Shaw in *The Changeling* at the Royal Court with Mary Ure, who he was about to
steal from under the nose of her husband, John Osborne.

Starring together in *A Terrible Beauty*, Harris became great pals with Robert
Mitchum who was a role model to budding hellraisers like O'Toole and himself.

Alan Bates simply exuded male beauty, a sort of cross between Tyrone Power and George Best. But he had to hide his bisexuality.

Connery and Shaw appeared in the television play *The Pets*, it was the beginning of a lifelong friendship, but also years of competitive rivalry.

The film *Billy Budd* made Terence Stamp a star at the first attempt. One critic said he was a cross between a Greek God and a rock 'n' roll idol.

T-shirts, being more used to the likes of Noël Coward and other better-scrubbed thespian types.

In spite of his living arrangements Bates found New York 'intoxicating', its culture, its streets, its ambience. He was invited to all the best parties and mixed in privileged circles with the intelligentsia and actors such as Richard Burton and Henry Fonda; Paul Newman and Joanna Woodward invited him to their Connecticut home for Christmas dinner. Missing Wyngarde no doubt, Bates was nevertheless sexually precocious in New York, indulging in brief affairs, careful, as always, to keep them discreet and neatly tucked away from prying eyes and wagging tongues.

24

Sense and Censorship

Back in London, Joan Littlewood was assembling a small cast of male actors for her latest stage production, *You Won't Always Be On Top* by Henry Chapman, an interesting play since it told no story whatsoever, no drama unfolded. Set on a building site on a rainy Monday morning, it merely presented a slice of working life. As Tynan said in his review: 'The extraordinary thing about this production is that it makes ordinariness fascinating.'

Luckily Joan's theatre was surrounded by building sites and the actors mixed in with real local labourers and brought a few newly learned skills directly onto the stage; Dudley Foster would lay a brick wall every night, Brian Murphy sawed and did joinery, there'd be a cement mixer mixing real cement, and Harris, well, he ran a wheelbarrow across the site when the mood took him. 'There was stuff going on the whole time,' says Philip Grout, who was also in the production. 'You had to act your socks off to get noticed.'

After *Macbeth*, which had been a real mishmash of styles, *You Won't Always Be On Top* was irredeemably Joan. As with Behan's *The Quare Fellow*, Henry Chapman's play was reworked, rejigged, and essentially taken over by Joan. 'And Henry sort of said, well as long as I get paid,' says Grout. 'He was a lovely man actually and sensibly realised that we knew more about his play than he did, we saw more of the potential in it.'

Joan didn't merely encourage her actors to ad-lib but positively demanded it, as if having a rigid format was abhorrent. For her, leaving a play open to fresh ideas was more important than polished repetition. Sometimes in rehearsals she'd cry out from the stalls to an actor,

'Yes, you've got it, you've got it, well done. Now do something different.' Or she might demand, 'Change it. Do something else. Do the opposite. Don't rely on what you did last night, that was rubbish.' To which the actor might respond, 'But you told me it was good.' Joan would shake her head, 'It's rubbish now.' It was her way of keeping things organic, and the energy levels high. 'I always felt with Joan that she was a sort of suppressed tornado,' says Grout. 'However nice and lovely she was, and she was utterly charming. But she could be very unsettling. And she had a very acerbic wit. She could be shatteringly complimentary: "You're going to give a great performance" – that made you more terrified than ever. In other words, you were constantly on your toes. We were terrified of her and sometimes we could kick her, but we all adored her.'

At one rehearsal Joan decided Harris should sing a song, park his wheelbarrow and just burst into an Irish ditty or something. Philip Grout remembers that moment well. 'He suddenly began to sing and everybody just stopped. There was this incredible voice, lyrical, penetrating, gentle, and it kind of *was* Richard, the essence of it. It was quite extraordinary. And I've never forgotten listening to him. There was a very gentle side to Richard, a very lyrical side, and that's the side that one actually found attractive. He wasn't a roaring Irishman who made a nuisance of himself all the time, there was a great gentleness to him and that's what made him so interesting.'

Midway through the successful run of *You Can't Always Be On Top*, two plain-clothes policemen were spotted in the stalls taking notes. 'Just so long as they paid for their seats,' said Gerry Raffles, not unduly bothered. The same pair was spotted again two nights later. It didn't raise any eyebrows at the time, but the repercussions of their visit would ultimately prove traumatic.

In January 1958 Joan got rehearsals under way for a new play. Harris and the usual mob were on stage when a pair of police officers barged into the auditorium. 'Yes, gentlemen?' said the assistant stage manager.

'Joan Littlewood?' asked the glummer of the two.

'At your service,' Joan replied from the stalls, bewildered but keeping her composure.

The other cop looked at the actors. 'Gerry Raffles, Richard Harris, we're here to serve a summons on you all.'

'What for?' asked Harris.

'That unlawfully you did present parts of a new stage play entitled *You Won't Always Be On Top* before such parts had been allowed by the Lord Chamberlain, contrary to section fifteen of the Theatres Act, 1843.' In other words, once a play had been cleared for production by the Lord Chamberlain's office, no unauthorised additions could be made. It looked as if Joan's method of encouraging her cast to ad lib had come a cropper, they'd obviously picked up rather too much 'colourful' building-site lingo. The date for the hearing was set for April.

There was a large intake of breath after the officers left and everyone looked at each other. 'Could they close us down?' someone asked.

'If they fined us heavily,' said Joan, 'they could sink us.'

That evening all those under threat of court action concocted a battle plan. First they needed a lawyer, which meant a large financial outlay they simply couldn't afford, so a series of begging letters went out. These met with a moderate response; Sean O'Casey sent two guineas, Michael Redgrave donated to the pot, as did Ted Willis and the Unity Theatre. As for the play Joan was currently rehearsing, it was dumped as every bit of spare energy was now needed to save the company.

Harris went into a production of Pirandello's *Man, Beast and Virtue* at the Lyric Theatre, Hammersmith. Friends labelled his performance a trifle overripe, but sitting in the stalls on the opening night was TV director Cliff Owen, then about to direct a drama for Granada television called *The Iron Harp* about the troubles in Ireland, a sort of sub-Behan thing. For weeks he'd been looking for the right person to play a key role, that of a blind poet and harpist, a role only recently essayed by Albert Finney when the play was performed at the Birmingham rep.

Struck by what he saw as Harris's booming passion, and being Irish obviously helped, Owen met up with the actor afterwards in the theatre bar and suggested he try out for the role the following day at Granada's head office in central London where auditions were taking place. Of course Harris overslept or something and feared he'd missed his chance. 'We had a gas meter,' recalls Elizabeth. 'And he raided that, busted it open, in order to get money to go in a taxi to get there fast because they were closing the auditions. So he got there and the director said, "I'm sorry we've closed the audition and we've already chosen who we're going to have for the part." Richard jumped over the desk and grabbed him by the throat and yelled, "I have raided my gas meter to get here and you're fucking well going to hear me. I'm going to read for you and you're going to see what I can do." And he did it and the director was blown away and Richard got the part.'

It was a fat fee, too: fifty pounds for a single TV appearance, more than he'd been paid for an entire run with Joan. 'I fell on my knees and kissed the ground at his feet for that loot.' The play aired live in March 1958 and Harris proved a screen natural, the TV critic of the *Daily Mirror* picked him out as someone to watch. After years of demanding attention, suddenly it was all there in his lap. But Harris wanted more. Maybe Associated British Picture Corporation would give it to him. Their casting director Robert Lennard was a keen spotter of talent, though unfortunately he was in the bath when *The Iron Harp* was screened. 'But his wife was watching it,' claims Elizabeth. 'And she shouted up at him, you've got to get out, come here, there's the most extraordinary actor. So he got out of the bath and sat and watched the rest of the play with a towel wrapped round him.'

The next morning Lennard was eager to sign the youngster up but didn't know who, if anyone, represented him. He picked up the phone with the intention of cold-calling every representative in London, trying his friend Jimmy Fraser first. By an amazing coincidence Harris was in Fraser's office that very moment, badgering the agent to take him on as a client. As Fraser was wondering how to get rid of this loud Irishman his phone rang. 'Did you see a young actor called Richard Harris on the television last night, Jimmy?'

'I did, Robert.'

'And do you know who represents him?'

A broad grin came over his face as he looked over at Harris. 'I do.'

Arrangements were made for a regulation seven-year contract. 'The only reason Richard did that was because I was pregnant,' reveals Elizabeth. 'Suddenly it hit him, more than me, that we now had responsibilities; he was much more struck by that than I was. So he signed that deal. He bought himself out of it later.'

Harris's good fortune was a far cry from what happened to Michael Caine when Lennard left a message with his agent saying that he wanted to see him. Caine was ecstatic at the prospect of being put under contract; a regular income at last. Caine floated into Lennard's office on a bubble of expectation that deflated faster than a hedgehog's balloon as the director looked up, smiled, and then proceeded to blitzkrieg every single one of his hopes. 'This is a tough business, Michael,' he began. Caine felt like saying, I know, I've been struggling at it for years. 'I've got a son, Michael, not much older than you. He's an accountant; looks a bit like you, too. He's got more chance of success in this business than you do.' Caine tried very hard to keep a smile on his face but inside he was in bits. 'This may sound unkind,' Lennard went on. 'But you will thank me in the long run. I know this business well and I can assure you that you have no future in it. Give it up, Michael.'

Caine thanked Lennard for his advice and walked out, more determined than ever to make it.

So Harris had a film contract, he also had a date at West Ham Magistrates Court, charged with breach of the peace for uttering and performing obscenities during performances of *You Won't Always Be On Top*. He sat in the dock, along with the play's author Henry Chapman, Joan and Gerry Raffles. The JPs looked like pillars of the establishment, while the public gallery overflowed with supportive fellow actors. The proceedings began with the two detectives reading from their notes. It was alleged that Harris had urinated on stage in full view of the audience while impersonating Winston Churchill, an act that was 'vulgar and blasphemous', in the words of the prosecuting council, while Dudley Sutton had stuck his fingers up in a V-sign. It was the end of civilisation. Harris and Joan could scarcely control their mirth at the pantomimic ludicrousness of it all.

Harris had his own theories as to why this prosecution had been mounted; it was all a plot to get rid of Joan. 'The workshop was becoming too popular, and it was anti-establishment.' He stood up and happily admitted that he was guilty of uttering, in his words, 'a dam burst of cock-sucking, cunt licking, arse kicking fuckology'. Joan and the others made similar admissions, as a protest against a law which 'prohibited theatrical free speech'.

Then a bit of good news arrived, it turned out that one of the magistrates had once been in the building trade, so the omens looked good. And despite the prosecution's case that the play was subversive, in the end they were given a mere token fine, a slap on the wrist more or less, and made to promise they wouldn't do it again. 'To the bar!' screamed Joan triumphantly on their return to the theatre, and as the celebrations began it was standing room only. 'That evening our smiling faces were in all the papers,' Joan recalled. 'Our victory was the first real blow at the ancient institution of censorship.'

The Lord Chamberlain's Office would stagger on until censorship in the theatre was finally abolished in 1968, by which time it had become a discredited and anachronistic institution. Jill Bennett was appearing on stage when the news broke, and must have been one of the first to hear about it. During her next scene she replied to one of the actors, 'Abso-fucking-lutely not!' stunning the entire cast. Obviously that new twist on the line wasn't in the script; she wanted to be the first to break the taboo.

25
Laughton's Party

Charles Laughton hadn't performed on the British stage for something like twenty years. The man who played Captain Bligh in *Mutiny on the Bounty* and Quasimodo in *The Hunchback of Notre Dame*, and had recently directed Robert Mitchum in *Night of the Hunter*, was eager to associate himself with the new wave of British playwrights, as Olivier had done to such crowning glory with *The Entertainer*. But Laughton was to make a grave miscalculation on his choice of play, an intense family drama called *The Party* in which he would play a father returning home after a mental breakdown, convinced that in its author Jane Arden he'd found a female Osborne. Ultimately she proved not to be in the same league and *The Party* trod fallow ground.

Laughton trawled the provincial theatres of England looking for his cast. Word had reached him of this young colt doing great things at Birmingham and so together with his producer Oscar Lewenstein he travelled up to watch Finney take on one of Shakespeare's classic roles – Macbeth.

Much had been happening in the life of Finney, not least getting married to the actress Jane Wenham. They'd met at a friend's house while she was appearing at Stratford and it had been a slow-burning courtship. Still, friends were surprised when they finally became engaged, not least because of Finney's own personal feelings about attachments of any kind. 'Personal relationships drain me,' he once confessed. 'And rob me of my concentration and aim and drive and everything. I'm very selfish. I demand a lot of attention and love, but I'm no good at giving it back.' The wedding was a low-key affair and there wasn't even a honeymoon, with Finney set to appear on stage that night.

Having earlier baulked at giving Finney a run out as Coriolanus, fearing he was too young, Bernard Hepton, now in full charge at Birmingham, took the gamble of casting him in the lead of a major production of *Macbeth*, even though he knew the actor was still not mature enough. Finney believed he was not only too young but also miscast, dubbing himself 'a juvenile delinquent in a kilt'. He'd spend hours in front of the make-up mirror to lend his face the age it needed. Conscious of the fact that he was utterly bereft of the life-knowledge required to play such a role, all he could offer was youthful enthusiasm and energy. All such reservations proved groundless, however, as the production was a great success, earning Finney a rave from the *News Chronicle*: 'His Macbeth has an authority truly astonishing in an actor of only 21.'

Paul Williamson appeared in this production as Macduff and rates Finney's performance as 'marvellously animal and savage, but he didn't really respect the verse very much, I seem to remember him tearing it apart. But that was offset by his terrific animal-danger quality.' As Macduff, Williamson had to fight Finney to the death in the famous climactic sword fight. 'They devised an extremely good fight for us and we were using what were almost large machetes, bloody heavy dangerous things. And I had to seize Finney by the head and slash my sword towards him which he then had to just dodge at the last second, with my back to the audience so they couldn't see, and I do remember thinking, God, I must be careful, this is Albert Finney.'

One night the inevitable crisis occurred when Williamson's grip loosened and his sword went flying out into the audience, and both actors stopped dead. 'Luckily it landed in the aisle next to an old lady, but I was then left with no sword and of course I was supposed to win. Fortunately I had a small dagger stuck in my belt which I grabbed as Albie came towards me slowly, looking fierce; it was all faintly ridiculous. I pushed him away and we somehow managed to return to the rehearsed fight and I dispatched him with my dagger. That's the bit of the pretend bit of acting which is really very funny at times.'

After another performance there was a loud rap on Finney's dressing-room door and in walked Charles Laughton, much to Finney's surprise.

'You were bloody awful!' the portly old thesp bellowed. 'But what can you expect at your age?' Finney wasn't put out by such bluntness; he knew Laughton had played the role back in 1934 at the Old Vic and been a terrible flop in it. Laughton introduced Lewenstein and the two men sat down and watched as Finney removed his make-up, including a great whiskery beard. 'And when those whiskers came off,' recalled Lewenstein, 'there was this marvellous young actor revealed to us.'

'My boy!' Laughton piped up. 'After Macbeth an actor needs a drink. And I should know.' A nearby hostelry was located and the men ate and quaffed heartily, before Finney made his bleary way back home. A few days later word reached him that Laughton wanted him for his play. Finney was allowed to leave Birmingham that spring with the good wishes of the entire company.

Laughton's decision to direct as well as star in *The Party* was another blunder since his unorthodox approach never found favour with his cast, especially his habit of speaking in abstracts. 'This scene is blue,' he told one actress, who was left scratching her head. 'And it's Bartók.' It was a difficult play for everyone to get their heads round anyway without Laughton, under pressure no doubt, creating an atmosphere of tension. Ann Lynn, playing Finney's girlfriend, described rehearsals as 'ghastly' and 'hell'. Laughton created no ensemble feel, instead was rather lordly over the company: 'You will bend to my will and my will only,' sort of thing. Yet Finney seemed to glide through it all with his usual self-assurance. 'Albie just seemed to get on with things,' Ann Lynn recalled. 'While the rest of us had suicide pacts about it.'

Everyone liked and got on with Finney. Lynn was particularly drawn to the fact that he was 'extraordinarily mature' for his age. Laughton too had grown extremely attached to the young actor, whom he found wonderfully unactorish; there was a paternal warmth that was unmistakable. Laughton's PA, Ann Rogers, felt their relationship was like that of Falstaff and Hotspur. 'You can tell a lot about what England is like today from Albert Finney,' Laughton told the press.

They shared only one scene in *The Party*, but it was a scene critics declared to be by far the best thing in the play, with Laughton's generally rather fumbling and over-the-top performance more earnest and believable in these exchanges. According to Tynan, here Laughton 'rose like a salmon to the occasion: few young actors have ever got a better performance out of their director'.

Finney did glow in this his West End debut. Michael Caine recalled seeing this production, the principal allure being Laughton's grand return to the stage. 'I enjoyed it, but the reason was a young actor nobody had heard of, who came on and acted Laughton right off the stage. Until that time anybody would have told you this was impossible, but that young unknown did it.'

26
Mayhem, Magic and Method

Out in Hollywood, Connery was relaxing in a hotel room when he received an anonymous telephone call, the voice was menacing, monotone and to the point: 'Get your ass outta town,' it said, then the line went dead. It all seemed like something straight out of a gangster movie, but Connery had no intention of playing the character who ends up shot to ribbons, so packed his bags and relocated to a motel out in the San Fernando valley and laid low. 'I didn't know what I was dealing with, and I didn't see any point in discussing it. Nothing did happen, but it was scary as hell for a while.' Just how had Connery got himself into such a mess?

It had been in the newspapers for weeks, the murder trial of Lana Turner's teenage daughter Cheryl. On 4 April 1958 she'd shoved a carving knife into the belly of Johnny Stompanato, fearing he was about to kill her mother. For weeks Lana had tried to break up with her hoodlum boyfriend; there'd been arguments, fights, but he'd refused to leave. One night Cheryl was eavesdropping outside her mother's bedroom when she overheard Stompanato threaten to cut Lana into little pieces. Cheryl went into the kitchen, grabbed a ten-inch carving knife for protection and was running back to the door at the moment Stompanato stormed through it, walking straight into the blade and collapsing on the floor.

With awe-inspiring heartlessness, Paramount rush-released *Another Time, Another Place* to capitalise on the scandal. The plan backfired when it was resolutely panned. 'Made in England, evidently as part of the current Go-Home-Yank plan,' said the *New York Times*. Connery blamed the movie's failure on an unsatisfactory script that was being rewritten as they went along and lacklustre direction. 'One's intuitive senses were saying that the director was an idiot. I'd no influence or authority at the time, so my protests went unheeded. But at least I learned from it.'

If nothing else, the picture proved Connery had star potential. Here was a relatively inexperienced working-class Scot, who'd only decided to become an actor five years before, holding his own against a screen goddess who ate hunky studs for breakfast – some achievement. Reviewers back home, however, gave him short shrift. The *Sunday Express* referred to him as 'a newcomer to films who will not, I guess, grow old in the industry'.

In the end Cheryl was found not guilty of Stompanato's murder, but during the trial Lana's love/hate letters written to him from London were released in court and splashed all over the press. Some of them detailed her growing friendship with Connery and their nights out together. When Stompanato's boss Mickey Cohen heard about them he wanted revenge; the demented goon had it in his head that his ex-bodyguard's killing had been orchestrated by unseen forces and was out to get those responsible. Connery was one of those in the firing line. It was all rather embarrassing since Connery had come to Hollywood to make a film for that doyen of family wholesomeness Walt Disney.

The film was *Darby O'Gill and the Little People*, a charming fantasy about leprechauns and pots of gold that had been a pet project of Disney's for years. Connery had managed to secure a place amongst a distinguished company of Irish thespians, some of whom hailed from the famous Abbey Theatre in Dublin. He couldn't believe his luck. It was his first major role in a film, the romantic lead no less, and his first trip to Hollywood. On the plane over he didn't realise all the food and drink was free. 'It took me for ages to order something.'

Filming took place at Disney's Burbank studio, with the main exteriors shot on a ranch in California, the fairy-tale landscapes courtesy of matte artists. It was a tough schedule. Director Robert Stevenson, the man later responsible for movies entire generations have grown up with such as *Mary Poppins* and *Bedknobs and Broomsticks*, was a hard task master, insistent on endless takes before he got the performance that satisfied him. In the evenings Connery and the rest of the cast let their hair down, roistering at a local Irish pub, knocking back the Guinness into the early hours. On his days off Connery hired a nifty sports car and drove himself round Burbank and up into the Hollywood hills. Sometimes he'd hang around the set and talk with Disney, a regular visitor, who took an almost fatherly interest in the young actor, taking him on a personal tour of the studio.

While he was in Hollywood, 20th Century Fox invited Connery to enrol in their charm-school programme; he told them where to go in no uncertain fashion. 'If you compromise your independence for any reason, there's not much use living. If you compromise it for something as fleeting as money you are already dead.' His presence in Hollywood did not go unnoticed by other power brokers and during his stay Connery was offered roles in numerous US TV serials, including the lead in *Maverick*. Again he declined. 'They might have earned me a fortune, but they'd have finished me as an actor.' Connery had no desire to be stuck in the rut of playing the same role week in, week out. Besides, he was keen to return to London and he missed Diane, surprised himself at just how much.

On his return friends noticed a change in Connery, many linking that change to his developing and serious relationship with Cilento. He'd hang around the pubs and clubs with his mates a little less frequently, while others felt a distance opening up. Connery was evolving both from a personal perspective and as an actor. On Diane's prompting he'd joined a movement class run by the Swede Yat Malmgreen, a former dancer with the Kurt Jooss ballet company. His hulking physique had hitherto helped him win tough-guy roles, now he used his body as a tool to help create and shape a character. Malmgreen's teaching method was all about expressing the inner state of a character through movement, an extension, it might be said, of the acting technique established by Konstantin Stanislavsky.

Connery found these classes, his first brush with formal dramatic training, a revelation and was invited by Malmgreen to join a small group of his best pupils to undertake the theory. These weren't physical lessons, more a discussion group where people wrote about and analysed the technique in relation to how it helped them in their acting. 'We used to meet I think on a Sunday,' remembers Ann Beach. 'And Sean was very good at the theory; I think he was top of the class.'

Since their first meeting Diane had fascinated Connery, while his effect on her could be put down to one thing, masculinity. 'Pure male authority. Absolutely nothing like all the actors I'd met before.' When it came time to meet the folks, Diane plopped down on a chair in that flat in Fountainbridge and kicked her shoes off as if the place were her own. While Sean and his dad popped round to the local for a few bevies, Diane and Effie sat chatting for hours. 'A wee smasher,' was Mrs Connery's verdict. Both parents suspected how special Diane was to their son, who, while living at home, had kept his romances as secret as possible, rarely bringing a girlfriend back to meet them.

Effie recognised in Diane a spirit very much like her Tommy: they were alike in so many ways, in mood and outlook. Like Connery, Diane was mistrustful of the press and the superficial aspects of stardom. Both were strong personalities, temperamental, but genuine. 'I'm a rebel,' she once said. 'I hate conforming.' Diane was said to be rude, a by-product of her Aussie straightforwardness, unable to hide her forthright dislike for some people, though always to their face rather than behind their back – another Connery trait. Both had a quality for honesty and gave prime importance to the real things of life, they didn't waste any time on those stupid little idiosyncrasies that can be characteristic of show business. They were made for each other, or so it seemed, but Diane didn't want to marry him. In fact, 'I didn't want to marry anyone. I'd just been through it and it hadn't worked.'

Diane saw marriage as a stifling institution, an act where one person claims ownership over another. More the traditionalist, Connery was sure they could make a go of it. But he was going to need all his powers of persuasion.

27

When Hellraisers Collide

By far the pinnacle of O'Toole's time at Bristol was his performance as Hamlet. Critics dubbed it the 'angry young Hamlet', with obvious reference to what was going on post-Osborne. Few who saw it ever forgot the experience, Sheila Allen amongst them. 'He was a roaring boy, Peter. Life was for living. And us girls, we used to think he got off scot free. There were late nights, and the late turning-up for rehearsals, or not turning-up at rehearsal at all. They were perpetual. He'd go to bed plastered and not hear the alarm go off or maybe he hadn't set it, and he'd be full of courtesy and apology on arrival. But we adored him. And then one day, I was sitting in the back of the stalls for the opening night of his *Hamlet* thinking, well, here goes, let's see, and I could swear that ectoplasm was coming out of him on that very first night; it was just extraordinary.'

In May 1958 Bristol staged an unremarkable production of an unremarkable play, James Forsyth's *The Pier*. O'Toole's role was prominent, as they were beginning to be by then, and at rehearsals he was struck by a new actor who'd joined the company, a fellow Irishman and, as O'Toole would soon discover, a kindred spirit – Richard Harris. It was to be the beginning of a lifelong friendship between the two men and countless marathon booze binges. Harris described this period as 'golden days. We kept each other up half the time, we never slept. It was days of chat and yarn-spinning and great, legendary boozing.'

During every intermission Harris and O'Toole propped up the bar of the local, managing to get back just in time for curtain-up in the second half. One matinee they overstayed their welcome and a stagehand burst into the saloon bar screaming, 'You're on!' Both men leaped to their feet and made it back into the theatre in fifteen seconds flat. O'Toole was the faster. Crashing into the wings, he hurtled past the backstage crew and tumbled onto the stage, almost falling head first into the audience. A woman in the front row sniffed his breath. 'My God, he's pissed drunk.' O'Toole lifted his head. 'You think this is bad, madam, wait till you see the other fella.'

After one mighty bender they returned to Harris's miserable bedsit totally rat-arsed and starving. In the cupboards there was nothing to be found, but in the fridge was a solitary pork chop; ancient it was, clearly it had been there a long time. They smelled it, looked at it, and thought better of it, so threw it through a window and went to bed. Come the morning they left the squat and under the window from which they'd thrown the chop was a chewed bone and a dead dog.

They also shared a passion for rugby and went to Twickenham whenever they could. 'O'Toole was a poet and a warrior,' said Harris. 'I loved every moment with him.' One prestigious bash they attended was presided over by Harris's father-in-law Lord Ogmore, who also happened to be president of the London Welsh Society. The room was, of course, full of Welshmen and Harris's continual interruptions of the speeches with cries of 'What about the Irish, then?' and dancing with O'Toole led to threats from society members to resign unless Ogmore ejected the pair. His Lordship duly complied.

Other laddish japes included the time both were competing for the affections of the same woman. After a night of drinking they said their farewells and went their separate ways, only to bump into each other twenty minutes later outside said maiden's block of flats. The game was up and so a deal was struck. O'Toole would try to smooth talk his way into her bedroom using the intercom, while Harris would climb the drainpipe up to the sixth floor and try to attract her attention that way. First come, first served, as it were. 'I nearly killed myself with my mountaineering efforts,' Harris later recalled. 'But eventually reached her balcony and peered in. Peter had literally that moment walked into the room to claim his prize. As they headed to the bedroom he looked back and saw my dishevelled figure and winked. I nearly fell down just from laughing.'

There is another version of this story, told from O'Toole's point of view. His memory was that both men dared each other to climb the drainpipe. O'Toole got up it first and, looking down, saw Harris struggling to navigate his way up. 'He must not have had my experience with drainpipes growing up in Limerick,' said O'Toole. When Harris began his ascent, about four storeys up the pipe broke away from the wall, leaving him dangling in mid-air. O'Toole helpfully summoned the authorities. Staring down from the balcony, the girl by his side, O'Toole watched as a patrol car arrived and the boys in blue manhandled Harris inside. 'Officers,' roared O'Toole. 'Arrest that drunken Irishman, he was trying to break into our home!'

Another time they drove down to a big seaside resort in O'Toole's rickety old car for a mini break, hooked up in a grand hotel and booked the presidential suite. They drank all weekend and went nuts on room service until finally Harris came to his senses: 'We've got to leave now, Peter. How much money have you got?' Nothing. Harris had nothing, either. They couldn't pay the bill. It was bucketing with rain outside, and the beaches were stormswept and dangerous. Harris had a brainwave. 'Take your clothes off, Peter, all of them.' Harris did the same. They rolled them up into a tight ball and threw the lot out of the window into a side street. 'Come on, let's pretend we're going for a swim.' On went some towels and they casually walked through the lobby towards the main doors. The manageress, a stern-faced woman, looked up from her work.

Harris smiled, 'We're going for a swim.'

The woman looked incredulous. 'A swim, in this! The waves are ten feet tall out there, the currents . . .'

'Yes we're going for a swim, we're Irish, we're tough. We can handle it.'

Once out of sight they quickly retrieved their clothes and made a bolt for it. Years later Harris was on a one-man concert tour and arrived in the very same resort to find that his promotor had booked him into that very same hotel. 'I recognised the lobby. Oh my God. And I signed my name and it was the same woman behind the desk. I hurriedly finished and made my way to the lift when, "Oh, Mr Harris?" I said, "Yes?" "We thought you and Mr O'Toole drowned."'

Harris was only at the Bristol Old Vic for that one production, which is probably the reason that the theatre is still standing; it probably couldn't have survived a whole season with those two. But their friendship carried on. 'They used to meet up every now and then and say, we can't believe we're still here,' Elizabeth recalls. 'They did burn the candle at both ends and in the middle. And enjoyed every minute of it. They were just like wild, naughty characters, but they weren't vicious. I don't think there was any hate, nothing malicious, the side-effects would be accidental, and half the time they wouldn't remember them. And when they were told about their exploits they'd be very contrite, but then the next day they'd go off and do exactly the same thing.'

Harris's Bristol career was cut short by an offer of a small role in what would be his first film, *Alive and Kicking*, a sub-Ealing comedy about the residents of an old people's home dissatisfied with their lot who abscond and set up an internationally successful knitting business. It sounds absurd, and it was. Director Cyril Frankel, when casting the film, recalled having seen Harris while still at LAMDA in a student production. 'And I came away with a deep impression of his quality as an actor, so when I was doing *Alive and Kicking* a little later I felt, well, I could use him. He had such a powerful personality and presence that he just absolutely stood out from the other students. It was his inner energy. He was a very instinctive actor; it came from somewhere very deep.'

Elizabeth also recalls going to see Harris at one of these student shows, maybe even the one Frankel attended. 'It was Chekhov's *The Cherry Orchard*, I think, and Richard was playing the gardener who kept coming through, and he seemed to be coming through an awful lot, maybe because all our eyes were glued to him.'

Frankel, who was interested in transcendental meditation and discovered Maharishi Mahesh Yogi long before the Beatles made him famous in the sixties, always looked for an almost spiritual intensity in the actors he worked with. Very few had it, this indefinable factor which many refer to as 'star quality'. Frankel saw it more as an intense human energy that's either inside a person or not, and the director's job as being to harness it and bring it out. 'If you're going to go out on a stage and face an audience you have to have this energy to capture them, and Richard had huge belief in himself, from the beginning, a great confidence. I thought he was a young Spencer Tracy.'

Of course, Frankel was already conscious of Harris's hellraiser reputation, 'so I had to surround him with people who were aware of it and to hold him back if necessary'. And although Harris didn't think much of the film at all he got on well with Frankel. 'Richard was highly appreciative of what I did for him. And years later when we met by chance walking along Piccadilly he came up to me and just embraced me.'

28

Shaw at the Court

For months now Robert Shaw had been living on acting scraps, facing the ignominy of playing the guest baddie in historical TV action shows like the one that had so blighted his career. This one was *William Tell* and its star, Conrad Phillips, had been at RADA with Shaw so knew all about his competitive nature. In one scene Shaw's character, in his quest to usurp Tell as resistance leader, challenges him to a fight which he is supposed to end up losing. 'So we rehearsed it,' Phillips remembers, all too clearly. 'And reached the point where Robert's panting on the ground beaten and I'm waiting for his line, "I've had enough. You win." He didn't say it. He wouldn't say it. He point blank refused to concede verbally that I had won the fight. I made a mock fuss, saying that he ought to stick to the script, but he still refused. As this was typical Robert, I laughed and went along with him on it.'

The climax to the episode had Tell capturing Shaw's villain after a treacherous deed and ordering him to be taken away and hanged. 'Robert suggested we cut this line,' says Phillips. 'Grinning, he said, "Don't you see, boy, I could come back and be a regular character. Be good for you, boy, to have a strong opposition. If I'm hanged, there's no chance." I grinned back at him, "No chance, Robert."'

Next, his agent sent him to meet director Cy Endfield, who was planning another testosterone-charged picture with his *Hell Drivers* star Stanley Baker. This one was called *Sea Fury* and was about rivalry between deep-sea tug boats. Suitably impressed, Endfield cast Shaw in just a minor part amidst an interesting cast that also featured veteran Hollywood slugger Victor McLaglen. In Baker, the undisputed macho star of British films at the time, Shaw found a willing partner in his idiotic challenges and sporting duels. At one party all the guests were in the top-floor bedroom watching the two maniacs challenge each other to see how long they could hang by their fingertips from the outside balcony before one gave up.

Fed up with what he was having to feed off as an actor, Shaw looked at what was happening in theatre and liked most of all what George Devine had been doing at the Royal Court: 'For me it was the most interesting theatre in England.' Shaw had worked with Devine at Stratford and no doubt given him gyp, so sat down and wrote a letter of apology for being such a pain to work with and enthusing about Devine's splendid achievements; essentially, it was a begging letter. 'I realise I had a reputation for being a difficult actor,' he wrote. 'But I've matured a bit and what with a wife and four children if you've got any work I promise not to be any trouble.'

Within the week Devine hauled Shaw down to Sloane Square and asked him to read for their new production. He was hired on the spot. The play was *Live Like Pigs* by John Arden, who had come to the attention of Devine and been commissioned to write specifically for the Court. Born in Barnsley, Arden had studied architecture at Cambridge and *Live Like Pigs*, about the conflict that results when a family of travellers are removed from a caravan site and forced into a council house next door to a 'respectable' family, was his first full-length play. It would establish him as 'The British Brecht', in the opinion of the *Guardian* newspaper. But it was not a happy production.

There were problems with the set, a large cumbersome house built on the stage that didn't work and frictions amongst the cast. The veteran Wilfrid Lawson, 'who was a very fine actor but he was on the booze too much', says Arden, went around complaining that the cast were 'acting like buggery'. But worst of all, it just failed to bring the punters in. The critics too didn't quite know what to make of the play. There was a hail of criticism from the left, complaining about Arden's attack on the welfare state, and then, feeling ignored, the right had a mighty dig, about the apparent endorsement of anarchy and immorality.

This was all grist to the mill for Shaw, who fell in love with the Royal Court; at last he felt he was doing real valid work and was an equal member of a company. He felt fully rehabilitated as an actor. Margaretta D'Arcy played opposite Shaw every night in *Live Like Pigs* and also happened to be married to John Arden. She doesn't recall any of the usual Shaw antics going on, the play-acting of his Stratford days appeared to have been laid to rest. 'I think Bob fitted in very well at the Royal Court. There was no sense of him lording it over the rest of us. He'd found his niche.'

It was a terrific cast: Nigel Davenport, Alfred Lynch and Stratford Johns. Shaw was particularly joyous about working with Lawson, who thought nothing of nipping to the pub next door not just before or after but often *during* a performance to down a swift pint and a whisky. A theatrical character, revered by the likes of Finney and O'Toole, Lawson was an alcoholic but amazingly remained in work, despite the perils his habit induced. 'He was nearly always drunk,' recalls Royal Court stage-hand Michael Seymour. 'Brilliant as an actor but totally unpredictable in his performance. There was a sequence in the second act where he gets into bed and would frequently lie there farting loudly.'

Shaw recalled visiting the pub with Lawson shortly before the evening performance and watching the veteran drink himself almost insensible. There were antics galore with Lawson. He'd taken a particular dislike to one of the actresses, whose main scene required her to make a grand speech then exit through a bathroom door. One night the actress was giving it her all when the audience was diverted by a large puddle of liquid seeping onto the stage. Lawson was behind the prop door taking a piss.

During the run Arden took quite a shine to Shaw and they often chatted during rehearsals. One afternoon Shaw opened up to the play-wright about an incident that had taken place during his days at Stratford, when he was performing in *Hamlet*; it was a lowly part but at the same time he was understudying the King. 'And he got a message at his digs one morning that the actor playing the King was ill and couldn't perform, and he was to play the part that evening. And Bob suddenly realised he hadn't learned a word of it, this was early in the production and he hadn't bothered. He said to me, "I ran to the theatre actually crying all the way because I saw my career collapsing completely." And once he got into the theatre the first person he saw was the actor who was playing the King who said, "I'm not going to let any of you young fellas take my part." And Bob thought it was a miracle.'

Arden and Margaretta invited Shaw for dinner one evening, when the main topic of conversation was the book he was writing. 'He made it very clear that he was more interested in being an author than an actor,' says Arden. 'Then his wife kept ringing him up and he told her all sorts of lies on our telephone about where he was and what he was doing. I've never heard anything quite so blatant. He was having a funny relationship with her. It was quite shameless, considering he was using our telephone. And then he made a joke of it afterwards; he was a very strange man.'

This odd episode is also remembered by Margaretta. 'Shaw told us that he had a compulsion to lie to his wife. What we have to consider is that maybe when he was in our house he was preparing for his role as Blackmouth in *Live Like Pigs*, who in the play is very much an outsider and would have lied and all the rest of it. Bob gave a great performance, I think precisely because of this outsider quirk, and a kind of consciousness that he knew he was an outsider in real life.'

Some of Shaw's notices, however, were not all that good; he was said to have been too overpowering for the rest of the cast. But Arden, like his wife, enjoyed Shaw's performance. 'He had an extraordinary voice, that was the thing I liked about him. Although it was sometimes a little difficult to understand what he was saying because his diction was quite peculiar. I sometimes wonder if he was rather like what Henry Irving would have sounded like; he too was always accused of having a very weird diction. It wasn't anything to do with Shaw's accent. He spoke what you call educated English in ordinary life. It was his theatrical technique. He was a Cornishman, of course, and had what you might call an alien quality amongst ordinary English people; because after all the Cornish are a different ethnic breed from most of us.'

Arden continued to write for the Court, becoming part of a new generation of young English dramatists gathered together by George Devine. But although the place has been much lauded for nurturing writing talent, Arden does not look back favourably upon his time there.

'The atmosphere there was fairly awful in my view. George was always under terrible pressure. He wanted to have a repertoire of good new plays and modern classics and all the time he was being pressured by the Board to put on something that would make money. They wanted successes but they didn't know how to get them. They wanted plays that were transferable to the West End, and a lot of the plays that George chose, including my own, were not transferable. The Board was always objecting. Ronald Duncan, a member of the Board, said in a loud voice after the first night of *Live Like Pigs*, and I heard him say it, he was in the audience about three seats away from me, he said to his companion; "This is exactly the sort of play they ought not to be putting on here and I told them so."'

29

Woodfall Rides the New Wave

With great fanfare, Olivier had taken *The Entertainer* to Broadway, where after the success of *Look Back in Anger* it met with critical and audience acclaim. While there Olivier decided to organise a good old cockney knees-up. It was a midnight cruise up the River Hudson, on the menu jellied eels and fish and chips served in newspaper. Osborne and Mary Ure, now man and wife, attended amidst a throng of some 200 party-goers and during a particularly lively rendition of 'Knees Up Mother Brown' the playwright bumped into Richard Burton. The two men had never met before and were immediately drawn to each other. Burton couldn't have failed to have noticed the dramatic changes happening back home instigated by the softly spoken gentleman before him, while Osborne was only too acutely aware of the criticism levelled at this mad dervish of a Welshman for having deserted the British stage and sold out to Hollywood, albeit the same man who once told 20th Century Fox to stuff their million-dollar contract to play at London's Old Vic for forty-five quid a week.

Osborne told Burton of his plan to turn *Look Back in Anger* into a feature but so far had faced shocking indifference from the British film industry; nobody was prepared to put a penny into it. How would he fancy taking a crack at Jimmy Porter? That was bound to perk up interest in Wardour Street. Burton agreed to the idea immediately.

Another new personality had entered Osborne's life, an enterprising Canadian impresario by the name of Harry Saltzman, and together with Tony Richardson they'd created their own film production company, Woodfall, named after the street on which Osborne lived with Mary Ure, and intended *Look Back* to be their first venture. Saltzman was an obvious bedfellow; a fanatical enthusiast of the play, he and Osborne had become great friends and together they'd wined, dined and caroused in the best restaurants and nightspots in New York and Paris. Though he'd failed to make any headway into the world of cinema, Saltzman was nevertheless a born showman and wheeler-dealer; most of all he was a visionary and sensed that a film of *Look Back* could be the start of something, as a few years later he sensed the same thing about the James Bond novels of Ian Fleming. Osborne would later say that without Saltzman, Woodfall would never have got off the ground.

Woodfall's policy ran parallel to that of the Royal Court, a basically naturalistic style, a sort of writer's cinema. 'To prove that good films, ones that showed British life as it really is, could be made,' in Osborne's words. To some extent this policy had already found expression two years before with the Free Cinema Movement, a group of would-be film-makers consisting chiefly of Lindsay Anderson, Tony Richardson and Karel Reisz, all of whom believed that the British cinema industry, like the nation's theatre, required a swift boot up the arse. And so they took their cameras out onto the streets, capturing a new naturalistic and unscripted look at England in three groundbreaking short films and documentaries. 'Free Cinema had a manifesto,' says Walter Lassally, who worked with them as a cameraman. 'It pointed out that the films were free in the sense that their authors were free to do what they liked, there weren't any pressures, either from front office or backers or anything of that kind. These films were made outside of the system, it was true independence and very unusual because there weren't many films of that kind being made in Britain or elsewhere in the world either.'

These shorts were shown one evening at the National Film Theatre back in early 1956 under the banner 'Free Cinema', a phrase coined by Anderson, who defined its aims as: 'A belief in the importance of people and the significance of the everyday.' Much to everyone's surprise the event drew a massive crowd who queued round the block; hundreds more were turned away. Its success led to similar programmes over the next few years. 'None of the people who participated and made those films were in the film industry,' stresses Lassally. 'We were trying to get

in. Tony Richardson had just started at the Royal Court and he was the
first of the directors represented in the first Free Cinema programme
who actually made it into the film industry. The opening of *Look Back
in Anger* at the Royal Court, that is really the key event that triggered
the progress into the film industry proper of the people concerned with
Free Cinema.' Indeed, Richardson was determined to use the stage
success of Osborne's play as a Trojan horse to break into the movie
business, which he viewed as smug, a closed shop and opposed to new
directors, and when Burton signed on they were up and running.

Osborne insisted, against resistance from Saltzman, that Richardson
be installed as *Look Back*'s director despite his having no experience whatsoever in features. Osborne knew he was the perfect choice, in his words,
'to lead Woodfall's opening assault on the suburban vapidity of British
film-making'. Burton too seized on the pioneering spirit of the enter-
prise, waiving his usual Hollywood salary. Osborne believed the Welsh
dragon took the part in order to appear current and restore a flagging
career. 'His most recent films, which had concentrated in CinemaScope
on his splendid knees beneath Roman kilts, had failed to establish his
surety as an international star.' He was also on his best behaviour, except
the time a startled actress came across him having sex in his dressing
room.

The screen version of *Look Back in Anger* was filmed in the autumn
of 1958. The part of Cliff was taken by Gary Raymond, who'd been at
RADA with Bates and all the rest and had stayed in touch with them,
going to Bristol to see O'Toole, popping over to Birmingham to watch
Finney. He also saw Bates in *Look Back* and remembers thinking how
he never had the sense that it was going to be THE play of the age. An
opinion that changed when he appeared in one of its stage revivals.
'When I played in it I thought it was wonderful. I thought the vitriol
and the power with which Osborne used words was remarkable.'

Raymond found Osborne, who was a regular visitor to the London
locations, a fascinating dichotomy. 'He was a mild sort of man when
you met him, not a flaring tearaway; he saved that for the pen.' Ann
Beach found this too when she appeared in his play *Under Plain Covers*
in 1962 at the Royal Court. 'The extraordinary thing about John Osborne

was he had this reputation of being an angry young man, but in person he was absolutely the opposite. He liked to think he was this angry young man. When he was interviewed and if you read his autobiographies he behaved that way, but actually in person he was lovely, a very sweet gentleman, quite the opposite of what he was portrayed as.' He wasn't to be messed with, though. Jonathan Miller was making his debut as director on *Under Plain Covers* and along with Ann and the rest of the cast had arrived at the conclusion that there was a particular section in the play that would be better omitted. 'Just leave it out,' Miller told his actors at rehearsal. 'He won't notice.' The next day's run-through was minus the passage. Osborne was in the stalls. 'Hey, hey, you missed out that bit,' he shrieked. 'He knew his play backwards,' says Ann. 'Every line was sacrosanct.'

The *Look Back* shoot progressed smoothly. Richardson on his first film was full of beans, he'd taken to it like the proverbial duck to water. 'He was wonderful,' confirms Raymond. 'He loved the whole business. He had power business breakfasts before anybody else, it seemed to me. He just loved it all. There was no sense from him of, oh God, what am I doing here, none at all. It was just something to be enjoyed.'

The film would end up a commercial flop, however, its failure unfairly put at Burton's door by Saltzman, who believed the star was miscast and at thirty-three too old to play Osborne's angry young man. Raymond didn't agree and had enjoyed working with him enormously. 'He was mad about actors and acting, Richard. Great fun to be with, very outgoing. But even then he was obsessed about the commercial side of the acting business, what could be made out of it. Richard told me once, "I sometimes get more pleasure out of a company report than a script." He really said that.'

Meanwhile, on Broadway, *Look Back* had just come to a close after 407 performances. Bates, however, had jumped ship early. 'I got stale,' he later confessed. 'Long runs are very bad for an actor, you just stagnate, and that's death in this business. I lived with *Look Back in Anger* for two bloody years, and it almost ruined me. Well, actually it made me, so I can't really complain about that!'

Fed up with the play, he'd also lost inspiration for Cliff and that's probably why he declined to appear in the film version. He also desperately missed England and so returned to appear in the British stage premiere of Eugene O'Neill's *Long Day's Journey Into Night*, which he'd seen on Broadway and been knocked out by. Bates brought an edgy emotional tension to the role of Edmund, the consumptive younger son of a tyrannical alcoholic father, played by Anthony Quayle. It was heavy stuff, certainly Bates's most demanding role yet and performances often left him physically drained.

The play opened at the Globe Theatre in September and the whole Bates family came to the first night. Peter Wyngarde, if he was there, was certainly kept at a distance, perhaps not even introduced. The relationship was still a secret from his family and the public in general. Recently they'd bought a delightful cottage in rural Kent as a sort of refuge; what little time for relaxation they had was spent there.

If one could relax in Wyngarde's presence, of course. By far, Wyngarde was the governing influence in the relationship, on a mission, or so it seemed, to toughen Bates up, to teach him about the business end of the profession. He told him what books to read, introduced him to important producers and writers, becoming for want of a better word a Svengali figure. Bates willingly took on this passive role, but quickly feared he might become utterly dominated. Later he'd recognise his own willing passivity and despise himself for it.

30
The Boy from Hull

Cameras were still rolling on *Look Back in Anger* when a young lad from Hull arrived at RADA in September 1958. His name was Tom Courtenay. Not much had changed in the old place since the heady days of O'Toole, Finney and Bates. Despite John Fernald's influence some teachers were still very much of the old tradition, as if John Osborne had been merely an aberration. There was still an over-emphasis on the 'proper' voice, scolding those who mispronounced their vowels or exhibited poor articulation. It thoroughly pissed Courtenay off. 'I spoke standard English at my grammar school in Hull, but at RADA they tried to improve it, so I put on the Yorkshire as thick as possible.'

It was as though the old mentality hadn't changed at all. 'We still had received pronunciation and the iambic pentameter and voice production lessons,' recalls Derek Fowlds, who befriended Courtenay at RADA. 'There was a bone prop which I used to have in my mouth to get the right vowels. We all had to do that. You clipped it in between the teeth and it was supposed to set your mouth in the right position to say the vowels. Now I wouldn't get a job in *EastEnders* even though I'm a working-class boy.'

While the mentality hadn't much changed, the pupil intake had; RADA was losing its middle-classness. The bulk of the teachers may not have been influenced by the revolutionary happenings in theatre but the people who wanted to go there had. 'When I joined RADA O'Toole, Finney and Bates had just left,' says Fowlds. 'And they were our heroes, really.' Actually Courtenay was rather disappointed, he'd rather hoped to have seen cravat-wearing toffs calling each other 'darling'; instead many of the students were just like him, including fellow northerner John Thaw, the son of a lorry driver from Manchester. The only students who came close to being of a classy sort were Sarah Miles and Edward Fox.

Tom Courtenay was born on 25 February 1937 and grew up in a small terraced house right next to the fish docks in Hull where his father Thomas worked painting and cleaning up the trawlers before they went back out to sea. It was lowly paid – 'The only way he could have earned less than he did was not to have worked at all,' his son used to say – so there weren't many luxuries in his early life, largely because his parents never wanted to borrow money or buy goods on the never-never. Until the house had a bath installed the young Tom was dunked in a zinc tub in front of the kitchen fire and always preferred using the outside lav in his grandparents' house nearby, 'because the newspaper hung in neatly torn sections on a piece of string'.

Thomas was filled with a desire to give his son the opportunities that he'd never had, but at the same time curiously begrudged him those chances and their relationship was consequently one of bitterness and anger. Far from the physical type, never as rough and tough as the other boys in the area, little Tom could never stand up for himself in playground rumbles, and it was this softness in his son that turned Thomas's stomach. 'What the hell's up with you?' he'd ask whenever his son came home in tears. 'You soft little sod.' It got so the beatings Tom took from the local bullies were as nothing compared with the unforgiving scorn he received when he got home.

His mother Annie was the complete opposite. She had an artistic bent but, alas, not the education to express on paper the myriad stories floating around her head, which she lamented all her life. Instead, though physically fragile, she worked long hours at home making heavy nets for the trawlers out of thick hard twine that arrived on huge wooden spools. To relieve the drudgery she and Tom would sing together or read aloud from books. Courtenay was grateful to her: 'The yearning to express myself I got directly from my mother, gift-wrapped.' She was an inspiration, 'a queen amongst shit', Courtenay's uncle would say.

As the UK's third-busiest port Hull was often the target of German bombers during the war who, after raids on its west-coast counterpart

Liverpool, were fond of dumping any leftover ordnance on the city before heading home. Courtenay was just a kid then and with no back garden, hence no air-raid shelter, would hide under the stairs with the family during raids then afterwards meet up with his friends to scramble over bomb sites looking for shrapnel.

The docks survived the battering of the Luftwaffe and Thomas continued to work there, as had generation after generation of Courtenays. This was an age when working folk never left the area where they were born and raised. Ordinarily it would have been taken for granted that Tom would end up as a stevedore too, but his mother wouldn't hear of such a thing for her sensitive lad with a gift for learning. Education would be his way out; the chance she never had.

Her belief in him was rewarded when Courtenay passed his eleven-plus, one of only two who did so in a class of fifty. So instead of staying at secondary school, where he'd be moulded into becoming just another navvy, it was off to the local grammar for a better class of education, endless possibilities and broadened horizons. It also for the first time made him conscious of his working-class status as the school's population consisted largely of lower-middle-class children. His parents couldn't afford to buy him the full uniform, just the cap and tie, and he was made to bloody well feel grateful for it, too, as he'd been made to feel grateful for most things, especially going to grammar school, even though that had been achieved by his sweat alone. Years later when Courtenay performed *Billy Liar* on stage there was a speech about gratitude, about what he was getting and the cost of it. It was so close to home that some nights he couldn't finish it. Finney, from whom he'd taken over in the role, came to see him one night and afterwards backstage said, 'That grateful speech, you don't get to the end of it, do you?' Courtenay shook his head, 'No, I get choked up.' The emotions were still raw, of his father reprimanding him that all his friends were now working on the fish dock earning money, 'and you're still at school'.

Seemingly out of the blue, Courtenay had what he later described as 'an absurd notion' to become an actor. Its early flowering was in school assembly, when he'd usually be asked to read the lesson because he did so more beautifully than anyone else. Here was something the big lads so good on the rugger field couldn't do, they'd stammer or clam up. 'The school hall would begin to fill. I would see all the girls gazing up at me. And I loved it.' It was his first audience.

No one from Hull docks became an actor, it was 'unthinkable', but he felt at home up on the stage and didn't have a nerve in his body when performing in school plays. After a trip to the theatre which had a juvenile in the cast not much older than Tom, he said, 'I'm better than that' to his dad as they were walking home. 'Don't you be so bloody clever,' Thomas senior shot back with a withering glance. 'Acting the goat is all you'll ever do.'

Having passed his exams with flying colours, Courtenay desperately wanted to pursue acting but felt obliged to his parents to further his education, so chose to read English Literature at University College London, a shrewd move since the building was in the same street as RADA and while there he could watch the drama students go in and out and see if he might fit in one day.

It was October 1955 when Courtenay set off from home with suitcase in hand, giving his mum Annie a hug and a kiss, both their hearts breaking. He shared digs in Muswell Hill with a school chum; the rent was cheap because the only bath was in the kitchen, though Courtenay was used to that. Miscast from the beginning at UCL, Courtenay kept despair at bay by joining the university's dramatic society. He also attended theatre as much as possible, going to the Old Vic, watching John Neville in *Julius Caesar* on his first weekend in London, sitting up in the cheap seats. After that he watched them all: Gielgud, Edith Evans and Sybil Thorndike.

During his first year Courtenay appeared in every production the drama society staged and his reputation as an actor of note spread quickly throughout the university campus. 'Everybody thought he was something quite special,' recalled fellow English student and later noted television screenwriter Andrew Davies. 'Tom went through a short James Dean phase.' In *Rebel Without a Cause* there was a scene in which Dean rolled a beer bottle across his fevered brow. 'I remember Tom doing that, only with a milk bottle,' said Davies.

In his second year Courtenay appeared in a substantial role in the drama society's production of *The Duchess of Malfi*. The director had a friend who was a student at RADA and invited him to see the play. Chatting later over drinks, Courtenay was offered words of encouragement: the director's friend said he could see no difficulty in him gaining admission to the academy. 'Though there might be plenty for the teachers to work on.' Undeterred, Courtenay knew he was raw; wasn't that the point in going? 'Actually there's a wonderful boy at RADA at the moment,' the friend went on. 'He's very charismatic. Strangely enough, you have something in common with him. You're not at all like him temperamentally and I can't really say why you remind me of him. But you do. I suppose you could be his younger brother.'

Fascinated, Courtenay asked, 'What's his name?'

'Finney. Albert Finney.'

Increasingly Courtenay began to apply himself less and less to his work – 'spending a year studying *Beowulf* seemed pointless' – and exerting more energy on drama. Finally he took the plunge and applied to RADA, receiving a date for an audition. But there was something very nasty on the horizon – National Service. In his mind he'd already wasted nearly three years at UCL and couldn't stomach the thought of wasting two more in the army. Courtenay sought advice from a doctor at UCL as to how to avoid it. The doctor agreed to help, and a letter was written on Courtenay's behalf declaring him emotionally unstable. Courtenay was excused.

Relieved, he turned up at RADA. For him it was not just for any old audition; 'this audition was for a lifetime'. In the small theatre, barely able to contain his nerves, he performed before seven people sitting some ten rows back in the gloom. As he spoke one of them leaned forward to speak to the others. Courtenay instinctively felt it was John Fernald, and that he liked what he was seeing.

Back out in the foyer the sergeant at the front desk asked if he wouldn't mind returning the following week to try for a scholarship. 'Does that mean I've got in?' asked Courtenay. 'I suppose it does.' A speech from *Hamlet* did the trick and the scholarship was his. He wasn't so lucky over at UCL, where he failed to get his degree. His parents were devastated by the news and Courtenay always felt a twinge of guilt over it;

they'd sacrificed so much to help him and this must have seemed like a kick in the teeth.

The long wait to get into RADA had sapped a lot of the confidence Courtenay exuded after leaving school and as a consequence he felt uncertain in his first term. He perked up later on when one of the new intake of teachers took a special interest in him and was full of encouragement. He'd also begun to make friends, including Derek Fowlds. 'I remember the first time we met because he was in a term below me, but we eventually caught up. I recognised Tom's talent at RADA. Even then he was a wonderful actor. He gets into the skin of whatever part he's playing and Tom would always make the part fit him and his strengths. And we've met off and on over the years and I've been a great admirer and a great fan. I knew that he would have a brilliant career and he has.'

31
Shake Hands with the Devil

Thanks to his film contract, money was now rolling into the Harris coffers so fast that he and Elizabeth no longer had to live on stews made of Oxo cubes and old carrots. He was able to pay off all their debts and furnish the flat to near-luxury standard. There was also a new propensity to brawl as frequently as he was able; and to go off on booze benders. One evening he awoke in a prison cell and when asked by the desk sergeant why he'd been arrested Harris replied, 'I haven't a fucking clue.' Harris was building up a mighty immune system to the hard stuff and not caring about the consequences.

Friends noticed that his temperament was starting to change and that, when unleashed, the Harris fury had become deeply frightening and something to behold. There's a story that when he returned home late one day tanked up, Elizabeth made a perfectly justifiable remark about his condition only to see him turn into a raging berserker. Grabbing a nearby wardrobe, he lifted it above his head and threw it at her. How long could such a marriage last? 'Everything would be going along swimmingly,' Elizabeth says of that time. 'And then for no apparent reason to you things would change and he'd be absolutely outraged at something that you couldn't see. It was part of his personality, and that never left him.'

The overbearing worry and concern about her future with Richard wasn't helped when she fell pregnant. But when she gave birth in August to Damian, Harris was overjoyed. Attending the birth he fainted and was dispatched to a nearby pub, on medicinal grounds for once, to recover. Swiftly returning, 'he just sat and stared and stared at his son', Elizabeth recalls. Then one of the nurses persuaded him to pick the child up. 'They both looked so vulnerable,' says Elizabeth.

In the end the couple would have three boys. 'And Richard was besotted and out of his mind about them. But he was never a nine-to-five father; then again we were never living a nine-to-five life. The boys always knew that Richard loved them and he was there for them, not every evening with bedtime stories, but where it counted you could always rely on him. If you were down, if you were in real trouble, Richard would be there for you. Half the time he got you in that position, but he'd always come and get you out.'

In September the young family flew to Dublin, where Harris had been cast by Michael Anderson in his film *Shake Hands with the Devil*. At his interview Harris had been blasé in the extreme, an act perhaps, then again maybe not. Strolling in, he'd told the director, 'Well, it's nice to see all you film folks, but I want to tell you up front, I don't do film, I only do stage work.'

Anderson looked up, puzzled. 'So why did you come?'

'I wanted to see what you was all about, you know, you hear a lot about films these days. I've read the script, it's a good script but no, I don't think so.' With that Harris started to walk towards the door when he turned round and said. 'Who's in it?'

'James Cagney,' said Anderson.

'I'll do it.'

The part was an IRA gun-runner and because the film was being shot in Ireland its subject matter caused a whiff of controversy. Though Harris was raw and unfamiliar with film acting technique, Anderson recognised in him a spark of talent. 'He had such a screen personality and put in gestures and little method things that weren't in the script but stood out a mile. He was unpredictable in a scene; you never knew quite what he was going to do, which made him so exciting. He was so different to someone like Burton, who I'd earlier directed and who'd been disciplined on the set; Harris was not.'

Already Harris was carving out something of a reputation for questioning his directors, not blindly following instructions but his own instincts, a habit that would lead to violent clashes in the future. Anderson was the first to confront it. 'After just a few days on *Shake Hands* Richard would come on the set and say, "I don't know if I want to do it this way," and we'd talk about the scene and once I'd persuaded him that's the way it should be done and the way I wanted it there was no problem. But near the end of the picture we were rehearsing a scene and Harris wasn't there. I put all the chalk marks on the floor where the actors would stand and the crew was making bets that Harris would never stand on those marks, he'd do something totally different. So Richard came in and said, "What are we doing, then?" I made up some bit of business and said, "I think if you go over to the window." He said, "I don't think I'm going to go over to the window, I think I'll come up here." And he went right on the marks that I'd put on the floor.'

Though he shared only a few scenes with Cagney, Harris was in awe of the Hollywood legend, remembering the days when he'd seen him in action, blasting gangsters to kingdom come at his local fleapit. 'I remember,' says Elizabeth, 'we were all on a quay waiting for a set-up and I was begging Jimmy Cagney, "Please do 'Yankee Doodle Dandy'," and there he did it for us, on the quayside; it was magical.'

Harris knew it was a great opportunity to see a master at work and he exploited it to the full. 'He was in awe of Cagney because he was such a big star,' Anderson recalls. 'Richard would watch him work. He was taking it all in.' Together with fellow actors John Cairney and Donal Donnelly, Harris formed what became known on the set as 'Mr Cagney's gang'. The Hollywood veteran liked nothing better than to have the trio sing Irish songs to him during his make-up session.

Neither has Cairney forgotten the way Cagney always made his entry onto the set each morning. 'He was a man of small stature, but powerful personality. He would come in very modestly, say his good mornings, and then, removing his coat, he would go into the corner of the studio, put two hands on the wall and tap dance vigorously for ten minutes, then would turn back to the cameras looking at least twenty years younger. He would then say, "Let's go, fellas." We were all most impressed. We tried the tap dancing, but all we could do was make a noise.'

Harris, Cairney and Donnelly were the rabble-rousers on the film, but their high jinks never got out of control, even though after every day's work in the studio back in England they'd scramble from their dressing rooms as quickly as possible and get driven in the unit car over to a little pub in Bray. 'On the bar,' says Cairney, 'there were three pints of Guinness already laid out and the trick was to get to them before the respective emblems on each dissolved in the foam. Donal had the shamrock, Dicky Harris had the Welsh leek, because of his wife, and I, of course, had the thistle. Whosever's emblem was still on show didn't pay for the drinks. Chalky White, the driver, wasn't allowed to join us, because he was cockney and not part of the Celtic triumvirate. He was also driving.'

32

Jungle Manoeuvres

Sometime in 1958 Oscar Lewenstein was asked to read a new play by a young author, Willis Hall, the son of a fitter in a Leeds engineering plant. It was called *The Disciplines of War* and dealt with a small band of British soldiers on patrol in the Malayan jungle during the Japanese advance of early 1942. It was Hall's own statement against the stiff-upper-lip war films then proliferating British cinemas, usually with Jack Hawkins doing something heroic on a battleship; no mock heroics here, but the dank sweaty odour of real conscripted men's experiences of fear, danger and death.

Lewenstein thought the play 'exceptionally well written and observed', and persuaded George Devine to put it on at the Royal Court. For director they took a huge gamble on Lindsay Anderson, an almost complete novice when it came to the theatre. His only previous experience was directing a Sunday-night workshop production at the Court at the invitation of Tony Richardson. Immediately Anderson ditched the title, replacing it with *The Long and the Short and the Tall*, taken from the lyrics of the 1917 song 'Bless 'Em All'.

Anderson began to cast the play with a brilliant eye. Finney, upon whose services Lewenstein had an option after *The Party*, was given the starring role of Bamforth, a bolshie cockney. Then, after Patrick McGoohan turned down the role of Sergeant Mitchem, Robert Shaw was cast. It was then that disaster struck.

Finney had taken it upon himself to form a special bond with the all-male cast by inviting them to the Bayswater flat he shared with Jane, who cooked them all a curry. The evening was a terrific success and rehearsals got off to a fine start the next morning. On the second day of rehearsals Finney arrived looking rather the worse for wear. A clearly concerned Anderson was hastily reassured that it was nothing more than the result of a late night. 'I'd been at a party and got through a bottle of Pernod,' said Finney. 'Mostly uncontaminated by water.'

The next day Finney's pallor was if anything even worse. The excuse this time was an over indulgence of Vermouth but Anderson wasn't convinced and urged the actor to see a doctor. When he did it turned out to be appendicitis and he was rushed into hospital for an emergency appendectomy, which might well have saved his life. When the news filtered back to Anderson he was deeply distressed, having been greatly impressed with Finney in those first few days of rehearsal and desperate not to lose him. But it quickly became obvious that Finney needed a great deal of time to recuperate and a replacement would have to be found.

David Andrews was the youngest member of the cast and recalls that dreadful day when everyone was assembled on the stage and told that Finney was out. 'George Devine came and gave us a pep talk, "We want you all to stay on, we don't want to lose you," and that was a wonderful thing to hear, especially for someone like me on my first really decent job, that you were part of what was already becoming a privileged cast. So we were put on a retainer for about a month; not much because even with its huge successes the Royal Court was not a wealthy company.'

Actually the search for a new Bamforth was already well in hand. Lewenstein recalled a trip to the Bristol Old Vic to see O'Toole, whom the impresario felt was achieving similar things there as Finney had done over at Birmingham. 'They were the two foremost actors of their generation, and the best examples of the new non-university breed of actors that the new times and plays were demanding.' O'Toole had actually been considered for the role originally and after reading the script raved about it. 'I wrote back saying whoever plays Bamforth will become a star, and please let it be me.' Now that the offer was on the table O'Toole turned it down; amongst former RADA students there existed a certain professional rivalry and O'Toole didn't want Finney's seconds. Ultimately, however, he saw sense and took the role.

By this time O'Toole had left Bristol and joined a company touring with a now-forgotten play called *The Holiday*, hoping for a West End engagement, but it broke down in the provinces. It did, however, prove to be a lucky break in one respect. Playing his sister was a striking Welsh actress named Siân Phillips, who, though married, had separated from her university lecturer husband. They began to date, Siân admitting she was 'dazzled' by O'Toole. They shared many interests, save alcohol; Siân didn't touch the stuff. The first thing O'Toole did to the poor girl was initiate her into the dark arts of boozing. During the tour he foisted whisky and beer upon her. 'I realised that an appreciation of Guinness was pretty essential in my new life,' she said. Evenings were spent invariably in a pub where Siân would sit sipping the black nectar, taking it down as a child might medicine, while O'Toole quaffed away like a man possessed. It was a strange life that she felt peculiarly drawn to; the O'Toole universe.

When the cast of *The Long and the Short and the Tall* returned to the Royal Court there was their new Bamforth, the wild swirling tempest that was O'Toole, and it wasn't long before he'd taken the young David Andrews under his wing. 'I found myself in Kenneth Griffith's flat, where Peter was staying, and we sat in the front room drinking and singing, and we'd hardly met. He was a lovely guy and incredibly charismatic, he had the most wonderful, sparkling, piercing blue eyes. That's one of the things that made me attach myself so closely to people like Peter and later Michael Caine, they were magnetic people, you couldn't resist them.'

For Anderson, still smarting from losing Finney, O'Toole at least ticked all the right boxes; he was working class, had a chip on his shoulder and didn't hail from the Home Counties. It's no coincidence that Anderson would go on to work predominantly with the likes of O'Toole, Harris, Malcolm McDowell and Alan Bates. He saw the north as free from 'the curse of middle class inhibitions'. He and O'Toole should have got along famously then, except it turned into a war of attrition from day one. Firstly, Anderson considered O'Toole 'too much of a star performer', while O'Toole thought 'Lindsay's idea of the working class was perfumed shit'. The relationship never healed. 'Peter hated Lindsay,' confirms Andrews. 'Thought he was rubbish. He used to pick up bits of script and pretend to wipe his arse with them.'

Neither did O'Toole and Robert Shaw prosper much. Tensions arose pretty quickly between the two of them during rehearsals. Shaw considered his role as the stern leader the best of his career so far, certainly the biggest, but he also realised that the bawdy, insubordinate Bamforth had many moments of great theatrics and O'Toole took full advantage. So Shaw set out to deliberately throw his co-star off balance, talking through his scenes or telling him where his performance faltered. More than once Anderson gave Shaw a strict dressing down but he didn't take any notice. 'Bob Shaw was a venomous bastard,' says Andrews. 'He was a really nasty guy and yet he had a sort of grudging liking for me. Robert, as a person was quite vicious. He was razor sharp in his ambition. He was very laid-back and relaxed. He had this wonderful, slightly Lancashire accent, and a very edgy voice. He was hard. He kept the company together, just by his presence.'

Shaw had come into the show bolstered by the success of his first novel, which had just been published. Entitled *The Hiding Place*, the story concerned two downed British airmen captured in a small German town and then kept prisoners of war in a cellar by a Nazi sympathiser. The man enjoys their company so much that he doesn't tell them when hostilities end and continues with the masquerade for years into peace-time. In 1960 the book was adapted into a TV play featuring Shaw himself and Sean Connery as the pilots.

Shaw was ecstatic with the critical response to the book. 'An exciting new talent,' said the *Daily Telegraph*. 'One of the most original novels of the year,' rated the *Observer*. In more ways than one the novel was a professional turning point. 'From having been treated as a stupid actor,' in Shaw's own words, friends and colleagues would now say things like, 'I never knew you could do that!' Shaw always loved surprising and impressing people. 'I began to be treated as intelligent.' After years of thinking his career had stalled, the novel also supplied him with a much-needed confidence boost. 'I became less temperamental and less vulner-able.' Using a sporting analogy, he equated it to a boxing match. As an actor he was just about out on his feet when 'that first book was like the punch that turned the fight my way'.

As the oldest amongst the cast, Shaw became an unofficial father figure, a position of responsibility he took to instantly; some of the actors under him were seven years his junior. It really was a terrific ensemble; besides

Shaw and O'Toole there were Ronald Fraser, Alfred Lynch, Bryan Pringle and Edward Judd, faces that were to become popular over the years with film and TV audiences alike. It was, according to Lewenstein, 'one of the finest all-round casts ever assembled for one of my productions'. Anderson brilliantly used the different regional accents of his actors to reflect the way the British army is made up of men from the whole strata of society; along with the army slang it added to the play's intense vitality.

As the youngest amongst them, David Andrews was certainly aware of the special nature of the production. 'I revelled in the fact that all these guys, although they were pretty fresh on the scene, were all so accomplished and so sure of themselves. I was horrifically insecure. All the actors were supremely confident and very inventive. And most of us had done National Service so we really knew quite a bit about what we were doing. I had to fire a Sten gun and that came almost as second nature to me because I'd been taught how to handle guns in the air force.'

The play opened in January 1959. As was his routine, O'Toole, along with Shaw and Ronnie Fraser, drank in the local pub prior to curtain-up. Sometimes with only minutes to spare they'd stampede back into the theatre, rub dirt over their faces and change into a khaki uniform looking as if they'd spent an hour in make-up to achieve the desired bedraggled jungle look. The trio made such a habit of sitting in the pub all possible hours that a line eventually had to be rigged up from the theatre so the stage manager's ten-minute call could be heard at the bar. Anderson was almost driven bonkers; 'I'm furious,' he'd yell at them. 'I've never known anything quite so monstrously unprofessional,' while the expert hired to make the actors look like real soldiers suffered a nervous collapse and left.

Siân Phillips had a theory about the bad behaviour, that it was quite deliberate, both a reaction and an attitude in order to distance themselves entirely from that breed of middle-class actor who after an evening performance put his cravat on and had a nice sherry back at his cottage in the Home Counties with his prim wife who looked like Celia Johnson. 'Plays were altering and the lads were going to show that they were the new breed of actor, born for the occasion; unconventional, bohemian, with no pretensions to belonging to the polite society of "civilians". No use expecting polite speech and middle-class behaviour from this lot.'

There was something deeper, too, a reaction against the times they were living in. 'We didn't have childhoods,' said O'Toole. 'They all came to an end when we were about thirteen or fourteen. There were many restrictions during the war – no meat, no food, no booze – and, of course, you didn't mind so much. But the post-war restrictions were worse, in a way, and we were told that it was our moral imperative to remain sober. Well, we had absolutely no intention of doing that. I keep reading about the dreary Fifties. Don't you believe a word of it, sweetheart!'

Even by the end of the decade Britain was still a country in the grip of harsh austerity measures. They had economic miracles in Germany and Japan while all we got in Blighty was successive Chancellors of the Exchequer telling everyone to tighten their belts. 'Bollocks to that,' hailed O'Toole. 'We wanted the roaring Twenties, please. There were some of us who saw it as our duty to be truants from the system. The drinking was liberation from the fear and the restrictions of the post-war years. The frivolity and the fun had gone. Booze was a way of recapturing it. We certainly had a bloody good time.'

O'Toole liked to quote the often-repeated line that if you could remember the sixties, you weren't really there. 'Well, we were doing that in the fifties. I can remember how the decade started, and how it ended but, sadly, nothing in between.' As students and then as young actors they had no money but what they did have was youth and stupidity in equal measure, so often to keep warm they'd have parties on the Circle Line on the London underground. It was warm, there were chairs and they'd take a battery-operated gramophone and play each other's records. 'We'd get off at stations, pop out to the pub, get some more booze and get back on again. Great fun! And the sixties were only a continuation of that.'

It didn't take long for word to spread around theatreland about the antics of these new actors over at the Royal Court. One Saturday evening, after *The Long and the Short and the Tall* had been running for a couple of weeks, the last tabs had dropped and the audience had departed, stagehand Michael Seymour was alone on the stage clearing things up: 'When through a door on the prompt side of the stage a man emerged. "I say," he said. "Where can I find the boys?" I assumed that he was looking for the cast, so I directed him where to go up the stairs. He thanked me, saying "Oh, my name's Noël Coward." I later saw him in happy conversation with them in the pub next door.'

Besides O'Toole, the other big boozer of the company was Ronnie Fraser. 'He was a very flaky sort of guy,' says Andrews. 'You were his great friend if you bought him a large Fraser special, which was about three vodkas, he'd be your great friend while you buy him that, but unless you were James Villiers or Peter O'Toole he would have absolutely no time for anybody. But it was wonderful watching his performance because it was so gentle and sentimental.'

Victor Spinetti knew Fraser well and did a play with him once in America. 'Flying out there, Ronnie was drinking so much on the plane that once we landed in Boston he was well fortified. The customs official said, "Can I see your passport?" And Ronnie replied, "I don't even want to come to your bloody country." Of course it was three days before we saw him again.'

According to Andrews, Lindsay Anderson had great difficulty controlling his burly male cast, unable to relate to them on either an intellectual, social or sexual level. Or put it another way, he was decidedly *not* one of the lads. 'Lindsay was a very unassuming man. Actually I don't think any of the cast liked him that much, but I was deeply impressed by Lindsay because I thought he was good about giving actors their head. I think Lindsay was slightly intimidated by the cast, but to have rallied that great group of actors together was quite an achievement, although he must have sensed that he wasn't the most popular person. He was from a different background, he was highly intellectual and came from a privileged environment, and some of those guys had nothing like that.'

Certainly the play hit a nerve with British audiences, still smarting from their government's post-colonial skirmishes in Suez and elsewhere, and its success launched Anderson's career as a theatre director. While not as revolutionary as *Look Back in Anger*, *The Long and the Short and the Tall* was still seen as a breakthrough, thanks to its earthy, naturalistic approach, like *Journey's End* with a knuckleduster.

And as Robert Shaw feared, O'Toole took the lion's share of the acting praise. Kenneth Tynan, who described the play as being 'performed in what, for the London theatre, is a new style of acting', singled out O'Toole: 'I sensed a technical authority that may, given discipline and purpose, presage greatness.' O'Toole went on to claim the London critics' award for Best Actor of the Year for Bamforth. He was the toast of theatrical London but society hadn't caught up with him yet. One evening he went to a restaurant near the Royal Court but wasn't allowed in, the reason – he didn't have a tie.

Soon O'Toole's phone was ringing off the hook with producers and directors wanting to set up meetings. At least Shaw consoled himself with having the biggest dressing room with the only toilet; age and experience did have its advantages. O'Toole had to make do with a big sink, and it was into this that he was merrily pissing one night when he heard an unmistakable voice behind him. 'Hello, my name is Katharine Hepburn.' O'Toole pretended to be washing his hands and quickly shoved himself back in his trousers. It was a momentous first encounter, after which Hepburn went around town singing his praises. For years O'Toole would bump into people who'd say, 'Kate Hepburn told me all about you.'

The Hollywood legend was in London filming *Suddenly, Last Summer* with Montgomery Clift, and one of the people she discussed O'Toole with was the movie's producer Sam Spiegel. Within days he was being ferried to Shepperton Studios for a screen test in a silver Jaguar driven, he'd recall, by a particularly surly chauffeur. Spiegel wanted O'Toole on standby, ready to take over at a moment's notice from the oft-ailing Clift, whom the producer doubted would be able to finish his role as a doctor in the film. Once at Shepperton O'Toole was hustled into make-up, dressed in a white coat and taken onto a sound stage where the set of a doctor's office stood. Holding an X-ray as a prop, O'Toole couldn't stop himself and cracked: 'It's all right Mrs Spiegel, but your son will never play the violin again.' O'Toole was quickly dispensed with, but Spiegel never forgot the insolence of the young actor. Just a few years later O'Toole's actions would come back to haunt him when the director threatened to scupper his bid to land the role of a lifetime.

33
Bates the Thug

In the summer of 1958 a high flyer from the world of Canadian television hitched up in London to take over as head of drama at ABC television, part of the ITV network. His name was Sydney Newman and he would quite literally change the face of British television. A brash and down-to-earth man, who might have been mistaken for the art critic of the *Observer* with his uniform of bow tie, crinkled jacket and suede shoes, Newman recognised that television was a mass medium that needed to appeal across the social strata but was all too frequently ignoring the masses by catering to the more highbrow elements in society. 'Damn the upper classes!' he raved. 'They don't even own televisions! Treat the common man seriously and you can find strong drama in their everyday lives. Do *Oedipus Rex* in Notting Hill Gate and you've got something very powerful.'

After catching a performance of *Look Back in Anger* during an earlier visit to Britain, Newman wanted to reflect what he saw as a changing nation with socially relevant drama specifically made for television that ordinary people could relate to. After all, where does most of the drama in life take place but in people's homes? 'Sydney was passionate about bringing working-class drama onto TV and that's what we did,' says director Philip Saville. 'Most of the plays were about ordinary people. Sydney Newman was a great pioneer of that.'

As his vehicle Newman used ABC's existing drama strand *Armchair Theatre*, which had been running for two years and presented different plays with a new cast every week. Newman's instincts were to prove not only highly prescient but profitable when by the close of 1959 *Armchair Theatre* was regularly placed in the week's top-ten rated shows with audiences of twelve million.

That evening at the Royal Court also introduced Newman to the talents of Alan Bates. After seeing him in *Long Day's Journey Into Night* the Canadian was keen that he swiftly make his dramatic bow on television. The project chosen was a play called *The Thug* about a rebellious youth kicking out at a society that he feels has somehow let him down. It was an attempt by playwright Jane Arden to gain, if not sympathy, then understanding for this new phenomenon of alienated gangs of teenagers, 'strays from the herd', she called them, whose wanton acts of hooliganism were their only way of expressing themselves. Husband Philip Saville merely thought his wife 'had an obsession with young men in leather on motorbikes'.

As a director for *Armchair Theatre* Saville was instrumental in getting Jane's play commissioned. She then set about writing it in her usual haphazard way, as Saville recalls. 'Jane was very careless when she wrote, using stray bits of paper or even loo paper, and I used to go around the house picking up these bits of work and we'd talk about it together in the evening.'

The play's central character was so key to the drama that it needed to be cast correctly. He wasn't just a hooligan, a thug, but 'anarchic, fearless, primordial, with a suppressed animalism', says Saville. It needed a special kind of actor. 'Actually the agents were thrilled to get this kind of character because they were sick and tired of casting chinless wonders; here was this real person at last.'

When Saville was introduced to Alan Bates for the first time the thing that struck him immediately was his beauty. 'He was incredibly good looking. He looked a bit like a cross between the film star Tyrone Power and George Best.' Saville would guide Bates through the two days of intense rehearsal and the actual day of recording. So green was Bates that he needed to be told where the camera was going to be. 'But he loved the whole process,' Saville confirms. 'And was a total natural. Unlike some theatre actors who didn't have a clue or simply didn't want to know where the camera was. Back then we were still drawing most of our actors from the theatre; there was no such thing as a television actor. Also back then some of the theatre lads tended to suddenly project their voices loudly and I'd have to keep on reminding them, which you don't today because actors are trained for television, that the camera and the microphone were close by and they didn't need to shout, they could talk quite normally. In other words, just be themselves. I didn't have to say any of that to Alan, so he was a complete natural.'

It showed on the screen. When *The Thug* was broadcast in February 1959 *The Times* raved: 'The production was exciting whenever Mr Bates was on the screen. His broodingly lonely and savage performance gave the part a profundity never suggested by the lines alone.' It was a hit with audiences, too, as Saville recalls. 'It was way up in the top-ten ratings and Alan was launched on television.' That kind of thing happened much more back in those days, with just two channels these kind of one-off dramas were watched by large swathes of the population and the next day at the office people would say, 'Did you see that new actor in that play last night, who is he?'

Certainly his fan mail soared as a result, letters from perspiring women who, of course, had no clue as to his complicated private life. 'In those days you didn't talk about that kind of stuff,' says Saville. 'Alan wasn't a hundred per cent gay because he did later marry and have two children.'

With telly success came the realisation that you can get very quickly typecast. The day after the broadcast of *The Thug* Bates was sent a script entitled, unbelievably, *The Brute*. He told his agent to decline it and instead agreed to join the ensemble cast of Arthur Miller's *A Memory of Two Mondays*, shown a little over two weeks after *The Thug*. The American playwright had always been fond of this one-act play about a disparate group of blue-collar workers scraping a living in a Brooklyn car factory during the Great Depression and adapted it personally for the ITV broadcast.

Harder to fathom is why Bates so quickly slipped back into hoodlum territory again that April as the leader of a gang terrorising a snack-bar owner in ITV's *Television Playhouse* production *The Jukebox*, co-starring Harry H. Corbett. Like *The Thug*, here was another sexually charged character that traded on Bates's brooding looks. Maybe this kind of typecasting was something he was just going to have to live with, though it tended to happen much more in film and television than his beloved theatre. From the very beginning Bates wanted a career of challenges, not safe ground.

Connery, too, was slipping back into familiar territory. After his casting as the romantic lead in the Disney picture he was once again playing a dullard of a part, a thuggish sidekick in a Tarzan flick taking pot shots at the rather ample chest of Gordon Scott, he of the loincloth and knee-trembling battle cry.

Hardly overawed by the material, Connery had accepted *Tarzan's Greatest Adventure* because it afforded him the opportunity of working with Anthony Quayle, cast against type as a psychotic killer tracking down a hidden diamond mine. In the end, Connery's doubts proved groundless; this was no formularised Tarzan movie but a thrilling action yarn in its own right, regarded by many as amongst the best in the long-running series. Gone were the clichés of yesteryear, there's no wailing Jane or cute animal interludes, though the traditional fight with the plastic alligator thankfully remains intact. It's also gratifyingly dark and a bit twisted; one female character dies in a pit of spikes. The *Los Angeles Times* was to call it 'A unique adult tale. I would single it out for its impact, even brilliance as cinema making.'

Filmed on location in Kenya using local tribesmen as extras, many of whom quickly adopted Western ways by staging a strike, the film wasn't burdened with the greatest of budgets. The producers certainly couldn't afford luxuries like a helicopter to ferry the cast and crew to the remote locations so everyone endured a two-hour drive by jeep from their hotel in Nairobi and then a further hour's walk over creeks and rough terrain until they arrived at the set.

It sounds just like a real-life adventure and that's exactly how actress Sara Shane, who played Tarzan's belle in this picture, remembers it. But it was tough. 'We would work for hours in the hot sun and by the end of the day I'd be knackered. One day, after we'd finished and were preparing to walk back, well, I started to sway a bit and Gordon Scott picked me up and flung me over his shoulder like I was a sack of potatoes and carried me an hour out of the jungle. Don't you just love it!'

One imagines that with lumbering hulks like Scott and Connery, there was plenty of testosterone flying around but Sara remembers only an atmosphere of high jollity and warm camaraderie. 'We all hung out together and ate together, we were like one big clan. It was a wonderful film to make, the most fun I ever had on a movie. Even though there was not much socialising. There were no places to go to, we stayed in the hotel mostly; if you went out you might get eaten by something!'

Back in London for studio work at Shepperton, Sara called all her friends in the movie business, producers, directors, to tell them about 'this incredible new actor called Sean Connery. You've got to meet him.' During their time together Sara had not only grown fond of Connery but been struck by his screen potential. 'My feelings about Sean were very strong. He was a tremendously talented fellow who was going to go far, it was obvious; it didn't require any brilliance on my part.' Some of Sara's friends took up her request but most didn't. 'A friend of mine actually tested Sean for a film called *Malaga* opposite Dorothy Dandrige, but in the end they gave the part to Edmund Purdom instead of Sean! What a terrible choice that was!'

Connery was still shooting the Tarzan picture when he lost out on another role. His agent managed to get him an audition for the lead in John Osborne's latest stage project, which was, rather bizarrely, a musical satire about Fleet Street gossip columnists *The World of Paul Slickey*. The lead required a fine singing voice and a strong sexual presence. As Osborne later confessed, 'I made a monumental misjudgement by dismissing Sean Connery, who turned up one morning looking like my prejudiced idea of a Rank contract actor. It was a lamentable touch of Royal Court snobbery.'

Actually the Royal Court was guilty of quite a bit of snobbery, more often than not reverse snobbery. When Peter Bowles appeared in a touring version of *The Long and the Short and the Tall* playing 'Smudger' Smith, a role first played by Bryan Pringle, Lindsay Anderson thought it ridiculous. 'In my opinion Bowles can't act,' said the director. 'I know because I've seen him wearing a suit.'

Actually it was a lucky escape for Connery, *Paul Slickey* flopped big time. The first night at the Palace Theatre was a calamity, with boos ringing out from the audience at the curtain call, so vitriolic that cast member Adrienne Corri stuck her fingers up and shrieked, 'Go fuck yourselves!' to an audience that included John Gielgud, Noël Coward and the Duke and Duchess of Bedford. As for Osborne, he was chased up Shaftesbury Avenue by a mob of hacked-off theatregoers.

34
West End High Jinks

Following its successful run at the Royal Court, *The Long and the Short and the Tall* transferred in April to the West End and the New Theatre, conveniently located next door to the Salisbury pub on St Martin's Lane. The cast drank there practically every night after curtain-down, slipping out of the back of the theatre, across an alleyway and straight into the pub's side entrance. Some of the actors partook of the brew before performances, O'Toole notably, which did no favours to his understudy who'd stew in suspense backstage as to whether he'd return from the pub in time. That understudy was Michael Caine and his agonies lasted three months. There Caine would be, not knowing if he was going to have to go on or not, when O'Toole casually breezed in, offering a hearty hello to the panic-stricken young actor.

It wasn't because he didn't know his lines that Caine was terrified of going on, it was because he thought O'Toole so magnificent in the role that he couldn't possibly come close to his performance. So he'd drip with perspiration every night as the clock counted down to curtain up. One evening his nightmare became a reality. The half went and O'Toole wasn't there. Caine was getting into a complete panic. Time went by and the quarter was called and O'Toole was still a no-show. 'By this time Michael was getting extremely agitated,' recalls David Andrews, who witnessed the whole episode. 'And eventually the stage director came into the dressing room and said, "You'll have to get the uniform on." And I can remember, Michael was trembling putting this stuff on and we were all thinking, Christ, is he going to cope with this? And then we heard the click on the tannoy as the microphone was switched on for the front of house announcement and thought, Christ, it's act one. So there we all were, waiting in the wings for the curtain to go up, and suddenly the stage door burst open and O'Toole rushed in and they grabbed him and put him in his outfit in record time. And Mike, there was sweat pouring off his face.'

So O'Toole made it, literally with seconds to spare. What had happened this particular night was nothing short of extraordinary. O'Toole had been at a wedding in Hampshire and presumably got smashed; by the time he looked at his watch it was getting very late in the day. 'Christ, how am I going to get back?' Luckily the father of the bride was a wealthy man and raced O'Toole over to Blackbushe, a small private airport nearby. 'And this guy chartered a four-engine passenger plane and got Peter onto it and flew him to Heathrow,' says Andrews. 'I don't know how true that story is, but it's the one Peter told.'

Another famous evening saw the curtain in the process of rising when O'Toole ran in screaming, 'Don't go on, Michael!' as he bounded into his dressing room, shirt and trousers cast asunder. 'He was changed within seconds,' recalled writer and friend Keith Waterhouse. 'And, pausing only to throw up violently out of the upstage window of the set – which the audience thought was part of the action – gave a flaw-less performance.'

Besides understudying, Caine's other functions were to bring in booze, find out where the best parties were and acquire girls. 'I'd have made a wonderful pimp,' he later joked. After last orders in the pub everyone usually headed to the nearest available party, all the young crowd, with a few veterans tagging along observing, like Willis Hall who at one house party was heard to mutter; 'Oh, awful. You know, white wine in cups and young girls being sick.'

One Saturday night after the show O'Toole invited Caine to a restaur-ant he knew. Eating a plate of egg and chips was the last thing Caine remembered until he woke up in broad daylight in a strange flat. 'What time is it?' he enquired. 'Never mind what time it is, what fucking day is it?' said O'Toole. They located their hostesses, two dodgy-looking girls who told them it was five o'clock on Monday afternoon. Curtain went up at eight. Luckily they were still in London and made their way to the theatre just in time. The stage manager was waiting for them with the news that the owner of the restaurant had been in and henceforth they were banned from his establishment for life. Caine was just about to ask what they'd done when O'Toole whispered, 'Never ask what you did. It's better not to know.' Ah, the voice of experience. After that, Caine made a point of never going out on the booze with O'Toole again.

The Salisbury pub remained the prominent watering hole for the cast. For years it had been a beacon for those in the arts to relax and drink, thanks to its location bang in the middle of London's theatreland. Back in the early fifties Osborne referred to it as 'The Rialto for loud-mouthed actors and lounging fairies.'

It really was a superb pub, with a buffet carvery at the end of the bar offering splendid roast beef at a not unreasonable price. 'The Salisbury also had a private bar entrance that opened straight onto the alley,' remembers David Andrews. 'And this room was always full of agents and managers, so you waltzed through on the way to the main bar hoping to get noticed, and if you were invited for a drink in there that meant you were going to get a job. The Salisbury really was the main hub of our social life; you would always meet the most amazing people there. Actors by the score would be pouring in; the better known they were the more likely you were to see them there, because it was a place to be seen.'

And then there were drinking dens and actor's clubs, the most popular of which was the Buckstone, situated in a quiet street behind the Haymarket Theatre across from the stage door. 'There was no dress code to keep out the riff-raff,' recalled Caine. 'Because we were the riff-raff and the club was for us.' Although that didn't stop O'Toole getting thrown out of the place once for bad behaviour. It served good cheap food, but most importantly drinks after hours. And there was always a fine array, of shall we say, female clientele. 'The Buckstone was a favourite hunting ground,' recalls Andrews. 'You could almost invariably find someone who would go out with you at least, if not actually hit the sack. I used to have lunch there with John le Mesurier. Also Ronnie Corbett used to work behind the bar for a time. There was a legend that Ronnie had to stand on a beer box. It was great fun. The

Buckstone's licence went till midnight, sometimes on special occasions they'd extend that to one or two o'clock. O'Toole would occasionally turn up there, also Michael and Sean. The other club we used to go to was Gerry's on Shaftesbury Avenue. One of the girls behind the bar we all called luscious. You could get a meal there, but the food wasn't as good as The Buckstone.'

The usual rule back then was to drink in the Salisbury till closing time, 10.30 or whatever, head over to the Buckstone and then if you were really desperate to carry on the obvious place to go was the Essex Serpent pub in Covent Garden. 'That's because it was open for the porters who brought all the fruit and vegetables into the market,' says Andrews. 'And it used to be populated at two or three in the morning by people in their evening dress who'd been to the opera and got sloshed. There were several pubs around Covent Garden that would stay open for the porters during the night. Some of the landlords were very strict and only allowed the porters in, others were more relaxed and didn't mind who went in, even actors.'

As the cast settled into a long run, David Andrews found himself sharing a dressing room with Caine and they became good friends. 'We'd sit in there having a plate of cold ham and salad that the company provided for us in between the matinee and the evening performance, and he used to tell me about his experiences in the Korean War. He was a lovely, good-humoured bloke, full of stories; even back then Michael was a great raconteur. And we had a little gramophone that only played 45s and we used to get all the latest numbers and play them. And he had star quality. You could see that he was ambitious, and he made sure that he got to know as many people in the business as he could.'

Leading the company once again was Shaw, still aggrieved that O'Toole had taken most of the limelight away from him. Competitive in life, on stage these two very different actors complemented each other to devastating effect, according to Andrews. 'Peter and Bob were breathtaking to act with. Shaw was exceptionally intelligent, while Peter was instinctively and intuitively intelligent, also clever and cunning and wily. To see them playing the same role night after night and always making it sound as if it were just happening for the first time, that they were under this appalling pressure in the jungle during the Japanese advance, it came over so clearly, it resonated so well.'

A month into the run Shaw's wife Jennifer decided to leave for Jamaica to stay with her parents for a while with the children. Lonely, Shaw often invited himself round to the home of Joan Plowright, with whom he'd been involved in a minor romance a few years earlier. 'I knew of his ambition to be a writer, which was far more important to him than acting,' Joan would remember. 'And we would spend Sundays, sometimes, working out plots for the play we might write one day.'

Shaw knew that Joan was currently separated from her actor husband Roger Gage and also conversant with the rumours that she was having an affair with Larry Olivier, his wife Vivien Leigh refusing him a divorce. One evening Shaw and a handful of other guests were at Joan's for supper, as she recalled. 'Robert, bent on mischief as usual, picked up the phone before I could get to it and I knew by the look on his face as he handed it to me that he had recognised the caller. "Who's the young blade?" Larry asked with some apprehension as soon as I answered.'

Another evening not long afterwards, Olivier called Joan and Shaw was there again, picking up the phone and reassuring the theatrical knight in jocular fashion that he had no cause to worry, that he and Joan were just old friends. It was that night that Joan told Shaw of her commitment to Olivier. He admitted to having heard the rumours but didn't know how serious it was. He then asked for her help in finding him a mistress who was 'on my intellectual level, but of course nice and dishy into the bargain'. After that Shaw made a habit of turning up at Joan's on Sunday mornings after playing squash with friends. To get him out of her hair Joan took Shaw to Hammersmith, where Tony Richardson held open house each week. And so began a new friendship that would alter the course of Shaw's life.

At a party that was too dull for Shaw's taste, and getting progressively drunker, he and Richardson began telling each other which actress they'd most like to bed. Richardson mentioned Mary Ure, the wife of Osborne. Shaw couldn't agree more; what a woman, he said, and began through the act of nauseating mime to demonstrate what he'd like to do to her behind closed doors. Shaw suddenly had a great idea. 'Why don't we both go round and see her this very minute?' The fact that it was two in the morning didn't deter him at all. A taxi was called and soon both men were deposited in the street outside the Osbornes' Chelsea residence. If their noisy presence had yet to be detected, Shaw made it obvious by crashing two dustbin lids together and serenading Mary to come out and see them. The door flew open to reveal Osborne in his dressing gown. Before the neighbours started to riot he invited them in, suggesting that next time they use the doorbell.

Shaw didn't waste time in telling Osborne that he had the hots for his wife; more than that, he wanted to give her one. It's true that Shaw could be a very uncouth man, often this was a deliberate stance to shock. Out with friends once at a restaurant Shaw asked one of the group's wives, whom he didn't know, 'Have you ever been buggered?' When she replied in the negative Shaw began to describe the operation in detail, 'You see, you have to be very hard, it's no good unless you're really hard.' The rest of the diners tried desperately not to listen.

Osborne responded to Shaw's bluntness by giving the two men a glass of whisky. Just then Mary appeared, in a white, near-see-through gown. This did not calm Shaw down at all, and he began to roll around on the carpet moaning. Mary thought it all terribly amusing and sat down, 'pleased as a welcoming dog', according to Osborne, who then gave Richardson a withering look and departed for bed. Shaw saw his chance and told Mary exactly what he'd told her husband, then gave her his phone number.

Was it merely sheer lust that goaded Shaw into such demonstrably outrageous behaviour, or something more? Mary was a popular and experienced actress. Born in 1933 in Glasgow, she'd played Ophelia to Paul Scofield's Hamlet and had just been cast in the film adaptation of D. H. Lawrence's *Sons and Lovers*, a performance that would earn her an Academy Award nomination for Best Supporting Actress. So she was going places. She and Osborne were also the golden theatrical couple of the moment. So was Mary a challenge, a game to Shaw, like winning Jennifer had been? Did he also want to kick Osborne off his throne as king of the Royal Court; he could never compete with him as a playwright, so he'd steal his wife instead.

These may not have been Shaw's motives, but they must have crossed his mind. The surprise for him was that Mary was so eager to be caught, returning his call within days. For some time she'd been unhappy in her marriage to Osborne, who'd been conducting a string of not too clandestine affairs. There were nasty rows and during a stay at Tony Richardson's rented home in LA she took an overdose of sleeping pills. Osborne and Richardson were out by the pool when Mary appeared utterly naked and dropped like a stone into the water. When she failed to surface Richardson turned to Osborne and said, 'Don't you think we should *do* something?' They fished her out.

O'Toole's evenings after he'd finished in *Long and the Short* were mostly spent walking around Covent Garden. Sometimes if he was in the mood he'd scale the wall of Lloyd's bank. 'Now for a little climb,' he'd say. The first time he took Siân on one of these nocturnal jaunts she was startled when he began his ascent of the north face of the building, thinking it to be 'mad, dangerous behaviour'. But after a few nights of it the actress came to accept this as unremarkable, as far as O'Toole was concerned.

Architectural mountaineering was a favourite pastime of O'Toole's. Delighted to hear one day that his old RADA chum Frank Finlay was in town and a guest at the local YMCA, O'Toole decided to pay him a visit only to discover the entrance locked, this being after midnight. Undeterred, O'Toole climbed his way up four storeys and, bottle in hand, manoeuvred his way along the narrow ledge to Finlay's room and hammered on the glass like a mad thing. 'Open up, open up!' A bemused but delighted Finlay was only too happy to oblige.

O'Toole and Siân were staying rent free with Kenneth Griffith, who admired O'Toole greatly but had grave doubts about the couple's wedding plans. 'You cannot marry this wonderful man,' he said one day to Siân. 'Understand, he is a genius, but he is not normal.' Siân started to get similar words of warning from quite a few of O'Toole's friends, and some of her own. She ignored them all. 'I was so deliriously in love

I couldn't understand why everyone around me was worried.' Their marriage in Dublin, which consisted of a pub crawl picking up well-wishers along the way, wasn't so much a ceremony as 'just an excuse for a piss-up' in Siân's words.

It was the sheer unpredictability of the man that had so attracted Siân to him in the first place. Quite often she didn't know what the hell he was going to do next. Once he showed up in a sports car yelling, 'Get your passport, we're off.' Heading for Rome, they took a wrong turning and ended up in Yugoslavia; the beginning of a grand mystery tour around Europe. For Siân each day was a challenge and a hilarious adventure, O'Toole was the perfect travelling companion. 'He had an aura, always. When we first went on holiday, we were mobbed. People wanted to travel with us, talk to us, but he hadn't done anything then. He wasn't famous. But even when he was nothing, as it were, you knew he was something.'

35
A Season to Forget

Finney was still coming to terms with losing out on *The Long and the Short and the Tall* when Charles Laughton contacted him again with another offer of work. After *The Party*, Laughton had gone back to Hollywood to make Stanley Kubrick's *Spartacus*, then been badgered somewhat by Stratford's supremo Glen Byam Shaw into appearing for a season at the memorial theatre. Laughton was open to the idea, provided they also engage Finney. Byam Shaw, who'd barely heard of the young actor, reluctantly agreed.

Finney would have preferred for Laughton not to have bothered; he didn't want to go to Stratford. 'I didn't really respond to the parts I was going to play.' But Laughton cajoled him, flattered him and Finney relented. It was going to be an important season, one to remember, not least the fact that it celebrated the theatre's centenary. 'A few people might have done a bit of Morris dancing on the walls a hundred years ago, and said a couple of speeches from *As You Like It*,' mocked Finney. It was also curtain-down on Byam Shaw's reign and he'd pulled out all the stops, assembling a stellar company of old pros – Laughton, Olivier, also just back from a stint in Hollywood wearing a toga for Kubrick, and Edith Evans, alongside young bucks like Finney, Mary Ure, Ian Holm, Vanessa Redgrave and Diana Rigg.

And there was the ubiquitous Robert Hardy, who remembers well the dressing room he shared with Finney. 'I was struck by him. He was obviously a very interesting actor but it never crossed my mind that he was going to be a great star, though I thought he was pretty damn good. It was very tight in that dressing room and there was another fellow, long dead, who was sharing it with us. At the very beginning of the season as we sat the three of us in front of our mirrors making up, he said, "I think I ought to tell you boys that I am a homosexual." And it's reputed that my response was to say, "Well, fuck me."'

Othello was first that April with Tony Richardson directing the great American singer and actor Paul Robeson in the title role and Mary Ure as Desdemona. During one matinee Finney was steaming drunk on stage. He'd been in the Dirty Duck downing Russian stout and just about staggered back before curtain-up. 'I was playing that terrible wimp Cassio. In the fight I drew my sword and couldn't control my sword arm and the broader edge of the blade struck one of my colleagues in the teeth. I started the sweats and I got the whirlies.' At the interval he took off his wig and make-up and stood under a cold shower in an attempt to get sober in time for act two. 'I've never been drunk again in performance.'

At Birmingham Finney had a reputation as a drinker. One landlady told the press that he was a wonderful man, to be sure, 'but a real devil. Drunk all the time!' Going on booze benders had seemed relatively attractive, to be the roaring boy. He'd gone through a period when he thought, oh yes, it's terrific to be like that. 'I found the idea appealing.' He just didn't have the system to cope with it, that's all, and so was never really part of that hellraiser crowd. When he did go on the lash with Harris, O'Toole and the lads he always ended up ill. 'When I got drunk with them all I used to have to go to the gents and throw up, then come back and pretend I hadn't been sick and buy another drink. It was silly.' He once had an all-day drinking session with Ronnie Fraser which ended with him getting the 'whirlies' in Fraser's dressing room at the Royal Court and throwing up everywhere.

Next up was *A Midsummer Night's Dream* directed by Peter Hall, with Laughton as Bottom. But Finney wasn't happy. At Birmingham there had been far more camaraderie, if anyone had a problem there was always someone available to talk you through it. Finney never felt that at Stratford; in fact he felt almost the opposite. Nothing seemed to be going right for him. He found difficulty in learning his lines, his actor's instinct dried up and he was less inventive. Richardson sympathised. 'He was just reaching the height of his powers and he didn't have the right parts. Albert was like a young stallion chomping at the bit, wanting that big, enormous role.'

Finney later admitted that his work at Stratford was the worst of his entire career. 'It was one of those times when you feel you're in a tunnel and there's nothing you can do to get out. My work was awful, just vile. Every time I went on stage I thought, oh get off, what are you doing.'

He suffered such a calamitous loss of confidence that Finney seriously considered giving up acting. It would be a lucky accident that made him change his mind.

36
Bates the Pin-Up

It was an interesting paradox, and a foreshadowing of how powerful and all-consuming television would become, that after appearing in *Look Back in Anger*, at the time (and perhaps still) the most significant British play of the twentieth century, and in a revered production of Eugene O'Neill's *Long Day's Journey into Night*, Alan Bates found himself fawned over by teenage girls all because of a couple of TV roles as a sub-Marlon Brando teen tearaway. The fan mail was pouring in and magazines labelled him a hot new face. *Picturegoer* went so far as to hail him 'The number one pin-up boy of British television.'

His next television play was *The Square Ring*, which aired on ITV in June 1959. Posing the question whether the sport of boxing is a noble art or mere barbarism, the action takes place in a dressing room as six boxers await their turn to enter the ring. Bates played young novice Eddie, alongside Sean Connery as Rick Martell, a crooked middleweight. George Baker led the all-male cast and recalls that rehearsals 'were great fun and what a wonderful cast. Sean Connery was not quite established but there was no question in any of our minds that he was extremely talented. And Alan Bates and I remained friends until his death.'

Like much TV drama from that period *Play of the Week* went out live. Some actors, like Baker, who admitted it was a nerve-racking experience, just got used to it. Not Bates: 'Live television was utterly terrifying – rep with a vengeance.' Bates had heard the horror stories, like the time an actor died on the set during a live broadcast and the rest of the company had to crawl over him and share his lines until the stage manager could drag off the corpse. Ann Beach experienced an actor's worst nightmare on a live production, an uncooperative prop. 'I had to shoot somebody and I was supposed to take this gun out of my pocket and fire, but I couldn't get the bloody thing out, so I pointed with my fingers and went – bang!'

It was still a pioneering time on television, a new world open to experimentation and innovation, if only certain hurdles could be over-come. 'In those days it was so exciting, all this television stuff,' says Paul Almond, like Alvin Rakoff another Canadian who came to work in Britain. 'We were all pretty new to it and we all loved what we were doing. Everybody today is kind of jaded. Back in the old days it was nothing like that; we were all thrilled and riveted by this relatively new and fresh medium. I came over to do a BBC TV play in 1958 and they were still using old-fashioned film techniques, the cameramen would mark on the floor their position, like you did in film, they'd chalk it on. And I got a stagehand and said, "Get your mop wet and go and wipe out all the chalk all over the floor, no chalk marks on this production." And all the cameramen were going, "You can't do that! What's going on here!" I said, "No chalk marks, you work according to where the actor is, you just go in and get the shots, you don't go to a mark." Talk about revolution.'

Even if they didn't go out live, plays were still shot 'as live', mistakes and all. But there was nothing quite like the real thing, the atmosphere in the studio was electric, a mounting feeling of anticipation and cold fear. The tension would sometimes become so much that Philip Saville recalls rushing into the toilet to throw up before going on.

Having set Bates on the path of TV teen idolisation with *The Thug*, Saville returned with a vastly more intriguing script entitled *Three on a Gas Ring*. Again Bates was to play, in Saville's words, 'a very northern, physical character and sex object', but this time not merely to one girl, but three, middle-class and 'with nice clean underwear', says Saville. They live together on a barge and Bates, as a randy sculptor, goes through the lot of them like grouse through heather. One of the girls, played by Sheila Allen – who enjoyed working with Bates: 'He was adorable. Such a gent. Real humility, real warmth' – falls in love with him and gets herself pregnant. Determined to have the baby, she pops the big question, 'Do you love me?' Showing no mercy, he tells her no, it was just a fling. Saville takes over the story: 'So she says, being quite outspoken, a potential liberated young woman, "Well, I'm not going to marry you." And the three girls decide to bring up the baby on the barge on their own. That was the denouement, this kind of a new England. Only new England wasn't having any of it.'

The play was never broadcast. ITV, which, beholden to their advertisers, was at the time far more conservative than the BBC, decided it was against the image of the traditional British family. Still, Saville enjoyed working with Bates again. 'Alan was deeply intuitive and also very much like the old school, coming to a scene totally prepared, but because he looked the new school, he straddled both. He was quite a unique person. I loved working with him.'

37

Harris Goes to Hollywood

On the verge of making his Hollywood film debut opposite Gary Cooper and Charlton Heston, Richard Harris worked for Joan Littlewood one last time in a production of *The Dutch Courtesan*, a Jacobean play written by John Marston early in the seventeenth century. Ann Beach hadn't been with Theatre Workshop long and this was her first experience of Harris. 'I remember he was very entertaining, but he was always pissed, of course. He had a very raw talent then, and that's what I think Joan liked, this natural Irishman. He was still finding himself, I think, as an actor. His personality could be overpowering, he was larger than life, but he told the most wonderful stories in the pub, terrific storyteller, in that wonderful Irish way.'

Ann also vividly recalls their big scene together, where they had to face each other on a steep staircase. 'After every few lines Richard kept moving up a step, so I'd move, then he moved again, so I was constantly having to move up this bloody ramp to keep up with him. He didn't do it on purpose I don't think, he was a great upstager because he was still a little bit raw.'

And then he was gone, never to act for Joan again but forever beholden to her tutelage and inspiration. They did make an odd pair, both combustible types; sometimes emotions ran high and they'd go hell for leather at each other, such as the time during *You Won't Always Be On Top* when Harris poured a sack of cement over her head.

Ann Beach stayed for years with Joan, but also flitted back and forth to the Royal Court, which Joan didn't look too kindly on. 'She thought, oh, those Oxford/Cambridge buggers.' Joan always had a thing against Devine and the Sloane Square mob while 'the Royal Court always thought Joan was populist', says Victor Spinetti, who had also just joined the Theatre Workshop. 'I remember after a performance of *Oh! What a Lovely War* and Lindsay Anderson was leaning against a wall just inside the foyer and I said, "Oh hello, Lindsay, did you enjoy it?" And he just shook his head very slowly. And then Noël Coward said a very funny thing about *Oh! What a Lovely War*, he said, "I got rid of World War One in my show *Cavalcade* in three minutes flat, you lot took two fucking hours!"'

This curious rivalry between Joan and the Royal Court is odd, given that their goals were the same: to get a different kind of audience into the theatre, to break the middle-class monopoly. 'Essentially it's the middle class that go to the theatre,' says Keith Baxter. 'It's never been the plaything of the aristocracy; the aristocracy by and large are too boneheaded to like it.' It was never the province of the working class either, and that's what Joan particularly strove to change, it's why her theatre was slap bang in the middle of a deprived and run-down area of London's East End. 'She was determined to entertain the local people with her productions, that was terribly important to her,' says Ann Beach. 'Her dream was for a people's theatre, she wanted a working-class audience, ironically she ended up with having the standard West End middle-class audience coming to see her shows.'

Once he began to get established in movies Harris would sometimes pop back to Theatre Workshop and catch one of Joan's productions. 'He sat in the box,' Brian Murphy recalls, 'and laughed uproariously. I told him, "Christ, Richard you behave more like a bloody star in the audience than you ever did on stage." Certainly he would make sure everybody knew he was there.'

On *Shake Hands with the Devil* Harris had made such a strong impression with director Michael Anderson that he cast him in his next production, the seafaring epic *The Wreck of the Mary Deare*. 'It was quite obvious Richard had a lot to learn. But it was equally obvious his acting possessed that special quality.'

The film was shot at MGM's Culver City studio, and Harris flew over with Elizabeth that June. It was a traumatic journey: one of the plane's engines burst into flames and they were forced to make an emergency landing. It was the Harrises' first trip to America and they couldn't believe the difference from the country they'd just left behind. It was a culture shock of the highest order, an experience Elizabeth has never forgotten. 'In the fifties the ambience in London was so different to anything you can imagine today. Because of the war England was still poor as a country. And the thing that first struck us about America was suddenly there was what seemed to us incredible luxury, the hotel and restaurants, and also the shops were full of things. London was austere in the fifties. If you watch any old newsreel you'll see the street lights are very dim; when we went to America suddenly the street lights were shiny bright. What was strange, back in England we didn't feel it was depressed because we weren't aware that we had been without things, that we had less than other people.'

Harris refused to be overawed by the fact that he was making his first movie in Hollywood. 'It was interesting,' recalls Anderson. 'When Harris first came on the set and I introduced him to Gary Cooper and Heston he said, "How are you, then? Nice to see ya." He wasn't at all impressed, that was Richard, he was his own man. As far as he was concerned he had his job to do, they had their job to do and he was certainly not intimidated by these big stars or anything else.'

Sparks flew, however, during shooting when Harris and Heston just didn't get on; it was a clash of personalities. Harris found epic cinema's leading man to be prudish and stuck-up. 'He'd played in Shakespeare and to listen to him you'd think he helped the Bard with the rewrites. He was a prick, really, and I liked tackling pricks,' he said later.

Elizabeth's recollection is that on arrival Cooper and Heston more or less ignored Harris, while the studio put the couple up in a shabby hotel on the wrong side of the neighbourhood, a message if ever there was one: you're a nobody in this town, boy; you ain't earnt your spurs yet.

It was well known amongst the cast and crew that Gary Cooper was gravely ill, and playing a ship's captain in an adventure story on the high seas obviously necessitated him being drenched in water much of the time. 'I thought, how strange,' says Elizabeth. 'There was Gary Cooper dying of cancer, he was very, very ill, getting into this freezing-cold water in a tank on the lot. And his wife and daughter used to come down every day of shooting because they knew how really ill he was and I thought, how weird this profession is. He was so ill but he'd still be on time, still be line perfect.'

After a few weeks Elizabeth returned to London and Harris was left to his own devices. In his spare time he'd explore LA and its dark under-belly, but there was no real hellraising. He knew this was a big chance and he might not get a second crack at Hollywood so pretty much behaved himself. And once again Anderson came away impressed with Harris the actor. 'He would improvise such wonderful things. We had a section of ship on the stage which was on rockers and he had to spit in this scene. So he spat overboard and with his head he turned as though he were watching the spit go down stream. Well, nobody in a million years would've thought of that bit of business, so you really believed that ship was moving. It was those little things that he would do out of the blue that were stunning, I'll never forget that.'

38
Stepping into Larry's Shoes

Albert Finney was still in Stratford, though wishing he were somewhere else, having come to the conclusion that he'd gone there not for the work – which he found dreadful: bad parts he didn't want to play – but because he'd been flattered into it by Laughton, whom he still liked a great deal and so suffered in silence.

The next production, *Coriolanus* with Olivier in the lead and Peter Hall directing, would make history. Larry had already played the part triumphantly at the Old Vic in 1937, but this would be the definitive interpretation. Few who saw it would easily forget his spectacular death scene as, spears driven into his flesh, Olivier hurled himself off a high platform, trusting a pair of soldier extras to catch his ankles at the last minute and suspend him upside-down in a death pose reminiscent of Mussolini's. It was breathtaking theatre.

Hall had Finney and the rest of the young actors in the company like Ian Holm and Julian Glover, play the citizens of Rome with broad regional accents, a brilliant idea that additionally made an obvious distinction between the acting generations on view. Finney was also installed as Olivier's understudy; so, no pressure, then.

During the run Olivier was required to begin work on the film version of *The Entertainer* and so after every Wednesday night's performance he'd leap into an ambulance and sleep in the back while he was driven all the way to Morecambe, where Tony Richardson had set up his cameras. With *Coriolanus* in rep, alternating with another play, Olivier had the luxury of staying in the Lancashire resort for a few days before he was needed back in Stratford.

The Entertainer was Woodfall's second film and despite the huge success of the stage version was a tough sell to investors, principally because the movie adaptation of *Look Back in Anger* hadn't done as well as anticipated at the box office. Saltzman got it into his head that the brewers Bass might put money into the film, since the lead character Archie Rice was permanently pouring the stuff down his neck. At one point the producer commissioned a twenty-foot cut-out of a bottle of Bass beer which he stood Olivier in front of during one of the scenes, no doubt to tempt the brewers with this early example of product placement. Olivier went nuts when he saw it.

He probably also went nuts at the suggestion that Vivien Leigh play Archie's wife Phoebe, an idea swiftly abandoned, and Brenda de Banzie was installed, reviving her role from the original stage version. As Jean, Archie's daughter, Joan Plowright was given her screen debut. The romantic leads were already lovers, and it was during the filming of *The Entertainer* that the union between them was sealed and they'd subsequently marry. Richardson was in no doubt that Olivier saw Joan as 'the epitome of the new world of theatre he had opted for'.

Richardson also handed out another big-screen debut, to Alan Bates, playing Archie's son. It wasn't a difficult role and Bates made as good an impression with it as he could have. He was shocked when he attended rushes. 'When I first saw myself on screen, so huge, it was a terrific shock. And then, for some reason that shock wilted entirely and I could judge it, change it, learn from it.'

It was a memorable shoot; Morecambe with its naff seaside cafés and crumbling music-hall-era theatres was the ideal location. It was a nostalgic return for Osborne, last there as an actor in rep when he'd finished writing *Look Back in Anger* on a deckchair. Richardson, now more experienced as a film-maker, loved shooting on location, using natural sound and light wherever possible. He'd come almost to despise working on a sound stage, believing the artificial conditions of a studio produced artificiality in the acting. Olivier was the complete opposite, preferring the safer and more controlled environs of a studio. In spite of that minor difference they worked beautifully in tandem and Olivier's performance earned him an Academy Award nomination.

Filming the now-famous tap-dancing scene, Olivier had been at it for hours and was tired. Richardson asked for one more take. Sighing audibly, Olivier agreed. And then snap, his old cartilage went. He was due on stage at Stratford the following evening, but the prognosis was not good. Rest was required, said the doctor; there was no way he would be able to perform. Word reached Finney that he'd have to go on for Olivier in *Coriolanus*. It was a moment of real drama, made even more sweat-inducing by the fact that his first performance would be the one in which Edith Evans returned to the role of Volumnia, Coriolanus's mother, after three weeks off following a car accident. At the run-through that afternoon Finney courteously introduced himself and asked, 'Dame Edith, is there anything I'm doing wrong? Am I in the wrong place at all?' She smiled deeply, 'Dear Albert, do what you like, go where you like, I'll get my face in somehow.'

Olivier's mishap turned out to be Finney's salvation, as all the difficulties he'd been experiencing at Stratford left him literally overnight. First off, he got through the performance unscathed. The only ace up the sleeve for any understudy is that the disappointed audience expects to see someone unprepared and unable to cope. 'So if you can get through with any degree of nous at all, they think you're very good,' Finney reminisced. 'But it's terrible to hear that announcement. You're in your dressing room putting on the make-up when . . . "Sir Laurence won't be playing . . ." And you hear a terrible groan throughout the auditorium.'

Robert Hardy was there that night, observing the panic coursing around backstage like blood pumping through a horse in the Grand National; all except for Finney. 'Albert never gave me the impression of being stretched or nerve-racked about it. And when he came on and did it I wasn't that impressed; although it took a lot to impress me in those days. But it was the making of him. All the critics came down to see him and away he went thereafter. I thought his acting was pretty raw at that time, but that was the beginning of an epoch when people wanted raw acting, they didn't want carefully carpentered and honed performances.'

Finney himself confessed later that he didn't believe he was very good as Coriolanus, that he failed to bring enough originality, enough of himself to the part. 'When you hear Sir Laurence's tones ringing in your ears night after night, it's very difficult for you not to be similar, because you're working from his blueprint.' At least for those six performances as Coriolanus Finney managed to escape that dingy dressing room he shared with Hardy and was allowed access to the much larger rooms of Sir Laurence. 'But then he came back,' said Hardy. 'His tail a tiny bit between his legs I suspect; back down to earth.'

Perhaps as a nod of gratitude, Finney was invited to play a small role in *The Entertainer*, that of Archie Rice's second son, the one not seen in Osborne's play. He appears in the film in a tearful station send-off to go fight at Suez, a conflict from which he will not return. It only took a single night to shoot, at Liverpool Street station, but it did mark Finney's cinema debut.

These were heady times for Finney, and not just professionally. He was having an affair with the actress Zoe Caldwell, who'd played Bianca to his Cassio in *Othello*, and had walked out on his wife and their one-year-old son Simon to stay at Robert Hardy's digs, lying in bed most of the day smoking like a chimney and hiding from Jane. Hardy finally had enough and turfed him out. It wasn't adultery that wrecked his marriage; it was over already, in fact never for one minute did it stand much of a chance. Wedded bliss, it seemed, didn't suit Finney. 'I felt I was in a cage, so I escaped. I was too young to get married anyway. I wasn't ready for it. Gas bills. Laundry bills. Everyone has them, but for me they're too much.'

Finney and Jane would divorce a couple of years later, with Jane granted custody of Simon, much to the distress of Finney's mother, 'who wagged her finger at me'. Finney tried to make light of the situation but actually his parents were appalled, coming as they did from a generation who stayed in marriages, even loveless ones, either because they respected their wedding vows or because they were too worried about what the neighbours might say. While he felt little guilt over the break-up, Finney deeply regretted that he wouldn't be able to raise his son in the same kind of warm, comforting environment he'd grown up in.

The affair with Zoe carried over into the next production in August,

King Lear, which had Laughton in the title role. As with *The Party*, Laughton's domineering presence fell once again upon the cast. He especially disapproved of Finney's dalliance with Zoe. 'He wanted the complete devotion of all of us in the cast,' she said.

The production was not altogether a success. 'Albert and I played Edgar and Edmund,' recalls Hardy. 'He was bloody good as Edgar, he was bloody good, but some of the critics said that we were wrongly cast, that I should have played Edgar and he should have played Edmund because he was rougher and tougher. But we got on pretty well.'

Laughton suffered badly, he was sixty and struggled with his *Lear*. Sensing a wounded animal, the critics weren't particularly kind and his failure in the role was crushing. It had been a mistake to take the part and he knew it but, unable to back down, his misgivings coloured his performances. 'Laughton played the worst Lear I've ever seen,' says Hardy.

Not long after that Stratford season Laughton's health deteriorated and he returned to the States, where he died at the end of 1962. Shortly before his death, Finney was invited by Laughton's wife Elsa Lancaster to visit their home in Los Angeles. Elsa had thought Finney 'sufficiently brilliant' to observe 'a giant going'. Finney stayed for half an hour at Laughton's bedside; alas, the great old actor never knew he was there.

39

O'Toole's Nose
Goes for a Burton

After his success in *The Long and the Short and the Tall* O'Toole began to receive movie offers. But even in those early days his behaviour and drinking had become legendary within the business and who knows how many potential film roles went down the pan because of it. On one occasion he went to see future 007 producer Albert R. Broccoli, who was looking, irony of ironies, to replace an actor who had a drink problem on one of his films. Alas, as O'Toole stumbled into Broccoli's office a bottle of whisky fell out of his overcoat pocket.

O'Toole's film debut was in Disney's *Kidnapped*, based on the classic Robert Louis Stevenson book. It was the star of the picture Peter Finch who recommended him for his small role. Maintaining his old Bristol habits, on his very first day O'Toole overslept. An angry film company rang to ask where he was. Kenneth Griffith answered with some ad-lib bullshit: 'This is a very large house, I'll see if I can find him.' Griffith raced upstairs and popped his head round O'Toole's bedroom door. He was fast asleep. 'O'Toole. You are forty-five minutes late.' Lifting his bedraggled head off the pillow, O'Toole asked if his car had arrived. 'No,' said Griffith, struck by the question. O'Toole's head crashed back onto the pillow. 'No car, no me.' And went back to sleep.

O'Toole had never wanted to be a film star anyway – 'What interested me was the £175 fee' – but the film world did intrigue him and he thought he'd have a bash at it. 'When I saw the rushes of my scene with Finch, I thought, I can do this.' So-called film technique wasn't so mystical, after all. 'It was like rehearsals for a stage performance chopped up into bits and so long as you kept your voice down to what you'd use on the telephone, you were all right.'

Finch was a mighty drinker, so not surprisingly the pair became great pals. O'Toole and Finch piss-ups were similarly mighty affairs and although they never made another film together little excuse was needed to indulge themselves. When Finch was working in Ireland in the early sixties O'Toole joined him one night for a drink but the pub refused to serve them because it was after closing time. Both stars decided that the only course of action was to buy the pub, so they wrote out a cheque for it on the spot. The following morning, after realising what they'd done, the pair rushed back to the scene of their bankruptcy. Luckily the landlord hadn't cashed the cheque yet and disaster was averted.

Even while he was still at Bristol O'Toole had come to the attention of movie makers, notably Joseph Losey. 'I thought that he had a tremendous talent. He also had the arrogance that goes with it when you are young.' Losey was setting up a film entitled *Blind Date*, a psychological thriller, and wanted O'Toole to play the police inspector, essentially the second lead alongside Hardy Kruger. Despite a nasty head cold O'Toole impressed Losey at the interview, but the financial muscle behind the picture refused to accept him because he wasn't a 'name'. So Losey had to look elsewhere, eventually casting Stanley Baker.

Still firmly believing O'Toole possessed talent, Losey recommended the actor to Nicholas Ray, then casting his film *The Savage Innocents*. Eager to work with the director of *Rebel Without a Cause*, the whole experience in the end turned into something of a disaster. Playing a Canadian trooper out to capture Anthony Quinn's Eskimo who has run foul of the laws imposed upon his Arctic homeland by white settlers, O'Toole hardly endeared himself to Ray. In one scene the two men have to make a sledge in order to escape the snowy wastes but the scriptwriter hadn't been able to figure out exactly how they were supposed to achieve this. O'Toole helpfully suggested the Eskimo eat his character and make a sledge out of his bones and skin. 'We want a happy ending,' said Ray.

Filmed on location in the north of Canada, interiors took place at England's Pinewood Studios, where the snow was in fact tons of salt mix. Two polar bears brought in from Dublin Zoo to lend a bit of local colour were ironically deemed not white enough against the salt so were covered in peroxide which drove them nuts. O'Toole left this sorry mess scratching his head and wondering whether he would ever make it in the movies, and whether he even wanted to, especially when he saw the final cut and discovered that his voice had been dubbed by an American actor.

A flop upon release, *The Savage Innocents* did throw up two important results. Its producer Joseph Janni used its failure as an excuse to return to making the kind of realistic, socially aware films he'd always wanted to do, a decision that eventually gave rise to such films as *A Kind of Loving*, *Billy Liar* and *Darling*. The other was the O'Toole hooter. A splendid beast it was, long, yes, crooked, yes, but magnificent, almost regal. According to Losey it was Nicholas Ray who persuaded O'Toole to have it fixed. And Losey wouldn't be alone in thinking it to have been a big mistake. 'It changed his personality, his interest for me. He didn't have an ugly or misshapen nose, it was just slightly bulbous on the end. He had more character that way. Then he became just another very good-looking actor.' David Andrews, O'Toole's *Long and the Short* co-star, was equally aghast when he saw it. 'Peter's nose was massive but it was beautifully proportioned, you could never say his nose was big, it was beautiful and I think they ruined it when they turned it into a horrible Hollywood snub.'

40

The Ginger Nut

Between film roles Harris returned to the theatre in a play he pursued fervently, *The Ginger Man*, based on the novel by J. P. Donleavy about bed-hopping, drunken Dublin student Sebastian Dangerfield, memorably described by Bernard Levin as 'making Jimmy Porter look like a Stakhanovite'.

The American actor Jason Robards had been named to star while Harris was offered a supporting role; sod that, said Harris and campaigned hard to play Dangerfield. Donleavy visited Harris in his flat on Earls Court Road. 'He showed me his fridge and pointed to the imprint of his fist embedded there. He held up the book and said, "Look here, this book is my life."' Reading for the part, Harris blew the producer and director away; they had to give it to him. And that's when the trouble really began.

Harris threw himself into the production, rehearsing forty hours nonstop, half-pissed, and then collapsing with exhaustion. 'I can't do the fucking thing,' he'd yell and storm off to the pub. Co-star and friend Ronnie Fraser was always the one sent to retrieve him.

For weeks on end *The Ginger Man* consumed Harris's entire being, took him over like no other role had. 'I think conveniently,' says Elizabeth. 'Because there was a lot of drinking and a lot of things that appealed to him; he was halfway there anyway. The character he was playing was absolutely up his street.'

The Ginger Man opened in September 1959 at the small Fortune Theatre in Covent Garden. It was hailed as another *Look Back in Anger* and Harris as theatreland's new angry young man. But the rave notices passed unnoticed by Harris: 'By the time we opened, I was living on

Pluto.' Sheer exhaustion and near-constant boozing had turned the Harris marital home into something of a battle zone. Unable to take living any more with Harris (or was it Donleavy's anti-hero?), Elizabeth left, taking one-year-old Damian with her. When reminded of this event years later Harris simply said. 'Did she? I wasn't fully aware.'

When the run finished in London Harris took the play to Dublin's Gaiety Theatre and a predictable disaster when it attracted a storm of controversy for its perceived sexual and religious profanity. On the opening night angry mobs tried to bar the actors from entering the theatre and there were shouts during the performance of 'take it off' along with boos and cat-calls. Next morning the *Irish Independent*, the country's most influential daily newspaper, damned *The Ginger Man* as 'one of the most nauseating plays ever to appear on a Dublin stage'. By the third night things had not improved and the management of the theatre demanded cuts. Donleavy and Harris told them where to get off and the play was pulled.

Predictably, Harris drowned himself in booze, happy at least to have thoroughly pissed off the moral majority. He drank every kind of alcohol but had a particular liking for brandy, which unfortunately brought out the worst in him. Mentally he was all over the place. After several weeks of convalescence Harris welcomed Elizabeth back home; she was able to restore a little welcome sanity into the Harris universe, although friends remained worried for her. Was Harris cut out for domesticity? He seemed to have a hankering for chaos. Even so, it seemed like the perfect time for a fresh start, and a fresh move.

David Andrews and his wife Tamara were looking for a flat and happened to be walking down Earls Court Road. Standing in an entrance between two shops was someone Tamara immediately recognised as 'Mickser' Harris. 'What are you doing down here?' he asked Tamara. 'We're looking for a flat.' They got chatting. 'Well, talk to Liz because we're just moving out of this place.' A deal was hastily arranged and David and Tamara moved in and remained there for three years. 'The reason I was told Harris was moving out was because his film contract required him to live in a more salubrious area,' says Andrews. 'At that time Earls Court was considered very bohemian.' One of the main features of the flat – it was unmissable – was a bar that Harris had made for the front room. 'And he'd left it for us,' says Andrews. 'It was free-standing, made of plywood and timber with shelving units. It was great because at parties you could set that up wherever you liked, although it took two people to shift the thing, it was pretty heavy, but very useful. You could put a barrel of beer on it, which we frequently did.'

One of the first friends Andrews invited round to the 'Harris Bar' was Caine. He'd just returned from a pre-West End run of a new play called *One More River* up in Liverpool. It was about a mutiny in which a crew puts its first officer on trial for manslaughter. Robert Shaw was also in the cast. Caine would recall that one day after a rehearsal the actors set out to look for somewhere nice to have lunch and came across a café where a band were playing, a group of teenage musicians attracting a size-able bunch of fans. Caine asked who they were. The Quarrymen, he was told. The group was just a few years away from taking over the world as the Beatles.

That October *One More River* moved into the West End, minus Caine but retaining Shaw, whose steely performance as the officer on trial drew much praise, even if the play itself was not a success. The produc-tion in Liverpool had been directed by Sam Wanamaker, but in London it was produced by Laurence Olivier's company and he installed the film director Guy Hamilton. 'I had worked with Larry for a few days on his film *The Devil's Disciple*,' says Hamilton. 'And as I was anxious to direct a play, my agent wangled it for me. Larry obviously thought that the five years I'd spent in the Royal Navy made me the perfect director for a yarn set aboard a dirty tramp steamer with a rebellious crew.' Hamilton found the whole venture pleasantly diverting and Shaw a pleasure to work with. 'He could not have been more professional or helpful to someone who was, in effect, an outsider.'

Shaw had recently moved into a large property on Abbey Road, big enough to accommodate his growing family. Forget new beds, chairs etc., the first item Shaw bought was a full-size table-tennis table which took up much of the front room. Most guests who visited were subjected to a fierce game whether they wanted one or not. Ronnie Fraser and Sean Connery were both told, 'Just not worth playing you, boy. Just not worth it,' after losing easily to Shaw. Philip Broadley once collapsed in tears after losing an epic hundred-set match.

Shaw's competitive nature extended far beyond his living room. Actress Barbara Jefford recalls an encounter that almost killed her: 'Shaw had to win at all costs and played all types of sports to the extreme, very hard. I remember getting involved in a game of squash at his squash club and nearly dying. I'd never played it before and it was a one-off, I never did it again.'

41
Stamp of Approval

Caine had been unable to come into the West End with *One More River* because he'd been asked to do the tour of *The Long and the Short and the Tall*, which was making its way round the country after finishing in London. After understudying O'Toole for so long he'd finally won the role of Bamforth and was able to make it his own. The other lead was played by Frank Finlay. While not a West End production, given the star role in a popular tour worked wonders for Caine's self-respect. 'It was my happiest and most valuable experience to date, and I identify it as my first step towards becoming a star.'

Also in the cast, taking the role David Andrews originally played of the radio operator, was an intensely shy young man by the name of Terence Stamp. This was his first professional engagement. Stamp never saw the original production but often walked past the theatre gazing at the photographs of O'Toole and Shaw on the hoardings outside. One night in the Salisbury pub he saw O'Toole holding court drinking, when an irate stage assistant burst in. 'Mr O'Toole, please, it's time. We're waiting to start, sir.' After more pleading the desperate assistant then grabbed O'Toole by the lapels and literally dragged him out. Stamp was impressed as many were who watched from afar, at this amazing quality O'Toole possessed. Was it endorphins that kicked in when he walked on stage, 'because an icy soberness becalmed him until the interval', said Stamp, 'when he was once again legless. I thought I could be pretty flash myself until I saw this fella.'

Because Caine knew the play back to front all the actors in the tour naturally gravitated towards him and he assumed the role of pack leader with a natural ease. On the train up to their first destination, Nottingham, he dominated the conversation, which revolved around 'birds' and little else. Caine mentioned one stunner he'd spied in the Buckstone one night. It turned out that Stamp knew her; better than that, he *really* knew her! Caine was impressed. 'So! You're one of the lads, then.' He leaned over and made a great show of shaking Stamp's hand. 'Blimey, I thought you were a poof.'

The two men grew even closer when Caine discovered Stamp's humble East End origins. 'Michael was relieved to find a fellow Londoner. A lad after his own heart, standing up to the invasion of actors from the north.'

There were remarkable similarities in their upbringings. Like Caine, Stamp had experienced the London Blitz, and had a bomb shelter in his backyard. Stamp would recall shopping with his mother one afternoon when the air-raid warning sounded and both were hustled into the basement of Woolworth's in Aldgate, squashed with other shoppers listening to the dance of death above until silence prevailed again an hour later. During the heaviest bombing the family moved to Yorkshire, vivid memories for Stamp; so too VE day, because that's the day his dad Tom came back from the war.

Stamp was born on 22 July 1939 in Bow, the eldest of five children, and lived in a typical East End home with his mother Ethel just about making ends meet on her husband's wages as a Thames tug-boat driver. When he was five the family moved to a slightly grander district where the young Stamp encountered the middle classes and for the first time in his life felt the black pang of jealously and dissatisfaction with what he'd got. It still remained a struggle for his parents to provide even the bare necessities, let alone the odd luxury or two, a sullen reminder of how much poorer they were than their new neighbours. And as more Stamp siblings arrived his mother was forced to work as a barmaid.

Stamp's mother played an important role in his life; she was the driving force in the home. In those days the strong moral structure of the family sprang from the mother. Their small garden backed onto another, much grander, property whose large pear tree overhung the fence. Every year it was heavy with pears, at a time when fruit was a luxury due to rationing, but it never occurred to the Stamp kids to take any; 'What you wanted, you had to earn.'

Ethel was also an avid film fan and often took Terence with her on trips to the cinema. She also instilled in him a sense that he was more special than most. Stamp later came to believe that his mother placed upon him all the dreams and aspirations she had sacrificed for a life of domesticity. 'For me there seemed to be born the most intense longing to show her that I wouldn't let her down, that somehow I would lift us all out of this squalor.'

And education was the way out. With his eleven-plus coming up, Stamp knew he was at a crossroads in his life; he didn't want to work at the Ford plant at Dagenham, as so many from his area did, their faces all smeared with gloom in the mornings. Problem was, he'd never really taken school seriously before, a habit that started in infant school when he quickly sussed out once your name had been ticked off on the register you could then quietly slip away to spend the day on the swings in the park.

Now he sweated and studied and, much to his own surprise, passed his eleven-plus; that meant he could go to grammar school, just as Caine had done. He also joined a local boys' club and one afternoon came across an amateur dramatic society rehearsing in the hall. He watched fascinated, and afterwards was called over by one of the actors who'd observed him staring from the sidelines and given an invitation to that evening's performance. It was the first proper play Stamp had ever seen, and it changed his life. Whenever the society turned up to rehearse another show Stamp was always there, hanging around, soaking it all up.

When he was sixteen he appeared in one of their productions at the East Ham town hall when someone dropped out at the last minute, playing of all things a sixty-five-year-old man. It was a complete disaster. By the final act he had succumbed so utterly to nerves that he started stuttering 'and transposing words in my dialogue which effectively made absolute gibberish of the text, let alone the plot!'

The critic of that august organ the *Stratford Express* was in the audience that night and in his review sang the praises of the entire cast, 'with the exception of Terence Stamp'. The offending review swiftly circulated around school and he was teased mercilessly. But something deeper had occurred, a psychological shift. 'The experience was so awesome that I swore it would be the last theatrical escapade I would ever embark on.'

At school he'd also slipped back into his old bad habits and left without passing a single exam. 'There'll always be labourers,' he remembered his teacher saying to him one day. 'And you, Stamp, will be one of them.' Hardly encouraging, but then he saw his contemporaries seemingly happy to follow that path into factory jobs. 'But if my mates had no ambition, I had.'

Rejecting local work, he got a job up West, as a glorified office boy for an advertising agency. His quick grasp of the advertising business, along with his personal charisma and wide boy arrogance, enabled Stamp to jump from agency to agency, getting further up the ladder each time, until he was earning decent money. Rather less charismatically, he still lived with his parents. They'd recently bought a television on hire purchase and many a night Stamp stayed in to watch the evening play, coming to the conclusion that most of the actors in them were rubbish. 'I could do better than that,' he'd say after sitting through another duff performance. 'I don't want you to talk about it any more,' his dad finally said one evening after Stamp had hurled another volley of insults at the box. 'I don't want you to even think about it. People like us don't do things like that!' Stamp came to believe that this was his dad's way of scaring off any thoughts he might have had of an acting career, fearful that he'd only end up disappointed. 'My Victorian father couldn't conceive how any son of his was going to be an actor.'

It was never spoken of again, but inside Stamp was boiling over. There was a fierce frustration within him, that he knew he had talent, he knew he could succeed, but that circumstances and his environment were against him. 'The doors have been closed so long to people like me that most of us have given up hammering.' Having gotten over his earlier stage calamity, Stamp now saw acting as an escape route out of the East End. He'd always felt he didn't belong there. 'It always felt a terrible mistake coming from Bow. Nothing wrong with Bow, it just didn't fit me.'

His acting ambition looked like being put on hold at the close of

1956 when it was time to do his National Service, but he failed the medical. 'You mean, I can't even volunteer?' pleaded Stamp, trying his best to look crestfallen. Inside he was bursting with relief. 'It was as if I'd accustomed myself to the idea of going to jail for two years and been reprieved at the last moment.' He caught the train home and mulled over exactly what he was going to do with the two extra years of his life he'd been given. Why not go out on a limb and try to be an actor, use those two years to really have a crack at it? If he failed miserably it didn't matter, he'd still be level pegging with his contemporaries coming out of the services. Mind made up, he told his dad that he had decided to become an actor. 'Turned queer then, have you?' asked Tom.

Deciding was one thing, but how to set about it was quite another. He had no idea of even the first step to take. 'I didn't know what RADA was. I thought that only Lords' sons were actors because they talked properly.' His friends were no more encouraging than his father had been: 'Who do you think you are?' Stamp already felt he didn't belong with them any more, in a place of 'narrow houses and narrower minds. And a lot of nits who think the world ends at Aldgate.'

Then someone told him about an acting class in Dean Street that taught The Method, just like the Actors Studio in New York where Brando and Dean had learned their trade. Stamp arrived to find it populated by an odd assortment of people all with one thing in common, a devotion to James Dean. The American had been dead for a year, but his films were still showing in London and this lot paid solemn visits to screenings as if they were attending church. One day in class a posh girl berated Stamp's acting approach, ending with, 'And your voice . . . if you think you can get to act anywhere with that, you won't even get past the door – well, perhaps, if they're looking for lorry drivers.' Stamp remembers thinking how strange the insult was, especially coming from a devotee of The Method, whose followers seemed to be blue-collar, earthy types. But then America was so very different.

The extent to which this generation of actors were influenced by Brando and The Method is a moot point. Certainly, the press picked up on it: Connery, Harris and Finney were each labelled at some point the British Brando. 'Of course we were very aware of The Method and the Actors Studio,' says David McCallum. 'But at the same time most of us ignored it. It was something that was very much a part of American culture at that time, it didn't really cross over to Britain. I was at the Oxford Playhouse during the height of all that Brando, method-acting stuff, and we developed a method of acting on stage which was called DOHTEM, which is method spelled backwards. I think it had three rules: look your best, learn your lines and speak distinctly.'

By now Stamp had left home and moved into a flat with a bunch of acting buddies in Harley Street, an expensive area, but as there were ten of them sharing it turned out to be relatively inexpensive. He'd tried to persuade some of his old school mates to come with him on this new odyssey, to get out of the East End, but none of them did. He guessed a lot of the reason was fear coupled with perceived inferiority: it was a common belief amongst the working classes that the people who owned or ran things must be geniuses, and they just couldn't compete. When he got out and began to mix, Stamp found that the bosses were more than fallible, that 'they didn't have an idea in their heads'. Moreover, they were crying out for new talent, for fresh blood. Stamp knew that some of the lads from the East End could walk straight in if they'd only get off their arses and try. Instead they were content to become clones of their parents. 'They are sentenced to lives in council houses.'

Stamp's thoughts turned to drama school, and how to obtain a place at one. When he heard that the Webber Douglas Academy of Dramatic Art awarded a scholarship biannually 'to students of outstanding ability and insufficient funds', Stamp went for it, giving up his cushy job in advertising. At his audition in July 1957 he gave the panel Mark Antony's 'Friends, Romans, countrymen' speech, inspired by watching Brando in *Julius Caesar*, followed by a piece of comedy for his modern speech which drew such applause that a flummoxed Stamp bowed, exited stage right and walked Clouseau-like into a brick wall. Composing himself, he left the room thinking, 'I've got this. I've bloody well got this.' Sure enough, later that afternoon came the phone call saying he'd been awarded the scholarship as their unanimous choice.

As at RADA, Stamp discovered that at Webber Douglas movie acting was looked down upon, and a career in film was no laudable ambition. Amongst his intake was Steven Berkoff, dressed usually in black, Penelope Keith and Samantha Eggar, whom Stamp lusted after from afar. As a student he largely subsisted on beans on toast and worked evenings at the Piccadilly Theatre as a general dogsbody, then backstage at Her Majesty's Theatre where the original London stage production of *West Side Story* was wowing audiences. Victor Spinetti recalls that at some time or another Stamp was his dresser during a London stage show and voiced a desire to meet Joan Littlewood. 'So I took him along and she told him he was too pretty for the theatre, that he should go into films.'

One afternoon on the tube Stamp found himself sitting opposite the old reprobate Wilfrid Lawson. Somehow Stamp conjured up enough courage to introduce himself. 'Mr Lawson, sorry to disturb you, sir, but I'm an actor, just starting. Is there any advice you could give me?'

'Advice.' The word seemed to take an aeon to enter his sozzled brain and for its meaning to be deciphered.

'Yes,' said Stamp. 'What's your technique; what do *you* do?'

Lawson's eyes rolled about in their bleary sockets and then fixed on Stamp like a hawk on a scampering mole. 'Oh, I just learn the wordies.'

In a production of *Othello* at Webber Douglas Stamp was cast as Iago. One of his friends knew top agent Jimmy Fraser and said he was coming to see it. Sensing this was his chance, Stamp put everything into the performance, acting out each soliloquy not in a passive way, but directly at the audience, as if each and every one of them was sharing in his secret villainies. After the show in the pub Fraser approached Stamp. 'My God,' he said. 'That's the sexiest Iago I've ever seen! Thank goodness you're not loose on the streets.' By the end of the evening Fraser asked Stamp to come and see him in his offices. 'You're good, and you're going to get better.'

It was decided that Fraser would take Stamp on and that he'd leave Webber Douglas early and start doing a bit of rep somewhere to gain proper experience. Within days Stamp had landed his first acting job, a role in the tour of *The Long and the Short and the Tall*.

After a few weeks on the road Caine had come to see Stamp as a younger version of himself while Stamp looked up to him almost as an older brother, for guidance and support. Caine constantly offered the youngster tips on how to craft his performance, make it more natural and make it play better for the audience, giving Stamp the full benefit of his six years' hard graft in rep. Caine was useful in other ways, too, telling him what the best aftershave was to wear to attract the ladies and loaning him his Ian Fleming paperbacks. On arriving in a new town the pair often put more effort into catching the local talent than their performances, but the show was a success in every venue it played.

Meanwhile, Jimmy Fraser was working hard for his new client, getting him an interview for the role of Paul in the film of *Sons and Lovers*. So buoyed by the news was Stamp that he decided to leave the tour early and head back to London. Never having experienced the hardships of being a struggling actor, the long stretches of unemployment, he was still finding it all terribly exciting. Caine wished him luck when he left; maybe they'd bump into each other in London.

42

Caine and Stamp Join Forces

In the late fifties the Oxford Playhouse was amongst the liveliest and most adventurous rep theatres in the country, nurturing the careers of, amongst others, Maggie Smith and Ronnie Barker. In the doldrums for many years, its fortunes had been revived by a bold and visionary new director, Frank Hauser. Beloved of his actors, Hauser's gift was for casting and he took a gamble by inviting Connery to play Pentheus, the tyrant Greek king in a production of Euripides' *The Bacchae*. One must commend Hauser as the first director to see Connery as an actor capable of playing historical figures, roles that would later loom large in his film career.

It was a fascinating production with a memorable climax when the king is slain and his head stuck on a pole. For this effect a plaster cast was taken of Connery's head and when it was brought on stage, all bloody and revolting, Connery recalled that 'a roar of anguished disbelief erupted from the audience'. His death scene was too realistic for one African tourist who fled the auditorium 'howling in abject terror'. The critics weren't impressed, however. *Plays and Players* magazine said, 'Connery's Pentheus was too much on the surface and his American inflections were often irritating.'

The critics were much kinder when he played Mat Burke once again in *Anna Christie*, this time opposite Jill Bennett. The *Oxford Times* thought him 'magnificent'. Lewis Gilbert, who'd directed Diane Cilento in *The Admirable Crichton*, had met Connery a couple of times on social occasions and watched him at Oxford: 'He wasn't always good on stage, but he always found some business within a role, he was always interesting – and that is something you cannot say of many actors in any sphere.'

That November Connery was seen in another period production, a television adaptation of Arthur Miller's *The Crucible*, playing John Proctor, a man of strong principle who chooses to be hanged rather than sign a false confession to devil worship. This was in fact the first television production of the play anywhere; Miller's drama was still seen as far too controversial for American home audiences.

Amongst the cast was a young actress not long out of drama school and making an early television appearance, Susannah York, who remembered well both the play and working with Connery. 'He was extremely personable and fun to work with, very generous and warm as an actor, very open, and a very sexy man; funny, too and very alive. He played the part superbly well.' It went out live, for Susannah her first bit of live telly. Connery by now was an old hand at it and enjoyed working on these classic plays; he felt the relative austerity of the production, as opposed to the films he was making, forced him to deliver of his best.

Stamp missed out on *Sons and Lovers*; Dean Stockwell got the job at producer Jerry Wald's insistence to help the film's chances of distribution in the United States. Richard Harris had also been up for the part, as indeed had Alan Bates, who was particularly miffed at losing out.

While walking in the West End following an afternoon drowning his sorrows, Stamp bumped into Caine, who after the tour had once again fallen on hard times. Stamp suggested he move into Harley Street, where there was a spare room going. Within days Caine was knocking on the door, suitcase in hand.

One morning he was rudely awoken by a couple of coppers, innocently let in by Stamp, and arrested for non-payment of maintenance. Caine was thrown in a police cell for several hours, an ordeal only slightly ameliorated by the fact that one of the officers recognised him from a recent episode of *Dixon of Dock Green* and gave Caine an extra bit of cake with his tea.

Such arrests were a regular occurrence in their early time together, Stamp would recall, 'Although the poor guy didn't even have the price of a pair of specs most of the time.' Once, hauled up before a magistrate, Caine suddenly regretted his decision to move to Harley Street. 'Rather a swish address for someone with no money, isn't it, Mr Caine?' said the judge.

'Look at it this way, guv,' answered Caine, thinking on his feet. 'Think of all the money I save on fares coming to court.'

Deciding to throw himself at the mercy of the court, Caine babbled on about his Dickensian life as an out-of-work actor, how he'd done two *Dixon of Dock Greens*, that if he went to jail how could he ever hope to work with nice Constable Dixon again. This went on for quite some time until the judge could stand it no longer. 'Shut up!' he yelled.

Spared breaking boulders, it was nevertheless drummed into Caine that if he faced the bar again for the same offence, prison it would be, Jack Warner or no Jack Warner. Patricia was in court that day; Caine hadn't seen her for a while and as he left he smiled at her. For a brief second there was a connection between them again as she smiled back. 'She's remarried, you know,' a friend told him a little later. 'He's another actor, but he earns a bloody sight more money than you ever did.'

The prospect of going to jail was a mighty stimulus for going out and getting a job. So it was back to phoning directors he knew and scanning the *Stage*. Stamp had learned that Caine's strategy was to stay in the hunt long enough so that when the big break arrived he was there and ready for it. To save money he walked nearly everywhere, not wasting money on the tube or buses. He'd been telling the magistrate the truth about that.

On the actor's grapevine Caine heard there was a play opening at the Royal Court directed by Lindsay Anderson about a bunch of teddy boys. It was called *The Lily White Boys*. Albert Finney was playing the lead and they were looking for an understudy. Caine auditioned, and failed. So Stamp had a go, a real go, turning up on stage and singing 'I've Got a Lovely Bunch of Coconuts', which so bewildered Anderson in the stalls he leaned forward in his chair and after an interminable pause offered, 'Ye-e-s. Thank you. We'll let you know.' Disheartened, Stamp returned to the flat, threw his jacket off (it was one the pair had specially made for auditions because it fitted them both), and said to Caine, 'I don't think his idea of cockneys is the same as ours.'

The Lily White Boys was planned to kick off the Royal Court's 1960 season. Socialist in content, it concerned three teddy boys who turn away from a ne'er-do-well existence, one becoming a successful busi-nessman, another a corrupt trade union leader and the third a policeman, only to find that their legitimate jobs are if anything more immoral than their petty thieving ever was.

With a few songs dotted about here and there, producer Oscar Lewenstein was convinced the play would make for a good satirical piece of Brechtian-style theatre and brought in the poet and playwright Christopher Logue as lyricist. He'd also hired Anderson and Finney, that actor's first appearance at the Royal Court, a company that suited his temperament and feeling for realism. Sean Kenny was set designer; later in the year his work for *Oliver!* and *Beyond the Fringe* set him on a path to become the decade's pre-eminent theatre set designer. Critics sang his praises by saying that punters came out of the theatre humming his sets.

Anderson quickly created a pleasant feel to the company and grew especially nurturing towards Finney, accompanying him to Paris to watch the Berliner Ensemble, a theatrical troupe founded by Brecht to present his work. The trip was Anderson's idea, a way of familiarising Finney with the style they were attempting, yet at the start of rehearsals the actor confessed to George Devine, 'You know, I'm not sure what Brechtian actually means.' Was this bravado or genuine sentiment? As Anderson would note in his diary, Finney learned, 'astonishingly fast, whether to sing, or to dance, or to play "objectively" that whole ironic, detached side of the part. Without a talent as outstanding as his, this show would be impossible.' Praise indeed, certainly warranted, but also coloured by personal feelings that Anderson had begun to harbour for his young star.

Professionally, Anderson was exactly the kind of director Finney was looking for at this time, one who encouraged his hankering for creative freedom and was determined to cut away the old-fashioned trappings of theatre. But inevitably as Anderson's feelings deepened, fantasising about more joint projects and perhaps even of sharing a home together, fissures opened up in their professional relationship.

In the end *The Lily White Boys* proved a personal triumph for Finney, but the audiences just weren't good enough during its six-week run to warrant a West End transfer, much to the disappointment of Lewenstein who thought it an excellent show, 'The nearest thing to a Brechtian piece of theatre created at that time in London.'

43

Harris Meets Mitchum

After his run-in with Heston on *The Wreck of the Mary Deare*, Harris faced the even more fearsome Robert Mitchum in his next film *A Terrible Beauty*, an IRA drama shot in Ireland. At first Harris disliked Mitchum but warmed to him when the Hollywood legend came to his aid during a pub brawl. Another time Mitchum sat drinking in a Dublin bar when a short Irishman came up and poked him in the ribs with a pencil. 'Hey, movie star, give me your autograph. It's for my wife.' Mitchum eyed the midget up and down with undisguised disgust. 'Will you look at the little leprechaun,' and then told him to wait until he'd finished his drink. But the man persisted. Finally, an exasperated Mitchum snatched the paper and pencil and wrote: 'UP YOUR ARSE – KIRK DOUGLAS.' The man was not best pleased and threw a punch, but Mitchum just sat there looking at him. 'If that's the best you can do, little lady, you better come back with your girlfriends.' The man did indeed return with some rather hefty mates. Mitchum head-butted one of them, sending him reeling before two more came into the attack. Harris leaped into the fray and a massive punch-up ensued resulting in the Guards being summoned to break it up.

As a couple, Harris and Elizabeth got to know Mitchum well and became friends. 'Mitchum was more of a rebel than any of them,' says Elizabeth. 'That's who they all gravitated to, O'Toole, Richard and the rest; they were all very much on the same mindset. And Mitchum wouldn't be bothered with authority; he didn't do authority.'

All these men played up to their boozy, brawling, madcap image; some resented the press label of hellraiser, others wallowed in it, turning it almost into a badge of honour and a second career. 'What that group of actors had was a fine madness, a lyrical madness,' said Harris. 'We lived our life with that madness and it was transmitted into our work. We had smiles on our faces and a sense that the world was mad. We weren't afraid to be different. So we were always dangerous. Dangerous to meet in the street, in a restaurant, and dangerous to see on stage or in a film.'

Elizabeth, of course, lived through it all and is today remarkably philosophical about that period. 'Richard was a hellraiser in the early days without the press following him. Then suddenly the press put that tag on quite a few of them. Actually the boys very rarely got bad publicity. The press were always very fond of them because they were very good with all the journalists, they'd go to hit them and at the same time put their arms around them and offer them a drink. There was a very good relationship with the press; if the boys were indiscreet about certain things they didn't publish it.'

Another thing, the press back then was not the enormous animal it is today with an insatiable appetite for gossip and tittle-tattle and irrelevances that can never be sated.

'That's why I think it was a good time for all of us that started back then,' says Rita Tushingham. 'You didn't have all the publications, all the television channels and all the gossip columns. You had some, but it's true, there were certain things that people would never print, and they weren't interested in it anyway because newspapers didn't want to have the kind of fodder that they have now. It was a much easier time to grow up in the spotlight.'

Certainly, Harris was a boon to the publicity department of Associated British Picture Corporation, whose stable of bland film stars didn't excite the press much, they were too well groomed and well behaved to attract their interest. With Harris the job became less about trying to get him press coverage and more about simply keeping pace with his antics. When the PR staff came into the office on Monday morning to find all the telephones ringing, the first thought would be, God, what's Harris done now?

That said, Harris always found that the UK media had a habit of taking the best out of him and throwing the rest away. Years later when he won an award he flew back to London and saw an *Evening Standard* billboard hailing 'British actor wins at Cannes'. Four days later he got into a fight in Covent Garden and the same newspaper's billboard read 'Irish actor in brawl'.

All this wild behaviour, of course, was fuelled by drink, lots of it, as Elizabeth was only too well aware. 'Richard didn't drink spirits; well, he did drink vodka, and then you just ran, got out of his way. In fact I wouldn't want to stay with him if he was on brandy, either. On the Mitchum film in Dublin he realised how dangerous he was with brandy, and he actually stopped himself drinking brandy. You just wouldn't mess around, you'd have to get out of the way he could be so violent. So he didn't drink spirits that much. Later on he just drank wine and beer. His drink of choice would be Guinness or beer.' Strangely though, there wasn't the level of violence that's associated with drinking now, with knifings and the like. 'There wasn't any of that,' says Elizabeth. 'They'd have a punch-up or a fight with someone and then they'd make up and go and have another drink. It was a totally different scene.'

In February Harris returned to television for director Alvin Rakoff in a version of Rod Serling's teleplay *The Strike*, produced on American television in 1954 with Franklin Schaffner at the helm. Retitled *Come in Razor Red* by Rakoff, since the word strike had political ramifications in Britain, Harris was perfectly cast as a tough commander of an American patrol lost in the jungle during the Korean War. Close to enemy lines, they come across an enemy artillery post that threatens to wipe out a full US battalion. Harris's commander faces a huge moral dilemma, should he order an air strike knowing full well that his own troops will end up as dead as the Reds. 'Richard was very, very boisterous, aggressive and self-confident,' Rakoff recalls. 'He wasn't going to take any shit from anybody. You could see it on his shoulder; the chips were bigger than his epaulettes. But that was part of his persona; it was patently clear that all you had to do was knock the chips off and you'd find a lovely soft guy underneath. Richard's persona was, don't get too close or I'll hit you, but that was just persona.'

Looking for as much realism as possible on screen, Rakoff rang up the US embassy to ask if they could loan him a platoon of Marines to act as extras. 'And to my surprise and delight, because television was very exciting to people in those days, they agreed. So these real Marines arrived. And I had this girl, no more than eighteen, just out of drama school, as my assistant, and of course the F-word was much in evidence during rehearsals with all these macho guys, nobody could tie their shoelaces without calling them the fucking laces. And Richard was a prolific swearer. And this girl's face was getting constantly redder; she must have come from a very sheltered background. So I got a big cocoa tin and put the words – the F box on it, and said, "From now on, anybody uses that word, it will cost them a penny and we give the money to charity at the end of rehearsals." That was the fuck box. I tell you, we gave quite a bit of money to charity.'

Richard, of course, was the principal benefactor. 'Alvin I want to talk to you.' Rakoff and his assistants would stand there while Harris ranted and raved and counted, that's one shilling, Richard, two shillings. One morning Harris yelled, 'Alvin I want to talk to you' then before uttering another word took out his money, several shillings' worth, put them in the can, and let rip.

Rakoff didn't have the same type of problems with Harris that Michael Anderson encountered on *Mary Deare*, a proclivity for not hitting his marks, but that was probably because this was live TV. 'And the director is absolutely in control in those circumstances,' says Rakoff. 'On film if the star wants to stand somewhere everybody adjusts accordingly, on live TV it's, you stand there because that's where the camera is and if you move somewhere else then I can't get your next shot on camera four, alright, so are you going to stand there or do I just forget about your close-up?'

44

Enter Pinter

With little film or television work around, Caine's agent sent him along to the Royal Court to audition for a small role in a one-act play called *The Room*, scheduled to open in March as part of a double bill with another one-act play *The Dumb Waiter*, both written by the same man. Caine recognised him the moment he walked in, only he'd known him when he went by the stage name of David Baron and both were desperately hard-up actors working in weekly rep. His real name was Harold Pinter.

Born in Hackney, Pinter was the son of working-class parents; his father was a tailor. After falling in love with theatre, Pinter studied in the late forties at RADA, which he condemned as 'a poof's paradise. There was a terrible atmosphere of affectation and unreality.' Feeling doomed as an actor, Pinter turned to writing plays and *The Room* was his first attempt, scribbled down over four days while performing in Terence Rattigan's *Separate Tables* in Torquay in November 1956. It was first performed the following spring by Bristol University's drama department in a converted squash court. Pinter watched pensively in the front row nursing a troublesome bladder. 'I wanted to piss very badly throughout the whole thing and at the end I dashed out behind the bicycle shed.' Thus began the career of arguably Britain's greatest postwar dramatist.

Though championed by the likes of Harold Hobson, theatre critic of the *Sunday Times*, whose glowing notices of *Waiting for Godot* and *Look Back in Anger* contributed to their success, Pinter still earned his measly crust as a jobbing actor and lived in a Hades-like basement flat in Notting Hill Gate with his pregnant wife, the actress Vivien Merchant. A chink of light appeared when a young theatre producer called Michael Codron was impressed with another Pinter play, *The Birthday Party*, and put it on at the Lyric Theatre in Hammersmith in May 1958. It wasn't just a disaster, it was a catastrophe. The critics savaged it. 'What all this means only Mr Pinter knows,' crowed the *Manchester Guardian*, while the critic of the *Daily Telegraph* sought to give cheer to one of the play's characters, a depressed deckchair attendant: 'He might have been a drama critic condemned to sit through plays like this.'

Pinter plunged into a very dark place, his wife tried to make things better by saying that he used to get far worse reviews as an actor. By the time Harold Hobson gave *The Birthday Party* a rave in the *Sunday Times* – 'I am willing to risk whatever reputation I have as a judge of plays by saying that Mr Pinter possesses the most original, disturbing, and arresting talent in theatrical London' – it had been forced to close after just eight performances where it had played to an average audience of twenty. Today the play is seen as a masterpiece.

By the time Caine became involved in the Royal Court production of *The Room*, Pinter's potential talent was beginning to be recognised in broader circles, with his plays being broadcast on BBC radio. And the actor sensed that he was appearing in something fresh and challenging, even something of greatness, in spite of the fact that he couldn't make head nor tail of any of it. One day at rehearsal Caine took his concerns to Pinter, asking precisely what the play was about. Pinter looked at him rather strangely before saying, 'How the fucking hell should I know?'

Caine would later describe Pinter as 'irascible. You could never change a line. Then after *The Room* he became this famous writer, and I was one of his biggest fans. He carried on writing for half a century – and never offered me another bloody thing.' It wasn't until the 2007 remake of *Sleuth* that the pair reunited.

Early in March Bates's agent contacted him with an amazing offer from the BBC to play *Henry IV*'s Hotspur in *An Age of Kings*, the most conceptually ambitious Shakespeare project ever attempted for either film or television, bringing all of the history plays to a home audience.

There was also an indecipherable play for him to read called *The Caretaker*. Over the next week Bates assessed both offers and then visited his agent's office. 'Well, there isn't much to say about all this, is there,' said the agent. 'Obviously you are going to play Hotspur.'

'I'm rather drawn to this Pinter play,' said Bates.

'Over my dead body,' replied his agent. 'The Arts Theatre? For six pounds a week. In a play which I find completely incomprehensible. I'm ringing the BBC now to accept Hotspur on your behalf.'

'Wait!' said Bates as his agent reached for the phone. 'I know the play is not easy to understand at first sight, but I've had an instinctive reaction to its poetry and humanity. I think it's a marvellous piece of writing – and I want to do it.'

Replacing the phone on the hook, the agent looked at Bates, as the actor would later recall, 'with an expression that seemed to suggest I would shortly be dropped from the MCA client list. Ten per cent of six pounds per week is not exactly what agents go into the business for.'

The Caretaker was born in unusual circumstances. After the debacle of *The Birthday Party* Pinter and Vivien moved with their newborn son into a distinctly modest first-floor flat in a house in Chiswick. The house was owned by two brothers, one of whom was a total introvert, suspiciously quiet with a dark secret; he'd undergone electric-shock treatment a few years back in a mental institution. One night he brought home a tramp and gave him shelter. He was there for almost a month, living in the house, dossing really, until after a bitter row the tramp was thrown out. Pinter, ever the observer, watched the whole tragic episode from the sidelines and an idea was born.

Out of this scrap of human conflict Pinter began to construct his play. It too featured two brothers, Mick and Aston, and a tramp called Davies whom Aston saves from a severe beating in a local pub and brings back to the near-derelict house he shares with his younger brother. Davies is allowed to stay on and pay his way by becoming caretaker for the property, but Aston's charity is offset by Mick's cruel baiting of the old man. When Davies learns of Aston's previous mental problems he turns away from him, then starts to manipulate the situation by playing one brother off against the other. When he goes too far and alienates them both he's thrown back onto the harsh streets once more.

Producer Michael Codron, who'd suffered huge losses on *The Birthday Party*, remained a strong advocate of Pinter, but realised he couldn't allow him another failure in the glare of the mainstream, so settled on the small Arts Theatre as *The Caretaker*'s perfect venue. He then set about the casting. First he sent the script to Donald Pleasence with a view that he could play the tramp. Pleasence was a highly respected actor who'd appeared at Stratford, worked for Olivier and Peter Brook and was beginning to carve a career in film and television. His response was immediate. 'It was like being handed *The Cherry Orchard* before it had been seen.'

After the casting of Peter Woodthorpe as Aston, the search was on for the perfect Mick. One evening Pinter was at home watching television when a play came on. 'I watched this actor leaning against a wall, smoking a cigarette, and at once I called the director and said, "We've found our Mick."' It was Bates, of course.

With just three weeks before opening night rehearsals were frantic, and a labour of love since the money was so lousy. Pinter attended almost every day and Pleasence would drive him back home at night, both living as they did in Chiswick, the actor using these occasions to probe the author for insights into the role he was playing. One particular night he asked about the tramp.

'Oh, I think he's still knocking around west London,' said Pinter.

'What did you feel about the old man at the end?' Pleasence asked.

'Thank Christ they got rid of the old bastard,' Pinter replied. It was this answer that helped enormously with Pleasence's characterisation.

As for Bates, he was disconcerted that the director Donald McWhinnie hadn't given him one single note during the entire rehearsal period. McWhinnie promised to do so and after the final 'technical' run-through Bates walked to the edge of the stage and anxiously asked, 'How was it?' McWhinnie simply gave him a thumbs up; that was the note. Each performance would be beautifully judged. There was something feral at the core of Bates's Mick, something dangerous and dark that was deeply unsettling. Like pure Pinter, the characters found the simple act of communication difficult, hence the now infamous Pinter pauses.

Ever since Osborne's breakthrough, theatre's function as a middle-class entertainment had become subverted by new playwrights. Before, audiences had gone to the theatre to get away from it all; now they went to see their own lives exposed and dissected. 'It was a very good moment,' said Bates. 'A very good time, and we were aware of it. We were aware of it as a change, as a difference. There was a new concentration on the social issues of the day, the underprivileged. There was no arena untouched, every area of life began to be explored.'

The public were hungry for different types of plays, not the usual stuff, but bold experiments in structure and technique. Audiences wanted their drama to be more like life: puzzling, sometimes annoyingly indecipherable and ambivalent. Pinter was the new architect of that, of being able to take normal events and shroud them in hidden and sinister meanings. With little plot to speak of, *The Caretaker* bristled with tension and an atmosphere of disquiet.

The Caretaker opened that April and the first night was a resounding success with the cast taking a dozen curtain calls. Afterwards Bates's agent came backstage to congratulate his client. 'It's wonderful, brilliant, and never listen to me again.'

The next morning the critics who had savaged *The Birthday Party* were forced to eat their words. 'Harold Pinter has begun to fulfil the promise that I signally failed to see in *The Birthday Party*,' wrote Kenneth Tynan. The *Daily Mail* judged: 'This is a play and a production which no one who is concerned with the advance of the British drama can afford to miss.'

After a month the play was transferred to the much larger Duchess Theatre. Coming from a fringe theatre into the West End, *The Caretaker* was now exposed to the scrutiny of the Lord Chamberlain. In the end there was just the one umbrage, the use of the word, arsehole. 'I doubt whether his Lordship has ever sanctioned an arsehole,' the Lord Chamberlain's Controller informed the producers, who could barely contain themselves. In any case, arsehole was banned.

Moving into the Duchess, the cast were concerned that the Orson Welles-directed production of Ionesco's *Rhinoceros*, starring Olivier and playing at the nearby Strand Theatre, might prove stiff competition.

'We thought we might get the overspill,' said Pleasence. 'But in fact they got the overspill from us.' *The Caretaker* broke the box-office record at the Duchess and was sold out almost every night for a year, catapulting Pinter into the spotlight. As for Bates, incredibly within the space of just four years he'd appeared in two of the most significant British plays of modern times.

Years later Bates would say: '*The Caretaker* was an unforgettable piece of good fortune, the only play I have ever done in which I have not for one second thought, oh God, I've got to do this again next week. It was sheer joy to play all the time.'

Bates's decision to favour *The Caretaker* over Hotspur in *An Age of Kings* left the BBC in a bit of a quandary. The role wasn't an easy one to cast. In the end someone suggested Sean Connery, who had recently appeared for the network in a Sunday-night live production of Jean Anouilh's tragicomedy *Colombe* opposite Dorothy Tutin.

Connery graced the series' first four episodes, which derived from *Henry IV, Part I*. His energetic performance, part rough-and-ready charm, part steely composure, made a big impact on audiences and critics. Robert Hardy played opposite Connery as Prince Hal. It was the first time the two men had met. 'I thought he was a very interesting man, and he was absolutely right for Hotspur. Sean had many of the attributes of Hotspur, he was single minded, a fighter and in a hurry. I mean, Hotspur's in such a hurry that he trips over his words and one of the joys with Sean's Scottish speech was that it sounded as if he were tripping over his words all the time; his thoughts were ahead of his tongue. I thought he was brilliant. And we had a hell of a fight together in the battle scene.'

An Age of Kings was the brainchild of, in Hardy's words, 'the most extraordinary, ebullient Yorkshireman', Peter Dews, a thirty-year-old stage director and former schoolmaster. It was a mammoth undertaking, a remarkably ambitious serialisation of Shakespeare's history plays in fifteen one-hour instalments shown fortnightly and stretching out over almost the whole year. The cast was enormous, including the likes of Julian Glover, Judi Dench and Eileen Atkins. It was Shakespeare for the masses, as Connery told the *Radio Times*: 'The most gratifying thing about the series has been the warm response to Shakespeare by people who would not normally go five yards to see one of his plays.' It was also the first BBC series to be exported to America, where it made quite an impression.

With the BBC's first purpose-built centre for television production currently under construction in Shepherd's Bush, it was hoped the prestigious *Age of Kings* would have been the first programme to be made there. Inevitably the place wasn't ready in time, so the first few episodes were broadcast from the BBC's Riverside Studios by the Thames in Hammersmith. David Andrews, who played Lord Hastings, recalls a huge door that divided the two stages; 'And Peter Dews broke all convention by having both stages opened up. He staged the battles there, with battlements built up in the studio and running six cameras from one control room, quite an adventurous thing to do.'

Andrews also recalls one amusing incident involving Derek Ware, then a bit-part actor who'd managed to convince Peter Dews that he was an expert stuntman and fully capable of performing a hazardous fall off a castle turret. Ware would go on to become a top TV and film stuntman, but at that time he'd never done anything like it before. When it came to the dress rehearsal Dews looked around the set. 'Where's Derek?' he blasted. 'I'm here,' piped up a figure in the background. 'And there was Michelin Man,' recalls Andrews. 'He was padded up to such a degree that you couldn't see any of Derek, you could only see this tiny head at the top.' Dews was not won over. 'What the hell?'

'I've got to have this padding,' insisted Ware. 'It's a legal requirement.'

'Well, all right, let's see you do the fall.'

Ware looked at the set and then the cardboard boxes meant to break his fall and said they weren't high enough. 'The boxes went up to about two feet,' says Andrews. 'And Peter, who was apoplectic at the best of times, well I thought he was going to explode. He got Derek to take most of his padding off and do the stunt and of course what does Derek do, he fractures two ribs and breaks his collarbone and was off for a week.'

It's certainly interesting to watch Connery in this highbrow environment. Here was a man that wasn't trained at drama school mixing it with Old Vic and Stratford veterans with their clipped, 1950s BBC Shakespeare voices; all proper vowels and posturing. By contrast, Connery is earthy and raw. 'I thought Sean was great,' says Andrews. 'But some of the more experienced actors who had come from the theatre pooh-poohed him, saying how dreadful, Hotspur shouldn't be played like that. But I thought he was great, I thought he had a lovely, lively sense of now in it; it was really happening as he played it. And a wonderful presence.'

'A Scottish presence,' affirms Hardy. 'He clarified his Scottish accent a little bit for film, those wonderful films he made later on, and whether he's playing a Russian submarine commander, or Hotspur or Robin Hood from Nottinghamshire, it's all Scottish, and all Sean.' Like Richard Burton, Connery's roots are in his voice; when he opens his mouth his whole life is there. 'But Richard learned the language of England and the language of Shakespeare,' argues Hardy. 'And with that absolutely superb voice of his he could play anything; it gave him a broader range than Sean was capable of. But they were both very alike, in both cases there was a very strong smell of testosterone about and nationalism. Richard, however far he travelled, never really left Wales and certainly, however much of his life he lived in Spain or the Bahamas, Sean has never willingly left Scotland.'

And like Burton, Hardy recognised in Connery a charisma and capacity to succeed. 'I never had any doubt he was going places. I would distinguish Sean and Burton as people who when I first met them I knew they would be stars straightaway. I didn't know it about Bob Shaw or Finney until it all happened in their cases later. With some actors when you're in their company, they just stand out. With Sean and Richard it had to do with their sheer presence.'

45
All the Rest Is Propaganda!

It wasn't just the theatrical knights such as Olivier and Gielgud who feared being kicked off their perch by this new breed of actor coming through, but the largely anodyne and terribly 'safe' British film star typified, one supposes, by the likes of Richard Todd, Kenneth More and John Mills. There was also the Rank matinee idol, pretty-boy actors like Dirk Bogarde who spoke with clipped accents and were sexually non-threatening on screen. Bogarde was the archetypal product of the Rank charm school, sexless and about as dangerous as a hamster in a coma. While shooting *Simba*, director Brian Desmond Hurst grew so narked at Bogarde's lack of passion playing a love scene opposite Virginia McKenna he yelled, 'Dirk, could you look at miss McKenna just once as if you would like to fuck her.'

Bogarde, though, was intelligent enough to see the new wave coming before it hit the beach. He wanted desperately to play Jimmy Porter in the film of *Look Back in Anger* but Rank's managing director, John Davis, who held Bogarde under contract, returned the script to him with a note saying that there was altogether too much dialogue.

He then tried to interest Rank in buying the film rights to a novel by new author Alan Sillitoe, something called *Saturday Night and Sunday Morning*, with the intention of playing the lead. Rank's head of production Earl St John refused. 'Dirk, how do you imagine that anyone could consider making a film which began with a forty-year-old woman inducing an abortion in a hot bath?'

Rank was the country's largest film-production company. Puritan in outlook and middle class in manners, it steered clear of subjects that might appeal to the lower orders chewing toffee in the stalls. John Davis liked to think Rank 'catered to the dress circle'. Is it any wonder they rejected Osborne and Sillitoe in spite of their top star's urgings. Interestingly, it was Bogarde's failure to get these films made that prompted him to leave Rank in 1961 in order to work on more challenging material like *Victim*, the first serious British film about homosexuality, and Jo Losey's *The Servant*.

One wonders what Bogarde would have been like as Sillitoe's anti-hero Arthur Seaton (pretty good, I reckon). It was never to be, though, and instead Albert Finney got the part and it made him a star.

Sillitoe had spent much of his youth in a council house in Nottingham, images he dredged up for his book. His hero Arthur Seaton, a boozy, rebellious factory worker who shags and boozes his weekends away, was inspired by a tale his brother told him about a young guy in a pub falling down the stairs one Saturday night after drinking eleven pints and seven gins. *Saturday Night and Sunday Morning* was continually rejected by publishers 'because it didn't fit into the preconceived romantic notions that people had about the so-called working class', according to Sillitoe. Too realistic for many people's taste, Sillitoe remained convinced he'd broken new ground and his optimism was eventually rewarded when it was published in 1958 to great acclaim.

Almost immediately the film rights were snapped up by producer Joseph Janni but no one he approached for finance rated its commercial chances, and so, unable to fund it himself, he reluctantly passed them over to Harry Saltzman and a grateful Woodfall. Despite the fact that he had never written or even attempted a screenplay before, Sillitoe was asked to adapt his novel to the screen. It was Woodfall policy always to get an author to carry out the adaptation himself; it made sense from an artistic point of view and also saved the cost of bringing in a professional and more expensive screenwriter. Sillitoe was delighted and got stuck in.

While it was taking shape, director Karel Reisz, another Free Cinema advocate given the chance to make his first feature, began casting. Saltzman wanted O'Toole to play Seaton, but Richardson and Reisz insisted on Finney, and when he was appearing as Edgar in *King Lear* at Stratford they both went to see him. After that evening's performance the men took a stroll around the town as Reisz explained the story and handed Finney the book and the script. It was a huge gamble they were taking with Finney, who'd only one night's previous film experience, his one scene in *The Entertainer*, but the general feeling was that here was an actor on the rise, ready to explode at any moment, and consequently the entire film was built around him.

With an unknown in the lead there was pressure to cast Diana Dors as Brenda, the married woman with whom Seaton has an affair and makes pregnant, but she turned it down, much to the relief of Reisz, who then went and got his first choice Rachel Roberts.

Meanwhile Saltzman was having trouble raising the finance. After reading the script, backers said their audiences wanted to see musicals, comedies or high adventure, not a story set in bleak conditions that most of them were already drearily familiar with. They wanted to spend two hours in the cinema escaping from reality, not having it rammed down their throats. Woodfall was also having trouble with the censor over the script, which was deemed to be far too violent with an overabundance of strong language. The word 'bugger' particularly riled them. One of the censors complained in writing: 'I know that "bugger" is freely used in such places as public bars and provincial pubs, but I doubt whether the average working man uses it much in his own home in front of his wife. That ought to be more the standard for us to adopt, even in films designed for the factory worker section of society.' Snobbish, or what!

Even with cuts the finished film was still landed with an 'X' certificate, restricting its audiences to those over eighteen. To the end of his life Sillitoe remained aggrieved that the compromises the film-makers were obliged to make watered down the essence of his story.

Eventually Saltzman managed to persuade Bryanston, an independent production company formed from the ashes of Ealing after the famous studio closed down in 1957, to put up 70 per cent of the tiny budget of £100,000. Bryanston was headed by Sir Michael Balcon, former head of production at Ealing. It's strange to think that without the aid of Balcon, one of the most conservative figures in cinema industry, one of the most radical of all British films would never have been made.

Filming began in April on location around the Nottingham streets of Sillitoe's youth; his mother enjoyed making tea for the actors. The factory scenes were shot in the very same Raleigh bicycle works where as a fourteen-year-old boy Sillitoe helped make not bikes, but ammunition, the factory having been turned over in 1942 to help with the war effort. Sillitoe toiled away on almost the exact spot where we see Finney working his lathe in the film. Finney was taught how to use the machine as though he'd been at it for years. 'And there may be people riding about on bikes that I helped make, or maybe come off them because I didn't do such a good job. But it was a wonderful thing to be able to concentrate on that reality; it takes the weight off the acting.'

This being essentially Finney's first film, and a lead role to boot, and Reisz's debut as a feature director, little wonder that both men were physically sick every morning before going to work, but their individual performances never let on that they were racked with nerves. Throughout shooting both enjoyed an intensely close working relationship, and during interior work at the small but efficient Twickenham Studios Finney moved into Reisz's Hampstead home. They never stopped discussing and analysing the film and the characters and so were fully prepared for anything that came up. They'd discuss how Seaton walked, how he talked, even how he smoked a cigarette.

Finney was to recall years later, with some amusement, that there were also discussions on set about how to present the sex scenes, 'Because the law then was that you had to have one foot on the floor, like in snooker,' said Finney. Much thought went into whether Finney should keep his vest on in bed and whether Rachel Roberts's slip should be seen. All faintly ridiculous today. But when the film came out those scenes of extramarital sex, a first for a British film, outraged people. It went too far, they raved, as Finney recalled, 'Reisz got an enormous number of hate letters, saying how disgusting it was.'

During filming, however, there was no real sense from anyone that what they were doing was going to break new ground, that for decades after it would be singled out as a major turning point in British film. All they knew was that it had been a back-breaking and gruelling six-week schedule and after the cameras stopped turning Reisz went to bed exhausted and slept for a whole week.

46

The Wild Man of Stratford

After the successful 1959 Stratford season it was all change at the Memorial Theatre. Twenty-nine-year-old Peter Hall had taken over the helm from the departing Glen Byam Shaw and was seen very much as the new shining light of the theatre world. A working-class boy from Bury St Edmunds, whose father worked on the railways, Hall won a scholarship to grammar school and Cambridge. He arrived at Stratford after running the Arts Theatre in London, a reign that included the English language premiere of Samuel Beckett's *Waiting for Godot*.

Hall brought to Stratford his own vision, less of the 'star' system that had prevailed since the war and more the creation of a true ensemble company. Peggy Ashcroft, with whom Hall had both worked and become friends, took the plunge first and signed on for three years. Her reputation meant others were less hesitant to follow.

Pretty soon Hall's first season, to begin that April, was shaping up very nicely with Paul Scofield agreeing to play two of Shakespeare's great roles: Shylock and Petruchio. Contracts were drawn up and duly signed. A couple of months before rehearsals were due to begin Hall received a letter from Scofield that sent him into a seizure. There it was, in black and white: Scofield wasn't coming. Yes he'd signed a contract, but he just didn't want to do it. 'Well, one's first reaction of course is fury,' Hall would recall. 'And solicitors and waving contracts.' In the end he decided to be very British and mature about it, but it did suddenly mean that he was fast approaching his first season with no leading man.

Hall recalled how mesmerised he'd been by a young actor playing Hamlet at the Bristol Old Vic, 'One of the most astonishing talents I had ever seen,' recalling particularly his 'enormous hooter of a nose'. Perfect for Shylock. It was O'Toole. It was a mad but inspired gamble,

Hall was offering him Scofield's entire line of parts. At twenty-eight, O'Toole would become the youngest ever leading man at Stratford.

To prepare, he and Siân went to Wales to stay with her relatives and relax before his hectic Shakespearean duties. But O'Toole managed to turn even a country cottage into a disaster area. One night he suddenly decided to do the cooking himself, although Siân had never seen him actually cook anything before. 'I can make the best French toast,' he stated. Minutes later the stove exploded into flames. They tried to extinguish the fire but it was impossible and both were driven out into the garden where they watched in the rain as the kitchen burned down.

When O'Toole finally arrived at Stratford for the first rehearsal Hall was shocked to see he'd had a nose job, that big hooter was no more. 'What have you done?' said Hall. 'I'm going to be a film star,' O'Toole answered back.

Siân also came to Stratford to lend support and they rented a house which she tried to make as comforting an environment as possible. But Siân, heavily pregnant, had concerns of her own as she gave birth to their daughter Kate during rehearsals for *The Merchant of Venice*. One night O'Toole turned up outside the maternity ward with several other drunken actors to serenade the new arrival. Siân was hardly in the mood to receive such a musical tribute. 'I lay silently in the dark, looking at the ceiling until they went away.'

O'Toole's folks visited, to wet the baby's head. Father and son got customarily slaughtered and as everyone retired to bed Peter lay spread-eagled on the floor; 'Not asleep, but crucified.' Patrick tried lifting his flagging son to his feet, but to no avail. Instead he opened another bottle and joined him on the floor. That's where the pair were found the following afternoon.

At the house numerous guests would appear without warning and Siân was expected to cook and clean after them. One arrival was fellow Irish thesp Jack MacGowran. He owned two goldfish called King Lear and Cordelia. Returning home after a pub crawl late one night a puckish MacGowran fried them both and had them on toast. Realising he perhaps had a drink problem, MacGowran bet O'Toole that he'd lay off the sauce for a whole month. 'You're on.' MacGowran's dry month was to begin the next morning; it lasted precisely seventeen seconds. O'Toole joyfully timed it. On another occasion during the Stratford season MacGowran got mightily hammered and arrived at the theatre barely able to stand, let alone play a matinee. Quick thinker O'Toole prepared a hangover cure to his own special recipe: a mix of beer, mustard and crushed cigarette butts. 'Great, old son, great,' said Jack and barnstormed his way through the play.

O'Toole was drinking a lot, too, and reckless about it. Siân would wake and find him asleep downstairs intoxicated in an armchair, having obviously driven back home from the pub drunk. With alcohol added to an already erratic driving style, Siân feared he may not live beyond the season, and would probably make his final exit wrapped round a lamp post. There were rows, sometimes lasting hours. After one heated argument Siân discovered O'Toole walking precariously on the roof of the house. 'Living from day to day was proving exhausting,' she later revealed. 'And almost impossibly difficult.'

The drinking was to some extent a crutch to keep the nerves at bay as the first night for *Merchant* drew nearer. O'Toole knew how important it was; it could make or break him. One morning it seemed the nerves had gotten the better of him. He stayed at home, cooped up in bed, rather than attend rehearsals. When the theatre rang to see if he was there, ill or dead, he refused to take the calls. On the morning of opening night the calls to O'Toole Villas were now more frequent and frantic. Still curled up in bed, O'Toole was not speaking, not even to Siân. By late afternoon there were, at last, stirrings. He dragged Siân into bed with him and an hour later was all energy and fireballs: 'How about a cup of tea?' 'What's the time?' 'Where's the car?' 'For God's sake everyone, get a move on!' Siân would later describe that day as O'Toole perched on the edge of a cliff, only at the last minute did he decide to pull himself back.

Of course the performance was a triumph; standing ovations, untold curtain calls. Siân sat there, tears welling up. At that moment she realised, whatever hell or madness this Irish sod would drag her through, that 'I was going to do everything I could to help cherish this talent'. It began straight away. Siân had organised an after-show party back at the house;

guests were crammed inside as she served them food and drinks, but of O'Toole there was no sign. He turned up hours later when everyone had gone. Where had he been? 'I went searching for that haystack,' he told Siân. 'The dung heap. It's not far from here at all.'

Playing Shylock one night, during the intense court scene, O'Toole spied a packet of fags close to the front of the stage. 'I was wondering what they were doing there, my cue came and I was off, "Now we have expressed our darker purpose . . ." It was the wrong play. I'd gone into King Lear.' Despite the occasional lapse O'Toole was a hit and critics hailed him as a major new talent. Bernard Levin called his Shylock 'a radiant masterpiece'. Peter Hall recalls that O'Toole was nothing short of a sensation. 'I mean, people were queuing up all night to see him.'

Even Elizabeth Taylor voiced interest in him playing opposite her as Mark Antony in *Cleopatra*, a role that eventually went to Burton. 'I'm marvellous. I must be,' O'Toole announced. The BBC sent an interviewer down to profile him but the man clearly hadn't done his homework.

'Well, what have you done?' he asked.

'Eh,' said a startled O'Toole.

'Let's see,' the interviewer continued, scanning his rough notes. 'There was that army thing. Come on, come on, what else have you done?'

O'Toole had had enough of this. 'Well, I played the dame in *Puss in Boots* once.'

The BBC man's face turned sour. 'Look, we don't have to do this interview, you know.'

'In that case,' O'Toole replied, 'I suggest you fuck off.'

One young actor lucky enough to see the production was Derek Fowlds. 'O'Toole is still the best Shylock I ever saw. It's a production that just lives for ever in my memory. I thought it was the most electric performance I'd ever seen. He was a very dangerous actor, very exciting to watch. And I was an enormous fan of Albert Finney and Alan Bates, all that lot were just amazing, and as a young actor coming out of RADA I was so in awe of these people. There was a change, you could feel it, it was working class, the acting was very exciting; it was just different.'

The regime at Stratford around this time, while not puritanical, was like a nasty dose of National Service, thirteen-hour days for stretches that might last months, with actors having to often rehearse during the day and perform that evening. Relaxation could be found in the green room which sold wine, bottles of beer and cigarettes. Back then most of the company would smoke, and the stench of cigarettes backstage was quite toxic. It was a case of pour down the old Guinness, hear your cue, stub out your fag on a saucer and go on before an audience of whom, ironically, a good percentage were smoking too. Many actors had a bottle of beer stored away for the interval; no one raised an eyebrow, it was the done thing.

The real drinking, however, came after the performance and usually in the nearby Black Swan pub, which had a special dispensation to stay open late for the actors. It became a popular haunt for O'Toole and his comrades and the place was given the nickname of the Dirty Duck. One night O'Toole broke the house record by downing a yard of ale (that's two and a half pints) in forty seconds. 'You only do that kind of lunacy because there's nothing else to do,' he excused. O'Toole went back to Stratford late in the sixties and on a visit to the Dirty Duck tried to repeat his earlier feat, without success. 'Either I wasn't that parched or my stomach had shrunk.'

It was at Stratford where O'Toole's reputation as a hellraiser was sealed. At one after-show party O'Toole held court on stage sitting on a throne, sustained by two pedal bins on either side of him, one full of beer, the other of hard liquor, into which he would alternately scoop a pint mug. Ex-RADA chum Roy Kinnear once watched O'Toole down a bottle of whisky without pausing for breath. 'There was so much bad behaviour during this season,' recalled Siân Phillips, 'that people flocked to the town to see what this outrageous bunch of actors were getting up to.'

Such antics didn't go down well with the entire company. Denholm Elliott, himself a boozer, was so nervous around the bombastic O'Toole that he could hardly bear to be in the same room. 'I get awfully nervous with the kind of actor who looks as though he might be about to hit you, even though he never does.' On stage there was little respite. Elliott found O'Toole 'very, very difficult' to perform with. 'He acts at you and it becomes a sort of battle. He is just completely overpowering.'

Another actor who found O'Toole, shall we say, a little intimidating, was Ian Holm, then just out of drama school and serving an apprenticeship of a kind with the company. Holm confessed to being 'terrified' of O'Toole. 'Probably because he was so melodramatically different, so alien to me. He had an independent manner, confidence, star quality and an air of ruined glory.' Holm recalled Peter Hall confiding in him that he thought O'Toole had the 'sparks of genius', even though, according to Holm, O'Toole was a loose cannon when it came to authority. 'There was something unconsciously gladiatorial and threatening about him. I developed into a company man and chipped in, whereas O'Toole never seemed as if he could take direction, just telling the director how he was going to do a scene, and then doing it. He was an enigma wrapped in charisma and sprinkled with booze.'

O'Toole's next performance of the season was as Petruchio in *The Taming of the Shrew* opposite Peggy Ashcroft as Kate, who, at fifty-three, was almost twice his age. In spite of that discrepancy – Ashcroft had thought Hall mad to put them together – their on-stage chemistry was electric and the production was another huge success. The *Evening Standard* critic described O'Toole as 'the most aggressive, virile, dominating Petruchio in years'.

Hailed the King of Stratford, it now looked likely that O'Toole would surge ahead and dominate the British theatre for years to come. But he had a destiny of an altogether different kind.

47

Steaks Through the Letter Box

In recent months Caine's earnings had jumped considerably after a smattering of film and television work, so he and Terry Stamp decided to move out of the Harley Street flat, which was becoming increasingly crowded with various artistic types and dropouts, and get a place together. They chose a small mews house near Harrods in Knightsbridge; so small in fact that it had only the one bedroom. One imagines they took it in turns sleeping on the sofa.

But acting is a precarious business, and work quickly dried up again; even with their combined incomes it became difficult to pay the rent and afford to eat decently. Luckily, Stamp was having an affair with a rich neighbour, who took to putting raw steaks through their letter box. Most of their idle time was spent eating in cheap cafés, watching the new Fellini at the National Film Theatre, listening to the latest pop hits at the HMV store or thumbing through books in Foyles. They'd also go and hang out on the King's Road, which was just beginning to get chic and the place to be seen, spending hours over a solitary cappuccino in one of the new coffee bars.

This was a time of great personal development for Stamp, and much of that derived from his friendship with Caine: 'He altered my whole cultural outlook.' David Andrews, who knew them both, saw first hand just how much influence Caine wrought over the young actor. 'Whenever we had a party Mike would always be there; it was very unusual for him not to be there, and we did give a lot of parties. And he always turned up with Terry. And Terry used to sit cross-legged in the corner while Mike would be there telling stories, being the life and soul of the party, and Terry never took his eyes off him. He used to soak Mike in, all the time. I remember that so vividly. And that's nothing against Terry, who is a wonderful, magical person. But Mike was a mentor of sorts to Terry; he introduced him to a lot of people.'

There was the odd audition and casting call, too. Caine set his heart on playing Bill Sikes in the Lionel Bart musical *Oliver!*, which was about to go into the West End. When he lost out to an ex-professional boxer called Danny Sewell, Caine was inconsolable for days. Work for Stamp was equally scarce. Since leaving *The Long and the Short* tour he'd been out of work for six months. Thoroughly exasperated, Stamp read for a part in yet another play about the evils of teddy-boy culture, this one called *A Trip to the Castle*, and when the director happily offered him a small role as one of the gang members Stamp put his foot down: No! I'll play the lead or nothing, you old bugger, or words to that effect. Nine times out of ten such impertinence would have been rewarded with swift directions as to where the exit was, this time his boldness got him the role, and his West End debut.

A Trip to the Castle was due to open in June at the Arts Theatre, and Stamp decided to attend the last performance of the play they'd be taking over from, just to check out the auditorium. The play stunned him, it was *The Caretaker*. 'As I walked home afterwards, I was assailed by a kind of envy. It was the feeling of being left behind. Something new was happening and I was missing the bus.' Indeed he was; *A Trip to the Castle* played to near-empty houses.

This sense of losing out while their contemporaries overtook them on the inside track was shared by Caine. Both received a metaphorical swift kick up the jacksy when news reached them that *The Long and the Short and the Tall* was going to be made into a film. Few actors knew the role of Bamforth better than Caine, but he didn't even get an interview. Stamp also lost out.

Others were overlooked, too. Michael Balcon was producer, having recognised the cinematic potential of Willis Hall's play and secured the film rights, and desperately wanted O'Toole to reprise his stage role as Bamforth. Failing that, he wanted Finney. But his American backers had different ideas; neither was famous enough and they insisted on a 'name' that would play in the US market, settling on Laurence Harvey, hopelessly miscast and giving an almost pantomimic performance only one level up from Dick Van Dyke's cockney in *Mary Poppins*. Robert Shaw also missed out; his stage role as the tough sergeant was taken by British war-film stalwart Richard Todd.

At least Ronnie Fraser was back from the original stage cast, and very happy he was too upon learning that Richard Harris was joining them, playing Corporal Johnstone, the role taken by Edward Judd at the Royal Court. Fraser and Harris had long been pub companions, and the regulars at innumerable Soho watering holes had gotten used to Fraser's omnipresent cry, 'More Fraser waters!' – quadruple vodkas – but their drinking was to reach near-lunatic levels when the cameras rolled in June with Leslie Norman directing.

David McCallum, cast as the young radio operator that David Andrews played in the theatre, was witness to the macho boozing that went on and the two very separate groups of actors that emerged within the cast: 'Basically there were the guys that drank and the few of us who didn't. That group (Harvey, Harris, Fraser) would go at lunch time every day to the pub nearby and they'd compete to see who could down the most alcohol, literally bottles and bottles of champagne. And they'd come back somewhat drunk and do the rest of the day. But those guys were always able to work even though they were massively inebriated. I never could understand how they did it because it would have killed me. But they were really an extraordinarily aggressive group of people.'

By far the worst yob of the trio in McCallum's estimation was Harris. 'I think Richard Harris was probably the most uncouth and certainly the rudest person I've ever worked with. He was quite horrible to people and made no bones about it. I don't know what it was, maybe bad parenting, and possibly the fact that he was aggressively Irish. You see, the Welsh get aggressively Welsh and get wonderfully lyrical like Anthony Hopkins, but Harris was a very violent person. A wonderful actor, though.'

Much of the Harris spleen was directed towards Leslie Norman, who was very much an old-school director who'd cut his teeth at Ealing, so an establishment figure in Harris's eye, something to butt his head against. 'Harris was extremely rude to Leslie the whole time,' McCallum confirms, 'and treated him with contempt practically, which was horrible to watch. It was not a happy situation.'

Norman's frustration with Harris focused solely around his drinking habits and it was never resolved according to his son Barry, the film critic and writer. 'Harris was a bit of a bully, and my father was not about to be bullied by an actor, so they were at loggerheads. In later years Harris avoided being interviewed by me because I remember him saying once, "I don't want to talk to him, his father hates me."'

As senior member of the cast Richard Todd took it upon himself to get things under some kind of control and one evening invited Harris for a chat in his dressing room. Todd ordered Harris, in no uncertain fashion, to stop behaving like an arsehole. Braced for a torrent of abuse, Todd instead watched in amazement as tears welled up in Harris's eyes as he apologised and promised to cut down on his drinking for the rest of the shoot. Todd later revealed, understandably so, that he had detested working on this film.

It was a surreal atmosphere all round, really. Plans to make *The Long and the Short and the Tall* on location in south-east Asia had been scrapped due to the political climate at the time, so a none-too convincing jungle set was built in the studio, ruining any sense of reality and suspense the director had hoped to cultivate. Even Balcon had to admit that the result was disappointing. It was also uncomfortable for the actors. 'They had to spray us down every day and make us wet because we were supposedly in the jungle,' remembers McCallum, who came up with quite a clever solution. 'I took my clothes away with me every day and back at home made them all wet with baby oil and so never had to be sprayed down; quite a relief, I can tell you.'

One positive to come out of the film was a friendship between Harris and Harvey that revolved almost exclusively around drinking. One game they enjoyed was to visit as many bars as possible and knock back a different drink in each one. The last man standing was the winner. Sometimes these pub crawls went on for hours as they went from regular pubs to nightclubs and then the all-night drinking dens Harris knew and loved. One famous session started at lunchtime, went through the night and found the pair still drinking at dawn in Covent Garden.

48

Golden Bollocks Hits the Stage

Well into his second year at RADA, Courtenay had certainly loosened up, and though still naturally reticent when it came to the girls happily indulged in a high-octane social life with the rest of the students. 'It was great,' remembers Derek Fowlds. 'We were all nuts really, we all had fun, we were kids.'

One term Courtenay and Fowlds performed together in a musical entitled *Shut Up and Sing*. 'I played the narrator with my guitar, singing all these songs,' says Fowlds. 'But the best part was the leader of this gang and that was Tom and he was totally brilliant in it. And John Fernald rather liked Tom and rather liked me.'

The show was open to agents, producers and industry insiders and afterwards in the pub playwright Ian Dallas walked up to Courtenay who was propping up the bar to exclaim, 'You're fantastic, you're going to be the next Albert Finney.' Indeed, the next day Courtenay's pigeon-hole was filled with letters from top agents wanting to sign him up. It was all very nice, especially their positive comments about him. One agent wrote that he had great natural timing. Puzzled by this, Courtenay asked his friend John Thaw what it meant. 'Well, kid,' said Thaw, sounding as if he was about to unlock the secret of the universe. 'I think it means that you've got a good sense of timing – you know – getting laughs and that, and it's . . . er . . . natural.'

His performance in *Shut Up and Sing* was a real game-changer for Courtenay and he knew it. Having arrived at RADA nervy and tense after what he felt had been wasted years at UCL, his progress had been slow and uneven. Now this. 'For the first time I felt certain that I had been right all along in wanting to become an actor. That my dream of being an artist was going to be fulfilled.' John Thaw started referring to Courtenay as 'Golden Bollocks'.

Of all the agents who'd contacted him, by far the biggest was MCA. 'Albert Finney has just signed for us,' he was told. There was that blasted name again. MCA really were the crème de la crème. David Andrews was represented by them: 'MCA's offices were in Piccadilly, it was like walking into an antique emporium, it was absolutely littered with Chippendale tables and theatre playbills. They were big. Their head office was in Los Angeles and there was a rumour that there was a Picasso in the lift, that's how affluent they were. And when I used to visit, the office was full of girls working there called Charlotte and Ermintrude and Desdemona, they were all thick as shit but terribly, terribly posh, and they all went to garden parties at Buckingham Palace and the Chelsea Flower Show.'

Next stop for Courtenay was Fraser and Dunlop in Soho. The man himself, Jimmy Fraser, met him and in a bid to try and keep his feet on the ground – 'don't get too big headed by all this fuss being made of you' – advised Courtenay to pack himself off to a theatre in the provinces after RADA to learn his trade. 'That's what Albert did.' In the end Courtenay went with his gut instinct and signed with the Christopher Mann agency, which had fine offices overlooking Hyde Park. He was now represented by a top firm, and still at drama school.

One of the classes Courtenay took was run by the actor Peter Barkworth and was all about technique. RADA did seem fixated more on the externals of acting, how one deports oneself, the voice etc., as opposed to what was being taught say at the Actors Studio where it was all introspection. Anyway, there was Peter Barkworth telling his class, 'If you are fortunate enough to get a West End job, you attend the first audition in a suit.'

As Courtenay didn't posses one this presented immediate problems. His donkey jacket and duffel coat would not suffice, and so, accompanied by John Thaw, Courtenay visited Burton's the Tailors in Tottenham Court Road and was suited up. He felt faintly ridiculous in the thing, but was pretty quickly able to put it to some use when Christopher Mann sent him to director Roy Ward Baker, then scouting for someone to play a young Spanish lad opposite Dirk Bogarde in *The Singer Not the Song*. He didn't get the part and when sent for another interview decided to go as himself, putting on his donkey jacket and a crew-neck pullover. Courtenay thought this was an awfully cool look but it didn't impress veteran producer Michael Relph and the interview went badly. 'I do think he might have worn a suit,' Relph complained to Christopher Mann. 'Who does he think he is?'

With new young guns arriving at RADA, notable amongst them John Hurt and Ian McShane, Courtenay approached his final term and the big forthcoming production *Doctor Faustus*, which would be his main swansong at the Academy. 'John Fernald asked me to stay on another term to do *Faustus* with Tom and I said, no,' Fowlds recalls. 'I'd already been there two years and I got a job and so had to leave. And Tom played Doctor Faustus with John Thaw playing Mephistopheles, both were brilliant and that was a real turning point for Tom.'

In the audience one night was the Old Vic's Michael Benthall. Courtenay had heard that the Old Vic were casting for a production of Chekhov's *The Seagull*, to be directed by John Fernald himself, and he was convinced one of the pivotal roles would be his: Konstantin, Chekhov's young, idealistic and desperate playwright. Fernald was instrumental in getting Courtenay an audition and after his reading Benthall asked him into his office. 'I was very impressed with your performance in *Faustus*, Tom,' he said. 'How would you like to play Konstantin?' Courtenay was stunned, lost for words. Then Benthall added, 'but not with those teeth'. The Courtenay gnashers had for some years now been of an irregular persuasion. They were to be modified as had been the O'Toole hooter. So, a course of dental work later, Courtenay became a junior member of the Old Vic company at fifteen pounds a week.

Just before going off to the Old Vic Courtenay appeared in his very last RADA production, which played in an open-air venue in Stratford. With O'Toole currently reigning supreme a trip was arranged for all the students to attend an evening performance. A couple of days later Courtenay was strolling along the river when he spied a familiar figure sitting on a wall outside the Dirty Duck. It was O'Toole. 'You're playing Konstantin, aren't you?' asked the Irishman. Courtenay nodded, he was too awe-struck to speak. 'He's a loser,' O'Toole carried on. 'He doesn't get the girl. Still, it's a nice part. Do it well and they'll be round you like flies round shit.'

That July Courtenay left RADA and began rehearsals at the Old Vic. The atmosphere he encountered there was not entirely welcoming. He felt a good deal of jealousy and bitterness directed towards him from other cast members who'd hoped to see themselves promoted to such a high-profile role, and here was this unknown and untested kid waltzing in and taking it. There was a snobbish element, too, according to Lindsay Anderson: 'When Courtenay played Konstantin in *The Seagull*, more than one critic commented scornfully on the impossibility of an actor in a play by Chekhov speaking with what was plainly a northern accent.'

Such dissenting voices were swiftly silenced after the first night when Courtenay was hailed as a major new find. Tony Britton was amongst the most experienced actors in the company and remembers the impact Courtenay made. 'It was a remarkable production. Tom was very innocent back then, very innocent, but certainly not naive. And his performance was astonishing, it showed that he'd learned an awful lot at RADA. Technically he was very good, but his talent was natural. He was brilliant casting for Konstantin.'

Years later, after Courtenay had gotten his knighthood, Britton bumped into him at the Garrick Club one evening. 'I hadn't seen him for a long time and jokingly I said, "Hello, Sir Tom," and he looked at me and said, "Don't give me any of that fucking nonsense." He was still the boy from Hull.'

Derek Fowlds saw the production and was mightily impressed, too. 'That was a really brilliant kick-start to his career; he was wonderful in that; it was the making of him, really. People were beginning to talk about Tom as being very like Albert, a pocket Albert Finney.' Fowlds has no regret missing out on *Doctor Faustus*, and what that might have brought, only a feeling of good fortune to have been around at all as an actor in those heady, wonderful days. 'We were so lucky leaving drama school then because there was so much work around. On TV we had *Armchair Theatre*, *Play of the Month*; there was a film industry, and also there were repertory companies all over the place. I started down in Worthing and did plays all over the country, plus the odd bits of telly and a film now and then. It was a very exciting period. Now I fear for all the kids coming out of drama school because I keep saying, what are they going to do? The repertory system is gone.'

In spite of the praise being heaped upon him, ever the pessimist, Courtenay wrote to his parents voicing his fears: 'I hope I don't spend the rest of the season disappearing into oblivion.' But already his performance was eliciting interest from the movers and shakers of the film industry. Woodfall were after him for a movie and Joseph Losey wanted to sign him up for a project. For now, though, he remained at the Old Vic and was handed the role of Puck in *A Midsummer Night's Dream*. Again a lack of self-belief rose to the surface. When asked to read for the part he stopped himself mid-sentence and called across the footlights, 'I'm sorry but I really don't think I can play this part.'

But play it he did, wearing ridiculous Spock-like ear extensions which he kept afterwards as a memento and loved answering the door to people with them on. Alec McCowan was playing Oberon and shared many scenes with Courtenay whose Puck is often at his side listening intently to his instructions. Getting bored with this, Courtenay began playing to the audience, moving his ears about like a rabbit, pulling faces and the like while poor McCowan did his best to get through his speech. One afternoon in the canteen McCowan gently but firmly informed the youngster that this was bang out of order. 'Look, one has to think about one's colleague as well as oneself on the stage.' It was a lesson Courtenay learned well, especially the way in which McCowan's warning had been issued, without venom or spite.

49
Silly Billy

During the West End run of *The Long and the Short and the Tall*, one of those rubbing shoulders with the likes of O'Toole and Shaw at the Salisbury tavern was novelist and *Daily Mirror* columnist Keith Waterhouse. The play had particularly caught his eye because it was written by an old friend of his. He and Willis Hall were working-class lads from Leeds and old youth-club chums but had lost touch, only to spookily find success at almost exactly the same time by drawing upon vastly different personal experiences: Hall as a squaddie in Malaya, Waterhouse as an undertaker's clerk in Leeds.

Waterhouse's class-conscious satirical novel *Billy Liar* had just been published to immediate acclaim. His central character, an undertaker's clerk named Billy Fisher who is a compulsive liar and daydreamer, was a fictional creation worthy of Kingsley Amis. Still living with his parents, Billy is bored with small-town existence and escapes into a Walter Mitty-style fantasy life, while at the same time pursuing an ambition to come down to London to find fame as a gag writer.

Out of the blue one afternoon Waterhouse took a call from Hall. Delighted to hear from his old pal, Waterhouse began reminiscing merrily when Hall perforated his nostalgic ramblings. 'Listen, this is business, luv. *Billy Liar* – fantastic. I think it would make a marvellous play. How do you feel about collaborating on it?' Back in their youth-club days both had worked on sketches together so Waterhouse was certainly game to give it a try and within three weeks they'd a finished product in which Oscar Lewenstein felt sufficiently confident to raise £6,000 to produce. It was Lewenstein's idea to ask Lindsay Anderson to direct and it was deemed only fair that Albert Finney play Billy. After losing out on the role of Bamforth, Finney had asked Willis Hall, 'Why don't you write a play for me?' It didn't take a genius to work out that *Billy Liar* would prove a great vehicle for him.

As rehearsals got under way Finney took a strange phone call, one that, if he had allowed it to, would have dramatically changed the course of his life. He was required to show up at the MGM studios in Borehamwood for a screen test. But this was no ordinary screen test; behind the camera was one of England's foremost directors, David Lean, whose last film had been the Oscar-laden *The Bridge on the River Kwai*. Sitting in a corner was Hollywood producer Sam Spiegel, responsible for such heavyweight pictures as *The African Queen* and *On the Waterfront*. If that didn't set Finney's pulse racing, then the role he was up for surely would, that of T. E. Lawrence in one of the most eagerly awaited productions in recent memory.

The enormity of it all struck Finney the second he walked onto the sound stage. Thousands of pounds had been spent on his test, with its elaborate sets and costumes, and it would take four days to shoot. However, by the final day Lean was shaking his head. 'I can't work with this beatnik,' he told Spiegel. 'He doesn't even wear a suit.'

Finney's test lasted a total of twenty minutes on screen, more of a short film than an audition, and Spiegel, if not Lean, was impressed. 'What do you feel about him?' the producer asked his director. 'Will you take him on?'

Lean screwed up his hawk-like face, still unconvinced. Finney was maybe too young. 'I think I can just about drag him through it, but I can't say more than that.'

Spiegel took the initiative, dangling in front of Finney a £10,000 fee and a £125,000 contract. Displaying enormous courage, Finney turned him down flat. When Lean heard the news he took it as a personal affront.

'Why are you doing this?' he asked.

'I think this may make me a star,' Finney replied. 'And I don't want to be a star.'

Lean was astounded. 'Why on earth not!'

'Because I'm frightened of what it will do to me as a person.'

In his dressing room at the Royal Court, Finney stars in John Osborne's groundbreaking play about Martin Luther, another working class rebel who defied the establishment – a medieval Jimmy Porter.

Tom Courtenay's haunted, hungry look seemed to perfectly fit the anti-hero roles of the moment. But he was far from an angry young man. 'I didn't have that attitude at all.'

Finding fame in *A Kind of Loving* meant Bates re-arranging his life. 'And that always costs,' says friend Keith Baxter. 'He had to maintain his private life.'

Filming *This Sporting Life* an infatuated Lindsay Anderson lost control of Harris, according to his wife Elizabeth. 'Richard gave him hell, knowing he could. He made his life bloody awful.'

Caine with his mum and brother Stanley during a visit home. A charlady, Ellen was your typical working class mum, devoted to her family and as tough as old boots.

Sharing digs with Caine, Stamp was always a favourite with the ladies, but with fame the succession of dolly birds turned into a flock, 'and I was the flight controller,' said Caine.

Like so many of his generation, Courtenay identified with Billy Liar's dream of coming to London to make something of himself. 'He was in every molecule of my body.'

O'Toole played Hamlet in the National Theatre's inaugural production in 1963. Before going on director Laurence Olivier warned, 'They're out there with their machine guns. It's your turn, son.'

Playboy hailed James Bond as the hero of the age, but Connery was trapped by the role for the rest of the decade.

It was a role Bates didn't want, that of a repressed writer, but *Zorba the Greek* turned into one of his most successful ever films.

Stamp was at the forefront of the new breed that played hard and worked hard, had no attitude about class and no prejudice. 'We're the new swinging Englishmen.'

In the early 60s Finney led a bizarre peripatetic life, boasting that he could get all his possessions into two suitcases – 'I may want to do a bunk.'

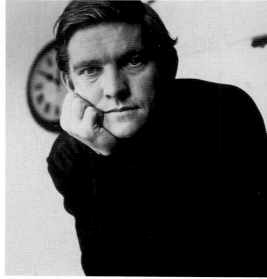

While the likes of Connery and Harris embraced Hollywood, Courtenay would be always weary of the place. He was still that little boy from Hull

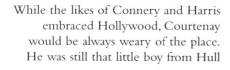

Caine takes a tea break while filming *Zulu* on location in South Africa.

This was Lean's recollection. Finney would offer something quite different, that it wasn't necessarily *Lawrence* he'd rejected, more the fact that the contract with Spiegel tied him down to other pictures later on. It was the seven-year contract he refused. Spiegel came back offering six years. Finney told his agent the answer was still no. Then five years – no. And four years – still no.

For someone who didn't know where he was going to be in five years' time, or even tomorrow for that matter, it was unlikely Finney would ever subject himself to becoming 'a property'. He hated commitment of any kind, be it women or cigar-chomping American film producers. Spiegel had even talked about a trip to his personal tailor to kit him out with a film star's wardrobe. Could anything be more unappealing. 'Go to his tailor!' thought Finney. 'It's a world I didn't want to know.' Another conversation with Spiegel that stuck in his mind was when the producer said, 'We probably wouldn't want to change your name.' Finney recalled thinking, 'Bloody cheek.'

There was an industry buzz about him now; Finney knew it, enough to start evaluating how to approach things. And he'd decided on total freedom, to embrace almost the unpredictability of his profession, to develop at his own speed. 'I started with nothing and if, at the end, I have fallen flat on my face, at least I will have had an exciting journey in my chosen way.'

So off he went back to *Billy Liar*, in the hope that he wouldn't live to rue the decision he'd just made.

The plan was to test run *Billy Liar* at the Brighton Theatre Royal for a week prior to it coming into the West End. Waterhouse drove Finney and Willis Hall down to the seaside town, managing to get lost on the way, with the result that Finney was late for the technical rehearsal. 'This did not endear us to Lindsay, who liked to run a well-disciplined ship,' Waterhouse recalled. Worse was to come.

For some time the team of Waterhouse and Hall had grown rather irked by the way Anderson was veering the play more towards farce than the generally sophisticated comedy route to which the writers had aspired. His approach to the immature Billy was to tip the balance over into infantilism, a quality which hardly suited the personality of Finney.

Things reached a head at the dress rehearsal when an admittedly well-lubricated Waterhouse and Hall, just back from a very nice lunch at a local hostelry, began hurling brickbats at Anderson from the dress circle. The director was having none of the criticism, referring the hooligans to what he called 'the underlying text', forgetting perhaps that he was actually dealing with the authors. 'Watch and learn!' he hollered. Waterhouse and Hall retired to their hotel.

The opening night of *Billy Liar* met with a decidedly frosty reception. There were mutterings and murmurings throughout and when the curtain came down a modicum of booing was heard. It was left to the dismayed theatre management to explain why. It was the overuse of the word 'bloody' that had got the prim Brighton audience's backs up; Billy's father punctuates practically every sentence with it.

It was hoped that there would be a more enlightened reaction in London as *Billy Liar* settled into the Cambridge Theatre, a huge barn of a place that Lewenstein feared was too big for their needs but was the only West End venue then free. The choice almost finished the play. When *Billy* opened reviews were mixed and business so poor that the management began drawing up plans to get rid of the show. 'You have to remember that at that point Albert's name didn't mean tuppence, really,' says Trevor Bannister, who played Billy's friend in the play. 'He had a reputation within the profession as one of the promising new actors, but the wider public didn't really know who he was yet.'

As with *Look Back in Anger*, it was the BBC who came to the rescue with its policy of broadcasting excerpts from current West End productions. Actually BBC executives had already dismissed *Billy Liar* as a candidate because of its swearing and chosen *A Man for All Seasons* instead, but when its leading man Paul Scofield objected, the Corporation's cameras were soon whisking their way to the Cambridge Theatre. Inevitably the BBC's switchboard was jammed with irate viewers complaining about the use of language. 'The fact that it takes fewer than a dozen calls to jam the BBC switchboard did not diminish the scale of the hullabaloo,' Waterhouse amiably observed. But there was more. Countless local newspapers were inundated with letters of complaint asking why such bad language was allowed and what were the churches doing about it? Vicars responded by denouncing the play from the pulpit. All of this, of course, was a godsend for the box office, as Bannister recalls: 'As a result of that TV excerpt there was a queue a hundred yards long outside the theatre the following morning.'

After the play had been running for a few weeks Anderson's feelings for Finney, strong and deep on *Lily White Boys*, abruptly changed. 'It's extraordinary how violently I have reacted against him,' he wrote in his diary. 'Not that there has been any overt friction between us, but somehow I became more and more conscious of the egotism under the charm.'

Maybe this sudden falling out of love with Finney, the dismantled prospect of them ever collaborating again along with his fantasies of them living together, was prompted by the discovery that he'd shacked up with Zoe Caldwell, then working at the Royal Court. Ann Beach, who played Billy's girlfriend Barbara in the play, always thought Anderson had been an odd choice for director anyway. 'You had these directors doing these plays with working-class actors in them about working-class situations, but they were the poshies. It went against the grain for some people, especially Joan Littlewood, that a lot of the directors weren't of the people.'

In October *Billy Liar* was given a further boost when the film of *Saturday Night and Sunday Morning* premiered and Finney literally exploded as an actor. Harry Saltzman, canny producer that he was, stage managed the opening amidst a blaze of publicity and audiences flocked to see it. 'It got its money back in the first two weeks of release, which scared the shit out of us,' said director Karel Reisz. Not Saltzman, whose tireless work tracking down a backer was rewarded with a very healthy payout, which he invested in an option on a series of books about a colourful British spy called James Bond and waved goodbye to Woodfall.

Reisz was so taken aback by the huge furore surrounding the film that he attempted an analysis of the reasons for it; maybe it was because the film showed a slice of English life that movie audiences had never seen before. And the character of Arthur Seaton was a blast of fresh air, too, perhaps for the first time a working-class person had been authentically portrayed on film. That's why its influence was so massive, it reflected the new breed of working man in Britain who had a healthy wage packet in his pocket come Friday night and a seam of anti-authority running through him wider than a coal mine; he wasn't going to be told what to do any more.

And Finney sympathised completely with Seaton's plight, having worked for a time in a factory as a student. He related to that feeling of wanting to break free, the fear of being chained to that machine until he was pensioned off. 'I was on his side.'

According to Lindsay Anderson, *Saturday Night and Sunday Morning* 'changed the face of British cinema overnight. It opened doors that had been nailed fast for fifty years.' But in America it ran foul of the Catholic Legion of Decency who vetted films for distribution. Reisz was asked to appear before them and was told by a monsignor that they were unable to give his film a certificate because Seaton went unpunished in the film.

'Unpunished for what?' asked Reisz.

'Adultery,' they spewed back.

Reisz scratched his head and said, 'Well, that's the story of the film.'

'You can change the story, can't you?' insisted the monsignor. 'You can create an ending where something bad happens to him.' Reisz just sat open-mouthed. The monsignor, no doubt oblivious to the nonsense he was talking, continued. 'Look, I'm not just talking as a censor, I'm also talking as a film critic. I think it would be much better if there was some retribution at the end.' What was he thinking – that one morning Arthur is gaily walking down Nottingham High Street when a piano falls on his head? This was absurd and Reisz told him so. Refusing to tamper with the film meant *Saturday Night and Sunday Morning* was refused a seal of approval, so scuppering its chances of widespread distribution in the US.

Still, as in Britain, American critics rated Finney as a vital new acting force. The *New York Times* saw him as having 'the seething animal vitality of Brando and the compelling abrasiveness of the young Cagney'. The *Daily News* said Finney couldn't be compared to any English actor, 'but is as unique as Brando is here'.

Is it any wonder that celebrities like Princess Margaret and Noël

Coward regularly paraded through Finney's dressing room at the Cambridge Theatre. John Gielgud, then planning to appear in *Othello*, was keen on Finney to play his Iago. 'I saw him last week in a funny play called *Billy Liar* in which he is superb,' Gielgud wrote in his diary. 'Now, of course, he's greatly in demand – turned down a film contract, for which I much admire him.'

According to Ann Beach all this success didn't go to Finney's head; he was more or less the same as he'd been when they'd first started, keeping himself largely to himself. 'He was quite a private person, and always interested in things away from acting, like horse racing. And because I'd been at RADA with Albert it was like doing the school play, really.'

There was just the odd display of Finney's idiosyncratic personality, such as the time during one performance when he suddenly turned on a chattering group in the stalls. 'I'm up here working, so if you won't shut up, go home. And if you don't, I'm going home.' That wasn't the only time the cast had problems with the audience. One night, act II had just started when a voice, a rather plum upper-class male voice, sounded from the balcony. 'Excuse me, could you start again, I missed the first bit.' Everybody in the audience looked up while the actors searched each other's faces for some kind of sign: 'What do we do?' And on another occasion a patron literally would not stop laughing, he was euphoric, but booming guffaws were spoiling it for the audience; during the interval the manager refunded his seat price and chucked him out.

More than once Finney himself had to step down towards the footlights and say to the audience in general, 'Could you please stop laughing. We can't really say the dialogue if you are persistently laughing all the time.' It got that bad sometimes. 'We got a bit of a reputation for being a rather strange show where we talked to the audience,' recalled George Cooper, who played Billy's dad in the play.

Finney stayed with *Billy Liar* for several months. During the run he agreed to be an usher at his old RADA pal Peter Bowles's wedding at Highgate church. Only he was late, having overslept, and arrived at the ceremony in his pyjamas, a raincoat hastily thrown over to cover his embarrassment. Finney was having such a good time at the reception that he decided to skip that afternoon's matinee, and phoned the theatre with a husky message: 'I've lost my voice.'

His parents also came down to catch a performance. He picked them up at the station and they all took a cab to the theatre. When they arrived Finney pointed up at the marquee where his name was emblazoned in lights. 'Look at that, not bad, eh? Come on, let's go and have some lunch.' Together Finney and his mum walked off but his dad stood rooted to the spot, looking up. Finney went back over, 'Come on, Dad.' But the old man – always the quiet one, gentle like, named Albert Finney just like his dad before him, so Albie was really Albert Finney III – wouldn't budge, just kept on gazing until finally he said, 'I never thought I'd see my name in lights.'

50
A Minor Mishap

Film history might have been very different had Sam Spiegel got his way and cast Marlon Brando in *Lawrence of Arabia*. David Lean wasn't so sure, anxious about the star's ego and that the film might turn into Brando of Arabia. In any event, Brando dropped out. Next on the list was Albert Finney, but, as we know, he refused.

This left Lean in an unenviable position, a juggernaut of a movie that had no leading man. Other star names considered included Anthony Perkins and Richard Burton. And every week Lean was pestered on the phone by Montgomery Clift begging to play Lawrence. Lean was becoming increasingly convinced that Lawrence should not be played by a star, with all that incumbent baggage. In life the man had been an enigma, even to himself; an unknown actor would more easily convey the required element of mystery.

Thoughts drifted back to a young actor he'd seen in a movie several months earlier. In an effort to escape the mounting pressure, afternoons were spent in West End cinemas, and at one particular matinee screening of *The Day They Robbed the Bank of England*, about a group of Irish patriots who plan to steal the British government's gold reserves, he was intrigued by a young actor playing 'a sort of silly-ass Englishman'. There was something about his face, something else, too, that indefinable quality that actors, however good they may be, either have or haven't got – a screen presence. Could he be Lawrence? Lean was convinced of it. The actor he wanted was Peter O'Toole.

Spiegel voiced caution; O'Toole's rowdy reputation was too much of a risk on so expensive a film. 'He thought I was a tearaway,' said O'Toole. 'He thought I lived up a tree. He didn't want to have to go looking for me every day with a net.' Finally the tycoon agreed to a screen test, which took place on the same set they'd used for Finney, though just one day was spent on it this time. O'Toole was even dressed in the same brown Arab robes Finney wore, supplied by Lawrence's biographer Anthony Nutting. They'd been given to the author by King Saud and ended their days cut into squares by Nutting's wife for their dog's bed.

Before the test was even complete Lean stopped the cameras; he'd seen enough. 'No use shooting another foot of film. The boy IS Lawrence.'

His fee was £12,500. Happy as Larry, O'Toole waltzed into the Salisbury pub and slammed £150 on the bar. For the rest of the day the drinks were on him. O'Toole still very much considered the Salisbury his home from home. 'This pub is a way of life to so many of us,' he told one reporter. 'It's my office. I get my phone calls and messages here. It's my bank. And sometimes I even sleep upstairs.'

A problem now arose. O'Toole was scheduled to appear again for Peter Hall and the newly formed Royal Shakespeare Company, which was opening its new London home at the Aldwych with a major production. Hall had managed to persuade Jean Anouilh to let him have the rights to his new play over the heads of West End managers. The play was called *Becket* and O'Toole would star alongside his old Bristol colleague Eric Porter. Then one day O'Toole strolled into Hall's office and dropped his bombshell. 'I've been offered the part of Lawrence of Arabia and I've simply got to do it.'

That Hall wasn't entirely happy with the situation is an understatement; he was depending on O'Toole and refused to release him from his contract. Spiegel, one of the wiliest negotiators in Hollywood, invited the RSC to sue. It was enough to make Hall think twice – did he dare risk a long and damaging court case? 'If an actor doesn't want to act for you, there's nothing in the world you can do to make him,' Hall admitted later. 'So Peter went off and became a film star and the rest, as they say, is history.' Christopher Plummer was hired as a replacement and Hall never worked with O'Toole again.

After signing his contract O'Toole was flown out to New York to meet the Columbia executives backing the project, an experience he didn't savour.

'When I look at you,' one of the suits said, 'I see six million dollars.'

'How'd you like a punch up the throat?' O'Toole replied. 'I hate that stuff,' he said later. 'It made me feel like a prize bull.'

With the role of Lawrence in his pocket, O'Toole settled down to celebrate Christmas with Siân, before going AWOL. O'Toole had a habit of vanishing for days on end without Siân knowing where or what he was up to. She'd almost gotten used to it. On Christmas morning he suddenly turned up with a brand-new Morris Minor with a huge ribbon tucked around it. Of course Siân had a horror of cars by now after so many terror-stricken journeys with O'Toole at the wheel, but was thrilled by the gift. It didn't last long. O'Toole commandeered the vehicle for a sentimental journey up to Bristol to bid the city farewell before leaving for Arabia. That night Siân received a phone call from the police. 'I'm very sorry,' said a voice, 'but I'm afraid we've had to lock Peter in the cells. We thought you ought to know.' O'Toole, rather the worse for wear, had driven the Morris Minor smack bang into the back of a patrol car. Sadly Siân never did see her Morris Minor again; it went to that great scrap heap in the sky of cars O'Toole had wrecked.

51
Tahitian Nightmare

When Marlon Brando declined the role of T. E. Lawrence he had in his sights that of Fletcher Christian in an epic remake of *Mutiny on the Bounty*. Carol Reed had been installed as director and not only cast hoary old Trevor Howard as Captain Bligh but a whole host of Brits in supporting roles: Hugh Griffith, Gordon Jackson, Percy Herbert and others. Reed also wanted Harris in there, attracted by his Irish ruggedness. In return Harris said he'd lick the deck of the *Bounty* for the chance to appear opposite his acting hero Brando. But when the script arrived Harris wasn't at all happy with the role on offer. It was too small, too insignificant, and he turned it down. Friends warned him of the risk he was taking – don't piss off Hollywood, for goodness' sake – but it worked. Reed came back with the much more prominent role of John Mills, chief mutineer alongside Mr Christian. Much better, you'd have thought, but Harris still wasn't satisfied and upped the ante even more by demanding star billing with Brando. A patent absurdity, they said, but agreed to increase his fee. Harris didn't want the money, he wanted the billing and stood firm.

Elizabeth remembers clearly the steely determination of Harris not to give in. 'He kept holding out for the billing and they kept adding the money and he kept turning the money down. He said, "No, I want above-the-title billing, with Brando and Trevor Howard." He didn't mind going below Marlon, he didn't mind going below Trevor Howard, but he was going above the title. And MGM came back and said, "But you're not as big a star as Howard." And Richard said, "Well, I'm as big today as Howard was when he was my age." Now that took them a while to work out.'

Meanwhile Elizabeth was getting ready to leave for Manchester where she was doing a TV play. 'And Richard came to see me off and he said, "OK, see you in London next week or see you in Tahiti next month." So I went off and then they caved in and they gave him above-the-title billing. And we had less money than all of the other actors who had much smaller parts because Richard kept turning the money down for the billing.'

Many thought Harris mad for pursuing it as far as he did. Elizabeth has her own theory as to why he was so stubborn on the issue. 'The first film he'd done when we went to Hollywood was *The Wreck of the Mary Deare*, and he was below the title, and I didn't understand why he was getting so upset – upset was a polite word. I mean something dark was gnawing at him and he'd get really angry, and I wouldn't have a clue what it was. But I'm pretty sure he realised he'd made a massive mistake because you don't go to Hollywood unless you go in through the right door. If you went there below the title, that's where you'd stay in those days. So he knew that the most important thing for him was to go in above the title. He was very astute. He thought things through; he had a very shrewd mind.'

What greeted Harris in the South Seas was a production in utter chaos. Brando seemed on edge the whole time, fluffing lines and dripping paranoia. He and Carol Reed argued constantly and stories began to emerge that when Brando didn't get his way he'd throw a hissy fit and walk off set, slowing the rate of production to a crawl. The weather didn't help either, with torrential rain and storms blighting the location site. There were scorpions and rats to contend with, too, and the cast and crew succumbed to dysentery and sundry other tropical ailments. But Harris revelled in the primitive conditions; it was a chance to be like Robinson Crusoe.

Elizabeth arrived in Tahiti on Christmas Eve. 'It was boiling hot and I'd brought a Christmas tree with me, one of those folding ones. I'd telegrammed Richard to say I was arriving on the twenty-fourth and I came with an au pair and Damian and I was pregnant with our second, feeling lousy, and it was a little tiny shed, not an airport. Pretty quickly everyone disappeared and there was just the au pair, Damian and myself, nothing else, except a few people closing down the little tin hut of an airport. Anyway, I managed to get a taxi to where the cast were staying, which were these huts with open sewage running between them. I found out that they were actually shooting and they wouldn't be back until the next day, Christmas Day. And because it was French Polynesia they had taken my four for a seven and they'd told Richard I wouldn't be arriving till the twenty-seventh. So he was allowed back and he welcomed us. He'd booked the house for the twenty-seventh so we were stuck in this weird, to put it mildly, complex.'

The rented house, when they finally moved in, was pretty good, by Tahitian standards. 'You had your own generator,' remembers Elizabeth, 'which unfortunately they'd built beside the cess pit which had scorpions in it, and every night Richard would turn the generator off and do a sort of kamikaze run shouting and screaming from there to the house. Cockroaches were just normal. And in the kitchen we had to put table legs into bowls of water with oil to stop the ants crawling up. So it was very basic. There was one road that went round the island and that was it. It was like Gauguin must have seen it, so I guess it was paradise. The men certainly thought that a lot of it was paradise because the women were very free. I remember all these beautiful girls with hair down to their waist, a lot of them were missing quite a few teeth because there was no calcium in their diet, so MGM gave them all teeth for Christmas. It was an incredible experience, but one that I was terribly glad to leave behind. The thought of having a child there, no way, so I had to come back to England.'

Pretty soon the whole cast and crew was being summoned home. With shooting running desperately behind schedule, MGM ordered the company back to Hollywood. Carol Reed, though, hadn't the stamina or nerve to carry on and he quit, or perhaps he was fired. Whatever the case, on hearing the news Harris groaned, 'We're in the hands of bloody philistines.' Reed was replaced by Lewis Milestone, a no-nonsense industry veteran who collided with Brando head-on, causing yet more friction and collective trauma. It appeared that Brando's behaviour if anything worsened when the unit returned to Tahiti to restart location work. Trevor Howard found the star 'unprofessional and absolutely ridiculous. He could drive a saint to hell in a dog sled.'

At least the weather had slightly improved, although filming on the *Bounty* itself was hellish as strong offshore winds constantly battered the ship, inducing mass seasickness. Howard said that every evening, after returning to his hotel, he continued to feel the ground heaving beneath his feet. 'And that was before I'd had a fucking drink!'

In the end Milestone couldn't take it any more and walked, leaving an assistant to shoot Brando's melodramatic death scene. 'It was shitsville,' said Harris, whose idolisation of Brando was battered to say the least. The constant rows with both directors and the star's absenteeism wore Harris out, and his frustration erupted during the filming of the scene where Brando's Fletcher Christian strikes Mills in defiance of his wish to mutiny. Absorbed with The Method and mumbling away, Brando's blow, when it finally came, was the dampest of squibs. Harris responded with a mock curtsy and waggled a limp wrist in the air. Brando didn't get the joke. Take two and again the blow was weak. Everyone waited to see how Harris would react. They weren't disappointed. Thrusting his chin forward he propositioned. 'Come on, big boy, why don't you fucking kiss me and be done with it!' Brando glared back, white with rage. Harris then planted a smacker on Brando's cheek and hugged him. 'Shall we dance?' Angry and embarrassed, Brando stormed off.

Tensions remained between the two men, not least Harris's irritation at Brando's insistence on multiple takes. Harris, Howard and the other British actors were used to working much faster, and Brando seemed to take perverse delight in wearing everybody else down. Brando had a theory that the next take was always going to be better, or better if done another way. One wonders how much of this was Brando seeking perfection and how much a deliberate ploy to hamstring his fellow performers, to render them invisible so it was he who ended up dominating the scene.

Harris had his own ideas about that. During one scene, after a dozen or more takes, Brando simply gave up the ghost and walked off set muttering, 'I don't know if it's going to work or not.' Harris was left agog. When it became obvious that Brando wasn't coming back Harris yelled after him, 'Damn you! Look at me! Act! Who the hell do you think you are?' On another occasion Brando moved the marks where Harris was supposed to be standing during a tense scene on the deck of the *Bounty*. During the course of the next three takes he'd change his mind and move Harris somewhere else. The Irishman knew Brando was just looking for a confrontation, so meekly went where he was told, and with a rictus smile on his face told his fellow actors, 'Forget your grand ideas, lads. We're just cabbages in this man's cabbage patch.'

Things eventually got so bad between Harris and Brando that they refused to appear on the same set together. Brando played his scenes opposite Harris's stand-in while Harris, adding insult to injury, used a packing case on which was drawn Brando's smiley mug. On the final day of shooting Brando sought reconciliation and requested Harris's presence on the set. The atmosphere was understandably tense. 'Would you mind giving me your lines?' commanded Brando. Harris refused, instead presenting him with the packing case. 'You'll probably get as much out of that as I got out of you.' The two men didn't speak to one another again for years.

Production troubles resulted in *Bounty* going millions over budget and six months over schedule, tipping MGM close to bankruptcy. Harris looked back on the film as 'nightmarish' and 'a total fucking disaster'. But at least he'd made his point to the Hollywood power brokers.

52

The Lass from Liverpool

Robert Shaw's relationship with Mary Ure intensified when they were cast together in the Royal Court's Jacobean tragedy *The Changeling* in February 1961. Shaw played the part of a servant in love with the mistress of the house who together plot to murder her fiancé. It was inspired casting by director Tony Richardson, who of course knew all about the affair between the two leads. It was common knowledge now amongst their friends and associates, while at the Court it was an open secret. The cuckolded Osborne's own chauffeur would ferry Mary to Shaw's bed at a little flat he'd taken near Sloane Square. Together on stage they radiated so much chemistry that when Shaw spoke the line 'I love that woman' it was with such passion that one night the audience apparently applauded.

Shaw's personal life had now descended into utter farce. Having made Mary pregnant he discovered a few weeks later that his wife Jennifer too was with child. Not only was he shuffling between a home life and his mistress, but now had to juggle two impending fatherhoods. Friends urged Shaw to stay with Jennifer, saying she was perfect for him and had been content to dump a promising career to be a wife and mother. Mary was still a working actress, strong and determined behind her fragile exterior. A timid creature to be sure, Mary could be tough. When appearing on Broadway she attended a party alone and was clumsily propositioned by Elia Kazan. She hit him in the face. So, Mary was unlikely to so easily take a back seat professionally. It would only lead to problems.

Things moved forward when Mary left her husband and took her own flat. Osborne paid a visit once, during which she talked about *The*

Changeling and then about Shaw, his talents as an actor and then, quite brazenly, his prowess in bed. It was then that she began to undress. 'Not as good as *you*, dear.' They ended up making love. When she was in the bathroom Osborne spied an open letter on the bedside cabinet, more than likely deliberately left there for him to read, which he duly did. It was from Shaw, explicit in its detail about his lovemaking activities with Mary in fathering their child. When she returned Osborne surreptitiously slipped the letter into his trouser pocket as he dressed. After a few cordial words, they kissed and he left. They would never see each other again.

Professionally, though, Shaw was on a high. *The Changeling* was a huge personal success for him, playing to packed houses, but it had a negative effect on his friendship with Richardson. They clashed during rehearsals when Richardson criticised Shaw's petty competitiveness, which he found adolescent and born of insecurity. They never worked together again. Nor, after the play closed in April, did Shaw ever step foot again on the English stage.

Hidden away amongst the more prominent supporting cast of *The Changeling* that included Jeremy Brett and Zoe Caldwell, playing a minor role as a sort of mad woman, mostly dragging chains around and making appropriate noises, was a young girl just arrived in London from Liverpool whom Richardson hoped to groom into a star. Her name was Rita Tushingham and she would become one of the faces of the sixties.

Woodfall had just bought the film rights to one of the landmark plays of the new school of kitchen-sink drama, *A Taste of Honey*. It had been written a few years earlier by the eighteen-year-old daughter of a bus inspector from Salford, Shelagh Delaney, partly to address social issues that she felt current theatre was not addressing. Her heroine was Jo, a seventeen-year-old working-class schoolgirl who meets and falls in love with a black sailor. When he returns to sea she is left abandoned and pregnant and finds lodgings with her best friend, a homosexual called Geoffrey. It really did tick all the boxes: class, race, gender and sexual orientation. Small wonder that Joan Littlewood was immediately attracted to it and put it on in 1958 to much critical success.

Finding the right girl to play Jo had become something of a problem.

Richardson and Osborne auditioned countless actresses only to be left with the distinct feeling that there was a dearth of female talent, certainly not of the quality of Bates, Finney, O'Toole and the rest. 'There was no equivalent of the so-called "northern" school of young men spilling out of drama schools or slogging away unseen in remote reps,' said Osborne. Then along came Rita.

While working at Liverpool rep behind the scenes as an assistant stage manager, Rita saw an article in the *Daily Express* titled 'John Osborne seeking ugly girl for *Taste of Honey*.' 'Go on, Reet, have a go, you're ugly enough!' her brother helpfully suggested over the breakfast table. Contacting Osborne by way of his literary agent, sending a letter and a photograph, Rita was invited to audition and then asked to make a film test. 'And luckily Tony picked me, because there was something he saw that he felt was right for the role, thank God. I've always believed that he saw something on screen that possibly he didn't see if I was in a room with him. I'm always surprised what the camera sees. The camera, if you let it, sees lots of layers.'

Before she took on the gruelling role in *A Taste of Honey*, which would be her film debut, Rita was put into the Royal Court company. 'Tony wanted me to familiarise myself with him and he obviously wanted to get to know me, so I did *The Changeling*. And that was a wonderful experience. I remember Mary Ure, she was a beautiful looking woman, very fragile, like porcelain almost. And I liked Robert Shaw a lot. He was quite extraordinary. I'd never come across anyone like that before. What you saw was what you got with Bob. And such a wonderful actor, great presence.'

The Royal Court and Woodfall didn't so much groom Rita as looked after her, welcomed her into the family, as it were. Woodfall also supplied her with a flat off the King's Road near to the theatre. 'Everyone was so wonderful to me. Mary Ure was very kind and supportive. And John Osborne was very good to me. And Tony, of course. I was very lucky to have them all because I would never have got on that train to come to London if I didn't already have a job lined up. I could never have come down on my own and looked for work.'

When *The Changeling* finished its short run *A Taste of Honey* began shooting on location in Manchester. It had taken almost a year for Richardson to raise the money. 'And the reason he couldn't get the money,' says cameraman Walter Lassally, 'was because the people who were most likely even to consider giving you any money were very conservative and they were not prepared to finance a film that was going to be made entirely on location.'

Richardson's previous films had been made entirely within the existing framework of the British film industry; exteriors were shot on location and interiors were all shot in the studio. But influenced by the French new wave, Richardson wanted to shoot *A Taste of Honey* entirely on location, to give the film a totally authentic look. The film bigwigs were having none of it. This was beyond radical and no one was prepared to gamble on it.

With so many films made on location today it's hard to comprehend why this idea was so impossible to sell to the financiers. But Richardson dug his heels in; it was what he wanted and he was prepared to fight for it. Why was he so determined? 'Because that was all part and parcel of the thinking,' says Lassally, who ended up photographing *Honey*. 'Bearing in mind what happened with the French new wave, all those people, Truffaut and Godard and some people in America, they were determined to get out of the clutches of the studio system because it promised a lot more liberty creatively. Studios were very oppressive and it hindered you all the time.' Lassally gives a perfect example. After the success of Theatre Workshop Joan Littlewood got the chance to bring one of her successful shows to the screen herself as director. She chose *Sparrows Can't Sing*. 'And she had a terrible time,' reveals Lassally. 'Because she was surrounded by people who were very eager to tell her what she couldn't do, but not at all helpful in the things that she wanted to do. 'Oh you can't do that, oh no.' On that film she suffered terribly as a result. I know because I was very friendly with her at the time.'

Also in that era the cinema industry was represented by very strong, almost militant, trade unions, as Canadian director Sidney J. Furie discovered when he arrived in Britain to work in 1960. 'The bane of everyone's existence was the sparks in the studio, the electrical trades union, they would throw the lights off in the middle of the take if you went past six o'clock. Then they'd negotiate overtime; they were in the wrong business. Once you escaped the studio you had great young guys who didn't give a shit, they were union members but it didn't matter, you didn't get that shop-steward mentality.'

Richardson did finally get backing and *A Taste of Honey* became the first British film shot entirely on location, a real milestone. And he managed to elicit a wonderful debut performance from Rita – there's no artifice there, she comes across as a complete natural. Richardson was, in essence, her teacher. 'I learned so much from him. For example, Tony didn't want me to go to rushes, and I understood why when I first saw the rough cut of the film because what you do is you look at all the wrong things, you look at the way you move your hands, what your hair looks like, stuff like that, so you're looking at you, you're not looking at the character. This is why I think Tony was so clever in saying, you mustn't come to rushes. And I've never been to rushes since either.'

Richardson, along with Karel Reisz, and later Lindsay Anderson, were at the forefront of this new British cinema. Walter Lassally is perhaps the best qualified, having worked closely with all of them, to compare and contrast their diverse talents. 'Lindsay was a very irascible person, very talented but very difficult to work with. Karel was completely different to Lindsay, Karel was very easy going, he never raised his voice, he never engaged in any kind of polemics, he was very laid-back and less emotional. Lindsay was a very emotional person and Karel not at all, certainly not on the surface. Lindsay had a tortured personality and had a terrible time as a sort of closeted homosexual. Tony was by far the most commercially minded of the group, he found it easiest to adapt and to do what was necessary in order to get in there. And Tony was by far the more sociable of the three, by far. And he was brilliant at casting, absolutely brilliant.'

Rita stayed on for the next couple of years at the Royal Court appearing in Arnold Wesker's *The Kitchen* and in the tour of *The Knack*, where in ultra-conservative Bath the bulk of the audience got up and walked out when Rita's character yelled out, 'Rape!' She also appeared in more films, becoming one of the very few British actresses to make an impact on screen at a time dominated by the boys. Why was this? The barriers were being dismantled daily but only the blokes were reaping the benefits. Maybe it was because this was a period all about anger, of smashing boundaries and kicking out against the system, predominantly male attitudes. And with the exception of Shelagh Delaney, the new playwrights who had the most influence were all male. The directors too, save for Joan Littlewood. In that sense it was quite a conservative revolution. Even in the play that started the whole ball rolling, *Look Back in Anger*, what did Osborne have its main female character doing most of the time on stage? Ironing.

53

Jesus and the Gypsy

Alan Bates was still appearing in *The Caretaker* when he was offered his first main role in a film, *Whistle Down the Wind*. The play's producers allowed him a month's leave and he travelled up to Burnley in Lancashire to start work. In his absence the role of Mick was taken over by Harold Pinter himself who, according to Donald Pleasence, was dying to play it. Actually Pleasence described Pinter's portrayal of Mick as far more malevolent than Bates's. 'He used to terrify me every night. Alan was not so frightening, but it was a much more subtle performance with Alan's own brand of malign understatement.'

In *Whistle Down the Wind* Bates plays a criminal fugitive who hides out in a barn and is discovered by a group of children. Startled out of sleep, when asked who he is, he replies with the expletive 'Jesus Christ!', which unfortunately is taken literally. ''E has cum back to our barn,' they blurt out innocently. Bates was fully aware when he accepted the offer that the children were really going to be the stars of the film, the main focus; his character merely becomes their focus, 'And that's why it was such a good part.'

Filming that scene in the barn proved a nightmare for Bates. Conscious of its importance to the narrative, when it came time to say 'Jesus Christ!' Bates just couldn't get anything out of his mouth. 'I became absolutely paralysed with fright, although outwardly I was still very calm. I think they finally took the Jesus from take nineteen and the Christ from take thirty-seven and put them together.' When it was all over, Bates packed up for the day and was driving home through twisty country lanes in the wintry landscape when he skidded on some ice and the car rolled over and landed on its roof, with him hanging upside-down inside. 'I think it was the relief of tension that it was over that caused the accident to happen.'

Based on a story by Mary Hayley Bell, wife of John Mills, it was inevitable that the film would star their daughter Hayley Mills, at the time the most popular child star in the world. Originally set in Sussex, the story was relocated to Lancashire after producer Richard Attenborough asked writers Willis Hall and Keith Waterhouse, in their words, to 'Northernise' it. Making his debut behind the camera as a director was former actor Bryan Forbes, who rendered stunning performances from the child actors and brought an almost documentary sharpness to the picture which the *New York Times* called, 'One of the most enjoyable and heart-warming films we've ever seen.'

While Bates had found his niche in cinema relatively quickly, Connery was still being badly employed under his contract. Cast in plays by Eugene O'Neill and Euripides on stage, and on television used in everything from Shakespeare to Arthur Miller, film producers lacked the same kind of imagination, categorising him as a brainless beefcake, nothing more. When Michael Winner wanted Connery in a film his producer point-blank refused, 'He's just a B-picture actor. You can't use him!' Here was the man destined to become arguably Britain's greatest film superstar and yet hardly anyone saw it coming. His next two cinema outings were a case in point, playing a thick-eared hoodlum and a dim-witted gypsy.

First was *The Frightened City*, a low-budget London gangland thriller that attempted to transfer the American gangster genre to a London setting. Today it looks terribly old fashioned with its smoky jazz clubs and clichéd characters, and even back then looked stale against the emerging kitchen-sink films. Then there was *On the Fiddle*. Director Cyril Frankel clearly recalls the reaction of his producer Ben Fisz to his suggestion of Connery appearing in this army comedy. 'He can't act,' Fisz blasted. 'He's just sitting around at the Pinewood canteen doing nothing and nobody will work with him.'

'Well, I've tested him,' Frankel said. 'And I know I can get a performance out of him.'

Reluctantly Fisz agreed. The part on offer wasn't any great shakes, but at least it offered Connery the opportunity to show off a bit of comedic talent as a slow-witted gypsy, effectively playing straight man to wide boy Alfred Lynch, an unashamedly working-class actor, the son of a Whitechapel plumber. 'So I invited Sean up for a drink,' recalls Frankel. 'And I told him about the film, that there was this cockney lad, a sort of spiv character, and then the gypsy who was more deeply based, so when they encounter the enemy it was the gypsy that came into his own and saved the day. And Sean said, "I have to tell you, I'm half gypsy, and if you're going to make fun of the gypsies I can't do it." And I said, "On the contrary, he's the hero, Sean."'

On the Fiddle is a quintessential British comedy of the period, jam packed with familiar faces like Stanley Holloway, Wilfrid Hyde-White, Bill Owen, John Le Mesurier and a young Barbara Windsor. During filming in April, Frankel was impressed with Connery's abilities, 'particularly his instinctive acting gifts'. Although he was cooperative and easy to work with, Frankel could sense a frustration burning away inside the actor that for the last few years he'd been on the verge of breaking through into the big league but it hadn't happened yet. It was obvious to Frankel that this rankled.

Some journalists were also starting to wonder whether stardom would forever elude Connery, one of those touted years earlier as 'the British Brando', remember. *Woman* magazine perceptively wrote at the time: 'It is a real mystery why no film company has built Sean into a great international star. He reminded me of Clark Gable. He has the same rare mixture of handsome virility, sweetness and warmth. His attractive speech has the vigour which many find lacking in the pinched vowels of London-trained actors.'

54
Lawrence Begins

Few actors have had more of a baptism of fire for their starring debut than O'Toole, not just a bugger of a role in one of the biggest pictures ever made, but having to appear opposite acting heavyweights like Alec Guinness, Jack Hawkins and Anthony Quinn. For a young actor it was intimidating, to say the least. Added to which, his character would appear in practically every scene. The film would live or die by his performance.

O'Toole's arrival in Jordan for the start of filming in May was accompanied by a massive hangover. Subsequently warned that he was now in an Arab country and that if he got drunk the authorities would throw him out, film or no film, he continued to knock it back, usually a bottle of champagne after a day's work. Guinness admired O'Toole's talent and charm but as he watched him drink to excess on location his appreciation cooled. Both were invited to dinner at some local dignitary's house where O'Toole got plastered, quarrelled with his host and threw a glass of champagne in his face. 'Peter could have been killed – shot, or strangled,' Guinness wrote to a friend. 'And I'm beginning to think it's a pity he wasn't.'

Many of O'Toole's scenes were played opposite another young, unknown actor, Omar Sharif. When first introduced to the Egyptian O'Toole murmured, 'Omar Sharif! No one in the world is called Omar Sharif. Your name must be Fred.' Henceforth Sharif was known as Cairo Fred. The two remained lifelong friends and at night after filming, when the cast and crew had finished dinner, they would adjourn to a makeshift bar and drink. 'It was like being in the army,' Sharif recalled. 'We sat in the bar and got pissed every night. There was nothing else to do.'

Both were obliged to film non-stop for three weeks, then have four days where they enjoyed the fleshpots of Beirut, then known as the sin city of the east. 'We had the use of a private plane to Beirut,' recalled O'Toole. 'This was in its better days, and misbehaved ourselves appallingly! Terribly!' The mind boggles. 'We'd just drink,' Sharif says. 'And try not to sleep too much so that we didn't waste any time.' Both took Dexedrine to stay awake. Gambling was another vice ruthlessly encouraged. 'We once did about nine months' wages in one night,' confirmed O'Toole. O'Toole was also prone to the odd jape during filming, not appreciated by everyone. Once he demolished the tents as the crew all lay sleeping. 'After a day's hard work in 140 degrees of heat, that wasn't funny,' said cameraman Peter Newbrook.

Lawrence of Arabia occupied a year and a half of O'Toole's life, filming in seven different countries. On the first day in the desert David Lean strode out of his tent, surveyed the scorched horizon, then turned to O'Toole. 'Pete, this could be the start of a great adventure.' Incredibly, before a foot of celluloid was even exposed, O'Toole spent several weeks learning how to live as an Arab, travelling across the desert with the Bedouin camel patrol, often sleeping rough under the stars, amidst utter silence, just as Lawrence had done. He even visited Bethlehem, but was unmoved by the experience, calling it 'Christ commercialised'. First job was to endure the heat of the desert, so hot at first it was actually physically painful, but he eventually adjusted to it. When sandstorms periodically engulfed the unit O'Toole and Sharif found that the best place to hide was underneath the make-up lorry.

Next O'Toole had to learn how to ride a camel, and after his first lesson blood oozed from the seat of his jeans. 'This is a very delicate Irish arse,' he warned his instructor. O'Toole came up with his own solution, some foam rubber which he cut to shape and placed on the saddle. Many Bedouins, incredulous at first, soon took it up and O'Toole described his invention as 'one of the most important contributions ever made to Arab culture'.

Eventually mastering the skill, O'Toole was almost killed during the spectacular sequence in which Lawrence's Arab army attacks the port of Aqaba. An effects gun loaded with small pellets went off too soon, hitting O'Toole in the eye and temporarily blinding him. Unable to control his camel the actor was thrown in front of several hundred charging Bedouins on horseback. Luckily the camel stood guard over the prone actor, as they are trained to do, shielding him from serious injury and probably saving his life. After being flown to hospital for treatment, O'Toole was back on the camel the next day.

Other injuries sustained in the line of duty included third-degree burns, sprained ankles, torn ligaments in both his hip and thigh, a dislocated spine, broken thumb, sprained neck and concussion. He also lost two stones in weight. It was murderous, the heat, the sandstorms, living in tents for months on end hundreds of miles from civilisation. Some of the crew couldn't take it and left. Even the army officer hired by Lean as the film's military adviser lost it, wandering out of his tent in the dark of night shooting at anything that moved across the landscape with live ammo. He had to be carted away.

Some feared O'Toole himself was close to a nervous breakdown more than once; would he crack, go AWOL? But Lean's confidence in him was unshakeable, even if the tyrannical director was deliberately hard on the actor, who found Lean's inability to offer any kind of praise whatever soul destroying. He begged Siân to come out and raise his spirits: 'Here, you have to be a little mad to stay sane,' he told her.

Filming in Jordan was also a logistical nightmare, not least the movement of equipment and people to distant location sites sometimes three hundred miles away from the production's base at the old sea port of Aqaba. In one of the more faraway regions, the stunning desert landscape of Tubeiq, Lean shot the famous scene where Lawrence goes back to rescue a man stranded in the desert. While shooting O'Toole and the Indian actor I. S. Johar riding together on a single camel, Lean saw that the men seemed to be having trouble staying on the animal. On closer inspection a large block of hashish was discovered; both actors were stoned out of their skulls. Shooting was abandoned for the day.

Lean was famously intense during the film-making process, highly strung, with all the foibles of a general atop a horse on a battlefield. He was also meticulous to an absurd degree, so a spot of improvisation was anathema to him. But when the scene where Lawrence is first given his Arab robes wasn't working as written, he took O'Toole to one side. 'There's something missing, Peter. What do you think a young man would do alone in the desert if he'd just been given these beautiful robes?' He pointed out towards the desert, O'Toole's eyes followed. 'There's your theatre, Peter. Do what you like.'

Suddenly the scene came to life with O'Toole's idea that the egoist Lawrence would immediately want to see what he looked like. With no mirror to hand, O'Toole improvised by pulling out a ceremonial dagger from its scabbard, holding it at an angle and peering at his reflection. 'Clever boy,' Lean muttered to himself. Such was the magic of the pose that it became one of the most used photographic images from the film.

After six months in the desert O'Toole was allowed to go back to Britain for a few weeks and immediately checked into hospital for rest and recuperation. Once out he went on the ultimate bender. 'After six months in the desert, I should think so.' Inevitably he got into trouble while visiting friends in Bristol. When police stopped his erratic drive down a street at four in the morning O'Toole stepped out of the vehicle and said, 'OK, skip. Let's go to the station. I'm drunk.' Spiegel was far from pleased. 'You're not supposed to get up to that kind of caper on a film like this!'

55

A Medieval Jimmy Porter?

The Royal Court was going through one of its periodic slumps. *The Changeling* had done well but not well enough to offset some heavy losses on other productions. At times of crisis *Look Back in Anger* was usually wheeled out but even that was becoming just a tad shopworn; so what better than a new John Osborne play? That would get bums on seats, especially since Finney had agreed to play the title role.

But what Osborne proposed took everyone by surprise: a historical play charting the stormy life of Protestant reformer Martin Luther. What?! Luckily there was more than a whiff of the angry young man in this intense psychological study of a flawed anti-hero, pitted against the world. One of history's greatest religious thinkers and revolutionaries, Tynan believed Osborne saw in Luther another working-class rebel who defied the establishment, demanded change, caused revolution and battled with the Catholic Church to set in motion the Protestant Reformation.

It was a strange subject to be sure, a bit heavy perhaps, even for the Court, but Devine was desperate to read it. When he got the play and finished it he couldn't wait to see Osborne, indeed hugged him publicly in the street outside the theatre, crying, 'By God, Boysie. You've done it! You've done it again!'

Brechtian in style, the three acts span twenty years of Luther's life. The highlight was three sermons delivered by Finney standing in a pulpit. Brilliantly, Osborne didn't fall into the trap of having a few benches and a motley band of medieval peasants; instead the audience were cast as the congregation, Finney preaching straight at them.

Luther was hotly anticipated by the theatregoing public. 'Osborne still exercised a mesmeric hold over his generation like a hell-fire preacher,' said Devine. But the production was held up for several months while Finney played out his commitment to *Billy Liar*. Devine and Osborne simply had no choice but to wait for him.

The play's inaugural performance was at a theatre festival in Paris, where Finney was awarded Best Actor for his part in it. Afterwards Osborne joined the whole of the cast back at their hotel, 'drinking into the night and listening to Albert Finney's whore-hunting adventures', he wrote. All the top English critics took the ferry over to see it. Tynan declared *Luther* the most eloquent piece of dramatic writing to have dignified the British theatre since *Look Back*, while journalist and critic Alan Brien said Finney's performance 'exhausts and yet hypnotises the eyes like the spectacle of a public flogging'.

In June 1961 *Luther* opened at the Royal Court and played to packed houses. Colin George, who'd been with Finney at Birmingham rep, remembers seeing the production and noticing a giant leap in Finney's abilities. 'He'd really grown enormously. The part required a lot, he makes this speech and collapses in anger and froths at the mouth. It's not to say that at Birmingham he didn't walk on stage with authority as, say, Henry the Fifth, but he'd really raced ahead as an actor. The part suited him so well. Luther was a common man and I think that's what made it for Albie.'

But there were a few detractors, amongst them Noël Coward, who wrote in his diary: 'I left the theatre knowing as much about Luther as when I went in. Fortunately there are some programme notes, which I read when I got home.'

When Finney left *Billy Liar* after enjoying great success many believed his shoes were simply too big to fill. Still, the search for his replacement began. Tom Courtenay had seen the play twice and loved it. He and John Thaw would sometimes see Finney eating at Lyons Corner House and come away awestruck. Like so many of his generation, Courtenay felt that Billy was speaking directly to him, this identification with heading down to London to make something of himself. 'It was a graphic illustration of how we lived. Billy Liar was in every molecule of my body.'

It was Courtenay's performance in *The Seagull* that made Lindsay Anderson think of him for Billy and one morning he was summoned to the Cambridge Theatre to audition.

Arriving early, Courtenay pottered about outside, unable to ignore the large photographs of Finney that hung on the walls beside glowing critical notices. Suddenly he sensed a presence behind him, it was Anderson, a broad smile on his face.

Quietly confident, Courtenay performed well; even better, Anderson took a liking to him and within a few days was offered the part. Generously, Michael Benthall agreed to release him early from his commitments at the Old Vic.

Rehearsals for Courtenay began as Finney played out his final few weeks in the role before going off to play Luther. Anderson was keen for Tom to undertake imaginative exercises, as he'd instructed Finney to do, such as to conjure up Billy's fantasy world of Ambrosia. Finney had drawn a map of the place and stuck it inside a cupboard on stage so as to be near it at all times. Character immersion such as this didn't sit well with Courtenay. He was more of a traditionalist who just learned his lines; the better he knew them, the more it seemed like he was speaking them naturally. 'And my imagination responded to the security I derived from knowing the text.'

Just a few days after taking over, Courtenay posed with Finney for a press photograph – the two Billys. Courtenay would later recall being on edge in his presence and perhaps self-conscious about the comparisons that had been made between them for so long. Strange, since they were so very different. 'Tom was much more open and easy going than Albert,' says Ann Beach, who was still in the *Billy Liar* cast. 'As people they were as different as chalk and cheese.'

Courtenay himself recognised this incongruity. 'Albert always gave the impression that he didn't give a bugger about anything. I worried about everything.' It was this almost schoolboyish reverence that Courtenay had towards Finney that he believes is the reason they didn't become friends until much later in life, indeed not until they filmed *The Dresser* in 1983. Although it was strange how throughout the sixties people would mix them up. 'I used to be congratulated for *Tom Jones*,'

Courtenay revealed. 'And Albert once got into a pub fight with a bloke who insisted Finney was me!'

Given that *Billy Liar* was such a monster hit and had helped propel its lead actor to stardom, Courtenay coped surprisingly well with all the incumbent pressures. 'I know that everyone is waiting to see me make a gigantic muck-up of it,' he joked. But deep down Courtenay knew that following Finney was a risk. He coped by trying, as best he could, to eliminate all the outside forces from his mind and to just see the play and the role for what they were. Courtenay hoped everyone would just shut up and let him do his job, which was to act.

After his triumphant opening night Courtenay quickly made the part his own, revelling in the freshness of the text, which was a wonderful release after all that crusty Shakespeare. 'It was such fun to talk in a language I could understand.' This was broad, everyday talk.

It was great for audiences, too. 'They want to see more about themselves,' Courtenay reasoned. 'They want to *know* about *themselves*. Nowadays ordinary people are being written about affectionately. And they respond. Hence *Coronation Street*, I suppose.' The television soap had made its debut the previous December, not that long after the impact made by *Saturday Night and Sunday Morning*. It was a kitchen-sink soap, you could say.

Ann Beach saw at first hand the smooth transition between Finney and Courtenay and the seemingly effortless way he coped. 'And I think Tom was better casting for it in a way. Albert was a very strong, big character, but there was something about Tom, that little-lost-boy thing, that suited the role better; he was more vulnerable. Whereas Albert had to play the vulnerability because his personality was so larger than life.'

Trevor Bannister was also still in the cast. 'I think Albert was much more of a leading man than Tom ever was. Tom always struck me as a bit more cerebral. I think it's down to balls, really, Albert's just got a bigger pair of balls. He had a slightly more showbizzy feel about it; he was more of a showman than Tom. But they were both wonderful to work with. There was nothing starry about either of them. Well, Albert did have a starriness but in the nicest possible way, in a very generous way. What was important to him was what we were doing, the play, and how we reacted to each other. He was terrific. And a great sense of humour, a twinkle in the eye.'

Certainly, the tempo of the two performances was different. 'They must have missed the panache and confidence of Albert's rendition,' Courtenay admitted. 'And the speed of it. Albert was going like an express. When I took over, George Cooper, playing Billy's dad, had to get a later train home.'

It's rare for an actor to take over a role from someone who has been a huge success in it and then not only make it his own but eclipse the previous performer. That's what Courtenay achieved, and he remains the one and only Billy Liar. When his old RADA pal Derek Fowlds got the part down at Worthing rep he approached Courtenay for advice. 'I said, "Tell me what you did in that play when your grandmother was dead." There was a marvellous sequence that Tom did which was so wonderful where he came back from his grandmother's funeral and he took a pea stick from the garden and that pea stick became everything from a gun to a snooker cue to a trumpet and in the end he did the last post, and Tom told me all and when I played it in Worthing it just brought the house down.'

As Courtenay went from strength to strength in the play and won plaudits and accolades back home his mother Annie, whom he still doted on, had fallen desperately ill with acute depression. Courtenay was outraged to learn that she'd been sent to a mental hospital for electric-shock treatment, waking up afterwards in a ward full of the shuffling near-dead. 'Lunatics, Tommy, you know, jabbering, slavering, mad people.' After the Saturday evening performance Courtenay always scampered over to King's Cross to get the last train north to stay the weekend. But what no one knew was that the cancer that would soon take her life was already beginning to spread through her body.

56
Stamp's Starring Role

At one of David Andrews' parties Terry Stamp met the playwright John McGrath, a passionate man of great charisma whose socialist beliefs were at the core of his writings. McGrath had just finished a play called *Why the Chicken*, about Britain's burgeoning post-war new towns and the violence amongst the disaffected youth living in such soulless places. McGrath was quite taken by Stamp and gave him the lead role. Lionel Bart was set to direct.

The hope was to get *Why the Chicken* into the West End but it died a death in the London suburbs. 'Our first night was in Wimbledon,' recalls David Andrews, who was also in the cast. 'It was a great barn of a theatre, and it was very poorly attended and it got terrible notices.' After a few days the cast assembled to discuss where things were going wrong. Lionel Bart stood up to reveal his master plan. 'We need to beat this show up a bit, boys. I tell you what we're going to do, we're going to put a musical number into the show.' He then produced a gramophone and played a record on it. 'I want you to learn this tune, boys and here are the lyrics you're going to sing to it – 'Do you know why, iy, iy, iy, why the chicken crossed the road, why the chicken crossed the road? To get to the other side.' The cast looked quizzically at each other, as well they might. 'So we all had to learn this bloody lyric,' says Andrews. 'And this band came along and did the musical accompaniment and it was incorporated into the show. But it was a straight plagiarism from this record Lionel played us, which was by a group called the Isley Brothers and the song was called "Shout", which was later a hit for Lulu. All he'd done was change the lyrics!'

Stage two of Bart's rescue job came next. 'I've been told that you should never talk about a character that doesn't appear,' he said.

'Yeah – Honkey, he doesn't appear,' said Stamp. There was a character in the play called Honkey, the brother of the Terry Stamp character who was always getting mentioned but never in the end ever turned up.

'Well, I think Honkey ought to be in this show,' said Bart.

Stamp and Andrews looked at each other, the same thought had entered their head. Caine was out of work – no change there – and was getting very low on cash – literally no change there. 'Mike,' yelled Stamp. 'Get Mike in, Lionel.'

So Caine was roped in to come on at the end and just say ten lines of dialogue. 'And it lifted the whole thing out of the theatre, it was amazing,' says Andrews. 'If they'd put Michael in at the beginning of the run it would have been a big success, because Terry was great in that show. He was undoubtedly a very interesting actor, Terry, he looked so pretty. And he was good fun, he came up with some very funny extra lines and we played off each other a lot, we just had a lot of fun on that. He's such a nice guy, Terry, and it's so unusual for people in this business to be that decent.'

Caine had also grown friendly with McGrath and was in his office one day when he saw a script lying on his desk. McGrath talked in glowing terms about it and that the BBC had asked him to direct it. The writer was a young guy from Canning Town who'd mostly written comedy material and this was his first serious play. His name was Johnny Speight, soon to create the immortal TV character Alf Garnett. It sounded interesting, thought Caine, and when McGrath left the room he picked it up and started to read. It was called *The Compartment* and Caine responded to it immediately. There were just the two characters: a strait-laced and terribly traditional businessman, briefcase, umbrella and pinstripe suit, the works; and then a cocky cockney type, dangerous, possibly mentally unbalanced. Two men poles apart who in normal circumstances would never meet, but here they are, alone, in a train compartment. Caine loved it, and he wanted to play the nutter. This was the chance he'd been waiting for, a lead part on television, the destiny of which was in the hands of a friend.

When McGrath returned Caine all but got on his hands and knees and pleaded for the role. 'It's perfect for me, John, you know that I can play it blindfold.' McGrath didn't need much persuasion, he knew Caine could do it, but how was he going to sell the idea to his bosses? Here was an actor who'd never even had a supporting role on television, let alone the lead. Only recently Caine had played a mere walk-on in a film and ballsed that up. The part was a policeman in the sci-fi drama *The Day the Earth Caught Fire*. When he fluffed his one line director Val Guest gave him a very public dressing down, followed by that old chestnut, you'll never work in movies again. What was even more galling was the fact that the star of the film was Edward Judd, one of Caine's drinking pals. More evidence that his contemporaries were shooting ahead of him in the game. 'It was all fine while we were all in trouble together,' Caine said. 'But now I started to feel increasingly isolated.'

That was why Caine was so anxious to get *The Compartment*. It might be his only chance. Luckily, McGrath managed to swing it with the BBC bigwigs and Caine was cast, with Frank Finlay playing the businessman. When the play was shown it was a great success and made something of an impact on the public, but in particular two men. One afternoon Caine and Stamp were walking along Piccadilly when they spied on the opposite side of the street Roger Moore, then a big television star. Just like fans they stood gawping at him when Moore caught their gaze and walked across the road straight towards them. 'Is your name Michael Caine?' asked Moore. Caine nodded. 'I saw you in that television play, *The Compartment*. I just want to tell you that you are going to be a big star.' With that Moore shook his hand vigorously and walked off. Caine was in a daze for several minutes, totally nonplussed. The two men would years later become the best of friends.

More importantly, watching at home had been Dennis Selinger, at that time probably the top agent in the country, who represented amongst many others Peter Sellers. Selinger wrote to Caine asking if he wanted representation. (Ironic, since Caine had been trying in vain to get the agent's attention for years.) Caine did, and would stay a loyal client until the agent's death in 1998.

★   ★   ★

While still performing in *Why the Chicken*, Stamp got a call from Jimmy Fraser asking him to meet Peter Ustinov at his offices in Golden Square to discuss his new film of Melville's *Billy Budd*.

'What's the part?' asked Stamp.

'The lead.'

'You must be joking. They must be scraping the barrel if they want to see me.'

'They are. They've already seen every young actor in town.'

Stamp attended the audition with a self-confidence bordering on arrogance, mainly because he thought he didn't stand a cat in hell's chance. Upon meeting Ustinov, whom he admired greatly and knew was not only the director but scriptwriter too, and would be playing the captain, Stamp almost went to pieces but managed to retain enough composure to warrant his attendance the next day at Elstree Studios for a film test. 'We'll send a car for you.'

Stamp rushed back to the flat to tell Caine everything. Pleased as punch at his friend's good fortune, Caine decided to lend a hand, and they went over his lines together for two hours. Less an instinctive actor than a master of technique, Caine also bestowed upon Stamp some of the brilliance of his admittedly minor film experiences. Most important, said Caine the teacher, was hitting your marks. He went into the kitchen and returned with several table knives which he placed on the carpet in various positions. 'Look,' said Caine. 'It's critical for any actor to hit the mark laid down. These marks are the cameraman's only way of keeping an actor in perfect focus. If you can't master it, you might as well give up right away.'

One can picture the scene, Stamp walking nonchalantly about the lounge and then halting just before his toes touch one of the knives. He'd recall that Caine never once spoke about what his character's motivation might be – no, it was practicalities, get those right first, said Caine, then you can build on them. Caine could hit his marks blindfold, Stamp remembered with unerring respect. 'He could feel a chalk mark through the crêpe soles of his desert boots.'

At the studio Stamp was hurried into make-up, then wardrobe, before entering the stage; for the first time in his life he was on a movie set.

Goosebumps time with knobs on. Once he'd shot the scene Ustinov wanted to do some improvisation with the camera still running; he was going to chastise him mercilessly – but whatever foul words he heard, Stamp was not to speak. Ustinov cried action and began. To get the right emotion Stamp conjured up the memory of when he was caned at school and had wanted to defiantly say thank you to his persecutor but no sound came out. That memory rose to the surface now. 'Cut!' said Ustinov, who walked out from behind the camera, right up to Stamp and rubbed his face with his chubby hands. 'That was, tumultuous.'

Although Ustinov saw that Stamp was 'extraordinarily nervous' during the test he was won over by his raw ability and 'hypnotic quality' and was determined to cast him in direct defiance of his backers. In Hollywood Allied Artists wanted Warren Beatty, Dean Stockwell or Tony Perkins, certainly not a complete unknown and someone untried on film. Ustinov's powers of persuasion were obviously mighty, since he got his way. Stamp had landed his first film job, and it was the starring role. The first thing he did after signing the deal was to treat himself to a top Savile Row suit.

Curiously, he'd kept his audition secret from his family, even the fact that he'd won the part. 'Gawd knows what they're going to think about this lot,' he told a reporter. 'When my mother hears about my contract she'll pass out. She's got used to me going home to scrounge Sunday dinner.' Their reaction when the news broke in all the papers was a mixture of shock and pride. His mother, though, burst into tears on discovering he'd have to bleach his hair for the film.

Filming on *Billy Budd* got under way in June on location in Spain, near Benidorm, then just a deserted stretch of coastline with one modest hotel on it. To build up Stamp's profile the studio had organised a publicity shoot. There he was one afternoon prancing on the beach with two local beauties on his arms supplied by the photographer. 'Don't want the folks in the US to think you're a faggot.'

Michael, later Lord, Birkett was first assistant director on the film and recalls a happy shoot with everyone working to a common purpose. There was also a Hollywood producer involved, no doubt keeping an eye on the money being spent. One day Ustinov mentioned to Birkett,

'Our producer doesn't like coming to sea.' All the scenes aboard HMS *Bellipotent* were shot on a real ship miles offshore and Ustinov sensed the American didn't care for the experience. 'I don't think he's much use to us you know, our producer,' Ustinov continued. 'Why don't you send him home?'

'Peter, he's not only paying my salary, he's paying yours as well,' Birkett answered. 'Are you sure about this?'

'Oh, don't bother about little things like that. You send him home.'

Birkett couldn't help thinking, well, that's a bit much for a first assistant director to tell the producer, go home. 'Anyway, I went over to the producer and said, "I don't think you're terribly happy here, I mean, you see rushes, but you'd be just as happy seeing them in Beverly Hills, wouldn't you?" And he said, "Yes, you're absolutely right, I would." And he was on the plane home the next day, he just went. So that was the end of the producer, so now Peter was producer, director, scriptwriter and star of the whole thing; lovely man, sweet man.'

David McCallum was amongst the supporting cast and found Ustinov a joy to work with. 'We were actually at sea for several weeks and Peter Ustinov telling stories constantly. After a while people were trying to find places to hide in order to get away from this wonderful repartee that never stopped. And Terence Stamp was a beautiful, innocent young guy, as we all were.'

Birkett in particular was taken by Stamp. 'It was a big movie and Terence was the young star of it, so he was understandably nervous. But he was awfully good in it, I must say, because he had a kind of childlike, almost angelic innocence, although he was very far from being a child. But he did have that sort of innocence about him which was essential for Billy Budd.'

The two men got quite pally and decided to drive back to Britain once location shooting had finished. 'We both stopped off in Rome,' recounts Birkett, 'and went out to dinner one evening and Terry said, "My Italian's getting better, you know." I said, "Oh good. How do you do that, have you been studying?" And he said, "No, I've got this machine that I put under my pillow at night, it's a little recorder, so I wake up in the morning speaking better Italian." I said, "Do you really?

That's amazing. I've never heard of that technique." So off we go to dinner in our taxi and the driver was your typical Roman, he went through every red light up the whole of the Via Corso, one of the main streets in Rome, and after a bit Terry turned to me and said, "When you've seen one red light, you've seen em all!" We got to the restaurant and I said, "OK, Terry, you order dinner now, good practice for your Italian." And I was expecting all sorts of wonders from him and Terry simply showed the menu to the waiter and said, "Eh cameriere, dinner." That was the extent of his Italian. I wasn't very impressed. He's a sweet man, Terry.'

57

Two Births and a Divorce

During the successful West End run of *The Caretaker* Bates managed to fit in the odd lead role on television, including another collaboration with Philip Saville, this time a period romantic comedy called *Duel for Love*. It was a chance for Bates to shed his leather jacket for once, a symbol of the tough, northern roles he'd been playing on television in recent years, and for viewers to see the softer side of his personality, as a dashing young Italian lover. 'Alan was curiously cerebral for an actor who was very earthy,' says Saville. 'He was very precise about his dialogue and had wonderful diction. And he still had those very boyish looks, right up to the very end of his career almost. He really was ideal for anything romantic because he had that kind of Celtic force. For someone who was bisexual he was incredibly masculine. Although he could come across quite . . . not camp exactly, but theatrical, let's say.'

Saville really went to town direction-wise on *Duel for Love*, aiming for a grand visual sweep, to allow his camera the freedom to wander. For the first time he'd come to see the clunkiness and technical limitations of television drama. 'I was very conscious of trying to create a television language for drama where the camera was used to tell most of the story. The power of television is that it's radio with pictures; it's different from film, which is largely a visual medium that tells you a story and omits things and lets the audience fill in the gaps to a certain extent. Television has to tell you and if you dither for a minute they're off onto another channel. You've got to grip them by the balls. And that's what some of us started to try and do, to use the camera.'

Saville wanted his cameras to flow amidst the action, rather than the standard procedure of shooting from a stock position facing or at the side,

314

but this was just not possible since they were large and extremely heavy objects; the crew called them 'iron men' because they rested on big solid pedestals. Another problem was the cables that operated them, three inches thick, they were, coiled about the studio floor like pythons; if you wanted the camera to move it took at least two stagehands to lift the cables.

One day on set Saville took the bull by the horns and ordered the camera to track the action, but the crew refused and dug their heels in. 'OK, then,' said Saville. 'I'm coming onto the floor.' That was another thing directors weren't supposed to do; they were required to stay in the control room during shooting and give all their instructions through the floor manager, or what is called today the assistant director. But Saville and a few others used to enjoy coming onto the set and eventually a lot of directors followed suit and monitors were specially hung up so they could watch and give instructions, just like on a film set. 'Anyway, I came down onto the floor and got hold of the camera, I had a bit of experience with movie cameras, but I was fairly shitting myself in front of the whole crew, thinking, "If I fuck this up . . ." I managed to focus and track and dolly and I said, "Look, if I can do it with what I know about cameras, surely you can do it." And of course they had to do it then. And there was a little polite applause. Anyway, nobody disagreed with me thereafter.'

As Bates prepared to return to Broadway that October with *The Caretaker* he heard the news that Peter Woodthorpe, who had played the role of Aston in London, had dropped out and was being replaced with Robert Shaw. Bates had never acted with Shaw before and was looking forward to the prospect and of returning to New York. As it turned out, the two men did not become close; if anything Shaw was more drawn to Pinter. Their friendship began with a test of strength and continued down the years greased by a competitive rivalry. During the pre-Broadway run of *The Caretaker* in New Haven the cast, along with Pinter, would retire after each performance for a meal and drinks. One particular evening Shaw did his usual thing and challenged someone, Pinter in this case, to a hundred-yard sprint, unaware that Pinter had been a champion runner at school. Supremely confident he'd win, Shaw stood rooted to the spot when Pinter bolted out of the blocks like a rocket. Halfway down, Pinter looked back wondering where his opponent was. He was nowhere to be seen. 'Why didn't you run?' he asked Shaw later. 'I didn't want to beat you, you bastard,' replied Shaw. Pinter was convinced Shaw didn't compete in the race once it had dawned on him that he was going to lose.

Shaw would describe *The Caretaker* as the most wearing play of his career, because he was so unlike the character he was representing. He was having to underplay all the time. At one point in the play Aston relates his tragic experience in a mental hospital. Shaw knew he could perform that scene in a way that would win him the sympathy of the audience, so it took a lot of honesty not to choose the easy option and instead interpret it the way Pinter envisaged, with as little theatrical effect as possible. This constant reining in of the emotional content left Shaw mentally exhausted at the end of every performance, but he loved the sheer challenge of it. 'My time of real development, both personally and professionally, came working with Pinter.'

His first time on Broadway, Shaw basked in the play's success, but his personal life was again bordering on disaster. Mary had given birth in August to a child, a son that the press reported was Osborne's, in view of the fact that they were still married, although a few journalists thought it strange that he was hundreds of miles away from his wife's bedside in Cannes. Osborne, of course, knew the truth: the child was Shaw's.

Shaw was delighted at having a son. All his children with Jennifer were girls and, though he loved them deeply, like Henry VIII it was a son he truly longed for. During the time both women were pregnant Shaw was telling friends how he was going to solve the problem, choosing between wife and mistress. 'I'll go to the one who gives me the boy.' Flippancy, perhaps, but poor Mary was distraught during the pregnancy in case a girl popped out. When five weeks later Jennifer gave birth Mary was in palpitations waiting for news of the child's sex. When she was told it was a girl, she fainted.

With a nanny in tow Mary and child arrived in New York, for a rest she told reporters, but in reality to join Shaw as *The Caretaker* began its run. It was now that the divorce petitions started flying. Osborne sought a divorce, citing Shaw; Mary did likewise, citing Osborne's frequent adultery. Speaking only through solicitors, their marriage was finally annulled amidst bitter recriminations.

The question now was, what was Shaw going to do? He chose Mary. Being in New York, cut off from his family and network of friends, perhaps helped make his mind up for him. Had he been in England with Jennifer and the children it might have been a lot tougher walking out on them.

It was ironic that his second novel, *The Sun Doctor*, had recently been published and that he'd dedicated it to Jennifer. Again it was well received. The *Daily Mail* felt it 'consolidates his place as a writer, whole and proven, and one of the powerful talents'. The most interesting aspect of the book is that the protagonist, after years in Africa working as a doctor, returns to his father's home in the Orkneys. Once there he slowly begins to understand his father, a man driven by his missionary work. It's not hard to see that Shaw, who almost certainly revealed more of his personal life in his books than he ever did in his acting, was coming to terms with his own father's death.

The novel won him the highly coveted Hawthornden Prize, Britain's oldest literary award. Shaw felt great pride to be counted amongst previous winners who included Sean O'Casey, Robert Graves and Evelyn Waugh. When asked why he wrote, Shaw once said, 'Because I have a childish desire for immortality.' More seriously, he viewed himself as a political writer. 'I genuinely love to shock my readership into something. I am always thinking of how I can get their attention, of how I can shock them out of their smug, middle-class ways. I want to shock them out of their stupor, to shock them into awareness, to make them think.'

Certainly Shaw was admired by his friends, too, as a writer of some distinction. None more so than Philip Broadley, who'd just begun writing for television, as David Andrews relates. 'Philip used to pick up the phone on a Saturday morning before he went to the Quill pub in Putney for a drink with myself, Bryan Pringle and Peter Bowles, and it would be Robert. "Hi, Philip." He'd say. "Yes, Robert, dear boy, what's going on?" Philip would ask, and Bob would answer, "I want to read you the latest chapter of my book." And Philip used to come to the pub almost in tears. "What's up, Philip?" we'd say. "Bloody Shaw has read me his book and I just think to myself, why can't I write like that."'

58

Bates Finds Schlesinger

Joseph Janni, who spoke with a rich, melodic Milanese accent, was still reeling from having had to give up the film rights to *Saturday Night and Sunday Morning*. As determined as ever to tap into the current vogue for working-class realist films, he bought an option on the novel *A Kind of Loving*, the story of a lad from an industrial northern town who gets a girl pregnant and is forced to marry her, and hired Willis Hall and Keith Waterhouse to write the screenplay. Now for the perfect director to bring it to life on screen.

Always on the lookout for new and exciting talent, Janni had been impressed with the work of a young director at the BBC on their documentary strand *Monitor*, notably his prize-winning documentary *Terminus*, a day in the life of London's Waterloo station. His name was John Schlesinger. 'I think I should like to discover you,' Janni said when they were first introduced. 'Be my guest,' replied Schlesinger. *A Kind of Loving* would mark Schlesinger's directorial debut and begin a partnership with Janni that would carry over into six films.

For backing, Janni went to a small but adventurous outfit called Anglo Amalgamated run by two shrewd Jewish businessmen, Nat Cohen and Stuart Levy. Anglo's output was mainly low-budget thrillers, like Connery's *The Frightened City* and seaside postcard-type comedies such as the *Carry On . . .* series. Cohen was a shrewd guy and prepared to take risks; he'd distributed Michael Powell's *Peeping Tom*, and was easily persuaded by Janni that the kitchen-sink-realism genre was current and lucrative.

When Janni and Schlesinger caught a screening of *Whistle Down the Wind* they believed they'd found their perfect lead actor in Bates, only to discover he was in his fourth week of a long run on Broadway with *The Caretaker*. But so taken was Janni by Bates's suitability he paid the theatre producers $10,000 to release him and he flew into Britain to start work on location in Manchester early in November. Janni immediately released a press statement proclaiming Bates to be 'one of the most important properties in British movies today'.

On Broadway, Bates was replaced by Alex Davion. Supremely nervous on his first night, during a silent blackout Shaw approached him from behind and forcefully goosed him. Davion just managed not to shriek out. 'Thought that would relax you, boy,' said Shaw.

In tune with other British new wave films of the time, *A Kind of Loving* was about working-class people and their everyday struggles and lives; it was about life as it was actually lived by millions around the country. That said, it departed from the norm in that Bates's character wasn't rebelling against anything particularly and seemed quite content with his lot. Bates is hardly a ranting and raving Jimmy Porter or Arthur Seaton type. Bates believed *A Kind of Loving* was the only one of that bunch of films which dealt with truly ordinary people. The characters in films like *A Taste of Honey* and *Saturday Night and Sunday Morning*, were, he felt, 'all rather extreme people in an ordinary background'.

Bates felt particularly drawn to his own character. Vic wasn't a million miles away from his own experiences: 'A boy from the Midlands who works at an ordinary job but feels that there is some other area of life he hasn't yet touched, and he is very rooted to his family.' Schlesinger also made a conscious decision to depart from the usual drab and gritty atmosphere of previous kitchen-sink films, to get away from the view that 'Up North' was unrelievedly drab and bloody awful. He also wanted to push the envelope in what a British film could show. There's one scene where Vic attempts to buy condoms at a chemist, an on-screen act hitherto unprecedented. Incredibly, even some members of the film crew thought this was beyond the pale. 'Fucking idiots,' Schlesinger condemned in his diary. 'When is the cinema going to grow up?'

Bates loved his time on the film, the whole experience, the sheer joy of it. 'There was such a sense of promise then,' he said wistfully years later. 'Such a sense of future.' Schlesinger, however, was plagued by insecurities from day one. Driving with Bates to the set on the first morning he saw the crew setting up and visibly cowered. 'Let's turn the car around while we still have time,' he said, 'and get the hell out of here.' Halfway through the first week those insecurities were still hovering. 'Oh God, I can't do this,' he muttered. 'It's all terrible. What was I *thinking*?'

Schlesinger considered Bates 'such a good, intuitive actor', and Bates warmed to Schlesinger, a director who was sympathetic to the acting process, having started out himself in the profession. Both men shared a similar mischievous sense of humour. Once in Paris they sat outside a street café speaking in broad Yorkshire accents and telling everyone they were miners, just aht from t'pit.

For Schlesinger, he rather hoped something more meaningful might develop between them. During shooting he nursed an intense crush on his leading man and, had Bates been willing, Schlesinger would have jumped in head first. As it was, Bates was still with Wyngarde and didn't in any case want the complexity of an affair with his director to cloud the work. With that out of the way they developed a firm professional bond and a deep lifelong friendship and would work together a further three times.

The eventual success of *A Kind of Loving* at the box office made Schlesinger's name. Looking back years later he realised it had been a very fortuitous time to start his career, with British cinema entering a renaissance, when new types of film-making were being explored and financing for home-grown product wasn't so fraught. 'There was such an energy, such an excitement.' He was saddened later in his career at having to move to America when the British film industry collapsed in the seventies. 'In the early sixties, it truly seemed as if British cinema would go on for ever.'

A Kind of Loving was also the making of Alan Bates, although fame was something he didn't altogether appreciate. 'In a way it's what you're looking for,' he said. 'Not so much fame as recognition for what you do.' But in other ways it troubled him, not least the publicity machine that surrounds star actors. He went out of his way to avoid personal publicity, gave few interviews and, when he did submit, refused to talk about himself in any depth. 'I was reticent about answering searching questions about myself. I was still asking myself searching questions and not getting very coherent answers.'

His complicated personal life might have played a part in this refusal to play the fame game. Success when it arrived didn't change Bates as a person, as he was never a vain man, but according to his friend Keith Baxter it meant changes in other areas of his life. 'When he found that celebrity Alan had to take a look at his life and he had to rearrange his life; and I think that always costs. He had to maintain his private life.'

59
King of Scotland

Sean Connery was awoken by the phone one morning and in his groggy state said yes to a strange offer to play the title role in a Canadian TV production of *Macbeth*.

The $500 fee was good, so Connery accepted without consulting his agent, requesting only 'a room with a good bathroom'. He'd been chatting away for about twenty minutes before it hit him that the call was coming from Toronto and his next thought was, my God, I hope he hasn't reversed the charges.

The 'he' in question was Paul Almond, a young Canadian director who'd managed to persuade CBC, the country's main television network, to let him mount an ambitious adaptation of *Macbeth* because he'd heard the schools in Canada were studying it that year. The real hurdle was finding a suitable actor to play what is arguably Shakespeare's most dramatic role. 'Back in the early sixties,' Almond recalls, 'Canada didn't have the richness of performers that we had later in the decade and in the seventies, so I rang my agent and said, "Look, I need a really good actor to play Macbeth and I want a Scotsman if you've got one. I know that's a tall order, but I don't want your average classical type actor." Although I'd been schooled in all that stuff at Oxford University, on television I like people to be real and honest.' After a couple of days his agent called back. 'There's this actor,' she said. 'He's a Scotsman, he's not classically trained or anything but he was very good in a BBC play about Alexander the Great.' Almond pondered on that a bit. 'Do you think he'll be good?' There was a pause. 'Absolutely.'

The BBC production being referred to was *Adventure Story*, which had been broadcast a few months back and Connery had made a distinct

322

impression in it. Based on Terence Rattigan's version of the life of Alexander the Great and directed by Rudolph Cartier, one of the pioneers of early TV drama, best remembered for *Quatermass* and *1984*, Connery had performed in a curly blonde wig with verve and unashamed energy. Conscious of the corrosive quality of power yet unable to resist it, Connery's Alexander grew from young adventurer to embittered tyrant, a compelling transition that drew striking praise from *The Times*: 'Certain inflections and swift deliberations of gesture at times made one feel that the part had found the young Olivier it needs.'

After agreeing to Almond's mad idea that morning, Connery's first thought was, Christ, what do I do first? Reading the damn thing might be handy, so he grabbed hold of a copy and after finishing it realised what he'd got himself into. 'It was monumental. I re-read it over and over on the plane all the way to Canada.' Rehearsals were already under way as Connery was taken from the airport to the studio to meet everyone, including his Lady Macbeth, Zoe Caldwell. To this day Almond recalls the moment he first caught sight of Connery in person. 'I remember thinking, my God this is just perfect. He was so right for the part; he was Macbeth standing there in real life. He was exactly what I would have thought Macbeth was. He was big and tall, good looking and rough. I could see him as the King of Scotland just in a flash. He was my Macbeth instantly.'

Incredibly, Connery had just ten days not only to learn the part but also conceive of a way to play Macbeth that was completely his own vision. He was already growing a beard. To have any chance of succeeding he needed to set himself a strict schedule: up at five each morning to rehearse lines while taking a shower, then a brisk walk to the draughty old abandoned factory Almond was using for a rehearsal room.

Confident his leading man would know his lines in time for filming, Almond then made the shocking discovery that Connery knew nothing whatsoever about the play, never having seen it performed or even read it before that early-morning call. Weren't the Scots raised on the text like porridge, Almond thought. Still, there was a silver lining: 'I didn't know that Sean had never studied *Macbeth*, but that was terrific because that meant he had nothing to unlearn, he'd no preconception of the play or the role at all. So Sean came to it totally fresh and went right into it, but of course he had to study like hell because he had to memorise it all.'

Almond stuck as close as he could to the original text and incorporated impressive set designs redolent of German expressionist cinema of the 1920s. He didn't want realism. 'On television you want a more symbolic approach, so we had a huge throne, and a huge staircase and then these huge beams coming right across the studio.' And because the production was intended to be shown in schools, as well as on national television, Almond ratcheted up the violence quota. 'I thought, those poor kids have all this awful Shakespearean stuff so let's have a good bit of violence in it. I also decided to make the witches very, very beautiful, because I was just so sex-starved in those days. We got three gorgeous girls from the national ballet of Canada.'

Having learned his lines, Connery was then hit by a vicious form of flu that almost floored him but still managed to battle through the last couple of days' rehearsal. One night walking home exhausted, muttering his lines, Connery was dazzled by lights and pulled over by the police. 'I had been taken for a bearded and perhaps demented vagrant.' It took some persuasion to get them to believe he was in Toronto to film a TV play and it took a late-night call to Almond to get him out of the cells.

Come the day of recording, the play was shot 'as live', so Almond couldn't go back and correct any mistakes. 'Sean did muff a few lines here and there, paraphrased them, but nobody noticed because we don't have those uptight sort of critics in Canada.' The production was then converted onto tape and subsequently went out on air as it was recorded. 'I was really delighted with Sean's performance,' says Almond. 'Because he made it a very physical Macbeth. The production designer gave Sean this huge broadsword and he was whacking away with it with great power; there was none of this little deft rapier-like swords, no, no – these were massive broadswords that Sean wielded with ease and power in his big fight scene. It was a very physical production and a great achievement by Sean to come over and give a great performance, learn all the moves and the dialogue and the sword fight, all in less than two weeks. I loved working with him, just great memories. He was totally unassuming, no big ego thing, just an actor working and wanting to do his best. And he worked like hell the whole bloody time. A total professional.'

When Connery returned to London he entered into crisis talks with 20th Century Fox. He wanted out. Having just played Macbeth in a distinguished television production he wasn't interested any longer in being loaned out to play yet more dimwit beefcakes.

Before cutting him loose, Fox asked if he'd play a cameo in one of their films currently shooting in France. *The Longest Day* was an 'event' picture from the very top drawer, a mammoth reconstruction of the D-Day landings, and the Mount Rushmore of war movies, with a terrific cast that included John Wayne, Robert Mitchum, Henry Fonda and Richard Burton.

Connery is seen only briefly as a bumbling private, speaking in a dense Celtic brogue that no one south of Dublin had much hope of understanding. Part of a double act with Norman Rossington, they're actually a joy to watch as both crack jokes while dodging bullets on the Normandy beaches. 'We did ad lib a bit,' said Rossington. 'Sean always liked to put things in, adding bits and pieces to a script. The scene where he jumps off the landing craft into the sea, he ad libbed there, but I think they cut a lot out. Sean was a very good comedian, very funny on film when he was allowed to be.'

Connery likened his days as a contract player to 'a man walking through a swamp in a bad dream'. At least he was getting paid handsomely on a regular basis, sometimes for doing nothing. But then the guilt kicked in, that he was earning more in a week than his old dad had earned in a year. There was arrogance, too. Connery showed up for rehearsals once on *An Age of Kings* in a brand-new car. 'What happened to the old one, Sean?' director Michael Hayes asked. 'That seemed OK to me.' Connery smiled, 'The ashtrays were full.'

Free at last of Fox, Connery breathed a huge sigh of relief, but according to director Guy Hamilton it had been a missed opportunity for both parties. 'Sean was a born star. He was a star before Fox even knew what they had on their hands. It was his loss and their loss that they didn't recognise what they had.'

With his destiny back in his own hands Connery immediately began tackling the kind of roles he felt his talent warranted. In the West End he appeared in Jean Giraudoux's *Judith*, a biblical play adapted from the French by Christopher Fry. As the Roman conqueror Holofernes, Connery was required in one scene to appear naked save for a loincloth. 'Never before, in my view, had the legitimate stage seen such remarkably graceful masculine physical beauty,' said his old mentor Robert Henderson. 'It was mildly sensational.' Negative reviews cut short the play's run but not before director Terence Young saw it. 'He was so good. He acted the play itself off the stage.' Young, of course, had directed Connery in the ill-fated *Action of the Tiger* in 1956.

He'd also been approached again by Rudolph Cartier to play opposite Claire Bloom in a prestigious adaptation of Tolstoy's romantic tragedy *Anna Karenina*, about a woman trapped in a loveless marriage who falls for a dashing army officer. Appearing polished and cultured, with just the right sort of aristocratic swagger as Count Vronsky, Connery matched his co-star with an intelligent portrayal of depth and subtlety, proof that he was now an accomplished actor and had eradicated the raw style which had marred some of his early performances.

Her television appearance in Cartier's bold production was Claire Bloom's first in four years after her success in Hollywood. When filming had begun in late June there was no question she was the star, but by the time it came to transmission, on the evening of 3 November 1961, it had been announced that morning in the press that Sean Connery had signed to play Ian Fleming's spy hero James Bond.

The question as to who should play the part of James Bond had been the male equivalent of the search for Scarlet O'Hara. Producers Albert R. Broccoli and Harry Saltzman scrutinised some 200 hopefuls in their quest to find an unknown whom audiences could accept unreservedly as Bond. Limited funds had scuppered earlier hopes to sign a star name like Cary Grant or David Niven.

Broccoli had become aware of Connery some months back in Hollywood when he watched a screening of *Darby O'Gill and the Little People*. It wasn't the ideal vehicle to show off Connery's potential as James Bond and an unsure Broccoli called up his wife Dana. 'Could you come down and look at this Disney leprechaun film. I don't know if this Sean Connery guy has any sex appeal.' Dana caught a cab and arrived at the screening room at the Goldwyn Studios. The lights dimmed and the movie began, and when Connery appeared 'I saw that face,' Dana was to recall. 'And the way he moved and talked and I said, "Cubby, he's fabulous." He was just perfect, he had such presence. I thought he was star material right there.'

At around the same time Harry Saltzman had also been pointed in the direction of Connery. Peter Hunt was carrying out editing duties for *On the Fiddle* when he was invited to dinner by its producer Ben Fisz at the Polish Club in central London. Halfway through their meal they were joined by Saltzman and his wife. By the time coffees arrived Hunt had secured the editor's job on *Dr. No*, the proposed first Bond movie, and discussions turned to how Saltzman was getting on with the tests to find a suitable actor to play the part. 'What about that Sean Connery,' Fisz suddenly said. 'Don't you think he might make a good James Bond?' A remarkable turnaround, since Fisz had battled so hard not to cast Connery in *On the Fiddle*.

Hunt agreed: 'We could send a reel up for Harry or Harry can see whatever he likes of the film.' Saltzman was keen on the idea. 'Yes, can you send me up some footage?' The next day Fisz and Hunt discussed which reels were the best ones featuring Connery and had them shipped over to the Bond office in Mayfair. 'Now, what influence that ever had on the actual choice of Sean I don't know,' Hunt said years later. 'But that's my part in the thing.'

According to *On the Fiddle*'s director Cyril Frankel, Saltzman called him up one day out of the blue to ask, 'You've just worked with Sean Connery. Do you think he could play James Bond?' Frankel thought about it for the briefest of moments before answering, 'Standing on his head and reading a newspaper.'

A meeting with the actor was hastily arranged at the producer's South Audley Street office, a meeting that has since passed into movie legend. Terence Young telephoned Connery the day before, urging him to wear a suit rather than his usual casual street gear. When he arrived for his interview Connery was wearing baggy, unpressed trousers, a nasty brown shirt, no tie, a lumber jacket and suede shoes. 'I never saw anyone come more deliberately to antagonise people,' said Young. Associate producer Stanley Sopel thought Connery the most appallingly dressed man he'd ever seen. 'He looked as though he'd just come in off the street to ask for the price of a cup of tea.'

Throughout the meeting Connery behaved with bloody-minded arrogance, repeatedly pounding on the desk, swearing and telling the producers in no uncertain terms how he intended to play Bond. It was all an audacious act; Connery had no intention of leaving the impression of a starving actor desperate for work. 'I think that's what impressed us,' Broccoli remembered. 'The fact that he had balls.'

Next, the thorny question of a screen test was broached. Connery shook his head. 'Sorry, but I'm not making tests. I'm well past that. Take it or leave it, but no test.' Broccoli and Saltzman rose to their feet to thank him for coming and said they'd be in touch. No sooner was he out of the room than they rushed to the window to watch him leave the building and cross the street. It was the way Connery moved that clinched it; for a big man he was light on his feet, 'like a big jungle cat', Saltzman observed. Broccoli said, 'He walked like he was Superman. The difference with this guy is the difference between a still photo and film. When he starts to move, he comes alive.' The producers had found their Bond. Barring falling under a double-decker bus, Connery was it from that moment. 'We'd never seen a surer guy,' said Saltzman. 'Or a more arrogant son of a bitch!' added Broccoli.

That both producers were not English but international (Broccoli was American, Saltzman Canadian) undoubtedly affected their final choice for Bond; neither wanted some cultivated actor with a theatrical background. Alert to the world market, they needed their Bond to be less Ian Fleming's Old Etonian and more of a brawling street fighter. Hence Broccoli's belief that Connery's virile, aggressive masculinity was crucial, arguing against the role being played by 'some mincing poof'. It was a view shared by Bond screenwriter Richard Maibaum. 'Sean was nothing like Fleming's concept of Bond. But the very fact that Sean was a rough, tough Scottish soccer player made him unlike the kind of English actors that Americans don't like. Sean was not the Cambridge/Whitehall type

– he was a down-to-earth guy. The fact that we attributed to him such a high-style epicure was part of the joke.'

Backers United Artists were less than convinced. Having refused to test, Connery was tricked into undergoing a few filmed auditions with prospective leading ladies. This footage was sent to the States and the studio response was blunt to say the least. 'See if you can do better' demanded one executive by telex. To their eternal credit, Broccoli and Saltzman stood by their man, intending to go ahead with Sean or not at all.

Having cast Connery, the producers were a little hesitant about telling Fleming that they'd found his dashing hero in the guise of a Scottish former milkman. On finally hearing the news Fleming wrote to a friend: 'Saltzman thinks he has found an absolute corker, a thirty-year-old Shakespearean actor, ex-navy boxing champion and even, he says, intelligent.' A meeting between Connery and Fleming was arranged at the author's cramped business office near Pall Mall. They talked and in the end Connery guessed Fleming regarded him as a compromise choice. 'Fleming had a veto,' the actor revealed years later. 'But I believe he is the one who approved me at the end of the day.'

Saltzman, however, knew Fleming was far from sold on the idea. 'I was looking for Commander James Bond, not an overgrown stuntman,' was one derisory comment from the author. Fleming feared that the working-class Connery didn't have the sophisticated persona to play Bond, but his mind was swayed by a female companion over lunch one day at the Savoy. At Fleming's table was Connery and the author's long-time friend Ivar Bryce, who'd brought along his teenage niece. After lunch she pronounced Connery as having 'IT' and that seemed good enough for Fleming.

When the producers finally presented the Bond offer to Connery he said it was 'like asking a boy who was crazy about cars if he'd like a Jaguar as a present'. This wasn't strictly true; he had severe reservations, knowing full well that if made properly *Dr. No* would be the first in a series and Connery was wary of long-term commitments, having been burned once before over at Fox. That experience had taught the actor a valuable lesson, what it felt like to be owned, and he was in no mood to let it happen again. 'Contracts choke you and I wanted to be free.'

For days Connery pondered the offer. In the end he talked it over with Diane. Should he accept or not? Connery often asked Diane's advice on matters of acting; he trusted her integrity and her honesty. She told him to sign. In today's climate of multimillion dollar deals it's striking to note that Connery's fee for *Dr. No* was a modest £6,000.

Colleagues found it all terribly amusing that Connery had landed the role of 007. 'It was a bit of a joke around town that I was chosen. The character is not really me at all.' What made Bond so appealing worldwide was that Connery was able to imbue the character with a classy and cool classlessness; apt for the age of the angry young man and the emergence of Finney, Caine, Harris and the rest. Connery's robust portrayal was the antithesis of Fleming's rather unappealing snob, whom audiences, especially in America, would have found unpalatable.

Showbiz bigwigs, too, were dumbstruck by the choice. One day Saltzman met his old producing partner at Woodfall, John Osborne, and told him of his plans to make a Bond film. 'And who do you think I've got as James Bond?'

Osborne scarcely knew the books but gamely played along. 'I don't know, Harry. James Mason?'

Saltzman stared back, dumbstruck. 'Hell, no.'

Osborne had another try. 'David Niven.'

'For Christ sake,' screamed Saltzman, before pausing for effect. 'Sean Connery!'

Osborne looked incredulous. 'Harry, he's a bloody Scotsman! He can hardly read.'

In many respects the casting of Connery as Bond symbolised what had happened over the last five years since the explosion of *Look Back in Anger*. If the Bond films had been made anytime in the fifties undoubtedly someone of the ilk of a David Niven would have played him. Now it was perfectly reasonable, indeed it made creative and commercial sense, to hire a working-class actor to play what was essentially an establishment figure, a servant of the state, a British hero.

The task of transforming the rugged Connery into cosmopolitan Bond largely fell at the feet of *Dr. No*'s director, the Eton-educated Terence Young. It was time to live up to the promise he'd made the young actor after the debacle of *Action of the Tiger*. He began by taking

Connery to his own tailor and shirt maker, in Savile Row, of course, and made him wear the new clothes everywhere to get the feel of them, 'because Sean's idea of a good evening out would be to go off in a lumber jacket'. Then it was off to fine restaurants and Mayfair gaming clubs to learn the basics of casino etiquette. Connery's hair and eyebrows were also trimmed. It was a total transformation, a feat of which Henry Higgins would have been proud. Connery was a man who preferred pints to champagne, egg and chips to foie gras. As for Aston Martins, a battered Jaguar was his choice of wheels.

Connery also had the wonderful advantage, one denied every subsequent actor in the role, of spending time with Ian Fleming himself. Together they discussed Bond the man and the world he operated in. Over time Fleming grew enormously fond of Connery and the feeling was reciprocated with genuine warmth. 'I liked Fleming, a terrific snob but very good company.' When *Dr. No* opened Fleming said this about the actor. 'He is not exactly what I envisaged. But he would be if I wrote the books over again.' When Fleming wrote his final Bond novel, *The Man with the Golden Gun*, published posthumously in 1965, Fleming paid perhaps his greatest accolade. 'At the end of the story Bond retires and Fleming gave him Scottish heritage. That's all a tribute to Sean,' said Bond screenwriter Tom Mankiewicz.

On 14 January 1962 the cast and crew of *Dr. No* arrived in Jamaica with little inkling that they were about to make cinema history. Composer Monty Norman had been hired by the producers to provide the score, and the all-important James Bond theme, and travelled to Jamaica in the hope of finding inspiration in the local music scene. The journey out there was memorable, to say the least, as he explains: 'Harry hired what must have been about the last turbo prop to cross the Atlantic with people in it. Everybody was on that flight; Cubby and his wife and Harry and his wife, the cameraman Ted Moore and his wife, Ken Adam and his wife, me and my wife, a lot of the actors, the stuntman Bob Simmons, and of course Sean Connery. And it became almost like a cocktail party, drinks were flowing and food, by the time we got to Jamaica I think we were all pissed. It was about a twenty-hour flight, it stopped in New York or somewhere. It was absolutely a historic flight.'

The Bond team shot up and down the island, in Kingston, Montego Bay, even the main airport. The classic scene where Ursula Andress as Honey Ryder steps out of the surf in a white bikini was filmed at Laughing Water, not far from Fleming's winter residence Golden Eye. Towards the end of location shooting Fleming paid the crew a visit, observing Bond and Honey hiding behind a ridge of sand while a machine-gun-toting motor launch sprays the place with bullets. He found it all rather amusing, writing about the experience to his friend Evelyn Waugh: 'The sand ridge was planted with French letters (condoms) full of explosive – by magic mechanism they blew up the sand in little puffs. All this endeavour was wasted because unluckily a detachment of the US navy entered the bay in speed launches and buggered it all up.'

After just a few weeks Young knew that everything was clicking into place, all the right ingredients were there: sex, action, style and also humour. Reading the script, Connery had found it seriously lacking a satirical edge and luckily Young agreed with him that the film would gain another dimension by injecting a bit of comedy, 'but at the same time to play it absolutely straight and realistically', said Connery.

Young also observed how Connery was tackling the role, like a man who knew this was his big chance. He was playing the character with just the right degree of menace and charm. Connery once revealed that the secret to playing Bond was to make the role dangerous. 'If there isn't a sense of threat, you can't be cool.' What Connery brought to the Bond role that no other actor of the day was capable of, with the possible exception of Richard Burton, was sheer animal sexuality and raw masculine power. As Peter Hunt described it, 'Sean really was a very sexy man. There are very few film stars who have that sort of quality, they virtually can walk into a room and fuck anybody.'

As suave and sophisticated as Connery could be as Bond, there was always a hint of the beast lurking beneath the tuxedo. Audiences believed that here was a man who would kill without hesitation. 'There is in Sean a sense of cruelty that suits the part admirably,' according to Terence Young. And there was the physicality that Connery brought to the role. A former bodybuilder, Connery looked formidable on

332

screen, the embodiment of Broccoli's edict that Bond be a ballsy, two-fisted spy. And the teachings of Yat Malmgeren were especially of help here – the graceful way he moved was part natural, part learned at those movement classes. 'One of the chief qualities, I think, that made Sean such a big star in those early Bonds, was his movement,' says Philip Saville. 'His hand movement, his agility, he was an altogether organic man. It's a very important quality if you're making action movies. Steve McQueen had it, he had that natural sense of forward movement and all his body coordinated. Connery had it, too, in spades.'

After *Dr. No* was in the can Connery knew he'd given it his all and that the picture had the makings of a hit. 'I just sat tight and waited.'

60
Running on Empty

After the runaway success of *Saturday Night and Sunday Morning* it was inevitable that Woodfall would film another of Sillitoe's stories, and they chose his novella *The Loneliness of the Long Distance Runner*, published in 1959. Its stark plot has as its central figure an unrepentant thief called Colin, an inmate in borstal and a natural athlete encouraged to take up running. When the liberal-minded governor hopes he will triumph in the first sports day arranged between the boy convicts and young gentry lads from a nearby public school, Colin shows utter contempt for authority by throwing the race.

One evening Osborne attended a performance of *The Seagull* at the Old Vic and afterwards called Richardson. 'I've seen your runner,' he said. Courtenay was asked to go to the Royal Court where Richardson was in rehearsal for *The Changeling*. He stood stock still on the stage while Richardson sort of peered at him for two minutes. 'You'll be absolutely marvellous in this part,' he finally said. 'And I couldn't believe my ears,' was Courtenay's reaction. 'And something told me he meant it and he would stick by it, and although it was over a year before the film was made I pretty well knew that I'd get it.'

Sillitoe couldn't have agreed more with Richardson's choice; if anything, Courtenay was nearer to his fictional representation of Colin than Finney was to Arthur Seaton. 'Tom was perfect. Albert was very good but physically Tom had that lean, hungry look.' Many critics were to point out that Courtenay's face seemed to fit perfectly the anti-hero roles of the moment. It had a wild and haunted look, with the permanent expression of a naughty schoolboy caught stealing apples.

Courtenay himself never felt comfortable pushed to the forefront of the new wave movement. 'I was absolutely not an angry young man, I didn't have that attitude at all.' He couldn't relate to the 'I hate everybody and everything' character of Colin in the way he had to Billy Liar. Nor did the political aspects of the film appeal. What drew him to the *Loneliness* project was the romantic element, a boy who had a gift.

Courtenay also believed it wasn't merely anger that fuelled his generation but something vastly more altruistic, and something that he himself had been a recipient of. 'The new wave in British film was to me simply the result of the 1944 Education Act whereby children of working-class parents got themselves educated and that's what produced books like *The Long Distance Runner*. And that group of actors came along because they suited the parts that the writers were writing.'

The 1944 (Butler) Education Act totally revolutionised the state education system in England and Wales, establishing as it did the right to secondary education for all. It also created state-aided scholarships to universities and drama schools, ensuring that education no longer remained the fortress of the privileged. In effect it transformed the social landscape of the nation, creating opportunity for the excluded working class and producing, in the words of Keith Waterhouse, 'An upstart generation who instead of becoming factory fodder had come up through the grammar schools and red-brick universities and was now ready to take the world on.'

Filming on *Loneliness* began in February. Courtenay was ready to face the cameras come Monday morning having finished his stint in *Billy Liar* on the previous Saturday night. His first day on his first film began at 5.30 a.m. when a Rolls-Royce picked him up at the flat he shared in Islington. Not quite star treatment, since the Roller in question was a little old and musty smelling, bought second hand by Woodfall. The car continued round London picking up various other actors including James Bolam and Julia Foster before finally arriving at the location. Everyone got out save for Courtenay, who remained inside, pensive, uneasy and nervous. There was a knock on the glass. 'Would you care to join us, sir?' It was the assistant director.

'What for?' asked Courtenay.

'For your first scene.'

Richardson again wanted to follow the example of *A Taste of Honey* and shoot entirely on location, believing actors responded better to working in real places. 'A lot of the discoveries that we made on *Honey*, the experience we had, filming on location and all that, held us in good stead when we made *Loneliness*,' says cameraman Walter Lassally. 'The films naturally followed on from each other.'

The hope was to film in an actual borstal but, sensing that the tone of the film might promote unrest among the inmates, the authorities refused and a large sweeping manor house complex in Surrey had to suffice. But a lot of the extras were actual borstal boys, on day release. 'And they were constantly hungry,' recalls Lassally. 'When we had lunch they kept watching us and if you left anything on your plate they used to say, can we have that? I don't think they fed them at all.'

Taking up some of the more prominent roles amongst the borstal inmates were a couple of Courtenay's RADA compatriots, John Thaw and Derek Fowlds. 'I'm going to cast a borstal repertory company,' Richardson had declared. 'And I was one of them,' says Fowlds. 'We were all mates in borstal with Tom and Jimmy Bolam. I was on the picture for about two weeks. It was great fun.'

Filming six days a week, it was back-breaking stuff. Courtenay, still nervous and unsure, would often dash over after each take to ask the crew if he was OK. 'They had to humour me in the end.' But his easy-going manner and sincerity won him the affection of everyone. 'Tom was somebody who had no edge to him,' says Lassally. 'He was always very quietly spoken, very cooperative, very laid-back. Sometimes he could be quite tense, but he made a tremendous effort to get into the part. He became that person.'

The tough schedule meant that Courtenay didn't have time, indeed wasn't allowed, to visit Annie, whose illness had deepened and was now in hospital. They wrote to each other, as they always had since he'd left home, but the enforced separation, especially at so difficult a time for both of them, put a huge strain on Courtenay, some of which he channelled into his performance.

One day Finney arrived at the location to see Richardson. Still in awe of the actor, Courtenay kept his distance, even though by now he'd gained a lot of confidence and had settled into the film-making process. Richardson had a lot to do with that. Courtenay recalls no shot lasting more than two takes and a degree of creative freedom. 'Tony gave me the impression that he was letting me do whatever I wanted, even sometimes asking me to *say* whatever I wanted. All very cinema verité, and not so technically demanding as filming usually would have been before the new wave.' Richardson made Courtenay feel special, the man of the moment, and the young actor lapped it up. 'Though some nights I would hold one of mother's sad little letters from hospital close to my chest and cry myself to sleep.'

When shooting finished Courtenay raced back up to Hull on a visit, but the change in his mother was heart-rending. It was Annie all right, he recognised her, of course he did, but she'd become a mere shadow of her once glorious self. Courtenay broke down. As he left the hospital a young nurse asked him to sign an autograph. His dad took him to the station to see him off, breaking the news that the prognosis for his mother was about as bad as it could be, and there was no chance of recovery. The tears welled up in him again and they held each other close. Courtenay said to his dad that if there really was no hope, Mum was better off out of hospital and back home. He then got on the train and waved as it pulled away, back off to London. He sat in first class, 'Not so much because I could now afford to, but because I reckoned that way fewer people would see my tears.'

61
Harris vs Anderson: Round One

Lindsay Anderson had been told by Osborne and Richardson over at Woodfall that should he ever come up with an idea for a feature he ought to bring it to them first. Reading the *Sunday Times* one morning, Anderson saw an article about a new young writer, a coal-miner's son from Wakefield in Yorkshire called David Storey, whose debut novel about the cut-and-thrust world of rugby league had won wide praise. It was called *This Sporting Life*.

When confronted with the book, Richardson voiced reservations that it was ideal material for Lindsay and refused any support, secretly planning to make the thing himself. In the end both were outbid by producers Julian Wintle and Leslie Parkyn, who ran Beaconsfield Studio and had a distribution deal with Rank. Their first choice for director was Karel Reisz, who said no on the grounds of it being too close in tone (i.e. grim and northern) to *Saturday Night*. But there was an ulterior motive. Reisz saw *Sporting Life* as a perfect opportunity to introduce his friend Anderson into feature film-making. 'Because of Lindsay's very articulate and rather vicious attacks in the press in his reviewing of the British film industry he was rather persona non grata back then,' recalls David Storey. 'And it's doubtful he would ever have got a film to be made. And Karel made it a condition that he would produce *Sporting Life* only if Lindsay directed and also had a free hand in casting. And J. Arthur Rank, who didn't really know what to do with the movie, agreed.'

Storey first met Anderson in a pub next door to the Cambridge Theatre, where *Billy Liar* was playing. Things didn't get off to the best of starts when Storey argued that Osborne wasn't a passionate writer, more a hysterical one, but the atmosphere settled down enough for

Anderson to ask Storey if he wanted to adapt his novel to the screen. It was a major gamble since the Yorkshireman had never written a screenplay in his life. It worked with Sillitoe, though, so why not?

Discussions quickly moved to casting. 'Albert Finney at one time thought of doing it,' says Storey. 'He was our first choice actually, and we talked with him about it on several occasions. It was quite clear he would do it very well, but Lindsay's involvement with Finney became very similar to the one that developed eventually with Richard Harris. Lindsay directed Albert in *Billy Liar* and I think he became possessive with Albert in the same way that he became possessive with Richard. But Albert wouldn't have it and just walked away from it in the end. Richard, being of a wilder temperament than Albert, never felt threatened by that kind of possessiveness, but rather enhanced by it.'

Next on the list was Sean Connery, whose virile physique suited the part perfectly, and Storey and Anderson visited him one night to discuss it. 'We both found Sean a very engaging and charming character,' recalls Storey. 'But we didn't think he was sufficiently robust mentally to play the book's rugby hero Frank Machin, or the aggression wasn't really at the surface, as it were.' Connery, according to Storey, was very keen, though.

With names bandied about like so much confetti, Storey was invited by Reisz one night to see *The Guns of Navarone*. Bit of an odd choice, thought Storey; why did Karel want to see a popcorn war adventure? But there was an actor in it Reisz wanted the writer to take a look at. 'He only had a very few lines to speak, a very minor intrusion on the narrative, and Karel said, "What do you think?" And we both felt there was something there just from that brief glimpse in the film.' It was Harris, playing a brief cameo as an Australian pilot effing and blinding to his superior officer. The distaste for authority oozed off the screen. Anderson wholeheartedly agreed on their choice, having seen Harris already in *The Ginger Man*.

Since Storey had yet to finish the screenplay, a copy of the book was sent to Harris, who was then in Tahiti making *Mutiny on the Bounty*. His response was one of complete enthusiasm. But when Storey's first draft was ready and duly sent over, the film-makers heard nothing back from

Harris except silence, a silence that lasted for weeks. Anderson took decisive action and flew to Tahiti to see what was happening. Once there he discovered that their potential star hated the script. The problem had to do with Storey's approach. Reluctant to simply rewrite the novel, Storey had deviated somewhat from his own source material and ended up with a rather watered-down version of the original. Harris had loved the book so much that he wanted nothing to do with this version. 'Why don't we just make a film of the book,' he told Anderson, 'and not the script?' For Storey, this was a turning point. 'It was Richard's sudden enthusiasm, quite obsessed with the book and the material, that brought it to life for Lindsay in a way that I'd been unable to do. It was really the introduction of Richard's energy and passion that galvanised the film and I went off and wrote a new script in about three weeks and just went back to the original novel.'

Something else happened out there in Tahiti between Anderson and Harris, something that was to have a profound effect on the film and on the lives of the main protagonists. Under that balmy tropical heat, amidst the palm trees and golden beaches, Anderson felt himself falling madly in love with the Irishman. The Harris he discovered in Tahiti was 'all warmth and ardour – so attractive that I found I responded to him with a wholeheartedness that made me tremble'.

So began one of cinema's most bizarre working relationships, one which Storey observed at close quarters with the keen eye of the writer. 'It was a combination of Richard's Celtic bravado and wildness and emotional commitment and Lindsay's homosexuality which he never really came to terms with and struggled with throughout his life. And in *Sporting Life* it came to a climax in the sense that Richard became the epitome of everything Lindsay desired in a homosexual relationship; the very powerful physical and emotional presence that Richard generated was completely intoxicating to Lindsay and he really had to hang on by his fingernails at times.

Harris knew what was happening and exploited the situation mercilessly as filming got under way in March, even resorting to physical violence to demonstrate who was boss. 'Stop smiling,' Harris hissed at Anderson one day on the set. 'I'll smile if I wish to,' the director replied.

'You'll smile when I tell you,' Harris bellowed before punching Anderson hard on the arm; an action that grew into a habit.

There was jealousy, too, on Anderson's part directed towards Elizabeth, whom he referred to as a fluffy blonde doll. 'He was polite to me,' Elizabeth says. 'But I was sort of in the way. I recognised he was very much in love with Richard. You'd have to be blind not to see that. So he had to tolerate me. And he was quite patronising, but I was very fond of Lindsay, I respected him enormously. Also you could see how much he cared, you could see how much he was being hurt, and he was powerless to do much about it. Richard was quite unkind, he gave him hell, knowing he could, that's the thing, that's where Lindsay made a big mistake. Richard made, I should think, his life bloody awful.'

The tension, combined with Anderson's inexperience as a film director, coloured the first few weeks of shooting. When the rushes didn't meet the required standards set by co-producers Wintle and Parkyn both expressed a desire to fire Anderson and replace him with Reisz, who, loyal to his friend, refused.

Anderson had found out perhaps too late that the Harris personality was too big for him to cope with. But he couldn't resist and was drawn ever inwards. 'This mixture of power and sensitivity, of virility and immaturity, of insinuating charm and aggressive domination – how can I be expected to resist?' Anderson confided to his diary. 'Whether he is embracing me physically, like some big warm dog, or ordering me to "heel" – I am at his service completely.'

Storey recalls a defining moment during the shoot, it was about three weeks in. Anderson walked over to where he was standing on the set and said, 'I think my relationship with Richard is evolving into the relationship between Frank Machin and Mrs Hammond and I don't need to tell you who's Mrs Hammond.'

In the story Mrs Hammond is Machin's feisty landlady, with whom he falls obsessionally in love only for that love to go unrequited, thrown back in his face, almost. And there was no question, Mrs Hammond was a terrific part for an actress to play, but first choice Mary Ure had already turned it down. When fiery Welsh actress Rachel Roberts came to audition she arrived with her lover Rex Harrison, who disapproved of the whole affair, especially the character Anderson and Reisz, whom he christened 'the little twits', were asking her to play. 'I don't believe dressing up in dirty clothes and pretending to be working class is something that show-business stars should do,' he said, and bloody well meant it, too. Rachel ignored him and accepted the role; it was a performance that would earn her an Oscar nomination.

Rachel couldn't help but notice the arguments that were going on between Anderson and Harris, relegating her to the sidelines. Sometimes she'd laugh it off as 'the boys doing their stuff'. Once though, after a particularly melodramatic row she yelled, 'When you boys have finished, I'll be in my dressing room.' That would be quite a considerable time and when things had finally settled down Rachel was nowhere to be seen. She arrived the next day at the studio and told Reisz, 'I went to the lavatory, pulled down my knickers, had a good shit and waited around until my arse got cold. Then I told myself, no one's going to treat the future Mrs Rex Harrison like this, and went home.'

Both Rachel and Harris were utterly committed to the project. 'Richard and Lindsay and Rachel used to stay out near the studio because they didn't want to break the atmosphere and what was going on,' says Elizabeth. 'It was so concentrated.' Harris above all put every fibre of his being into it, one of the reasons he was cast in the first place, according to Storey. 'We chose Richard because of his emotional volatility, he was very accessible emotionally and had none of those traits of a conventional actor, or even a conventional leading actor. And his enthusiasm was total, he was completely committed, verging on the edge of insanity in some respects, and that became infused in the film itself. Richard then was at his best in the sense that he was very desperate to attach himself to some new experience and saw with Lindsay that was definitely on the cards.'

To get into shape for *Sporting Life* Harris trained hard, afraid he wouldn't measure up on the pitch to the professional rugby players hired as extras. Shot on location in Wakefield, on the first day the local rugby league team congregated on the pitch while Harris was in his caravan. 'He was spending ages on his make-up,' recalls Storey, 'with his false nose, his dark eye lenses to make him look more mysterious, and his mascara. And then when he came out and saw all the players standing at the other end of the pitch going, oh Jesus, look at this flower coming out, he just took one look at them and ran down the whole pitch towards them. And as he ran he got faster and faster until they suddenly realised with horror that he was going to run right into them, which he eventually did. It was that initial gesture of total physical commitment, almost indifference and carelessness that caught the players' admiration and they really took to him in a major way.'

Some of the game play was filmed at live matches. Because they couldn't afford a host of extras they would turn up at half time and ask over the tannoy whether everyone in the crowd would mind staying on the terraces while they did a bit of filming. 'I know Richard was really nervous when he had to kick goal once,' says Elizabeth. 'He was dying. He'd been practising for ages but he was so nervous about it. He knew the crowd was going, oh yeah, he's just an actor trying to play rugby, and they were ready to laugh. It was a hell of a moment, but he pulled it off, he got that ball over.'

The rugby scenes are bone crushing in their intensity; hyper-realistic. In the scene where Harris is roughed up behind the scrum, rugby league legend Derek Turner was doing the punching. Before one take Anderson took Turner to one side and asked him to make the contact look real. So he did. He punched Harris square in the face and knocked him out. Shooting for the day had to be stopped while Harris recovered.

So Anderson could dish it out, too. 'It was a masochistic relationship in many respects that exploded and went over the edge several times,' admits Storey. 'They came to blows and Lindsay rather liked it. And it was great credit to Lindsay's inner sturdiness or intellectual sobriety that he managed to hold on to what he thought it might achieve for the film, but it very nearly broke him.'

Many times Anderson simply lost control of the situation and had no choice but to call in the cavalry, in the shape of Elizabeth. 'I remember I had to go into hospital and Lindsay then rang me up and said, "Can you discharge yourself? Richard is just going wild, I can't do anything with him. Can you come back?" And I discharged myself from hospital. Richard would go down to the pub, he'd have his friends around and they'd be joking and laughing and Lindsay would be the butt of the jokes and the laughter. By the end Lindsay felt he'd lost control of Richard.'

62

'Pontefract with Scorpions'

Sam Spiegel was spitting blood, increasingly fed up with David Lean's lethargic pace shooting *Lawrence*. He'd been over a year out in the desert and Spiegel feared he'd never get him out of it, let alone see a finished film. He'd become despotic, paranoid, a perfection fetishist. Filming a landscape of windswept sand dunes, if he spotted a footprint he'd get someone to brush it out; his Arabia had to be virginal. For scenes involving O'Toole and Sharif riding camels as mere specks on the horizon, you'd have thought stand-ins would be used, but that wasn't good enough for Lean. He got the bloody actors out there and insisted they do it themselves, even if from the audience's point of view it could have been a chimp wearing a top hat.

Amidst loud protestations Spiegel took the extreme step of closing down the movie and forced Lean to move his unit to the more manageable Spain, which O'Toole dubbed 'Pontefract with scorpions', and told him to finish the damn thing with all haste. After a few weeks there Spiegel paid the production a visit on his yacht and summoned O'Toole to his cabin, where he gave the actor a severe dressing down. Whether this was meant to spur him on in the final stages of filming O'Toole never discovered. 'I left the yacht feeling dreadful,' he later recalled. 'Just as ever, destruction was Sam's game. I couldn't bear that man.' Pissed off, he looked for a bar to drown his sorrows in and found one already propped up by the film's art director John Box, who'd got the same rough treatment from Spiegel. After consuming several bottles the pair decided to have their revenge and climbed up the anchor chain onto the tycoon's yacht, crept into his private quarters and stole all his prize cigars.

Some of the film's key moments were shot in Spain, including Lawrence's capture and torture at the hands of the Turks and his death in a motorbike accident. To achieve this famous opening sequence O'Toole sat on a bike that was strapped to a trailer and pulled along behind the camera car. During filming the bar connecting the trailer to the camera truck snapped and the only thing preventing O'Toole hurtling out of control into the road was a flimsy piece of rope. The car abruptly stopped and the crew breathed a heavy sigh of relief to see O'Toole still in one piece. 'I think it was only Lawrence up there, teasing,' he said.

In Spain the riotous friendship between O'Toole and Omar Sharif continued, though could have ended up stranded on the rocks when O'Toole supplied Sharif with a woman for the night who had recently undergone a sex change operation; a discovery the Egyptian actor only made after he'd been to bed with her. And there was a new best pal in Jack Hawkins, arriving in Madrid to play General Allenby. A heavy drinker himself, Hawkins became enormously fond of O'Toole and together they indulged in many a boozing session.

For everyone the *Lawrence* adventure was almost coming to an end. After Spain they'd moved on to Morocco, staying for three and a half months, and then it was home. For most it had been the experience of a lifetime, seared on their memory; that desert would never leave them. O'Toole guessed that Lean would have been happy to stay in that sand paradise ad infinitum, cranking his camera over and over, never stopping. While shooting the final scene O'Toole sat in an army jeep with old RADA classmate Bryan Pringle driving, his feet in a bucket of ice because it was so hot. 'And David just shot it and shot it and shot it. He was amazingly reluctant to let go.' It had become a way of life.

O'Toole felt very differently; he didn't much care if he ever saw another blasted sand dune in his life. En route back to England he stopped off in Casablanca, arriving at their version of the Dorchester. Waltzing through the big swing doors into a large packed lobby he screamed at the top of his voice: 'The fucking picture's finished!'

It was over, at last it was over, but it hadn't gone away. 'LAWRENCE!' O'Toole wailed when he got back to Blighty. 'I became obsessed by that man.' Two years, almost, making the film – that was two years thinking about nothing but T. E. Lawrence, in essence *being* him, and that's how it was day after day. It affected him personally, how could it not? 'And it killed my acting later. I was emotionally bankrupt after that picture. That filming for that length of time, and having all the responsibility for the performance but none of the control.'

Lean was back in London, too, settling down with his team to edit the mammoth movie in time for its Christmas opening, but still he couldn't let go of O'Toole. A call went out: he was needed for one more day. The famous appearance of Sharif, arriving astride a camel from out of a mirage as if by magic, had been one of the earliest things in the can, shot in an arid desert landscape. Lean now required a close-up of O'Toole haranguing Sharif: 'Sheriff Ali, so long as the Arabs fight tribe against tribe . . .' And so he was hauled into a studio, put in an army costume, covered in sweat and sand and stood against a blue screen. When the sequence was spliced into the existing footage O'Toole was amazed. 'I was twenty-seven in the first shot and then eight seconds later, there was another close-up of me when I was twenty-nine years old! Eight goddamn seconds! And two years of my life had gone from me! The difference was astounding. I'd lost the bloom of youth. We're in a strange situation, film actors. We can watch the decomposition of the flesh.'

63
Richardson's Romp

Isn't it about time, Osborne and Richardson thought, that we made a film with no social message whatsoever, no contemporary problems laid bare, just a good old-fashioned romp, a hoot. The result was *Tom Jones*, the perfect antidote to long-distance runners and Jimmy Porters, a film that was to capture perfectly the burgeoning sixties vibe, and a move away from the 'it's grim Up North' school of black-and-white naturalism.

It was going to cost, though. Woodfall had never attempted anything on this scale before. Several potential backers withdrew when they heard the budget would be north of half a million pounds; too much of a gamble, they thought. Did the public really want to see an adaptation of Henry Fielding's period romp about the adventures of an amiable rogue, even if it was Albert Finney playing him? Luckily, United Artists thought differently. The American company had begun to make inroads into the British film industry by green lighting the first James Bond movie and took a punt on the talented Woodfall team. Only later did they realise they might have made a terrible mistake.

A romp it certainly was, but Richardson would still not bend to film convention; he wanted to incorporate the freewheeling style he'd employed on previous films and see how they worked in a commercial picture. It was an approach that didn't find favour with some of his colleagues. 'The great Oswald Morris was the originally chosen cameraman,' says Walter Lassally. 'But he and Tony drifted further and further apart because Oswald kept saying to Tony, "Look, *Tom Jones* is a big colour production, you can't make it in the way you made *Taste of*

Honey and *Loneliness*." and Tony kept thinking, well, why not. So eventually Oswald resigned and I was brought in.'

So why did Richardson feel so compelled to give *Tom Jones* such a modern slant? Lassally again: 'A very important decision was taken very early on, that was that if the costumes and the art direction were impeccably eighteenth century, then the camera style could be very modern.' Put alongside other period Hollywood epic films of that era, *Tom Jones* looks completely different, and that's all due to the style, with Richardson bringing in techniques such as Godard-like jump cuts, hand-held cameras, characters talking to the audience and assorted other tricks.

And there isn't the glossy sheen usually associated with period films, either; it looks as authentic as if a documentary team had shot it all for real. Richardson didn't want too much glamour, he wanted an earthy realism. One day on set Richardson surveyed one of the actresses coming out of make-up and told her, 'Sheila, you look too pretty, you've got to have snot coming out of your nose.' And so the requisite gunge was administered.

Shot over a glorious summer in the counties of Dorset and Somerset, Richardson organised a party on the first day for the whole cast and crew, telling them of his intention to make the film a fun and sexy piece of entertainment: 'Now, let's all go and have a lovely ten weeks' holiday.' Diane Cilento, cast as a hearty wench, never forgot the experience. 'They always had a huge American car, boot filled with champagne, and everyone was drinking away and having a good time and we had great big barbecues. It was wonderful.'

Richardson's talent as a director lay in his relationship with his actors. He liked to work closely with them and always encouraged them to show him first what they wanted to do in a scene. The classic moment where Finney and Joyce Redman devour plates of food in an inn as a sort of prelude to sex was largely improvised by the actors, according to Lassally: 'That was an excellent example of the advantages of leaving enough elbow room for the actors to enhance a scene.'

That's certainly how Susannah York remembered it. 'There was a kind of spontaneity in the making of it which was very exciting. People coming up with ideas, trying them out and seeing what happens.

Certainly we the actors were all game to try anything. A lot of wonderful scenes came out often from what Tony saw in the actors and what the actors were doing in the moment. And the fact that the actors felt free to improvise or were encouraged to improvise. It wasn't all plain sailing, but I felt it was very much a picture made in the right spirit.'

Finney also thoroughly enjoyed making the film, although he didn't think the part was taxing enough, not like Arthur Seaton, which had made demands on his acting ability and his creative imagination. Tom Jones was more of a personality role and at that time in his career he was still anxious to prove he was a serious and proper actor as opposed to just a personality. 'But he tackled the movie with great enthusiasm and skill and good humour,' says Lassally. 'And it was fun, but it was very hard work, too. In those days movie making tended to be fun – not all the time, but that's an element which has almost completely disappeared, mainly because of pressure of time.'

Richardson had assembled a veritable cavalcade of great acting talent: from Edith Evans to David Tomlinson, Hugh Griffith to Joan Greenwood. Griffith was a colourful character to be sure, a born eccentric with a predilection for the hard stuff that often led to tortuous incidents, such as the time he fired a shotgun at Richardson's Thunderbird. Or when instead of climbing off a horse he slid and then fell off the animal, a take that survived into the final print. 'It was very funny,' recalls Lassally. 'When that happened Tony turned to an assistant and said, "Go and look to see if he's dead, darling." Of course he wasn't, not even hurt.'

Finney and Griffith, it's best to say, had a strained relationship. 'They came to blows at one point during a night shoot,' says Lassally. 'Hugh was chasing him with a whip and Albie said, if you touch me with that whip I'll lay one on you – and he did. They made up, though.'

With *Tom Jones* under his belt Finney spoke of a hankering to direct. After his stints in the West End he'd come to feel that the actor was at best a hired hand, and that all the creative power was with the director. So he sent off letters to the top rep theatres in the land offering his services. Only one bothered to reply: Glasgow's Citizens Theatre. He could direct Pinter's *The Birthday Party*, they said, provided he also appeared in the title role of Pirandello's *Henry IV*. Finney agreed. He was on twenty pounds a week.

For the next two and a half months he lived in a sparsely furnished flat near the Clyde, with a pair of bongo drums and some jazz records for company. It was symptomatic of his way of life at the time. Back in London he lived in a one-bedroom flat, 'where I can reach everything without getting out of bed'. He bragged about the fact that he could still get all his possessions into two suitcases. 'I may want to do a bunk.' He smoked at least five cigars a day, had kippers and champagne for breakfast and wore a battered leather jacket even to the most formal gatherings. He was his own man. But one few had been able to truly find the centre of. Friends would talk of Finney having two distinct personalities, one moment direct and friendly, the next complicated and guarded. It's one of the reasons he became an actor: 'When you are on stage you are in disguise.'

64
Tom and Julie

It always seemed likely that *Billy Liar* would be turned into a film. Even at rehearsals for the original stage production Finney and Anderson would say things such as, 'Oh, we'll do that in the film.' And it always seemed likely that Woodfall would make it; indeed, Oscar Lewenstein was already working closely with Tony Richardson to that effect, lining up Finney to reprise his role with Anderson in the director's chair. But Waterhouse and Hall had not forgotten their creative disagreements with Anderson, and while Lewenstein, Richardson and Osborne were in Acapulco for a film festival the authors sold the film rights to Joseph Janni.

Janni still wanted Finney as his star but not Anderson, preferring to stick with John Schlesinger. Loyally standing by his director, Finney refused to make the film without him and walked. After an insane idea to bring in Anthony Newley, Janni saw sense and cast the only other obvious candidate, Courtenay.

After the success of *A Kind of Loving* Schlesinger and Janni were able to entice a much healthier budget from Nat Cohen for *Billy Liar*. They needed it. While on stage Billy had merely acted out his fantasy world on the drab solitary set of his parents' living room, on screen Schlesinger wanted to actually show it. This was an approach that Courtenay resisted at first, wanting to keep his portrayal as faithful to the play as possible, but ultimately he realised it was what audiences wanted to see. His employers, funeral directors Shadrack & Duxbury, not seen in the play, were also brought to life for the movie, with Leonard Rossiter cast as Billy's mostly exasperated boss and a pre-Likely Lad Rodney Bewes as his workmate.

Curiously it was the part of the free-spirited Liz, who offers Billy his only real chance to escape to London, that posed the greatest casting problem. During his days directing documentaries for the BBC, Schlesinger made a film about the Central School of Drama in London and recalled how one of the students left a striking impression on him. Her name was Julie Christie. Besides a bit of TV and a couple of small roles in minor films, she hadn't really done very much, but Schlesinger tested her – only to then cast someone else, Topsy Jane. She'd appeared as Courtenay's girlfriend in *Loneliness* and the thinking was that audiences wanted to see them back together in another film. Within a few weeks of shooting Topsy fell ill and had to drop out, forcing Schlesinger to go back to the tests. There he saw Julie again and thought, 'My God, we're mad! Why didn't we cast Julie?' The film made her a star.

In many ways the film of *Billy Liar* follows the tone of the original novel more closely than the play. And like *A Kind of Loving*, Schlesinger departs from the by now rather clichéd tenets of kitchen-sink drama. He also tried to make the shoot fun. During one scene where Billy fires a gun into the air Schlesinger got the prop man to drop a dead duck on Courtenay's head from the studio rafters. Yes, the film is still based up in the grim north and has a rebellious and angry young man as its protagonist, but this time he's not trapped by his class, only by his own narrow reach, the choices he himself makes. The film's famous ending has Billy finally catching the train bound for London with Liz, only to get out at the last minute; it's heartbreaking. 'The longing and fear of going to London was what I brought to Billy,' said Courtenay.

Like a dutiful son, Courtenay still went back to Hull most weekends, travelling by train first class, 'because of the peace and quiet', he said, then complained to a reporter, 'But no matter how posh the clothes I'm wearing, they keep on coming to check I've got the right ticket, You realise this is first class, sir?' It used to upset him, drive him mad, then it just made him laugh.

One weekend he walked into the kitchen to see his dad, his face a mask of pain and hopelessness. 'Your mother's bad,' was all he said. Her bed had been moved into the sitting room where she'd been propped up, her head slightly lolling to one side. 'It's Tommy, Ma. I've come to see you.' There was no response, just a haunting silence. Unable to make the previous weekend, Courtenay's heart took a direct hit when his dad talked about how lively she'd been then, behaving like a child. 'What a shame you couldn't come last weekend.'

There were moments during his stay when his mother came out from behind that wall of silence but never once did she acknowledge or seem aware of her son's presence. She spoke to her husband, sensed his presence alone. Courtenay could only watch, racked with guilt that he'd perhaps missed his last chance, but ever hopeful those eyes might recognise him and they could talk one last time. Both men were in the room together when they heard Annie breathe her last. A week later *The Loneliness of the Long Distance Runner* opened. 'But she knew I was on my way,' said Courtenay. 'And Father had a theory that's why she lived as long as she did.'

As with *Saturday Night and Sunday Morning*, *Loneliness* fell foul of the censor. 'This story is blatant and very trying communist propaganda,' wrote one BBFC adviser. And they weren't very happy with the use of bad language such as 'bugger', 'sod' and 'Christ'. The censor complained that 'bleeding' and 'bastard' were used eleven times and that one of the borstal boys had the sheer effrontery at one point in the film to stick his two fingers up. But times they were a-changing, and the producers were able to get away with much more than they had on *Saturday Night*.

Opening in September 1962, *Loneliness* was greeted less enthusiastically by the press than its predecessors. Noting the influence of the French new wave, especially François Truffaut, they complained that the stylistic devices were too derivative. But today it's rightly seen as one of the most important films of the period. In the mid-sixties Walter Lassally belonged to a British Film Institute programme that presented movies in prisons. They were invited to Brixton, 'And when we arrived we were invited to the governor's office, with the cans of film under our arms, and he said, "Which picture are you showing?" And I said, *"Loneliness of the Long Distance Runner."* And he went, "Oh my God!" Of course it went down a bomb.'

Courtenay's performance, however, was rightly hailed for what it was, a simply stunning debut. Lauded as Britain's latest star, Courtenay began to feel that success had struck him a little too fast for comfort. He feared he lacked the self-confidence to cope with it. It disturbed and excited him in equal measure. Nor did he think he'd acquired the proper experience yet; he was a star but did not yet consider himself an actor. 'I was an odd mixture of arrogance and insecurity. I was very thin skinned, really, so it wasn't that good for me, being discovered.'

65
The Walking Aphrodisiac

'I think the kitchen sink has had it. Now we're going in for nouveau riche pictures like *Dr. No* with Ursula Andress stripping off.' In his own inimitable way Terence Stamp had put his finger on the pulse. When the first James Bond movie opened in London at the beginning of October 1962 it changed not only the entire landscape of British film, but movie making around the world.

Before its premiere Connery was greeted with snide comments from the press. In interviews journalists asked him questions like, 'Would you call yourself an Old Etonian, Mr Connery?' And, 'How did your training driving a milk truck prepare you for this picture?' One doesn't have to look too far into just when Connery's career-long mistrust and plain hatred of the media began. His performance, too, drew a mixed bag of notices. The snobbish critic of the *Spectator* ridiculed him as being nothing more than a superannuated Rank starlet. Though the *News of the World* felt he fitted Fleming's hero 'like a Savile Row suit'. Ultimately it was the public who decided and they liked what they saw enough to turn *Dr. No* into a global smash hit.

Terence Young put the first Bond picture's success down to opening at exactly the right time when a particular mood was beginning to envelop Britain. Just a day before its London premiere the Beatles released their debut single, 'Love Me Do'. Things were starting to swing, the sixties were about to get into top gear. 'I think people were getting tired of the realistic school,' said Young. 'The kitchen sinks and all those abortions.'

Zena Marshall, who'd played a deadly spy in *Dr. No*, accompanied Connery to the first night and watched as Hollywood starlet Anita Ekberg sat close by them in the dress circle but never, it seemed, watched any of the movie: she couldn't keep her eyes off Connery. 'Whatever effect he'd had on women up till then was doubled,' said Zena. 'James Bond made him a walking aphrodisiac.'

Sensing his professional career was now on the runway and cleared for take-off, Connery set about sorting out private matters. First off he'd decided to marry Diane, she was the one, he was sure of it now, 'the girl who has the most inner sex appeal for me'. With Bond doing wild business in London they decided to get hitched overseas to avoid the inevitable media circus. It was a top-secret affair planned with all the cunning and deception of an MI6 operation. Friends and relatives were told the date, 29 November, and the location, Gibraltar, and sworn to secrecy. After the ceremony the happy couple toasted each other as the sun faded behind the old harbour in the distance, the warm breath of Africa, across the straits, caressing their faces. All very romantic, except they'd overstayed their welcome; both were trapped deep inside a military base and the gates had clanged shut. With only a few gibbering Barbary apes for company, it wasn't until past midnight that a kindly sentry relented and let them out.

Back in London, they moved into a new home, a four-storey former convent just off Acton High Street. Thousands were spent converting it into a family residence. The chapel became a 37-foot long drawing room with piped-in hi-fi and there were five bedrooms, including one for Diane's young daughter Giovanna. There was plenty of space for a nursery, which was just as well since Diane was close to giving birth to their first child, Jason. It was the perfect sanctuary for the busy couple, somewhere to relax away from the pressure of a workload that seemed to be piling up. Diane had been commissioned by George Devine to translate a Pirandello play for the Royal Court, while Connery was gearing up for another outing as 007.

Even by West End standards the premiere of *Dr. No* had been something of an occasion, with high society turning out in droves – Paul Getty was there; Ian Fleming, of course – but it was eclipsed two months later when *Lawrence of Arabia* took over the Odeon, Leicester Square.

Guests of honour were the Queen and Prince Philip. Noël Coward was there and afterwards hunted down O'Toole at a party held at the Grosvenor House Hotel in Park Lane. 'You were very good, Peter; congratulations.' O'Toole smiled back, it had been an evening of congratulations. 'Yes, very fine indeed,' Coward continued. 'And far, far more attractive than Lawrence could ever have been. If Lawrence had looked like you, Peter, there would have been many more than twelve Turks queuing up for the buggering session.'

The British critics raved. Alexander Walker in the *Evening Standard* hit the nail on the head when he called *Lawrence of Arabia* 'an epic with intellect behind it'. Just as James Bond propelled Connery into stardom, the role of Lawrence did likewise for O'Toole; both their faces were now amongst the most recognised in the world. 'I woke up one morning to find I was famous,' said O'Toole. 'I bought a white Rolls-Royce and drove down Sunset Boulevard wearing dark specs and a white suit, waving like the Queen Mum. Nobody took any fucking notice, but I thoroughly enjoyed it.' O'Toole had a whale of a time in Hollywood promoting the film, his antics leading one columnist to commiserate with readers: 'Too bad O'Toole won't be spending a lot of time in Hollywood – his personality is reminiscent of Errol Flynn.'

After LA it was off to New York, where his behaviour was even worse. Predictably he hit the bars fast, where he was subjected to his first encounter with American Martinis. 'I'm a whiskey drinker, like every good Irishman, and I thought I was drinking lemonade. It was a memorable experience.' Most of his nights out were spent in the company of actor Jason Robards, so much so that he was barred from the house by Mrs Robards – none other than Lauren Bacall! As Sam Spiegel observed, 'You make a star, you make a monster.' Lean concurred, writing to a friend: 'I think it has all gone to Peter's head and already people are getting a bit fed up with him not showing up for appointments. Sam and I did one TV show with him in New York and he was a real dope.' It's that fame thing; it either gives you a nose bleed or it doesn't. 'Stardom is insidious,' said O'Toole, in reflective mode. 'It creeps through your toes. You don't realise what's happening until it reaches your nut. And that's when it becomes dangerous.'

While in America O'Toole befriended the controversial stand-up Lenny Bruce. One night O'Toole took Omar Sharif to see the comic perform and afterwards the boys hit the town. In the early hours of the morning they staggered back to Bruce's home where the comedian shot up in front of his two guests. The next thing they knew the living room was full of cops and they were being bundled into vans and taken to the local precinct house. The drug squad had had the place under surveillance for some time.

A sober Sharif decided to use his one phone call to contact Spiegel for help. It was three in the morning and the producer was fast asleep in his suite at the Beverly Hills Hotel.

'Sam, it's Omar.'

'Omar who?' The producer was still half unconscious.

Sharif identified himself and dropped the bombshell that he and O'Toole had been arrested for drug possession and were in the cells. 'You're nuts,' yelled Spiegel. 'You kids are going to ruin me.' The producer sent his lawyers to bail the pair out but O'Toole was so taken with new friend Lenny that he refused to leave without him. 'Sam was going out of his mind,' Sharif recalled. 'And finally we got Lenny Bruce released with us.'

A worldwide box-office smash, *Lawrence of Arabia* would eventually win seven Oscars, including Best Picture. O'Toole was nominated but at the time of the ceremony was treading the boards in London. Spiegel attempted to buy every ticket for that night's performance so O'Toole could fly to Hollywood, but the theatre management said it would be impossible to reach all the patrons for refunds. O'Toole lost out to Gregory Peck, anyway, for *To Kill A Mockingbird*.

Lawrence of Arabia has never truly left O'Toole's life, in the same way that Bond has stayed with Connery. The identification is too strong, their performances too perfect. Years later O'Toole would say the most important influence on his life was David Lean. 'I graduated in Lean, took my BA in Lean.' When O'Toole had a son, much later in his life, a father at fifty, he named him Lorcan, Gaelic for Lawrence.

66
Fame for Stamp

The fag end of 1962 saw the birth of yet another star – three in a row, quite some going. After being delayed for months, *Billy Budd* finally opened in December and Terence Stamp received the sort of adulation few actors have basked in before or since. The *New York Times* described him as 'a new English actor with a sinewy, boyish frame and the face of a Botticelli angel'. Renowned film journalist Donald Zec said he was a cross between 'a Greek god and a rock 'n' roll idol'.

They said he was quite a good actor, too, but it was his looks that most critics focused on. Stamp had always been very self-conscious about his looks, but in recent years took to glancing at the mirror with a little less trepidation. 'Terry was pretty bright, so I shouldn't think he was unaware of the fact that he was a fairly attractive fella,' says his friend Lord Birkett. 'But he never showed it or ponced about with it. He was very charming, very quiet and gentle. A very gentle soul, Terry was.'

With recognition came certain advantages, a degree of wealth that brought with it more independence. And women, quite a few of them. Stamp hadn't done too badly in that department before, 'But now the succession of individual dolly birds turned into a flock and I was the flight controller,' according to Caine.

The pair had since moved to bigger premises, large enough for them to have a bedroom each. No more sleeping on a mattress in the living room. They also hit the town together, going to the new nightclubs that were starting to spring up in places like Wardour Street, where Christine Keeler and Mandy Rice-Davies numbered amongst the dancers. Things were changing, a new era was flowering, populated, according to Stamp, by a new kind of Englishman. 'People like me, we're the moderns. We work hard and we play hard. We have no class and no prejudice. We're the new swinging Englishmen.'

Caine was naturally delighted with Stamp's success, but there was a feeling of watching it all from the wings. What must have been going through his mind, seeing all of his contemporaries, the rogues he'd drunk pints with down the Buckstone and the Salisbury, exploding around him: Connery was Bond, O'Toole was Lawrence, Harris had been to Hollywood and worked with Brando, Finney was a stage and screen star, Courtenay, a spring chicken by comparison, was being raved about. Bates, too, had got his movie breakthrough. And now his own flatmate, to whom he had bestowed all his worldly wisdom, was the new hot thing. Everybody, it seemed, within Caine's orbit was hitting the big time except him.

Never once, though, did it damage Caine's friendship with Stamp. 'They really were big friends,' says Lord Birkett. 'There used to be a huge ramp in the middle of Hyde Park and they used to race up in their cars and leap off the top and hurtle down the other side.'

There was, however, a degree of guilt on Stamp's side; understand-ably so. 'I mean, he took me under his wing and guided me. When it all happened to me, I was a little embarrassed because he was my guru and I thought he would make it. I couldn't see how anybody could fail to see his talent.' Everyone was still wearing shades, obviously. And so Stamp decided to try and push things along. James Woolf, one of the top film producers in the country, the man who masterminded Laurence Harvey's rise to fame, had taken a keen interest in Stamp. They'd become inseparable. As Woolf began to map out a career path for him, Stamp tried to interest him in doing the same for Caine. But Woolf couldn't help. Yes he liked Michael a lot, thought he was a capable actor. 'But he hasn't got what it takes.'

And time was running out. Caine had always told Stamp that if you hadn't made it in the business by the time you were thirty you never would, and now that milestone was only a few weeks away. He wasn't looking forward to it.

67

Council Property

It was Harold Pinter's own idea to turn his hit play *The Caretaker* into a feature film, bringing in Clive Donner as director. The budget was a measly £40,000, which Michael Birkett, acting as producer, had raised in America. Bates and Pleasence were to reprise their now famous roles, as would Shaw.

Forgoing a studio, the film-makers hired a house in Hackney from the local borough council. 'It was the most ghastly place,' Lord Birkett remembers. 'The wires were coming out of the walls, there was damp everywhere, it was just awful, and the council said, that'll be fifteen pounds a week, some modest sum like that. I phoned the council and said, "Are you sure about this fifteen pounds a week? Wouldn't like to reduce it to twelve pounds, would you, because it's in pretty dreadful condition, and it's a very low-budget film." And Hackney borough council said to me, memorably, "Well, it's a bloody sight cheaper than Pinewood." So I thought, OK, you win. So I paid up the fifteen quid.'

Filming was due to start by the close of the year; with just a week to go the American backers started making demands on Lord Birkett. 'They said, we want a script supervisor and I said, not with Harold Pinter, you don't.' And so they pulled out, leaving the film on the brink of collapse. 'We'll have to find the money privately,' Birkett announced the next day to the stunned cast. 'Let's go simply to friends who might back it. And I'm sorry but we can't take money from friends and pay ourselves with it, so you don't get paid.'

Bates, Pleasence and Shaw all agreed to forgo their fee, as did Donner, Pinter and Birkett. The plan was that they'd all get 50 per cent of the profits, while the backers got the other 50 per cent; provided the movie made money, of course. 'So I went out and got new backers,' says Birkett. 'And they were so distinguished and so famous that I put them on the screen before the cast, actually; you know, the producers would like to thank . . . We got Noël Coward, Peter Hall and Harry Saltzman.' Within days Birkett had scraped together £30,000; all he needed was another £10,000. 'So I went to Richard Burton, whom I knew admired *The Caretaker*, and he and I and Elizabeth Taylor had lunch at the Connaught Hotel.' It was a memorable encounter, to say the least.

'I think probably a bottle of Dom Pérignon, don't you,' said Birkett, opening the bowling.

'Absolutely,' returned Burton.

Birkett then went into his pitch, told them what they were doing and that the budget was £40,000.

'I'll give you the lot,' said Elizabeth without any prompting.

'No, Elizabeth,' replied Birkett. 'Can't do that. I've got thirty thousand already, all I need is ten.'

A little put out, Liz answered. 'Oh well, you can have that, anyway.'

'What makes you so keen?' asked Birkett.

'It's my production company, you see. It's called Elizabeth Taylor Productions, based in Rome, and it's for supporting young and enterprising films like this.'

'Oh, good,' Birkett interjected. 'We're young and enterprising.'

'The trouble is, you see, I've only got two entries on the books so far.'

'What films are those?' asked Birkett, genuinely interested.

Liz pulled a face. 'I'm afraid that's the problem – the only two items on my books are both fur coats.'

Birkett got his £10,000 and the film was back on. During his search the cast had been rehearsing in the house. It was a Friday when Birkett arrived at the property to tell them all the good news. 'We're OK, you can shoot on Monday, I've got the money.'

It was certainly an enterprising solution to raising funds. 'Done out of pure love of the piece,' said Bates. 'To record it and make sure people could see the cast that had done it.'

Bates saw the film as essentially a piece of theatre, a deliberate translation of the play to celluloid. 'But I don't want to call it filmed theatre.' He knew, as the others did, that the play needed opening out in some way. 'But we knew very well,' says Birkett, 'both Harold and Clive and I that what we mustn't do was to open it out in such a way that it lost the claustrophobia of being in this awful old house.'

A few exterior scenes were added, including a high-angle shot of Aston and the old tramp walking back together at the very beginning of the film. This was done on Hackney High Street, Pinter's old stomping ground. The company hired a cherry picker and up went Donner and camera operator Alex Thompson high above Hackney. 'How does the shot look to you?' Donner asked. 'I don't know, Clive,' replied Thompson. 'I've got my eyes shut, too.'

Birkett also thought the film required a brand-new opening sequence. In the play the old tramp mentions that he got fired from his job – 'they give me the bullet'. It was a famous speech. 'Well,' Birkett said to Pinter one day, 'we ought to see him getting the bullet.' So off went Pinter and wrote a twelve-page addition to the script. 'I read it and then I had the slightly agonising task of phoning Harold and saying to him, "I think it's a marvellous script, I'm fascinated with it, but actually I don't think we should use it." And to my immense relief, Harold said, "You're absolutely right, we shouldn't." And I thought, that's one hurdle got over.'

Midway through the production Noël Coward made a visit to the set, turning up outside the Hackney dump in a burgundy Bentley. Birkett's production office was down in the basement and boasted just three items of furniture, all of which came from the local junk shop: a chest of drawers, an old battered filing cabinet and a chair. There was no carpet, just a square of linoleum that didn't quite fit. In walked Coward, looked around and said, 'My word, how slap-up.'

Coward ended up staying for two days watching the filming, Birkett recalls. 'And we had such a small room, I mean, the sound department was in a cupboard on the landing because there wasn't room for them. So Harold gave up his seat so Noël could sit down and have a look.' He also came to rushes at a little viewing theatre in Soho. He seemed to be greatly enjoying himself and was genuinely sad to go, but go he had to. 'I'm sorry,' he said to Birkett at the end of the second day, 'but this is the last time I can come. I'm going to have to go home now to Switzerland. I hope it goes well and let me know how it all progresses.'

'I'll send you a postcard from time to time,' said Birkett. 'And tell you all about it.'

'Oh do. I'll love that.'

'Except I don't have your address in Switzerland,' said Birkett.

'Oh, don't worry about that. Just address it to "Noël Coward, Switzerland".'

Coward's involvement in *The Caretaker*, like that of Olivier in *The Entertainer*, was another case of the old guard embracing the new wave. Philip Saville tells a nice story of the time that he was rehearsing a play in a big hall off Tottenham Court Road, 'And next door was another space and there were these two men, in their sixties or something, and they came in and stood looking at us in the corner. After a while I asked my assistant to go over and find out what they were doing. And he came back, pulled me aside and said, "It's Sir John Gielgud and Sir Ralph Richardson." And I went thundering over to them, "Do come in, my God what an honour it is etcetera." And Richardson said, "We were just looking to see how it's all done by you new chaps." I'll never forget that.'

Of course these great actors weren't stupid, they could see what was happening and were clever enough to realise they couldn't stop it. 'Both Larry and Noël were highly intelligent and so of course they saw the light, they saw what was coming and what was in vogue at the time,' says Birkett. Let's also not forget that in their own time both Olivier and Coward were pathfinders, groundbreakers. Look no further than Coward's play *The Vortex*, which caused a huge furore when it opened in 1924, shocking sensitive West End audiences. It spoke in as vehement a tone to its contemporary generation as Osborne. Where *Look Back* and its ilk was labelled 'kitchen sink', an outraged Sir Gerald du Maurier called *The Vortex* 'dustbin drama'.

As filming continued, the performances began to take shape. Bates's unpredictable Mick seemed even more of a menacing portrayal on screen; 'The closer you are, the more sinister Mick is, because you see much more of his mind.' Bates had already mastered the different worlds of stage and screen acting, the smaller gestures, conveying feelings with just a look, a nuance. 'Alan never came on with the pyrotechnics,' says Birkett. 'He just played his part, very laid-back, but always terrifically impressive, you couldn't take your eyes off him.'

Bates was never a showy actor like O'Toole or Olivier. But then that's what made him such a good film actor; there was so much going on in his face without much visibly happening. His skill, on show in early films like *Whistle Down the Wind* and *The Caretaker*, lies in saying so much without revealing anything. 'And that was very much part of Alan's personality, too,' says his friend Keith Baxter. 'Not revealing things.'

For Donald Pleasence, having already played the tramp for such a long time on the stage, making the film was almost a luxury. He understood the character so well, he instinctively knew what the tramp would do in any situation. During filming he enjoyed walking about the streets of Hackney in character.

Robert Shaw's most famous scene in the film is the monologue in which Aston describes what awful treatment he was subjected to in hospital. Donner's idea was to do one long tracking shot into Shaw's face, followed by two more long takes, nine minutes in total. 'And we did three takes of that,' remembers Birkett. 'And on the third one Bob became quite emotional, and in the course of the scene he started to cry. And he was immensely proud of this, he thought it was just wonderful. Later at rushes I said to Clive, don't use that take, use take two, which was absolutely calm in its delivery. So we did and I don't think Bob ever quite forgave us.'

With just a five-week schedule the work was tough and disciplined, with the three actors getting stuck in and causing no problems whatsoever. The only thing that raised their concern was their individual billing. 'There are only three of you in the film, for heaven's sake,' said Birkett. To which they replied, 'Yeah, but who comes first?' Birkett took them all upstairs into a tiny attic that the crew used as a sort of green room; there was barely enough space for the three of them to fit in. Birkett then shut the door on them, turned the key and announced, 'You don't get out until you've decided the order in which you're going to appear on the screen, because I don't care, I don't mind a bit which of you comes first, it means nothing to me at all. But you three care, so you decide, and when you've decided I'll let you out.' Eventually they agreed Pleasence really ought to come first, since he was the star of the play, and that Shaw should come next because he was more famous than Bates. 'It was an arrangement everyone was perfectly happy with,' recalls Birkett.

Everyone was perfectly happy with the finished product, too, especially Pinter, who believed that an ideal balance had been struck. 'We were all patting ourselves on the back afterwards saying, we got that right,' says Birkett. 'It was a very disciplined film, we didn't muck about with it at all.' *The Caretaker* still stands amongst the finest examples of a stage play's transition to the screen. 'It almost looks like a stage play without perhaps being stagey,' says Birkett.

By this time Shaw and Mary Ure, who had produced a second child, had moved out of London and set up home in Amersham. It was a haven, a fun-filled place where all Shaw's children could spend time together. 'I used to go and see them,' says Lord Birkett. 'They lived quite close to me in Buckinghamshire. He had a huge swimming pool and he was forever plunging into it and swimming up and down, to preserve his physique, of which he was quite proud. Understandably, because he was a very good-looking man. And Mary was lovely and I thought they were ideally suited.'

Friends were forever dropping in and guests were always challenged to a game of Shaw's choosing. Subbuteo, which he was never truly to master, was one of them. Once, when Shaw's opponent earned himself a penalty kick, Shaw moved his goalie so vigorously that the entire table tipped over. Henceforth whenever an opponent threatened to score, Shaw would hurl over the table 'accidentally' to prevent a goal. This obsession to win, more accurately an obsession not to lose, never truly left him and often he'd resort to plain old-fashioned cheating if his skill didn't match up. He was quite brazen about it, too. As for the games he never mastered, they were dumped. He once decided to take up badminton and bought all the equipment: rackets, net, the works. Unlike tennis, which requires bullish force and energy, badminton is more suited to finesse and subtlety, qualities lacking in Shaw, and when a friend roundly beat him the badminton equipment was put away, never to see daylight again.

68

Kitchen-Sink Sinks

As 1963 began Harris was gearing up for the release of *This Sporting Life*. He knew it was the best thing he'd ever done, and might ever do, but the tide was beginning to turn away from this kind of film-making. Harris had quite simply missed the boat. The huge success of *Dr. No* and *Lawrence of Arabia*, colourful epics with a sheen of exotica to them, demonstrated that audience's tastes had changed dramatically. As director Carol Reed observed, 'Cinemagoers no longer want to look for an hour or two at a kitchen sink, the greasy dishes and the mental and moral miasma of certain elements in society.'

When *Sporting Life* opened towards the end of January the critics still lauded the picture, well most of them, but the public stayed away in droves and the film was a commercial disaster. According to David Storey *Tom Jones* would later that year take more money at one West End cinema than *Sporting Life* did in the whole of Great Britain. Anderson took its failure particularly hard, not making another film until *If* in 1968.

Sporting Life's measly profit return prompted John Davis, managing director of the Rank Organisation, to say that he would never again finance a British new wave movie, nor make such a 'squalid' film again. Neither did he want any manager of their chain of Odeon cinemas to show them. 'We cannot play films which are unacceptable to the public as entertainment,' he said at a dinner for exhibitors. 'This would lead to disaster for everyone.' He also put out a warning to independent producers to heed the public's demand for more mainstream and commercial fare and stop making grubby little films about pregnant girls in Grimsby: 'The public has clearly shown that it does not want the dreary kitchen-sink dramas.'

It was time for change; maybe the black-and-white images of terraced houses and smoky factories had become something of a cliché. As Keith Waterhouse observed, 'At that time, it seemed you could not climb over a slag heap without encountering two film directors squabbling over who had logged the chimney-stack horizon extreme long shot first.' The culture had moved on, too. Amongst the new generation of artists, be they actors, musicians, painters, whatever, there was less interest in contemplating the old provincial milieus which so many of them had left behind. They wanted to celebrate Britishness in a new and more dynamic way.

So while the methods and style of the British new wave remained influential, gritty and socially realist topics were frowned upon. But *Sporting Life* didn't connect with audiences for another reason. While other kitchen-sink movies contained at least some spark of human warmth and hope amidst the grimness, Anderson's picture was unremittingly bleak.

Put out that the public were shunning it, Harris still bathed in the critical glow of terrific notices. He was also delighted to have been nominated for Best Actor at the Cannes Film Festival and duly attended. Drinking steadily in the hours leading up to the ceremony, Harris was well gone by the time he heard his name called out as winner and bounded onto the stage. But when actress Jeanne Moreau handed him his award, in the shape of a plain box, Harris barked. 'What's this?' Momentarily stunned, Jeanne composed herself. 'Cufflinks,' she said. 'That's what the Best Actor gets.' Harris clearly thought, fuck that, and grabbed the biggest trophy he could see, said thank you and darted off stage. Two gendarmes attempted to retrieve the statue but Harris barged them aside and escaped into the night. The Festival Committee demanded the return of the statue, which was inscribed for best animated film, and Harris finally relented. The cufflinks were duly sent on to him. He kept them for years but the incident still rankled. 'Who gives cufflinks to an Olympic medallist?' he moaned.

No one was more acutely aware of Harris's drinking than Elizabeth, who lived with it on a daily basis. 'And yes, it was difficult, and in the end it was too difficult to cope with, but you live with it for so long that it sort of becomes your life. First of all, your hours are different to most people's. If the curtain comes down at eleven, then these guys had to unwind, and then they go out and have something to eat and drink, so you're not going to bed until three and four and then you sleep later in the day. So you're out of kilter with everybody who isn't in your world. And you think that's normal life. Film was a different scene, but then they used to allow drink on the set in those days.'

On the American press tour for *Sporting Life* Harris got so bored with the endless interviews that he left his plush New York hotel to hang out with the bums and the tramps down in the Bowery. 'I spent four days down there while my studio was going crazy.' He even shared some of their awful, paint-stripping brew and was as sick as a dog afterwards. 'But it was wonderful.' Harris was near to being out of control.

69

The Perfect Birthday

With Stamp the new golden boy of British movies it was only fair he chipped in most of the rent, and also slipped Caine the odd bit of cash to keep him going through what was becoming another barren patch. Meanwhile Caine's agent Dennis Selinger hatched a battle plan, to send his client up for roles that were artistically worthy rather than jobs that paid the most or seemed the most commercial. Caine wasn't sure about this and even less sure about Selinger's decision to put him in a play called *Next Time I'll Sing to You*. Yes, it was one of the leads, but he didn't understand what the hell the play was about and he was afraid if it turned into a long run he'd miss out on any potential film roles.

Under protest, Caine opened at the Arts Theatre in January and very quickly reached the opinion that Selinger had made a terrible mistake. Some members of the audience clearly hated it and weren't shy in letting the actors on stage know. 'That's because it was a very difficult play and very avant-garde for its time,' says Denys Graham, who was part of the company. 'Nowadays you'd say it was very Pinterish and Beckettish. The part I played was an old hermit and at the end of the play the actors murdered me with words. I died on stage from words, not by physical violence. It was an odd piece, but Michael was great in it. The problem was, because it was called *Next Time I'll Sing to You* many people who came thought it was a musical and they used to walk out.'

After the performance the cast, as they usually did, went to a nearby tavern and Graham remembers one night a man approaching them in the street. 'Have I seen you lot in that play across the road?' he said. The actors smiled and began to reach for a pen to sign autographs when he yelled back, 'I've never seen such a load of fucking rubbish in my life!' and stormed off.

'I did get very annoyed with the audience because they didn't seem to be enjoying the play,' says Graham. 'Towards the end, before I get killed, I had a marvellous speech where I screamed "You bastards!" I was shouting at the cast but I always said it to the audience.'

There was one admirer, however, and quite a notable one: Harold Hobson, the chief critic of the *Sunday Times*, took a real shine to the show and gave it a rave and then proceeded to mention it in some way practically every week in his column. A buzz suddenly circulated around it, audiences grew in size and became more responsive. To his own astonishment, Caine was suddenly in a hit show.

One evening after the performance there was a rap at his dressing-room door. In walked Stanley Baker, whom Caine hadn't seen since they'd worked together in *A Hill in Korea*. Baker was very complimentary about Caine's performance and told him that he was in the process of starring in and producing a movie that had a cockney character in it. 'If you're interested in trying for the part, Michael, go and see our director Cy Endfield; he's holding auditions tomorrow morning at ten in the bar of the Prince of Wales Theatre. Good luck.'

Caine was ecstatic and thanked Baker. 'Oh, what's the name of this movie, Stanley?'

'*Zulu*.'

Caine arrived dead on ten to find Cy Endfield sitting alone at the bar with an apologetic expression on his face. 'I'm sorry to have wasted your time, Michael, but we've given the part to James Booth. We figured that he looked more cockney than you do. Sorry, kid.' Caine knew Booth, who'd worked for Joan Littlewood and was a good actor. 'That's OK,' he said, and turned on his heels to walk out; another opportunity gone, another of his contemporaries surging ahead of him. Just as he was close to the exit there was a voice in his ears. 'Michael, can you do upper-crust English?' Caine walked back. He'd give it a damn good bash. Cy looked him over. 'You know, you don't look anything like a cockney to me. My idea of a cockney is a little, downtrodden, working-class man. You look like one of those snotty blue-blooded English guys.'

The role Endfield was thinking of was Bromhead, a caddish, slightly effeminate lieutenant. Just then Baker arrived and Endfield mentioned his idea. Baker liked it and they got scripts out and read through a few scenes. After further discussion it was agreed Caine should do a screen test. This took place at a little studio in Fleet Street and Caine was a bag of nerves, drenched in sweat in his tight-fitting military uniform. Baker was also there, feeding him his lines off-camera, a remarkable show of professional courtesy that Caine never forgot.

Somehow he managed to soldier through, but when he left the studio Caine knew it hadn't gone well. For years he'd bragged that if he could stay in the game long enough his chance would come, the trick was to be ready for it. This had been that chance, but Caine was convinced he'd blown it.

The decision wasn't going to be made until the Monday so Caine decided to hit the town on the weekend and get bombed. On the Saturday evening he went to a friend's party and who should he meet there but Cy Endfield. For the whole evening Caine kept looking over for a sign, a clue, the merest hint, but Cy continually blanked him. Things looked bad. When Endfield got his hat and coat and was about to leave he finally walked over to Caine. 'I've seen the test,' he said. 'It's the worst one I've ever seen.' Caine's guts fell to his kneecaps. 'But I have a feeling there's something there, so you've got the part. We go to South Africa in three weeks. Congratulations.' With that he left and Caine rushed to the toilet to throw up. It was the night before his thirtieth birthday.

70
The Pagan Poet

There had been much speculation as to what O'Toole would do after *Lawrence of Arabia*; just how do you follow one of the most revered and successful films of recent times? For a start he scoffed at the idea of himself as a handsome leading-man type, preferring to mould his image into that of a 'star' character actor, so it was important what he chose as his next project. He had various roles in mind, one of them a hankering to play in a film version of *Waiting for Godot* that he wanted to produce himself with Samuel Beckett. There was also talk that he was up to play Professor Higgins in Warner Brothers' *My Fair Lady*, but Jack Warner wanted Rex Harrison to repeat his stage performance. Finally, he decided to go completely left field and what he chose surprised everyone.

Oscar Lewenstein was in his office one day when O'Toole barged in. He'd a super idea: he wanted to put on Bertolt Brecht's play *Baal*, about a wastrel poet who leaves tattered and broken lives in his wake. It had never been performed in Britain before. Would Lewenstein produce it? Unfamiliar with the play itself, O'Toole's enthusiasm was so boundless and his marquee value so strong that Lewenstein couldn't refuse.

Siân Phillips was in no doubt that doing *Baal* was O'Toole's direct response to his sudden superstardom. He looked truly ghastly on stage, with ragged clothes and scabby make-up, a conscious effort, thought Siân, to appear dreadful after looking so wondrous as Lawrence. It was a worthy effort, some thought, bringing Brecht's first play to a wider and new audience, but the more general view was, why did he bother? 'If you could keep awake in that you were a very avid theatregoer,' remembers David Andrews. 'I didn't like it, I couldn't understand much of it for a start, and all I could see was Peter appearing to indulge himself with it. I'm sure he wasn't, but it looked like he'd chosen it because he was never off the stage and I think that slightly demeaned him because he didn't need to be like that; he could walk on with one line and he'd steal the whole bloody thing.'

O'Toole's pal Harris also thought it an odd choice, especially after his success as Lawrence. Anyway, he decided to see it, but incognito, otherwise the front-of-house manager would tell O'Toole he was in. 'So I went to a costumiers and I got dressed as a Roman Catholic priest, with the rosary beads, the hat and the collar and all that. I went with a mate of mine and we sat up in the gallery and O'Toole was unbeliev-ably brilliant. So I had to go back and tell him he's great, but I couldn't go back dressed as a priest or he'd ask me why. So my friend and I swapped clothes.' The next day one of the newspapers said there had been a commotion during the matinee of *Baal* where a Roman Catholic priest was seen to undress in the gallery. Anyway, Harris went to see O'Toole and not a word was said. Fast-forward seven years and Harris had a number-one single, 'MacArthur Park', and decided to go out on a one-man concert tour. 'I went up to the north of England, to Scunthorpe where no one could see me break it in. I'm singing a song and I heard a commotion at the back of the hall, so I stopped the orchestra, "What's going on out there?" And a voice said, "I'm Peter O'Toole, I'm here dressed as a nun."'

Lewenstein himself believed the production as a whole was a gallant attempt which didn't quite work. 'O'Toole was extremely nervous towards the end of rehearsals and wanted to postpone the opening for a day or two. It would not have helped, although perhaps two extra weeks of rehearsal might have done.' According to Siân, the director William Gaskill was shunted to one side by O'Toole, who invited George Devine to come in and try to 'fix' the production. But as with every-thing O'Toole touched, there was high drama. 'His dresser, on the night of the final rehearsal, screamed, "This show is cursed," flung the clothes on to the floor and fled out of the Phoenix Theatre and into Charing Cross Road, never to return,' recalled Siân. The play itself, due to tech-nical difficulties, sometimes ran way over. People walked out rather than endure any more.

Amongst the supporting cast was Gemma Jones, then a young actress making a very early West End appearance, who looks back on *Baal* with nothing but fondness. 'It was an extraordinary production and there was a huge focus of attention on it because of Peter and *Lawrence of Arabia*. It was a wild cast, a lot of drunken Irishmen. They treated me with great respect because I was very young and very green. And Peter was very nice to me. It was a rather surprising thing for him to do because it's quite an academic piece really and Bill Gaskill brought a very intelligentsia approach to it. But then on the other hand there were these lecherous Irishmen who'd use pornographic playing cards in the card-playing scene. So there was a lot of levity as well.'

Those cards became a bone of contention during one performance. During a scene in a café it was obvious that the actor's cues weren't coming in properly. Upstage sitting round a table were a bunch of men playing cards. 'And that's when we discovered that the stagehands had given them some pornographic cards instead of their normal playing cards,' says Gemma. 'So they were so distracted by these cards that they weren't listening to their cues.'

For many, *Baal* was the play to see at the time. John Gielgud was unsure, though, writing to a friend: 'Sounds an awful piece, but Peter does a lot of romping in it and his performance sounds worthwhile. And he is so very dishy.'

Gemma does recall having a love scene with O'Toole which was all extremely chaste, 'except that he used to unzip my chemise, which meant that when I got out of bed I had to wrap this thing round me so it didn't fall off. It wasn't part of the act; he just used to do it as a practical joke.'

The play did attract a certain amount of notoriety for the large number of scantily clad actresses adorning the stage at various intervals. Gemma shared a dressing room with one of them. 'Guinevere Roberts was her name and she had a very, very luscious figure and the number of actors who would knock on the door by mistake – oh sorry, wrong room – hoping to catch Guinevere in her undies. There was a lot of riotous goings-on backstage to counteract the fact that we were in such a serious piece of drama.'

With his *Lawrence* stint bringing in the money, O'Toole purchased a town house in Hampstead, installing the children into a top-floor nursery, a room that one suspects he rarely trod. According to Siân, he paid a visit one night when his daughter was feeling ill. Days later the child asked, 'You know that man who came to see me, Mummy – who is he?' After that Siân made a point of putting up facial shots of O'Toole in whatever film or stage role he was inhabiting to avoid any further misunderstandings.

Elsewhere the house was lavishly furnished and renovated, so much so that it exhausted all his funds. 'I'm skint,' he declared. And not for the first time. 'The only difference now is that I am luxuriously broke.'

71

Harris vs Anderson: Round Two

Lindsay Anderson still hadn't managed to flush Harris out of his system and in March directed him in an adaptation of Gogol's *Diary of a Madman*, put on at the Royal Court. During rehearsals their *Sporting Life* relationship rose to the surface once again, 'varying between friendship and creativity on the one hand, and resentment, fear and nervous bullying on the other', Anderson wrote. One night the director was alone on the stage with Harris when the actor's booted foot came crashing down on his instep and a hand grasped him around the throat. 'A hallucinating moment.'

It was an odd choice for the pair, Gogol's tale of a lowly government clerk's descent into insanity during the overbearingly bureaucratic and oppressive era of Tsar Nicholas I required Harris to be on stage alone the entire time. Critic Clive Barnes was to call his performance a tour de force that 'struck me as one of the greatest things I have ever seen in the theatre'. However, Karel Reisz saw the production and condemned it as 'a disaster'.

David Storey attended the memorable first night. 'The house lights went down and the lights came up on the stage and absolutely nothing happened. It looked as though Richard had done another of his walk-outs. It might have been five or ten minutes before he eventually sauntered onto the stage and began what was virtually a monologue and worked his way through it. Richard wasn't an actor really, in the sense that Gielgud was an actor, he was what you would call a performer, and he gave you a performance.' No longer in the theatre, though, with his film career now truly up and running Harris would not appear on the stage again for another twenty years.

His working relationship with Anderson also came to an end, though perversely both men still pursued projects that the two of them could work on together. It was intended that Gogol's *Madman* would be followed by two more plays at the Court featuring Harris in the title roles under Anderson's direction: *Julius Caesar* and *Hamlet*. Two weeks into rehearsals for *Julius Caesar*, having already dithered over signing the contract, Harris accepted a film role and withdrew from the play. Anderson was devastated, even getting fellow Royal Court director Anthony Page to drive him past Harris's house one night to see if the lights were on and he was at home.

There was also talk of a film of *Wuthering Heights* with Harris as Heathcliff. 'It would have been marvellous,' says Elizabeth. 'They used to say Richard would do Heathcliff and Lindsay would then come on as Cathy, and this used to be a standing joke between everyone.' Alas, that also withered and died, a situation Storey felt was probably for the best. 'Several films were offered to them after *Sporting Life* but I felt that the producer in each case wasn't powerful enough to control the wildness and ferocity of the relationship between Lindsay and Richard, which had become quite obsessional really on both their parts, particularly on Lindsay's.'

For years, even into the seventies, Anderson would be tempted to have another go with Harris and use the hindsight of his previous experience to control and contain the relationship. 'But Richard would then do something which reminded him that he couldn't really cope with him and it was wiser not to get involved again,' says Storey. 'But Lindsay remained vulnerable to it all his life, yet he realised that Richard very nearly broke him completely and it would be very foolish to get as deeply and as profoundly involved in the relationship again.'

As for Harris, there would be times, usually after a few bevies, when he'd be consumed by guilt over his behaviour towards Anderson and as late as 1990 he still occasionally telephoned the director 'when I feel dreadful'. When Anderson died Storey invited Harris to speak at his memorial service, which took place at the Royal Court. 'He turned up and he came with prepared prompts on a series of blank postcards, phrases and words, which he held in his hand, and he attempted to read from them but couldn't quite cope. So he just threw them down and said, "Oh well, bugger this, I'm really here because I love him and that's what I've got to say." It was quite emotional.'

72

With Some Guts Behind It

On 26 March 1963 Caine and the rest of the cast and crew of *Zulu* touched down in Johannesburg after a gruelling twenty-hour flight from London. While preparing to leave for the location Caine acquired a rather unusual lucky charm from actress Liz Fraser, who'd appeared with him in *Next Time I'll Sing to You*. It was a dead mouse. Caine kept it right up to the world premiere. Fraser sat next to him in the auditorium and asked about the mouse but got a non-committal answer. When the curtains closed and the audience was on its feet applauding, only then did Caine turn to Liz and say, 'Here's your mouse back.'

Zulu's executive producer was the American showman Joe Levine, who'd gone nuts when Endfield told him who he'd cast as Bromhead: 'He's not right, it won't work, he's not suitable.' In the end he'd reluctantly put Caine under contract, but it was hardly a boost to the actor's confidence. Ultimately it just made him more determined to prove the Hollywood suits wrong. Firstly, he was confident about the accent thanks to his years in rep, 'where you were always playing Lord Ponce or some bloody part like that'. However, for the physical bearing of an officer Caine carried out a bit of research. As a private in Korea he'd observed officers up close and seen and also been at the receiving end of how they behaved to the lowly ranks. What he didn't know was how officers interacted with each other, invaluable for Bromhead's close relationship with Baker's character Lieutenant Chard. Caine solved this little dilemma by having regular long lunches at the Royal Guards officers' mess near Buckingham Palace, just to watch how they all behaved with each other.

Such dedication, however, swiftly fell on stony ground. Caine had come up with a couple of deliberate gestures for Bromhead. Firstly, he'd decided to have his helmet pulled down slightly so it shielded his eyes, so that when his character needed to make a point he'd tilt his head a bit and flash those blue peepers. At the first rushes he ever attended, one of the crew yelled, 'Why's that stupid bastard wearing his hat in front of his face?' Shell-shocked, Caine ran outside and threw up in the toilets. Never again has he attended rushes on any of his films.

His next gesture was something that he'd seen the Duke of Edinburgh employ on state occasions, that of crossing his hands behind his back while walking, which Caine felt displayed a sort of inbred aristocratic authority. The American backers didn't think so, firing off a telex to Endfield and Baker – 'Suggest you fire actor playing Bromhead, doesn't know what to do with hands.'

By accident Caine saw this telegram and feared the worst. 'Is it true they're going to fire me?' he asked Baker the next day. 'I completely understand and I'll go at once.'

'Who is the producer of this movie?'

'You are, Stan,' said Caine.

'Have I said that you're fired?'

Caine mumbled a 'no'.

'Well, just get on with your job,' said Baker. 'And stop reading my fucking mail or you *will* get fired.'

Weeks of anxiety and self-doubt floated away. Caine knew he was on the movie for keeps – for better or worse. It also taught him a valuable lesson. 'I thought, I'm dealing with dummies here. I can make a career in this business because I'm actually smarter than the guys who are running this show – they don't know what I'm doing.'

Midway through the film it was obvious Caine had star potential. A British journalist visited the location site and struck up a conversation with Jack Hawkins, playing a supporting role as a missionary. 'If I were you,' said the veteran actor, 'I'd go over and talk to that young man,' singling out Caine from the others.

'Who is he?' asked the reporter.

'Michael Caine,' replied Hawkins.

'I've never heard of him.'

Hawkins smiled. 'You will. He's the best thing in this film. Just you wait and see.'

Maureen Endfield, Cy's wife, also quickly realised that Caine was one to watch when she attended rushes with her husband. 'I remember my heart stopped the first time I saw Michael – the demeanour and his bearing were incredible. It was obvious there was a star.'

The cast and crew were all holed up in nearby hotels for the duration of the shoot. Caine shared a room with Ivor Emmanuel, whose moment of glory in the film is when he rallies the men into a spirited rendering of 'Men of Harlech', as the Zulus prepare to attack. He recalled Caine saying once, 'God, I want to be a film star – look at the money they get!'

As for socialising, there wasn't an awful lot to do. Fraternising with the locals was right out, especially the female ones. With apartheid still in full force, everyone was obliged to sign a form saying they would not have sex with black women. If they were caught doing so they faced prison or twelve lashes. Upon learning this Baker asked the chief of police, 'If I get caught, can I have the twelve lashes while I'm still doing it?'

Glynn Edwards, who played Corporal Allen, remembers actually having it written into the actors' contracts that there should be no sexual intercourse with the natives. 'With a basically all-male picture it should have been OK, until the day a hundred beautiful dancing girls arrived on set with the sun glistening on their dark nubile bodies. Stanley Baker was to be heard saying, "Remember your contracts, lads," which I am pleased to say we all did.'

Edwards also recalls the day the Zulu extras arrived, 'but Stanley could not get enough of them for the long shots of the Impis coming over the hills, so someone had the bright idea of nailing ten shields to a long piece of wood with a Zulu on each end so for every two warriors we had twelve, but if you freeze-frame the film you will notice that quite a few of them are legless'.

Back in London, Caine looked forward to the release of the film and for Levine to honour his contract and find other projects for him to appear in, maybe even star. When he was summoned to see Levine at his office Caine arrived brimming with confidence. It didn't last long, Levine was terminating his contract with immediate effect.

'Didn't you like me in *Zulu*?' Caine asked.

'Loved you, Michael. But there's one thing I gotta tell you.' He drew heavily on his cigar. 'I know you're not, but you gotta face the fact that you look like a queer on screen.' Caine couldn't believe his ears and was thinking of getting Stamp along as a witness to the contrary when Levine started up again. 'There are a lot of queer stars out there who look butch, and that's fine, but you're the other way round, Michael, and it's the wrong way round. You'll never be a romantic lead.'

What to do now, save face the drudgery of doing theatre or small roles on TV again as he waited for *Zulu* to open and the hope of what that might bring? Then news reached him of an opportunity, not just a job but the title role in a play heading into the West End after a successful run at the Mermaid Theatre. John Neville, who'd been playing it to critical acclaim, was unable to continue any more and Caine's name had been put forward by the Mermaid's owner, the actor Bernard Miles, and seconded by the show's leading lady Glenda Jackson. Sadly, the financial backers thought they knew best and rejected Caine out of hand, 'We've never heard of him.' The play was called *Alfie*.

73
Connery and Shaw Do Battle

Delighted with the success of *Dr. No*, Connery was enjoying playing James Bond, for now. 'After all, I can kill any son of a bitch and get away with it.' He knew that, handled the right way, Bond could set him up for life. And he had the full support of Diane, although she believed the role of Bond, from an artistic standpoint, was beneath his talents.

Reporters had also descended upon his childhood home to interview Joe and Effie, obviously proud parents who had photographs of their famous son adorning the walls. Effie was always quick to point out that fame had not gone to her son's head. 'He comes in that door every time with his usual "Hello, Mum", and film star or no, he's just the same laddie he always was, daft as the devil. Nothing could change our Tommy. He's not swell-headed. A wee bit better spoken maybe, but he has to be.'

Connery had tried coaxing them to join him in London but they wouldn't budge, preferring to stay amongst people they knew. Joe wouldn't retire, either. 'I'm not the sort that would like to sit around and let a son take care of him.' Instead, Connery set up a trust fund for them and bought the latest hi-tech fridge as a gift, a huge thing it was that barely fitted into the small flat. It remained there looking faintly ridiculous, proof of a son keen for his parents to share in his new wealth.

The next Bond, he was told, would be *From Russia with Love*, the producers cleverly exploiting the fact that John F. Kennedy had recently revealed it to be amongst his favourite novels. Connery's agent Richard Hatton was able to negotiate a few more perks for his client and also suggested to Broccoli and Saltzman another of his clients who might be perfect for the role of Red Grant, the psychopathic assassin out to kill Bond, a certain Robert Shaw.

Offered the part, Shaw was of a mind to turn it down, calling the script 'rubbish'. More than likely he couldn't face the prospect of playing a supporting role to his old rival and table-tennis nemesis Connery. It was Mary, only a few months into being Mrs Shaw, who urged him to swallow his pride and take it. Undergoing the humiliation of having his hair bleached in a beauty parlour, Shaw also wore lifts to boost his 5′ 11″ height.

The boys' big scene together is an almighty dust-up aboard the Orient Express which must rank among the greatest ever scraps in cinema history; it's fast, frenzied and satisfyingly vicious. Connery and Shaw insisted on handling most of it themselves; only in a few shots were they replaced by stunt doubles during the two days of filming. Never have we feared for Bond's life so much as at this moment; it's white-knuckle stuff. Though it must have galled Shaw to have to lose, for Connery it was sweet payback for the time Shaw played a mean practical joke on him the first time they worked together, on a live television play called *The Pets*. Playing two airmen, the actors had to bail out of a studio-bound plane, but Shaw had fixed Connery's straps so that when he jumped out they became entangled, leaving him embarrassingly dangling in mid-air.

In the small but crucial role of spy planner Kronsteen was Polish actor/director Vladek Sheybal. Back in 1960 Sheybal was directing Diane in a BBC TV play and that's when he'd met Connery for the first time. He'd pick Diane up at the rehearsal studios and they'd all go to the pub together. 'Vladek, look at Sean,' Diane would urge. 'Cast him in your next production. Isn't he sexy, handsome and charming? And he can act.' Vladek could sense Connery was acutely embarrassed by this, 'but I never had any doubts about Sean becoming a star with his outstanding charisma'. The only thing that concerned Sheybal was his accent, which could still be overpowering to the uninitiated. 'I thought his accent would limit the parts he would be offered.'

By 1963 Sheybal had grown tired of acting and had given it up completely when his agent sent him the script for *Russia*. He read it and hated it. He especially hated the part he was being offered: just a few scenes and ending up killed with a poisoned spike. Thanks, but no thanks. His agent kept pressing him but Sheybal was insistent, he didn't want to do it.

An hour later his phone rang. It was Connery, his voice barely under control. 'You complete idiot,' he raved. 'How dare you turn down this part?' This was Bond, it was going to be huge and every actor in town would sell their grannies to be in it. 'And another thing,' Connery continued. 'I feel personally hurt. I suggested you to Harry and Cubby. I told them you would make this part important, vibrant. You are going to ring your agent and you are going to play this part!' Then Connery slammed down the receiver. Sheybal had no choice, and Connery was right, the exposure kept him in employment for the next three decades. As Sheybal arrived on the set for his first day, Connery was waiting for him outside the sound stage with a simple message: 'Welcome to James Bond.'

With a budget of $2.2 million, more than double that of *Dr. No*, *From Russia with Love* went before the cameras in April, with location work in Istanbul, where Mary Ure was a regular visitor, as was Fleming himself. When they were filming at Pinewood Connery often invited Sheybal back to his house for dinner and according to the actor would walk through the door booming to Diane, 'We are hungry!' slump in his favourite sofa, hug Jason, and then yell, 'Where is my beer?'

Diane had fallen very much into the same dilemma afflicting Siân Phillips; her career was in limbo as she was left literally holding the baby. O'Toole had voiced his aversion to Siân working, and here was an actress who'd won awards and rave notices. Their rows were such that she installed soundproof doors in the house to prevent the rest of the family hearing them. Like many of this acting group, O'Toole was something of a chauvinist and had no intention of changing his ways now. 'If you don't like me, leave me,' he'd say to Siân. He'd grown up in a male-dominated household and so expected his Hampstead sanctuary to run to his volatile whim. If he came in drunk at four a.m., it seemed only reasonable that his wife should make him breakfast.

Connery's thinking wasn't a million miles away from this, either, at least so far as housewifery was concerned: 'No, no. You can't work any more. I don't want you to work,' is how Diane remembers it. 'After we married Sean suddenly reverted to being, I suppose, the Scottish husband.'

74

The British Invasion

Today *Billy Liar* is rightly regarded as a classic, but at the time both Schlesinger and Janni felt the film hadn't quite come together as well as *A Kind of Loving* had. And the critical reaction when the film opened that summer mostly proved them right, although America's *Variety* dubbed Courtenay 'probably the best of Britain's new wave of young actors'. But *Time* magazine perhaps summed up the overall public mood: 'Moviegoers are getting a bit bugged by that same scummy old roof-scape and the eternal kitchen sink-drome. They sometimes find it hard to believe things are really all that bad in merry England.'

It's true, *Billy Liar*'s failure at the box office (Nat Cohen said it never made back its cost) did point towards audience apathy towards working-class subjects, even those laced with an affectionate humour. But there are glimpses of the future amidst Schlesinger's grey mise en scène. Britain is emerging as a very different world from the one Arthur Seaton inhabited in *Saturday Night and Sunday Morning*; city centres are being regenerated, the back-to-backs torn down to make way for high-rise flats. Courtenay's own childhood street would soon be demolished, that whole community gone, the fish docks gone, his old school so much rubble beneath the developer's wrecking ball.

Billy Liar was nevertheless nominated for six British Academy awards, including Best Film. It was also shown at the Venice Film Festival, with Courtenay in attendance. Sitting in the theatre, as the screen flickered into life with his big malnourished face on it, he began to slide down his seat in excruciating embarrassment. All he saw was how lousy he was. 'I just didn't see the magic, just the mistakes. I wanted to get out of that cinema as fast as I could.' When the credits rolled the applause was thunderous. Arriving at the festival an unknown on the continent, Courtenay was now fawned over by the European press and glamorous women. 'A bit of success and the birds flock around you,' he told British reporters. 'Well, I'm dead chuffed, naturally. Although look at me, I'm no great catch now, am I? I don't have the sort of dash that Finney or Stamp has got.'

Even so, Courtenay had definitely arrived and was, it seemed, beginning to get a handle on the fame game; he employed a chauffeur, for a start – 'I'm working so hard I can't frig about catching buses,' he excused – though he confessed this to be his sole luxury. 'I don't live it up because I trust this business as far as I can throw it.' He really wasn't interested in premieres and the adulation, much preferring to conduct interviews down the local pub. There was no film-star glitz with Tom Courtenay.

At the same time, what was important for him at this juncture was not to become too identified with his roots. He didn't want to beat his chest or build a career around being northern or working class.

Alan Bates had arrived at much the same conclusion. The danger of kitchen-sink movies was that they created images for the actors which were self-perpetuating. Early in his career Bates had a paranoia about image and typecasting. He wanted to play a variety of roles in films, as he'd been allowed to do in theatre. It was a shrewd and deliberate choice after he saw how willing producers were to push him into prototypes of earthy regionalism.

So what better than a comedy, something he'd never tried before, and one that concerned itself with the new Britain, a land of empty affluence, with its TV ad consumerism and colour supplements? *Nothing But the Best* featured Bates as an ambitious young estate agent, determined to rise in the world but trapped by his accent and class. Denholm Elliott plays the amiable scoundrel who teaches him how to beat the toffs at their own game.

The film's leading lady was Millicent Martin, who after appearing in sundry stage musicals like *South Pacific* had become a well-known face thanks to her singing skits on the hit TV comedy *That Was the Week That Was*. She adored working with Bates and was delighted to discover that he'd made a vow to have fun on the movie, no matter how gruelling the schedule. 'Alan was a terrible giggler,' says Millicent, 'and we got into awful trouble. The director Clive Donner used to get angry with us and send us off the set, "Go away, you're like children. Compose yourself and come back again." And Alan would get upset that he was upsetting Clive. But we had a lot of fun. I think the two of us enjoyed the fact that we could have giggles but still get the job done.'

Millicent had now worked with two of the most sexually attractive leading men Britain had produced in years, Bates and Connery. And yet she never once sensed that either of them took that particularly seriously or felt their looks were important. 'They were certainly aware of how attractive they were, but I think it didn't sort of mean anything. If you do sexy, which a lot of people do, then it isn't sexy or sensual. If they're aware of it every time they move, the way they sit and the way they speak, it becomes a performance, it's not something that is naturally in them. And with Alan, I think the fact that he was so caring and so warm, that was what made him so attractive, it was really this lovely behaviour of his, it was very, very attractive. Also he was so genuine, there was absolutely no other side to Alan.'

Within months of working with Millicent Bates found himself on the island of Crete making a movie that would seal his international reputation – *Zorba the Greek*. Its director Michael Cacoyannis first saw Bates at the Royal Court in *Look Back in Anger* and singled him out as an excellent actor with a great presence. 'I invited him to dinner and he was delightful company, a very nice person but rather shy,' Cacoyannis recalls. Over the next few years Bates would take holidays in Greece, staying at the director's home, so by the time of *Zorba* their friendship had become very close. 'I was following Alan's career with great interest, hoping one day we would collaborate. I thought it would be a blessing for me to have him in one of my films.'

Bates plays a middle-class writer, a repressed intellectual, who travels to Crete on business and finds his life turned around by a lusty Greek peasant played by Anthony Quinn who, according to Cacoyannis, came away impressed with the young English actor. But there were frequent on-set clashes between Quinn and his director, principally over Quinn's tendency to chew the scenery. 'He could be impossible,' says Cacoyannis. 'But I found ways very early on to get around that because he was co-directing the film with me and I wasn't going to put up with that.'

This was Quinn's way, as cameraman Walter Lassally discovered. On the first day Quinn marched over to the crew to announce brazenly: 'Look, it's up to you technicians to get things properly prepared because I only do one take, I'm always best in my first take, so get things ready. I do my take, and that's it.' Lassally strolled over to the star and said, 'Mr Quinn, we don't work like that here!' And there was a look of total amazement on his face. 'Shortly afterwards it became very obvious that he was dying for a bit of resistance, because he was surrounded by yes men. I remember once at rushes an assistant was sitting behind him and tapped him on the shoulder and said, "That was really nice, Tony." And he said, "Isn't it always?" And she said, "No, it's not always." And he loved that because everybody else said: Tony, you're the greatest; Tony, that was fantastic. He was thoroughly sick of it.'

Bates, of course, was the complete antithesis of Quinn. 'He was very skilful,' says Lassally. 'Very pleasant, never a cross word did one hear from Alan Bates. I would say the term that best describes Alan Bates is an English gentleman.' For Cacoyannis it was Bates's unstinting generosity towards his fellow players that left the deepest impression. 'But sometimes I would find him not looking in the right direction because he was admiring the actor or actress playing in the scene with him. So he'd be looking at them instead of at the camera for his close-up. I'd say to him, "The camera is centred on you, Alan." And he'd say, "I know, but aren't they wonderful?" For most actors, it is enough that they manage one mood with competence. Alan reflected three or four moods at the same time.'

As Finney geared himself to open in *Luther* on Broadway in September 1963 a po-faced American Equity attempted to block his work permit on the grounds that he wasn't 'an artist of exceptional ability'. The show's indomitable producer David Merrick wasn't standing for that and personally appealed to the US Immigration Service and won. The play went ahead and Finney was nominated for a Tony award for his performance.

American Equity's gripe was a case of over-zealous nationalism. There had been a veritable infestation of British shows and actors on Broadway in the last couple of years, and even more galling was the fact that they'd been so successful. It was an invasion of British talent, long before the Beatles ever boarded a plane. Alongside *Luther* there was *Beyond the Fringe*, *Oliver!* and Arnold Wesker's *Chips with Everything*, about RAF conscripts and the class system, about as parochial as you can get, and all were faring well.

The Brits on Broadway were a close-knit bunch, supporting each other and forming a community almost. 'We had a ten-pin bowling league,' recalls Derek Fowlds, who was in *Chips with Everything*. 'We used to bowl against *Luther*, and bowl against *Oliver!* It was a great period over there. Very special. And I saw Albert in *Luther*, he was brilliant in that. Certain productions in those early years you remember, they stand out, and *Luther* was certainly one of those.'

Things changed radically in October for Finney, still appearing as Luther, when *Tom Jones* opened in America and went through the roof. 'It was a phenomenal success,' says Walter Lassally. 'Which wasn't expected, least of all by Tony Richardson. One of the problems with Tony was that because he was his own producer, when it came to the stage of nearly being finished in the editing, he was much too close to it, he couldn't see the wood for the trees. If there had been another producer, that producer, if he was wise, would have picked Tony up bodily and taken him away from the editing room and sent him to the Bahamas for a fortnight because Tony thought nothing worked, the film wasn't funny, the pace wasn't right. He was completely and utterly worried about it, so the enormous success of *Tom Jones* came as a total surprise to Tony.'

Forget Richardson, the film's success came as a total shock to United Artists. When their executives first sat down and watched it they hated the damn thing and were convinced it wouldn't make a dime. Finding popularity in Britain first, it was American audiences who embraced it like no other British film before, turning it into the highest-grossing foreign-made picture ever released in the US up to that time. 'It was a liberating kind of film,' says Lassally. 'I think that accounts for its universal success. The last line in the film is, "Happy the man, and happy he alone, he who can call today his own. He who, secure within, can say, Tomorrow, do thy worst, for I have lived Today." That caught the spirit of the time and the public mood perfectly.'

Combined with the success of *Lawrence of Arabia* and the first two James Bond films, American companies saw potential in British movie-making and the Hollywood studios made a stampede for the UK, leading to an explosion in British cinema that would last for the rest of the decade.

Nominated for ten Academy Awards, *Tom Jones* would end up winning Best Picture, Best Director, Best Screenplay for Osborne and Best Original Score. Osborne and Richardson stayed well clear of the cere-mony. 'I had quite enough of prize giving at school,' scorned Richardson, who nevertheless soon accepted an offer to direct his first Hollywood movie. It was a move that effectively ended his association with the Royal Court; never again would he direct there. His defection to Hollywood also affected Woodfall, sapping much of the company's creative energy, and although it did come back fleetingly a few years later it wasn't the dynamic entity of its formative years.

Tom Jones made Richardson and Osborne millionaires overnight. The rewards Osborne received from his hit plays paled into insignificance compared to the cash *Tom Jones* generated at the world's box offices. With all this newfound success Osborne metamorphosed into part of the landed gentry with a house in the country and one in Belgravia, a Bentley and a Rolls, a chauffeur and live-in nanny. Osborne got into the habit of keeping a fridge in the bedroom to save him the inconvenience of going downstairs to fetch champagne. The cry of this particular angry young man had been muffled in velvet. 'Osborne was extraordinary,' says Philip Saville. 'All this great anger towards the upper class and the privileged, and of course what happened was, like in life, we become what we resist, and he became very established. He bought a beautiful pile in the country and lived like a country squire. But there's no ques-tion that Osborne made a huge contribution to turning things around.'

And Finney was laughing all the way to the bank, too. In a bid to keep costs down he'd agreed, shrewdly as it turned out, to a modest fee for *Tom Jones* in exchange for a large slice of the profits. After all the money was counted, Finney's profit share was enough to make him a dollar millionaire. The world was his oyster, as the old showbiz adage goes, and he could walk into any part in any film. But once he'd finished his obligations to *Luther* Finney intended to disappear off the face of the planet.

75

O'Toole Opens the National Theatre

When it came to booze Peter O'Toole rarely met his match. But he did in Richard Burton. O'Toole immediately latched on to the Welshman as a soul mate. Both came to the film *Becket*, a historical drama focusing on the relationship between Henry II and his Archbishop, with notorious and well-deserved reputations. Burton had seen O'Toole at the Bristol Old Vic and had written in his diary: 'He looked like a beautiful, emaciated secretary bird. His voice had a crack like a whip. Most important of all you couldn't take your eyes off him.'

During filming there were wild lunches, lasting hours, full of hearty quaffing of champagne and brandy and verbal fencing, both men lobbing Shakespeare soliloquies at each other. During one pub crawl around the drinking dens of Soho, O'Toole and Burton got seriously sloshed. 'Richard was in a bad state,' O'Toole later recalled, 'worried about his career. "Oh, Pedro, what am I doing?" That night he had fallen into a bottle of Scotch and I wasn't far behind him.' Staggering home at three in the morning, O'Toole tried to carry his friend but he was too heavy and both men stumbled and fell into the gutter. Somebody stopped beside them on the pavement. It was Alan Bates, so the story goes. 'Peter,' he said. 'Today I've just signed up for my first commercial picture.' O'Toole and Burton looked at each other, and then up at Bates. 'You coming down to join us, then?'

During one of the innumerable liquid lunches taken on the set of *Becket* by O'Toole and Burton discussions turned to *Hamlet*. Both had played it and both hated it. 'Let's be masochists,' said Burton. 'Let's do *Hamlet* again and get it out of our systems.' The plan was for one of them to play the Dane on Broadway, the other in London. They discussed their common admiration of Laurence Olivier and John Gielgud, then fell to arguing which of the duo they would like to direct them. In the end, they tossed a coin. O'Toole ended up with Olivier, who had recently been appointed director of the newly formed National Theatre.

So legend has it, Olivier was in his makeshift offices of the fledgling NT, wondering what to come up with to launch the company upon the world, when O'Toole barged in demanding he direct his Hamlet. There is another tale told: that it was Olivier who sought O'Toole out and at first he didn't want to do it. 'But have you ever tried to argue with Olivier? He's the most charming, persuasive bastard ever to draw a breath.' Of all his generation, O'Toole held the old guard in the most reverence, Olivier above all. 'I mean, he's done it. He's sat on the top of Everest and waved down at the Sherpas.' But he had misgivings about the man running the National Theatre, that he should waste his time and talent there; surely all his energies should be focused purely on acting. 'He belongs in the stable, as head stallion.'

Whatever the truth about who asked whom first, Olivier was glad to have a major star grace the National Theatre's first production beginning that October. Less impressed were John Dexter and William Gaskill, whom Olivier had brought in as assistants, after George Devine couldn't be prised away from his beloved Royal Court. Both men were against O'Toole coming in, Dexter because he didn't like him, while Gaskill was opposed on principle, seeing this as turning the NT into a sort of Hollywood system of star names rather than a company of equals. Olivier tried to win them round by saying that the great British people were bound to ask of their *Hamlet*, 'But who's in it?'

It was decided not to wait for the construction of a new building to house the National Theatre but to take over the Old Vic, scene of some of Olivier's early stage triumphs. Quickly he set about changing the place, putting in a new revolving stage and taking out the first two rows of the stalls so that the stage could be extended beyond the proscenium arch. Into this building-site chaos came the *Hamlet* rehearsals. Max Adrian remembered starting work while 'the whole place was still littered with rubble and mortar and there was a bloody enormous hole in one wall which allowed the wind to blow straight in from Waterloo Road'.

O'Toole was not intimidated in the least by the heritage of Olivier, who had made theatrical history playing the Dane, but according to Joan Plowright there were disagreements between the two men on how the part should be played. Never once did it degenerate into hostility, she was quick to point out, although it's rather telling that the two men never worked together again. In 2000 O'Toole won the Olivier award for outstanding achievement, presented by Joan Plowright. During his speech O'Toole reminisced about the *Hamlet* experience. Turning to smile at Joan he said, 'Larry and I got on very well,' then turning to face the audience – 'at first.'

Much to O'Toole's dismay, Olivier wanted to do the full text, four and a half hours, performed six nights a week and two matinees. Losing that battle, O'Toole announced his Hamlet would have a beard. 'Why should I be the only man in Elsinore with a razor blade?' Oh no, said Olivier, not in my production, ducky. Again O'Toole lost out. He'd play Hamlet clean shaven, with his hair dyed blonde and in tights, the full bloody works.

In rehearsal Olivier and O'Toole never hit it off as both thought and imagined they would, with O'Toole simply refusing to bow down and bathe in Olivier's living legendhood. 'At first glance I could see through him, and he could see through me, and he knew that I knew that he knew.'

Olivier had surrounded O'Toole with an experienced bunch: Michael Redgrave, Rosemary Harris as Ophelia, Robert Stephens, even his old RADA buddy Frank Finlay as the gravedigger. And there was twenty-three-year-old newcomer Michael Gambon as a spear carrier, who described O'Toole as 'a god with bright blonde hair'.

John Dexter had carried out some of the casting; he happened to know Derek Fowlds well and got the young earnest actor an audition before Olivier. 'And John said to me afterwards, "Right, you're in the company, your first part is Laertes in *Hamlet* opposite Peter O'Toole." And I said, "Gee whizz." A few weeks later I got a call from him, it was bad news. "You can't join the National Theatre because you look too young and we can't cast you in the other plays." That was always my problem, I looked about fourteen when I left RADA and played juvenile roles for about forty years. When I was doing *Yes Minister* I was nearly fifty then! Anyway, I was very upset. And Derek Jacobi got the gig instead of me. So he played Laertes and all the rest and stayed at the National for ten years and had a wonderful career and I went to work with Basil Brush.'

Rehearsals continued under huge stress and chaos, as building work continued nosily all around them, and the company looked to O'Toole as the rock to cling to. He rose to the task majestically, seemingly immune to the near-catastrophic tightrope the production was walking. He even indulged in practical jokes, like the time he filled all the dressing-room showers with ice. But as opening night arrived the tension got to him and he was seen pacing around backstage, a big ball of nerves.

The first preview didn't do those nerves any good whatsoever; it was an utter disaster. Peter Cellier, playing Rosencrantz, has never forgotten it. For one thing, about halfway through the performance, the revolving stage seized up and refused to budge. 'The curtain came down and we the actors didn't know what to do. And Olivier, dressed in his tuxedo, came out to the front of the stage, sat on the edge and just chatted with the audience. He told them what a wonderful thing it was to start the National Theatre, what he hoped to achieve with it, that kind of thing, he talked like an old friend to them for about twenty minutes while backstage there were these frantic attempts to mend the stage going on. I thought it was pretty brilliant of Larry.'

The performance resumed, but not long afterwards the stage lights went off and there was this one solitary bulb downstage right still on and everybody was flocking towards it to say their lines and so be seen by the audience. 'It was very funny,' admits Cellier. 'But an actor's nightmare, of course. I recall that my aunt was in a play with Donald Wolfit and the gun refused to go off and the actor gave him a great kick up the balls and faced the audience and said, "Luckily the sole of my boot is poisoned." It's all you can do, really.'

On the first night proper, as the curtain started to rise, Olivier grabbed O'Toole in the wings just as he was about to walk on stage. 'Are you ready?' he said.

'For what?' O'Toole replied.

'For them. They're out there with their machine guns. It's your turn, son.'

The opening night met with a lukewarm critical response and over the next few days O'Toole's performance fared hardly better. 'I don't understand why Peter was criticised,' says Cellier. 'Because I thought he was a very good Hamlet, most excellent. It was a clear-cut, interesting and vital performance. And the audience reaction was ecstatic.'

But, as Siân had to admit, 'This Hamlet was a pale shadow of the performance he gave at the Bristol Old Vic.' Olivier's own personal assessment was equally damning. 'It was tragic actually. If O'Toole had given on the first night the performance he gave on the last dress rehearsal it would have been an absolute sensation.' The problem according to Olivier was that O'Toole departed from his precise stage directions, he was changing the pace and the rhythms that had been carefully mapped out, so going his own sweet way. 'And he wouldn't understand that he was absolutely fucking up his chances. I mean he would not understand that. He wouldn't. I couldn't talk to the dear fellow.'

The stress of performing the full version every night and two matinees was punishing. Yet O'Toole still persisted in partying away. At someone's house for a shindig and feeling depressed about performing the following day, a woman gave him a green pill from a fancy silver pillbox. 'I was on the ceiling for forty-eight hours. I was cuckooing and crowing from chimneys, hurtling about and gambolling and skipping – and I never stopped talking. I wept at weather forecasts.'

And he was drinking heavily, often before a performance, scaring the wits out of Derek Jacobi, who had to perform a delicately orchestrated sword fight with him. 'If he gave me a wink, and he usually did, this wild Irishman, it meant a very hard fight. It was even dangerous to be sitting in the front row when he flashed out his sword like Douglas Fairbanks.'

At one matinee O'Toole was informed that Noël Coward was going to be out front. The play was going well when O'Toole entered to perform the 'To Be or Not to Be' speech. He was only a few lines in when there was faint laughter coming from the front row. Gamely he continued, and then there it was again, chuckling. What's going on, he thought. O'Toole staggered through and at one point raised his hand to his face. Oh crap, he was still wearing his horn-rimmed spectacles. They were special ones, made for his photo-phobia, with lenses that turned almost pitch black when exposed to direct light. He'd been wearing them off stage and forgotten. And there was Noël in his chair in convulsions. At the end of his speech now, O'Toole roared the line, 'There'll be no more marriages,' took off his glasses and threw them at poor Rosemary Harris.

In the end Olivier decided to take the production off after just twenty-seven performances, although he did invite Tom Courtenay to succeed O'Toole as Hamlet, but it was an offer seen as just too daunting at this early stage in his career.

As for O'Toole, he scurried off to lick his wounds. 'Of course, I think it's the worst bloody play ever written. Actors do it out of vanity. I only did it because I was flattered out of my trousers.'

At least Olivier's baby was off the ground and running. 'This was the beginning of the National Theatre so we were all very conscious that we were making history,' says Cellier. 'And we would have done anything, we'd have died for one another to make it a success, there's no question about that.'

76

Stop the World,
I Want to Get Off

Still on Broadway playing *Luther* as 1963 passed over into 1964, Finney was getting itchy feet. He wanted out – and how. Not just a break, he wanted to jump ship literally, perform a complete disappearing act. This desire had been festering within him for a while; he'd been telling friends that after eight years of constant slog he desperately needed 'to just run away' from it all. Everything had come to a head in New York with the success of *Tom Jones*, and the man playing Luther realised he couldn't quite cope with the supreme adulation coming his way, or didn't want to cope with it.

It was probably a good time to take stock as Finney's private life was all over the place. Divorced, he'd had an affair with Samantha Eggar and been cited in actress Judith Stott's divorce and ordered to pay costs in the case. Asked if he now had any intention of marrying Miss Stott, Finney replied, 'I don't intend to marry anyone.'

It was a terrible risk he was running; people warned him that taking so much time off after *Tom Jones* was dangerous. 'Audiences will forget you,' he was told, other new actors would come along and take his place. Finney didn't seem to care. 'If nothing turns up all it means is that I'll have to give up Monte Cristos and go back to Woodbines.' So instead of exploiting the success of *Tom Jones* Finney, characteristically, was intent on doing the exact opposite. He'd mapped out an epic voyage for himself, taking in the eastern states of America, across the border into Mexico and then following in his childhood hero Captain Cook's footsteps around Hawaii. For a while it looked as if he wouldn't be coming back.

When his old Birmingham rep cohort Colin George heard what Finney was doing he had to take his hat off to the guy. 'I thought, what a fantastic thing to do, not just hanging around in Hollywood going to all the right parties but actually to educate himself in a way he hadn't had a chance to when he grew up. That sums up the man to me.'

It was almost a year-long odyssey of sightseeing, beachcombing and putting his feet up.

He found the perfect place; an almost deserted little island nestled between Tahiti and Bora Bora, and just flopped on the beach, swam a little or slept under a palm tree, not a care in the world, quite happily turning down gargantuan film offers. 'I am not going to act again until I need to,' he said. 'I don't mean financially. I mean until my body physically needs to act.'

In the mornings he'd stroll round and stare at the reef, quaffing on a liberally spiced Bloody Mary. Then he'd have lunch. Afternoons? Well, usually he'd go down to the reef to see if it was still there. Even reading a book seemed like a chore. 'You get to the state where even turning over the page is too much effort.' Instead he unwound utterly, 'and I found out about myself'.

But all this soul searching, looking for his inner self type of stuff did begin to wear him down and day upon day of idleness became mind numbing. 'I realised that I was so wound down that I was about to fall apart.' Other islands he visited were invariably inhabited; loneliness was a problem, then he'd run across an island very definitely populated with a fair number of female diversions. Finney would claim that, while making love to a native girl once on a beach in Hawaii, only one thought crossed his mind: 'I'm doing this not just for myself but for all the Finneys who never got here.'

Other close encounters with the Pacific female population weren't so romantic. 'I met this Fijian girl. Big girl, and I mean BIG! I asked if she'd spend some time with me. She said, no, no! But then she said, "What I would like is to take you to my father's island and build us a house." That's when I got nervous.'

Despite Finney going AWOL, the British invasion rolled on. The Bond movies were breaking records across America and *Zulu* had just premiered in London with Michael Caine hailed as a brand-new star;

for the first time British actors were seen as hot properties, combining popular appeal with serious acting credentials. 'Never before have we been able to match up to those great faces of Hollywood – Brando, Quinn, with all their raw peasant vitality,' showbiz journalist Roderick Mann wrote. 'Now suddenly we can. We are producing them: Finney, Harris and Stamp. And not before time.'

Then there was the Beatles, made up of four working-class lads from Liverpool, who'd just played to seventy-three million Americans on the *Ed Sullivan Show* and were at the forefront of a British music revolution.

The Oscars were a perfect barometer of this success. Previously *Lawrence of Arabia* had swept the board in the 1962 awards, and now *Tom Jones* looked likely to do the same for 1963 with ten nominations, including Finney up for Best Actor competing with Harris for *This Sporting Life*. Hedda Hopper, that doyen of Hollywood bitchery, had the actual effrontery to complain about the number of Brits on the ballot: 'I'm not going to be narrow enough to claim these fellows can't act. They've had plenty of practice. The weather's so foul on that tight little isle that, to get in out of the rain, they all gather in theatres and practice Hamlet on each other.'

Finney quickly surged ahead in the Best Actor race, ahead of Harris, Sidney Poitier (for *Lilies of the Field*) , Rex Harrison (*Cleopatra*) and Paul Newman (*Hud*), but still on his desert island he couldn't give less of a toss and adamantly refused to return to Hollywood and campaign. When the Oscars were presented in April 1964 he wasn't even watching, instead enjoying a cruise around Pearl Harbor while dancing the hula-hula with his Hawaiian girlfriend and knocking back coconut milk and cognac. One keen reporter had hired a raft and paddled furiously after him, armed with a short-wave radio that was broadcasting the Oscar ceremony live. Coming alongside the anchored vessel the reporter spotted the actor up on deck and shouted at the top of his voice, 'Mr Finney, was that a good performance by Sidney Poitier?'

Finney leaned over the side, 'Indeed it was.'

'Because he's won the Oscar,' replied the reporter.

Finney just smiled and raised his glass in a toast, 'To Sidney, well deserved.' Then he grabbed his girlfriend, 'C'mon, baby; let's dance.'

Bibliography

The Theatres of George Devine by Irving Wardle (Jonathan Cape – 1978)

A Better Class of Person by John Osborne (Faber and Faber – 1981)

At The Royal Court edited by Richard Findlater (Amber Lane Press – 1981)

Peter O'Toole: A Biography by Michael Freedland (W. H. Allen – 1983)

Sean Connery: A Biography by Kenneth Passingham (Sidgwick & Jackson – 1983)

Sean Connery: His Life and Films by Michael Feeney Callan (W. H. Allen – 1983)

Charles Laughton: A Difficult Actor by Simon Callow (Methuen – 1987)

Stamp Album by Terence Stamp (Bloomsbury – 1987)

Coming Attractions by Terence Stamp (Bloomsbury – 1988)

Olivier by Anthony Holden (Weidenfeld & Nicolson – 1988)

Almost a Gentleman by John Osborne (Faber and Faber – 1991)

Albert Finney: In Character by Quentin Falk (Robson Books – 1992)

Loitering with Intent: The Child by Peter O'Toole (Macmillan – 1992)

What's It All About by Michael Caine (Century – 1992)

Long Distance Runner by Tony Richardson (Faber and Faber – 1993)

Robert Shaw: The Price of Success by John French (Nick Hern Books – 1993)

Kicking Against the Pricks by Oscar Lewenstein (Nick Hern Books – 1994)

The Making of Lawrence of Arabia by Adrian Turner (Dragon's World – 1994)

David Lean by Kevin Brownlow (Richard Cohen Books – 1996)

Harold Pinter by Michael Billington (Faber and Faber – 1996)

Loitering with Intent: The Apprentice by Peter O'Toole (Macmillan – 1996)

Bibliography

Dear Tom by Tom Courtenay (Doubleday – 2000)

Mainly About Lindsay Anderson – A Memoir (Faber and Faber – 2000)

And That's Not All: The Memoirs of Joan Plowright (Weidenfeld & Nicolson – 2001)

Public Places by Siân Phillips (Hodder Headline – 2001)

Behaving Badly: The Life of Richard Harris by Cliff Goodwin (Virgin Books – 2003)

Acting My Life by Ian Holm (Bantam Press – 2004)

Edge of Midnight: The Life of John Schlesinger by William J. Mann (Hutchinson – 2004)

Richard Harris: Sex, Death and the Movies by Michael Feeney Callan (Robson Books – 2004)

Zulu: The Making of the Epic Movie by Sheldon Hall (Tomahawk Press – 2005)

John Osborne: A Patriot for Us by John Heilpern (Chatto & Windus – 2006)

Michael Caine: A Class Act by Christopher Bray (Faber and Faber – 2006)

Otherwise Engaged: The Life of Alan Bates by Donald Spoto (Hutchinson – 2007)

Being a Scot by Sean Connery and Murray Grigor (Weidenfeld & Nicolson – 2008)

Ask Me If I'm Happy by Peter Bowles (Simon & Schuster – 2010)

I'd also like to thank the wonderful staff at the British Film Institute library and the Westminster Reference Library.

Picture Credits

Plate Section 1

Robert Shaw © Popperfoto / Getty Images
Peter O'Toole © Daily Mail / Rex Features
Sean Connery and Patrick McGoohan © ITV / Rex Features
Michael Caine © ITV / Rex Features
Richard Harris and his wife Elizabeth © Getty Images
Albert Finney © Getty Images
Peter O'Toole © SSPL via Getty Images
Sean Connery © Mirrorpix
Mary Ure and Robert Shaw © Getty Images
Robert Mitchum and Richard Harris © Everett Collection / Rex Images
Alan Bates © Getty Images
Sean Connery and Robert Shaw © ITV / Rex Features
Terence Stamp © Rex Features

Plate Section 2

Albert Finney © Time & Life Pictures / Getty Images
Tom Courtenay © Everett Collection / Rex Features
Alan Bates and June Ritchie © Everett Collection / Rex Features
Richard Harris © ITV / Rex Features
Michael Caine © Getty Images
Terence Stamp © Getty Images
Tom Courtenay and Julie Christie © Everett Collection / Rex Features
Peter O'Toole © Getty Images
Sean Connery © J. Barry Peake / Rex Features

Picture Credits

Anthony Quinn and Alan Bates © Twentieth Century Fox / Everett / Rex Features

Terence Stamp © Getty Images

Albert Finney © George Konig / Rex Features

Tom Courtenay © Shaun Gordon / Rex Features

Michael Caine © Getty Images

Index